NGOs in International Law

Efficiency in Flexibility?

Edited by

Pierre-Marie Dupuy

Professor of International Law at the European University Institute, Florence, Italy

Luisa Vierucci

Researcher in International Law at the University of Florence, Italy

Edward Elgar

Cheltenham, UK • Northampton, MA, USA

Published by
Edward Elgar Publishing Limited
Glensanda House
Montpellier Parade
Cheltenham
Glos GL50 1UA
UK

Edward Elgar Publishing, Inc.
William Pratt House
9 Dewey Court
Northampton
Massachusetts 01060
USA

A catalogue record for this book
is available from the British Library

Library of Congress Cataloging in Publication Data
NGOs in international law : efficiency in flexibility? / edited by
Pierre-Marie Dupuy, Luisa Vierucci.
    p. cm.
  Includes bibliographical references and index.
  1. Non-governmental organizations—Law and legislation. 2. Nonprofit
organizations—Law and legislation. I. Dupuy, Pierre-Marie. II. Vierucci,
Luisa.
  KZ4850.N46 2007
  346'.064—dc22

                                                              2007017596

ISBN 978 1 84720 560 5

Typeset by Cambrian Typesetters, Camberley, Surrey
Printed and bound in Great Britain by MPG Books Ltd, Bodmin, Cornwall

Contents

List of contributors   vii

Introduction: a normative or pragmatic definition of NGOs?   1
Christine Bakker and Luisa Vierucci

PART I   NGOS AND INTERGOVERNMENTAL ORGANIZATIONS

1.   Beyond consultative status: which legal framework for an enhanced
     interaction between NGOs and intergovernmental organizations?   21
     Emanuele Rebasti
2.   Domesticating civil society at the United Nations   71
     Olivier de Frouville
3.   NGOs and the development policy of the European Union   116
     Valentina Bettin
4.   Controversial developments in the field of public participation
     in the international environmental law process   135
     Attila Tanzi

PART II   NGOS, INTERNATIONAL COURTS AND COMPLIANCE
          REVIEW MECHANISMS

5.   NGOs before international courts and tribunals   155
     Luisa Vierucci
6.   The legal status of NGOs in environmental non-compliance
     procedures: an assessment of law and practice   181
     Cesare Pitea

Conclusion: return on the legal status of NGOs and on the
methodological problems which arise for legal scholarship   204
Pierre-Marie Dupuy

Appendix 1   *Questionnaire on the legal status of NGOs in*
               international law   216
Appendix 2   *Selected documents relating to recent developments*
               relevant to NGOs' status under international law   220

Participatory status for international non-
governmental organisations with the Council of
Europe Resolution Res(2003)8   220
Communication from the Commission, towards a
reinforced culture of consultation and dialogue –
general principles and minimum standards for
consultation of interested parties by the
Commission, COM (2002) 704   227
Guidelines for the participation of civil society
organizations in OAS activities, CP/RES. 759
(1217/99)   248
Statement of the Free Trade Commission on
non-disputing party participation, NAFTA, 7
October 2003   257

Selected bibliography   260

Index   269

Contributors

Christine Bakker, PhD in International Law (European University Institute, Florence, Italy).

Valentina Bettin, PhD in International Law (European University Institute, Florence, Italy). She is currently co-operating with the chair of European Union Law at the University of Florence.

Olivier de Frouville, Professor of Public Law at the University of Montpellier 1.

Pierre-Marie Dupuy, Professor of International Law at the European University Institute, Florence.

Cesare Pitea, Researcher in International Law at the University of Parma.

Emanuele Rebasti, PhD researcher at the European University Institute, Florence.

Attila Tanzi, Professor of International Law at the University of Bologna.

Luisa Vierucci, Researcher in International Law at the University of Florence.

Introduction: a normative or pragmatic definition of NGOs?

Christine Bakker and Luisa Vierucci

NGOS AND MAINSTREAM INTERNATIONAL LAW

It is today beyond doubt that Non-Governmental Organizations (NGOs) play a prominent role in international law-relevant fields, from treaty making to rule implementation; from support to courts to aid delivery. However, the increasingly active stance of these organizations on the international plane still raises questions concerning their position under international law, which is the subject of a continuing debate amongst legal scholars. In the last decade this debate has focused especially on the question whether NGOs have international legal personality.

In legal doctrine an entity with international legal personality is usually described as an entity endowed with legal rights and/or obligations and legal capacities directly conferred on it under international law. Sometimes the legal capacities are specified as including procedural capacity and/or treaty-making capacity. While states clearly enjoy all aspects of international legal personality, this is not necessarily the case for other entities. For instance whereas International Governmental Organizations (IGOs) usually have treaty-making capacities, they cannot invoke the contentious jurisdiction of the International Court of Justice (ICJ) or of regional human rights courts. Legal scholars have not reached a consensus on the question whether NGOs also enjoy (some components of) international legal personality. Moreover some authors have examined the legal status of NGOs, rather than their legal personality. The term 'legal status' has been efficaciously defined as 'a broad concept, which embraces all kinds of provisions and practices which explicitly take account of NGOs or which can be used by these organizations for acting in the international legal context, irrespective of which field of international law the material belongs to'.[1] The content of this status may vary according to the circumstances and needs to be specified for each particular entity.

---

[1] Anna-Karin Lindblom (2005), *Non-Governmental Organisations in International Law*, Cambridge: Cambridge University Press, p. 116.

This approach appears to be particularly fitting to NGOs, since it encompasses the components of the traditional concept of international legal personality, while at the same time admitting that other elements or practices may define their international legal position. Nevertheless, as the following overview will demonstrate, most legal scholars continue to address the international legal position of NGOs in terms of 'legal personality' or of 'subjects' under international law.

Four main standpoints can be distinguished in international legal literature representing, as it were, a gliding scale in the recognition of NGOs as international legal subjects.

Reluctance to Accept International Legal Personality of NGOs

On one side of the spectrum there is strong reluctance to attach any international legal consequences to the existence and activities of NGOs. While some scholars expressly deny that such organizations can have any legal position in the international sphere,[2] others do not mention this possibility at all in their discussion of the subjects of international law.[3] This attitude is in line with the traditional conception of international law, according to which the subjects of international law are narrowly defined as comprising states, international organizations and a few historic legal subjects, such as the Holy See and, according to some, the Sovereign Order of Malta.

This stand reflects a positivist approach to international law, having its roots in the Westphalia inter-state system. As is well known, however, the ICJ had dismissed the position that states are the only subjects of international law as early as 1949 in its advisory opinion concerning the *Reparations for Injuries* case. The Court was asked to clarify whether the United Nations, as an organization, had the capacity to bring an international claim against a government regarding injuries that had been caused to the organization by that state. On the question of international legal personality, in an *obiter dictum* the Court held that 'The subjects of law in any legal system are not necessarily identical in their nature or in the extent of their rights and their nature depends upon the needs of the community.'[4]

---

    2 S. Sur (1999), 'Vers une Cour pénale internationale: la Convention de Rome entre les ONG et le Conseil de securité', *Revue Générale de Droit InternationalPublic*, **103**(29), 35–8.
    3 Cf. Ian Brownlie (1966), *Principles of Public International Law*, Oxford: Oxford University Press, 5th edn, 1998, pp. 57–61; Jean Combacau and Serge Sur (2006), *Droit International Public*, Paris: Montchrestien, 7th edn, pp. 309–25.
    4 *Reparations for Injuries Suffered in the Service of the United Nations*, ICJ Reports, 1949, p. 178.

Even though this opinion concerned IGOs, the Court clearly laid down the more general principle that also other entities than states can have international legal personality. It is therefore somewhat surprising that some scholars continue to be reluctant to accept the possibility that non-state actors, other than IGOs, may also be regarded as subjects of international law.

Admittedly, to date no clear pattern of rules has evolved which determine the legal personality of NGOs as a 'category', their rights and obligations under international law or their legal standing before international courts and tribunals. On the other hand it cannot be denied that certain NGOs have explicitly acquired legal personality, either by entering into agreements with IGOs or as a result of specific treaty provisions.[5] Moreover one could argue that the reality of increasing involvement of NGOs in the international context requires some form of legal recognition of these organizations and possibly legal regulation as well.

Open Attitude towards NGOs as Subjects of International Law

At the other end of the spectrum, a number of authors have instead adopted an open attitude towards recognizing NGOs as international legal subjects. Those authors argue that following 'a more "liberal" delimitation of subjects of international law' could lead to the conclusion that 'an entity can be considered a subject of the international legal system if it has rights and/or obligations under that system'.[6] A clear example thereof is the direct endowment of certain rights and responsibilities to the International Committee of the Red Cross by the four Geneva Conventions of 1949.[7]

A variety of legal arguments have been put forward to support an open

---

[5] This is in particular the case of the International Committee of the Red Cross.

[6] A. Reinisch (2005), 'The changing international legal framework for dealing with non-state actors', in Philip Alston (ed.), *Non-State Actors and Human Rights*, Oxford: Oxford University Press, pp. 37–89, at 70.

[7] See Articles 9 and 10 of the First, Second and Third Geneva Conventions; Articles 10 and 11 of the Fourth Geneva Convention. On this point see Ch. Dominicé (1994) 'La personnalité juridique internationale du CICR', in Christophe Swinarski et al. (eds), *Etudes et essais sur le droit international humanitaire et sur les principes de la Croix-Rouge en l'honneur de Jean Pictet*, Geneva: CICR and The Hague: Nijhoff, pp. 663–73, and P. Reuter, 'La personnalité juridique internationale du Comité International de la Croix-Rouge', ibid., pp. 783–91. They both conclude for the international personality of the International Committee of the Red Cross not only on the basis of the Geneva Conventions but through the analysis of practice (the Committee entertains quasi-diplomatic relations with States, enjoys immunities typical of intergovernmental organizations and enters into agreements with states).

attitude towards NGOs under international law. Some legal scholars[8] have affirmed that, especially in the human rights field, international rights and obligations are not only conferred on states, but also on individuals and other non-state actors. This view is increasingly adopted by international human rights monitoring bodies.[9] For example, the UN Human Rights Committee first affirmed in 2000 the binding nature of the core of human rights obligations for all members of society, including NGOs.[10]

Other scholars have upheld that NGOs inevitably play a role in the modern, democratic law-making process, which is no longer exclusively reserved for states, beyond the human rights area.[11] According to this view, non-state actors directly participate in the formation of so-called 'media-law' which is created alongside 'state-law' that is built through traditional channels.[12] By 'media-law' Reisman refers to the process through which NGOs, together with political and social pressure groups as well as individual commentators, directly contribute to the continuous process of rule creation, which is communicated through the media. With this assertion Reisman seems to imply that NGOs have already gained some degree of *de facto* international legal personality (at least in terms of law making), without the need of any formalization of that capacity. Although such an approach highlights the complexity of normative developments under modern international law, it may be questioned whether the abovementioned category of 'media-law' meets the criteria for genuine law making in terms of accountability, representation and clarity. Therefore, the assertion that NGOs play a key role in the formation of international law is somewhat weakened by limiting this role to a process which could also be considered as merely 'normative pressure' exercised by civil society.

Finally, some scholars go so far as to question the appropriateness of the

---

[8]   In particular Reinisch, *supra* note 6, at 71, stresses this point by referring to art. 30 of the Universal Declaration of Human Rights, UN G.A. Res. 217 (1948), Article 30: 'Nothing in this Declaration may be interpreted as implying for any State, group or person any right to engage in any activity or to perform any act aimed at the destruction of any of the rights and freedoms set forth herein.'

[9]   Reinisch, *supra* note 6, at 69–72. On this point see extensively Andrew Clapham (2006), *Human Rights Obligations of Non-State Actors*, Oxford: Oxford University Press.

[10]   UN Committee on Economic, Social and Cultural Rights, General comment No. 14 of 11 August 2000, U.N. Doc. E/C.12/2000/4, para. 42 .

[11]   M. Reisman (2005), 'The democratization of contemporary international law-making processes and the differentiation of their application', in Rudinger Wolfrum and Roeben Volker (eds), *Developments of International Law in Treaty Making*, Heidelberg: Springer, pp. 19–20.

[12]   Ibid., pp. 24–6.

traditional view that there exist only 'subjects' and 'objects' of international law; subjects being those elements bearing, without the need for municipal intervention, rights and responsibilities, and objects being the rest.[13] In particular, one authoritative scholar, Rosalyn Higgins, has proposed to regard international law as a dynamic decision-making process in which a variety of actors take part with the objective of maximizing certain values. Instead of 'subjects' and 'objects' in this model there are only participants. Along with states, international organizations, multinational corporations and individuals also NGOs would then be considered as participants in the international legal order.[14] Similarly, another commentator has held that 'the intensely debated but largely sterile question as to whether or not NGOs [. . .] have emerged as new subjects within the international legal order' can be avoided by using a constitutional or functional approach to international law.[15] According to this approach, NGOs can be 'elegantly integrated into a broader concept of "international community"',[16] if one would consider that NGOs make the public opinion and public conscience of a cosmopolitan civil society heard in international relations.

Despite the differences among these views, the fundamentally favourable approach towards recognizing the role of NGOs in the international legal order does attempt to come to terms with the ever-increasing proliferation of actors at the international level. Such an open attitude has the advantage of clarifying the status of these non-state actors which are currently operating, at least to some extent, in a legal vacuum.

Cautious Recognition of NGOs' Legal Personality under International Law

Two positions cover the middle ground of the aforementioned conceptual scale. Firstly, some scholars favour a cautious recognition of legal personality for NGOs, albeit within the traditional international legal framework.[17] While

---

[13]   Rosalyn Higgins (1994), *Problems and Process; International Law and How We Use It*, Oxford: Clarendon Press, p. 49.

[14]   Ibid., p. 50.

[15]   D. Thuerer (1999), 'The emergence of non-governmental organizations and transnational enterprises in international law and the changing role of the State', in Rainer Hofmann (ed.), *Non-State Actors as New Subjects of International Law*, Berlin: Duncker & Humblot, p. 53.

[16]   Ibid., p. 53.

[17]   R. Falk (1995), 'The world order between inter-state law and the law of humanity', in Daniele Archibugi and David Held (eds), *Cosmopolitan Democracy; An Agenda for a New World Order*, Cambridge: Polity Press, pp. 163–79; Christian Tomuschat (2003), *Human Rights: Between Idealism and Realism*, Oxford: Oxford University Press, p. 231.

stressing that states continue to be the principal subjects of international law, even though the central role of the state is eroding,[18] these commentators acknowledge that non-state actors, including NGOs, are playing such an important role in overall governance structures that they have become part of the international legal order.

It has been argued that such a cautiously favourable approach is also reflected in the final Articles on Responsibility of States for Internationally Wrongful Acts,[19] adopted by the International Law Commission in 2001.[20] Article 33(2) stipulates that the part of the Articles dealing with state responsibility 'is without prejudice to any right, arising from the international responsibility of a State, which may accrue directly to any person or entity other than a State'. Although the legal personality of non-state actors is not expressly afforded by this provision, according to the Commentary to the Articles such a development may not be excluded in the future.[21]

The second attitude consists in a more flexible recognition of the role played by NGOs in the international legal order without attempting to place them in a fixed legal framework.[22] According to this view, legal rights and responsibilities should be accorded to NGOs on a case-by-case basis, and only if this is 'functional' to the pursued objective.[23] The rationale behind the functionality requirement is that, in the current situation, NGOs effectively participate in various fields of international concern, despite the limited legal regulation of such participation. It is therefore not necessary, according to this reasoning, to endow all NGOs with international legal personality, or to treat NGOs as such as a new

---

[18]   Falk, *supra* note 17, pp. 166–7. Falk distinguishes, however, between fields in which inter-state realities persist, and where inter-state law provides for control (for example, war/peace, environmental issues, transnational economic activity) and fields in which non-state actors are gaining an increasingly important role, and where they already contribute to the formation of the 'law of humanity', a development which he strongly supports; ibid., p. 167.

[19]   UN Doc. A/56/10 (2001).

[20]   P. Alston (2005), 'The 'not-a cat' syndrome: can the International Human Rights regime accommodate non-state actors?' in Philip Alston (ed.), *supra* note 6, at 24.

[21]   The Commentary to the Articles states that they do not deal with the possibility of the invocation of responsibility by non-state actors but at the same time it notes that some procedures may be available enabling a non-state entity 'to invoke the responsibility on its own account and without State involvement', Report of the International Law Commission to the General Assembly, Supplement No. 10 (A/56/10), Commentary to Article 33, at 234–5.

[22]   R. Wedgwood (1999), 'Legal personality and the role of non-governmental organizations and non-state political entities in the United Nations system', in Rainer Hofmann (ed.), *supra* note 15, at 21–36.

[23]   Ibid., at 36.

category of subjects of international law.[24] The proponents of such a view
further argue that the question of subjects of international law should be
approached in an undogmatic way. For example, Thuerer states that '[w]e should
use a functional approach according to the Roman proverb "ubi societas, ibi ius"
and conclude what the law is from social forces'.[25] According to Wedgwood,
'the interesting inquiry, each time, is whether according rights of participation
and address, or imposing some form of direct responsibility for non-state actors
in the international community, will usefully increase the capacity to resolve
conflicts and enforce standards of human security'.[26] In her view, the role of
NGOs has been seen as beneficial and creative, subject to suitable cautions.

The functional approach combines the recognition of the role of NGOs with
some flexibility in terms of legal regulation, taking account of the diversity of
actors and the complexity of decision-making processes at the international
level. The inconvenience of such a flexible, case-by-case approach could be
the uncertainty of all actors involved in when and how an NGO may be
awarded rights and obligations under international law, or when and how an
NGO could be held internationally accountable for its actions.

These various approaches clearly demonstrate the existence of a recurrent
dilemma haunting modern international law: on the one hand, the perceived
benefits of regulating an existing and progressing practice of NGO involvement in the international legal order; and, on the other hand, the perceived
risks of legalizing the participation of these non-state actors in the traditional,
state-dominated system.

OBJECTIVE AND SCOPE OF THE VOLUME

The diversity of views among academics, which has been sketched above
concerning the international legal position of NGOs, called for the collection
of empirical data on the part of NGOs themselves in order to complete the
picture. This was the starting point of the project which was the foundation of
the present volume. In 2002, a workshop was convened at the European
University Institute, bringing together representatives of various NGOs and
specialists in public international law; that is, both practitioners and scholars.
The workshop aimed to address the issue of the status of NGOs in modern
international law, by focusing in particular on the modalities of NGOs' cooperation with IGOs and international courts or quasi-judicial bodies.

---

24 Thuerer, *supra* note 15, at 91.
25 Ibid., at 91.
26 Wedgwood, *supra* note 22, at 36.

The workshop consisted of two parts. First, NGOs' representatives presented the modalities of their organization's cooperation with IGOs and international (quasi-)judicial bodies, commenting on the degree of legal formalization of such cooperation. With a view to steering the debate towards a qualitative assessment of the existing cooperation mechanisms, participants were asked to make their presentations by answering a questionnaire which had been distributed in advance (see Appendix 1). The questions were designed to withdraw the veil over practitioners' perception of the status of their respective organizations, with a view to comparing the 'formal picture' of NGOs under international law to their real functioning in practice.[27] The second part of the workshop hinged upon the legal status of NGOs from a more theoretical perspective, leading to a debate sparked by the answers provided by the practitioners.

Throughout the workshop, a clear distinction was made between, on the one hand, cooperation between NGOs and IGOs and, on the other hand, the interaction between NGOs and international courts and quasi-judicial bodies. The main results of the NGOs' practice concerned the variety of forms taken by their relationship with IGOs, ranging from formal participatory rights or consultative status to informal contacts with individual IGOs' officials. Indeed, the informal relationship appeared to be quite effective and appreciated by the great majority of NGOs.

On the other hand, the possibilities for cooperation between NGOs and international tribunals or (quasi-)judicial compliance mechanisms appeared to be more limited, the most important modalities being *amicus curiae* intervention and, in some cases, provision for *locus standi* before international bodies. Participants in the workshop pointed to the need for further regulation in this field, in particular for *amicus curiae* intervention, in order to better protect the rights of the defence in criminal trials or the position of the applicant in other types of international proceedings, and to ensure the legitimacy of the NGO presenting an *amicus* brief.

Given these differences, the same subject-matter division has been maintained in this book which has been built upon the main findings coming out of the workshop. The present volume aims to provide some preliminary answers to the following question: is there a need for a revised legal status for NGOs in international law? In other words, does the increasing international role that NGOs de facto play require a reconsideration of their de jure position or, on the contrary, does the flexibility currently enjoyed by NGOs constitute the most effective and desirable solution for all international actors involved?

---

[27]   The questionnaire was mainly elaborated by Anna-Karin Lindblom, now in charge of the human rights division of the Swedish Ministry of Foreign Affairs, who is the author of *Non-Governmental Organisations in International Law*, *supra* note 1.

In order to answer such questions, the first part of the book addresses issues connected with the relationship between NGOs and IGOs. It provides an empirical analysis of the various legal positions which formally define the scope of NGO activity within different IGOs, in particular within the United Nations system, but also the European Union.

Emanuele Rebasti first examines the different forms of cooperation between NGOs and IGOs, ranging from consultative status to purely informal bilateral contacts and then evaluates whether legal formalization has so far provided an effective framework for cooperation between IGOs and NGOs. The chapter shows that, while there clearly is a gap between the concrete dynamics of the interplay between NGOs and IGOs and the legal definition of this relationship, it is much debated whether the emerging paradigm of NGO/IGO relations should be crystallized in a new legal regime or rather left to self-regulation. The author argues that the two opposing approaches will finally combine to provide tailored solutions to the problems raised by civil society's enhanced participation in IGO activities. He analyses the reforms recently introduced or proposed by a number of intergovernmental organizations, such as membership of NGOs in the African Union, ECOSOC; extended NGO participation in UN organs; streamlined and depoliticized accreditation procedures within the UN; renewed self-regulation and self-organization of NGOs in their relations with the UN; an innovating participatory status for NGOs in the Council of Europe; and informal participation and administrative facilitation for NGOs at the EU. Three models of interaction are identified, responding to the needs raised by the nature of the contribution NGOs seek to make to the intergovernmental process, by the field of action in which NGOs' participation takes place, and by the specificity of the intergovernmental organization at stake. Finally the author opens new avenues for exploration by shifting the question of the legal status of NGOs in international law from a legal personality perspective to the functioning of IGOs. In this light, civil society participation is increasingly perceived as a parameter of IGOs' good governance.

In the second contribution, Olivier de Frouville takes a closer look at the emergence of what he calls a 'servile society', namely NGOs who serve a state rather than public interest. He analyses the relationship between the United Nations and an increasing number of government-oriented NGOs or 'GONGOs', who claim to represent independently the civil society of their country, while in reality maintaining close links with the national government and pursuing the interests and policies of the latter. Some examples of GONGOs are represented by Chinese 'mass'-organizations, which openly admit a link with the government, but also by civil society organizations pursuing a certain goal which at the same time constitutes a foreign policy priority of the government of their country, such as Islamic organizations actively following the situation of Kashmir, and pursuing the same objective as the Pakistani government. The author strongly criticizes the way in which various United Nations bodies, in particular the Human Rights Commission and ECOSOC, have established a more or less formalized relationship with these organizations, and proposes some measures to improve this situation. It remains to be seen if and how the newly established Human Rights Council will be willing and able to address the above shortcomings.

Valentina Bettin examines the evolution of the role and legal status of NGOs in the framework of the European Union Development Policy. The author takes into consideration the relationship between the EU and NGOs in both the implementation and the formulation of development policy. She demonstrates that the cooperation between NGOs and the EU is well advanced as regards the implementation of development policy, through the formula of co-financing. However, the analysis also reveals a tension between the formalization and non-formalization of the NGO involvement in development policy. Such a tension does not exist in the framework of the Cotonou Agreement, which regulates the development cooperation between the African, Caribbean and Pacific states (ACP states) and the EU. This agreement requires consultation with NGOs on the formulation of development policies and strategies. The author concludes that the formalization of NGO consultation in the context of the relationship between the EC and the ACP states has been possible because the formal NGO involvement affects an international institutional framework and not the internal decision making of the European Union. In other areas of development cooperation, as well as in the other sectors covered by the EC Treaty, the Commission has been reluctant to formalize the relations with NGOs. As a result, NGO involvement in the EU and its policies mainly takes place on an informal basis.

Attila Tanzi concludes the first part of the volume by presenting his findings on the participation and status of NGOs in the field of international environmental law. After examining the international instruments on sustainable development, in particular the Aarhus Convention, he underscores the recent shift of emphasis in the role of NGOs in the environmental process, from decision making to the implementation phase. He concludes that, while public participation through NGOs is fairly well established in national environmental law processes, such participation is significantly weaker at the international level. The case-by-case approach followed in the various international environmental fora, such as the UN, the UNECE Pan-European Framework and the mechanisms envisaged by the Aarhus Convention, is inherent in the scattered setting of the international environmental institutions. According to Tanzi, both states and NGOs seem to have, for opposite reasons, a strong interest in avoiding formal regulation of public participation in international fora. He argues that states are wary of binding themselves for the future to afford certain rights of public participation across the board, even though they have accepted such participation in a specific context. For their part, NGOs appear not to be interested in having a fixed legal framework either, since this may limit their participation in international environmental fora. In a less regulated context, NGOs may be able to increase their participation on a case-by-case basis.

Taken together, these contributions demonstrate that there is a clear need to rethink the traditional forms of cooperation between NGOs and IGOs. Nevertheless, the question whether a new legal regime is also required is controversial. Indeed, it appears as if a certain degree of informality (hence flexibility) in the relationships between these two types of organizations is rather appreciated by NGOs and IGOs alike, albeit for different reasons.

The second part of the book addresses forms of participation and standing of NGOs before international courts and quasi-judicial bodies. The first contribution, by Luisa Vierucci, examines the status of NGOs before international courts and tribunals, in particular the regional systems of human rights protection, international criminal tribunals and the WTO dispute settlement mechanism. It attempts to assess whether NGOs are satisfied with the access to justice they are currently experiencing, and whether it is desirable to suggest changes *de lege ferenda* in order to make their participation in international justice more effective. Distinguishing between direct (*locus standi*) and indirect (*amicus curiae* intervention) participation, the author first sets out, for each of these two modalities, the international courts and bodies to which NGOs have access according to their respective rules. Subsequently, she presents and comments on the desirability of further regulation of NGOs participation, analysing the advantages and disadvantages of increased formalization. In particular the author identifies two conflicting interests that must be weighed: on the one side, the need to ensure that those issues that can be put forward or properly dealt with only by NGOs have an avenue for presentation before the international judge; on the other, the necessity to limit the risks that uncontrolled participation of NGOs may constitute for the rights of the parties to the case. Considering the importance of these different interests, the difficulties in finding a balance between them, and the formalism that is inherent in the very nature of international proceedings, it is concluded that a more formalized legal status for NGOs' participation, whether direct or indirect, in international adjudication seems unavoidable. The author presents arguments in favour of both informal and formal regulation of the participation modalities, and formulates some ideas on how to address two major concerns related to NGOs' participation before international courts and tribunals, namely representation issues, and safeguarding the rights of the parties.

Cesare Pitea next addresses the participation of NGOs in compliance review procedures in the environmental field. By way of a case study, the analysis focuses on the key role played by NGOs in the compliance review procedure under the Aarhus Convention. The author notes that, despite some positive experiences, the governmental view still prevails according to which NGOs' participation, in particular their power to initiate compliance review procedures, may undermine the non-confrontational functioning of those procedures. However, he concludes that the positive impact of the formal involvement of NGOs within compliance review mechanisms in terms of increased efficiency and transparency is becoming evident. He finally points to some possible further developments in terms of regulation of NGO participation.

Thus, the analysis in this second part of the volume indicates that increased regulation, be it formal or informal, would be appropriate, both in terms of NGOs' direct (*locus standi* or access to compliance committees) and of indirect (*amicus curiae*) participation. It also demonstrates that the level of formal regulation is a function of the degree of participation. The ideas put forward in the separate contributions on possible modalities of such regulation will certainly contribute to the discussion among legal scholars and practitioners on the creation of a new legal regime for increased international involvement of NGOs in international legal proceedings.

Drawing on the various contributions, Pierre-Marie Dupuy derives some conclusions on the desirability of further regulation of the status of NGOs, considering, inter alia, whether, in the international legal order as it is currently evolving, maintaining a certain degree of flexibility in the relationships between some of its increasingly influential actors or participants may be more beneficial and efficient for the achievement of its fundamental goals.

DEFINING THE INDEFINABLE: NGOS IN INTERNATIONAL LAW

Although legal scholars have already been debating the issue, it is surprising that lengthy discussions can be held and elaborate papers can be written about NGOs and their legal status, without defining the term 'Non-Governmental Organization' itself. Neither at the EUI workshop, nor in the contributions to this book, has the need to determine such a definition been prominently brought to the fore.

Even in the absence of an agreed normative definition, both experts and the public at large constantly use the term, confident that others know what they are talking about. One could therefore wonder whether it is necessary at all to determine a generally accepted definition. In other words: should the flexibility which seems to be desired by all actors in the relationships between NGOs and IGOs be maintained with regard to the definition of such organizations as well?

In order to address this question, a brief look will first be given to the attempts which have been made to define the term 'NGO' in international legal literature, as well as the different definitions adopted by various IGOs. After examining some negative consequences of the 'normative loophole', the specific situation of NGOs before international courts and tribunals will once again be addressed, in order to establish whether a normative definition would be required.

Inexistence of an Agreed Definition in International Law

Although the term 'NGO' appears in an increasing number of international legal instruments and so-called 'soft-law' instruments, only a few of them include a definition of this type of organization. Moreover the few existing definitions show some important differences. For example, the term 'non-governmental organization' is included in Article 71 of the UN Charter, but no definition was provided.[28] A definition was subsequently established by ECOSOC in 1950, according to which, for the purposes of consultative arrangements, an NGO is understood as '[a]ny international organization which is not created by intergovernmental agreement'.[29] A more elaborated definition was adopted in 1996,[30] and a number of conditions were enumerated for the establishment of consultative relations with an NGO. These conditions include that the aims of an NGO shall be in conformity with the spirit, purposes and principles of the UN Charter; that it has a democratically adopted constitution as well as a representative structure with appropriate mechanisms of accountability; and that it shall be of recognized standing within the particular field of its competence or of a representative character.[31] The relevant ECOSOC resolution refers neither to a non-profit making aim nor to a national legal personality.

Within the Council of Europe, consultative relationships with NGOs have

---

[28]   According to this provision, 'The Economic and Social Council may make suitable arrangements for consultation with non-governmental organizations which are concerned with matters within its competence.'

[29]   E/RES/288(X), *Review of consultative arrangements with non-governmental organizations*, 27 February 1959, para. 8.

[30]   'Any such organization that is not established by a governmental entity or intergovernmental agreement shall be considered a non-governmental organization for the purpose of these arrangements, including organizations that accept members designated by governmental authorities, provided that such membership does not interfere with the free expression of views of the organization', E/RES/1996/31, *Consultative relationship between the United Nations and non-governmental organizations*, 25 July 1996, para. 12.

[31]   Ibid., para. 2 and paras 9–12.

been established since 1951,[32] although no definition of such organizations had been adopted at that time. However the 1986 Convention on the Recognition of the Legal Personality of International Non-Governmental Organisations[33] does provide several elements of a definition of NGOs. It enumerates some conditions which 'associations, foundations and other private institutions (hereinafter referred to as NGOs)' must satisfy. Contrary to the 1996 ECOSOC resolution, these conditions include the requirement of a non-profit aim, which must also be of 'international utility'. The explanatory report to the Convention indicates that a trade union is an NGO, while a commercial organization is not.[34]

Finally, in 1999, the Organization of American States (OAS) adopted new Guidelines for Participation by Civil Society Organizations in OAS activities,[35] which define civil society organizations as 'any national or international institution, organization or entity made up of natural or juridical persons of a private nature'. This definition is broader than the one previously adopted, which was limited to an organization made up of natural or juridical persons of a private nature.

Given the absence of a universal definition of NGOs in the primary sources of international law, several attempts have been made in legal doctrine to define the seemingly indefinable category. Although the proposed solutions often indicate what NGOs are not,[36] some authors have tried to single out those elements which identify such an organization. Thuerer seems to accept the legal definition provided by Macalister-Smith, whereby NGOs (i) are not established by a government, or by an intergovernmental agreement; (2) are typically private institutions: associations, foundations, federations or other unions founded on the basis and under the regime of the private law of a state;

---

[32]   Council of Europe Resolution (51)30F, *Relations with International Organisations, both Intergovernmental and Non-Governmental*, 3 May 1951.
[33]   Council of Europe, *European Convention on the Recognition of the Legal Personality of International Non-Governmental Organisations*, ETS No. 124, entered into force on 1 January 1991.
[34]   *Explanatory Report on the European Convention on the Recognition of the Legal Personality of International Non-Governmental Organisations*, Strasbourg, 1986, commentary on art. 15 of the Convention, http://www.uia.org/legal/app411.php#bn1a, accessed 4 January 2007.
[35]   CP/RES. 759 (1217/99), *Guidelines for Participation by Civil Society Organisations in OAS Activities*, 15 December 1999.
[36]   For example, NGOs are not established or controlled by states, they do not seek to overthrow governments by force, they do not aim to acquire state power, they do not seek financial profit for their own sake; see M. Kamminga (2005), 'The evolving status of NGOs under international law: a threat to the inter-state system?', in Philip Alston (ed.), *supra* note 6, at 96.

and (3) have concerns, purposes and objects which are, in contrast to the origins of NGOs, of a public nature.[37] Kamminga points out that 'NGOs are usually thought of as having an international character, with members and branches in more than one country and with objectives that are not limited to one State.'[38] All these elements are also mentioned by Reinisch, who further adds the requirements of a minimal organizational structure, and of established headquarters.[39] Lindblom distinguishes between NGOs with an international character and those of a purely national nature. She also considers that an NGO does not use violence for promoting its interests, that its internal structure must be democratic, and that it normally, but not necessarily, enjoys legal personality under national law.[40]

Even though these definitions do not differ dramatically, the fact that not all the mentioned requirements are taken up by every commentator demonstrates that to date no consensus has been reached among legal scholars on an exact definition of NGOs.[41]

Negative Consequences of the Normative Loophole

Whereas the non-existence of a clear and common definition of NGOs may have some benefits in terms of flexibility, some negative consequences should also be highlighted. In the first place, the abovementioned GONGO phenomenon is a direct effect of what could be regarded as a normative loophole. Despite their lack of independence from national governments, GONGOs may benefit from the arrangements existing within the UN system and destined for genuine non-governmental organizations. In reality, those organizations pursue policy or political goals of the state where they are registered; they are sometimes state-controlled and they often lack adequate accountability mechanisms. As demonstrated by Olivier de Frouville in his contribution to this volume, the relationships established between GONGOs and IGOs are based on a broader definition of NGOs than those discussed in the previous paragraphs. Their involvement in the work of the UN and other IGOs, and even their participation in NGO platforms regrouping several NGOs pursuing

---

37   Thuerer, *supra* note 15, at 43.
38   Kamminga, *supra* note 36, at 97.
39   Reinisch, *supra* note 6, at 40, note 19.
40   Lindblom, *supra* note 1, 48ff.
41   Kamminga notes that a broad definition of NGOs, such as the one adopted by H. Rechenberg (1997) 'Non-Governmental Organizations', in Rudolph Bernhardt (ed.), *Encyclopaedia of Public International Law*, vol. 3, Amsterdam: North-Holland, at 612, may encompass multinational corporations and even national liberation movements; *supra* note 36, at 95.

certain common aims, may negatively affect the functioning and impact of genuine NGOs. Indeed, one of the main strengths of NGOs is precisely their independence from governments, which allows them to provide information, to carry out analyses and to formulate positions in their fields of expertise without any political bias, or at least in disregard of state interests.

The lack of clarity about the type of organizations that may legitimately be considered as NGOs also leads to legal uncertainty in cases where NGOs are granted certain rights. The question is then which organizations may benefit from such rights and which may not. Such uncertainty may arise particularly with regard to their participation before international courts and tribunals. For example, when NGOs have *locus standi* before a regional or international judicial body, can any organization considering itself as non-governmental bring a case before that body and act as a party in the proceedings? Or, on the other hand, should certain standards be set ensuring, for instance, a minimum degree of representation? Similar questions can be asked concerning indirect participation before international tribunals. Should each and every NGO be permitted to present *amicus curiae* briefs to these judicial bodies in all circumstances? These points are addressed in detail in the contribution of Luisa Vierucci.

It is, however, clear from the outset that, depending on the definition of the term 'NGO', participatory rights of civil society organizations may be dramatically expanded or curtailed. In other words, each element of a possible definition will undoubtedly exclude certain organizations and bar them from access to international courts. On the other hand, the formal nature of (international) judicial proceedings and well established international rules regarding the rights of the defendant require a certain regulation with respect to the parties before international tribunals. Moreover, unlimited participatory rights for all types of NGOs would further increase the already important workload of these judicial bodies, ultimately leading to reducing access to justice altogether.

It would therefore seem that a certain form of regulation is indeed required with respect to the participatory rights of NGOs before international tribunals. On the other hand, in the broader context of flexibility as regards the relationships of NGOs with IGOs, and taking account of the wide variety of NGOs and the interests they support, it might 'by definition' be impossible to formulate a uniform definition. However, is it really necessary to have an agreed universal definition, or would it not be sufficient to agree on a generally accepted list of minimum requirements for an organization to qualify for the category 'NGO'? As the various contributions to this volume demonstrate, the nature of the phenomenon of NGOs itself, as it has evolved in practice, does not allow for excessive formalization. Moreover there appears to be circularity in the effort to define NGOs. In practice, a wide range of organizations has evolved, their diversity stemming from the very absence of prior regulation. As a result, it is extremely difficult (possibly not workable) to find common features making it possible to mould all these elements into one definition.

The solution may lie in a dual approach, maintaining flexibility in both the legal status and the definition of NGOs for their relationships with IGOs in general, while at the same time introducing some degree of regulation of NGOs for their participation before international (quasi-)judicial bodies. Flexibility may indeed be the best recipe for efficiency in the role of NGOs in the international legal order. However, such a flexible attitude should nonetheless allow for a minimum of formalization in the judicial field.

PART I

NGOs and intergovernmental organizations

1. Beyond consultative status: which legal framework for enhanced interaction between NGOs and intergovernmental organizations?

Emanuele Rebasti

INTRODUCTION

Interaction with intergovernmental organizations (IGOs) is a central part of NGO's (non-governmental organization)[1] activity at the international level. The institutional structures of international cooperation provide NGOs with the forum they need to make their voices heard beyond the boundaries of the nation-state and with a political target for the exercise of their non-governmental diplomacy. Thus it is not surprising that NGOs have hardly been indifferent to intergovernmental institutions: either confrontational or cooperative, NGOs' action is often defined with reference to IGOs' policies or aims at influencing the outcomes of intergovernmental processes. Similarly, IGOs have increasingly

---

[1]   As is exhaustively explained in the Introduction to the present book, the notion of a Non-Governmental Organization is not univocal in international practice or in academic debate. While it is commonly understood that NGOs are organizations established by private initiative, formally free from any governmental influence and without a profit-making aim, it is much more debated whether in that category may also fall organizations which promote professional or class interests; which represent social or ethnic groups; which lack legal personality in their national law order; which have a political or religious nature or which carry out their activity in the territory of a single state. In practice, every IGO which establishes a formalized relationship has its own definition of an NGO. In recent times, however, IGOs have been promoting cooperation with a larger and larger range of non-governmental actors, including local authorities, business companies and private organizations performing public functions (see *infra* the third section and conclusions of the present chapter, respectively at pp. 46 and 62). As a consequence, reference is increasingly made to the more inclusive concept of 'Civil Society Organizations' (CSOs). In the present study we use the notion of NGO with reference to the traditional category of private, non-profit making organizations, while we adopt the concept of CSO when a broader notion is necessary. The expression 'civil society' is used in a non-technical way, as a synonym of the first or the second category, depending on the context.

looked at non-governmental organizations as strategic allies to ensure the success of their policies and programmes, either by disseminating information and raising public awareness or by means of direct action on the ground. This convergence of interests has led to the development of forms of NGO–IGO cooperation since the time of the League of Nations.[2]

Following the example provided by Article 71 of the UN Charter, a growing number of intergovernmental organizations has adopted formal arrangements to enter into relationships with non-governmental organizations: subordinated to specific requirements and to an accreditation procedure, NGOs are granted a bundle of legal positions which formally define the scope of their activity within a given organization and which are properly defined as status. Thus the forms of institutionalized cooperation between civil society and IGOs represent a model of reference in the continuing debate on the need to define a legal status for NGOs at the international level.

In this chapter we will try to evaluate whether legal formalization has so far provided an effective framework for the cooperation between IGOs and civil society.[3] It will be shown that the impressive growth in the quantitative and qualitative dimensions of NGO participation which followed the 'NGO revolution' of the early nineties has resulted in a significant gap between the legal definition of the IGO–NGO relationship and the concrete dynamics of their interplay (first section, *infra* p. 23). However, while it is clear that the time has come to rethink the traditional forms of cooperation, it is much debated whether the emerging paradigm of the NGO–IGO relationship should be crystallized in a new legal regime or rather left to self-regulation (second section, *infra* p. 37). In the third section (*infra* p. 46) we then turn to examine the reforms recently introduced or proposed by a number of intergovernmental organizations and we show that in practice the two opposing approaches of institutionalization and self-regulation combine to provide tailored solutions to the problems raised by civil society's

---

2   See B. Seary (1996), 'The early history – from the Congress of Vienna to the San Francisco Conference' in Peter Willets (ed.), *The Conscience of the World – The Influence of Non-Governmental Organisations in the UN System*, Washington, DC: Brookings Institute.

3   The present study does not deal with NGO–IGO cooperation at a purely operational level. The specific aim pursued in this form of interaction (operational implementation) affects the structure of the relationship which is structurally bilateral and mostly relies on private law instruments since it implies the assumption of reciprocal obligations, the definition of respective responsibilities and a detailed regulation of the activities that will be performed by NGOs. Thus it is not surprising that operational cooperation has been integrally regulated outside the framework of existing consultative statuses, through the conclusion of operational agreements and, to a lesser extent, through the acceptance of self-regulation codes developed by NGOs themselves. For an inventory of NGO–IGO operational agreements, see Anna-Karin Lindblom (2005), *Non-Governmental Organisations in International Law*, Cambridge: Cambridge University Press.

enhanced participation in IGOs' activities. We identify different models of interaction which respond, with a decreasing degree of institutionalization, to the different needs raised by the nature of the contribution NGOs seek to make to the intergovernmental process, by the field of action in which NGOs' participation takes place or by the specificity of the intergovernmental organization at stake. To conclude, we show that, although flexibility in the design of non-governmental participation appears to be a characteristic feature, some common trends in the evolution of the NGO–IGO relationship can be identified. We finally derive from the practice analysed the conclusion that non-governmental participation is strongly emerging as a parameter of good governance for IGOs.

CONSULTATIVE RELATIONSHIP: A NARROW LEGAL FRAMEWORK FOR ENHANCED NON-GOVERNMENTAL PARTICIPATION

One of the major achievements of non-governmental action at the San Francisco Conference in 1945 was to build up a broad support for strengthening the role of the proposed Economic and Social Council (ECOSOC) and for adding to the UN Charter an express provision establishing the basis for a formal relationship between that organ and NGOs.[4] In particular, non-governmental representatives succeeded in promoting the idea that 'some orderly channels should be established whereby national and international organizations of a non-governmental character could bring their views to the attention of the Organisation'.[5] This proposed pattern of relationship expressly departed from the informal system of close cooperation with NGOs adopted within the League of Nations,[6] which had demonstrated itself to be unable to resist changes in the attitude of member states and of the League bureaucracy.[7]

---

[4]   Article 71 of the Charter reads: 'The Economic and Social Council may make suitable arrangements for consultation with non-governmental organizations which are concerned with matters within its competence. Such arrangements may be made with international organizations and, where appropriate, with national organizations after consultation with the Member of the United Nations concerned.' For an assessment of the role of NGOs at the San Francisco Conference see Pei-heng Chiang (1981), *Non-Governmental Organisations at the United Nations – Identity, Role and Function*, New York: Praeger, pp. 39ff.

[5]   Pickard, informal paper for the International Secretariat on the arrangements to be made for international non-governmental organizations in the UN system, London 1945, quoted in Seary, 'The Early History . . .', *supra* note 2, at 26.

[6]   Seary, 'The Early History . . .', *supra* note 2, at page 26; Pei-Heng Chiang, *Non Governmental Organisations . . .*, *supra* note 4, at 34.

[7]   In the early years of the League an informal relationship allowed NGOs a high

In 1946, ECOSOC implemented the system of formal relationships conceived at San Francisco with the adoption of the first comprehensive resolution on consultative arrangements with NGOs: from that date, the main features of an institutional framework destined to become a model for other IGOs were set up.[8] The system was built up on a basic assumption: the Organisation formally recognizes that NGOs have a role to play in the intergovernmental process and vests them with a corresponding legal status but retains control on the access through an accreditation procedure and limits participation by defining its modalities. As for the role recognized for civil society, it is defined as a consultative one.[9] The term is deliberately intended to exclude non-governmental organizations from the decision making process: NGOs have the right to attend meetings and, to a certain extent, to circulate statements, to speak and to propose agenda items,[10] but it is made clear that

---

level of participation in all the League's activities. NGOs' delegates – called 'assessors' – were considered as 'participants without vote' in the League's organs and therefore allowed to speak, present reports, propose resolutions and amendments and be assigned to sub-committees. In fact, non-governmental representatives were placed upon an equal footing with IGOs' representatives. However, the League later showed a growing tendency to withdraw from collaboration and cooperation. Assessors were replaced by 'correspondents' with reduced privileges. Participation upon invitation and selection became the rule. Among the factors which seem to have influenced the change in the League's attitude there are the growth in the number of NGOs seeking participation, the refusal of the League to take action on sensitive political issues to which NGOs were committed and the consolidation of a bureaucracy which increasingly perceived non-governmental participation as a threat to its prerogatives or as a source of additional work. See Lyman Cromwell White (1951), *International Non-Governmental Organizations: Their Purposes, Methods, and Accomplish-ments*, Rutgers University Press, pp. 252–5; see also Bertram Pickard (1956), *The Greater United Nations*, New York: Carnegie Endowment for International Peace, p. 54.

[8]   See E/43/Rev.2, *Arrangements for consultation with non-governmental organizations*, 21 June 1946. The system was first reviewed in 1950 (ECOSOC Resolution 288(X), *Review of consultative relationship with non-governmental organizations*, 27 February 1950), then in 1968 (Resolution 1269(XLIV), *Arrangements for consultation with non-governmental organizations*, 23 May 1968) and finally in 1996 (Resolution 1996/31 *Consultative Relationship between the United Nations and non-governmental organizations*, 25 July 1996). The ECOSOC model informed to a great extent the arrangements for civil society participation adopted inter alia by the UN Specialised Agencies, by the Council of Europe and by the Organisation of American States.

[9]   Despite the numerous revisions of the arrangements for NGO participation – see *supra* note 8 – the paradigm underpinning the ECOSOC model of *consultative* relationship has not been modified in its fundamental character. The most relevant changes have concerned the specification of the condition for an NGO to be granted consultative status, the treatment of national NGOs and the adoption of rules for NGOs' participation in international conferences convened by the UN (E/RES/96/31 part I, para. 5 and part VII).

[10]   ECOSOC resolutions provide for a differentiated status for NGOs as a function of their involvement in the work of the Council. According to Resolution 96/31,

their status cannot be equated to 'participation without vote' which is reserved for member states which do not have a seat in the ECOSOC;[11] in short, since any possibility for NGOs to engage in negotiating functions is excluded, they are more correctly referred to as observers than as participants. The accreditation mechanism is conceived as a political filter: an organ composed by representatives of member states is established to assess a predefined set of admission conditions which are drafted in non-restrictive terms but are general enough to 'shut the door'[12] when required by political considerations.

In general terms, 'consultative relationship' has proved to be an effective tool within the narrow limits of its declared scope. The presence of non-governmental representatives in meetings and their participation in debates has influenced the agenda and shaped the policy approach, for example by adding a human rights and environmental dimension to a number of political issues. Information provided by non-governmental organizations has become fundamental for the functioning of specific ECOSOC bodies or other UN organs which had adopted similar participatory mechanisms. The number of NGOs applying for consultative status has steadily grown, thus demonstrating the interest in formal participation. The model itself was exported outside the UN and adopted by UN Specialised Agencies, the Council of Europe, the Organisation of America States and other IGOs.

However, from the 1980s and especially after the 'civil society revolution' of the 1990s, NGO–IGO interaction has progressively acquired new qualitative and quantitative dimensions. On the one hand the conditions have been established for an increased non-governmental activism at the international level: globalization and the development of new information technologies

---

NGOs may be accorded general consultative status when they are concerned with most of the activities of the Council and can demonstrate that they have substantive contributions to make to the achievements of the objective of the UN. *Special consultative status* is granted to those NGOs which have a special competence in only a few of the fields of activities covered by the Council. Finally, non-governmental organizations which can make useful but only occasional contributions to the work of the ECOSOC can be accredited in a special list: the *roster*. All three categories of organizations are allowed to attend the public meetings of the ECOSOC as observers. Only NGOs with general or of special status may submit written statements in their field of competence, albeit of different length. Only NGOs of general status may make oral presentations to the ECOSOC and propose items for ECOSOC agenda. See E/RES/96/31, *supra* at note 7, paras 28 to 32.

[11]   See part III paras 1 and 2 E/43/Rev.2, *supra* at note 8. The principle is restated in the subsequent revisions of the arrangements for NGO participation. See for instance paras 18 and 19, E/RES/96/31, *supra* at note 8.

[12]   See J. Aston (2001), 'The United Nations Committee on Non-Governmental Organisations: guarding the entrance of a politically divided house', *European Journal of International Law*, **12**(5), 943–62.

have provided the political ground and the advocacy tools for the mobilization of a growing global public opinion. International non-governmental organizations multiplied in number and fields of activity and advanced a stronger claim to participation. On the other hand, the revitalization of intergovernmental organizations after the end of the cold war brought to the fore the issue of the effectiveness and accountability of their action. In the debate which followed, a greater involvement of civil society in the intergovernmental process started to be perceived both as an effective tool to put pressure on policies implementation by states and as a possible new source of legitimacy for IGO action.

As a result, not only have NGOs become even more important operational partners in the implementation of IGOs' programmes and projects but they have also proved to be able to shape rather than to observe the intergovernmental decision-making process in a growing number of fields. NGOs have started playing a crucial role in setting the international agenda, in influencing international rule making and in contributing to the implementation of international norms. They have proved to be a driving force in some of the major innovations undergone in the international system (such as the establishment of a permanent International Criminal Court) but also vital partners in the day-to-day enforcement of international standards and programmes.

It is worth noting that these substantial changes in NGO involvement have not been matched by a consequent evolution of the existing consultative statuses. While appearing more and more influenced by non-governmental action in their decision making, governmental institutions resisted any attempt to provide a formal recognition of the new role played by NGOs. For instance, the reform of the ECOSOC arrangements in 1996 was limited to secondary changes and simply restated the paradigm of 'consultative relationship'.[13]

As a result, a significant gap has emerged between the legal definition of the NGO–IGO relationship and the concrete dynamics of their interplay. On the one hand consultative status no longer provides IGOs with an effective tool to control non-governmental participation. In the first paragraph of this section, it will be shown that formal limits to participation and formal requirements for participants are ineffective in practice and can be easily circumvented. On the other hand the existing arrangements do not satisfactorily answer the problems deriving from the new dimensions of non-governmental participation. Since consultative status fails in facilitating non-governmental participation, the informal dimension of the NGO–IGO relationship gains importance and new modalities of interaction are experienced (see the second paragraph).

---

[13]   See *supra* note 9.

Consultative Status as an Inadequate Means of Controlling Participation

Practice shows that strict rules on access to IGOs or specific IGO organs do not represent a serious limitation to NGOs' interaction with international organizations. To start with, the lack of formal provisions concerning NGOs' participation in the activity of a specific organ has not prevented NGOs from having informal relations with it. A good example is represented by NGOs' relationship with UN organs other than ECOSOC. While the existing consultative status is expressly limited to ECOSOC and ECOSOC bodies, and any attempt to establish formal relationships with other major UN organs has so far failed,[14] informal cooperation has been developed with both the General Assembly and the Security Council.

This is the case of the UN General Assembly.[15] In November 1993, during the debate on preparations for the International Conference for Population and Development (1994 Cairo Conference), the second Committee of the GA

---

[14]   In the aftermath of the Rio Earth Summit, ECOSOC decided to undertake a general review of the consultative arrangements with NGOs as set out in the 1968 ECOSOC Resolution 1296. Particular attention was devoted to the broader question of NGO participation 'in all areas of work of the UN', the purpose primarily being to extend the consultative relationship to the General Assembly and to Specialised Agencies. The topic proved to be highly controversial. The United States feared that, once the consultative relationship was extended to the GA it would have proved difficult to contrast NGOs' attempt to participate in Security Council meetings. In order to avoid the blockage of the negotiations, the working group responsible for the review finally decided to separate the two issues: while the new ECOSOC resolution would have dealt only with procedures in ECOSOC and international conferences (ECOSOC Resolution 1996/31, 25 July 1997), a decision would have recommended the GA to examine the 'question of the participation of non-governmental organisations in all areas of the work of the United Nations, in the light of experience gained through the arrangements for consultation between non governmental organisations and the Economic and Social Council' (ECOSOC Decision 1996/297, 25 July 1997). Emphasis was put on the fact that the proposed recommendation fell within the competence of the GA as set forth in article 10 of the Charter, thus excluding from the following debate within the Assembly the issue of NGOs' participation in the Security Council activities (UN Press Release ECOSOC/5684, 25 July 1997). The GA endorsed the ECOSOC recommendation with its decision A/52/453 and the open-ended working group on UN reform set up a sub-group on NGO participation in January 1997. However a new political confrontation arose on the scope of work: while Northern countries wanted it limited to GA matters, the Group of 77 and the Non-Aligned Movement insisted that 'all areas . . .' also meant Bretton Wood institutions. This proved to be fatal for the sub-group, which was finally disbanded.

[15]   See P. Willetts (2000), 'From consultative arrangements to partnership: the changing status of NGOs in diplomacy at the UN', in *Global Governance*, **6**, 191–212 at 197.

formally suspended the meeting while the delegates stayed in the room to hear from the head of the NGO Planning Committee.[16] The same procedural device has since then been used several times.[17] A more far-reaching practice was established in 1997 during the 19th GA Special Session convened to review the implementation of Agenda 21 (Earth Summit +5). In that occasion, taking account of the role major groups had played in Rio and with the precedent of the procedures of the Earth Summit, the president of the Assembly, for the first time in the history of the UN, invited NGOs' representatives to take part and to speak in the main plenary debate. Although it was expressly stressed that the Earth Summit +5 experience would 'in no way create a precedent for other special sessions',[18] NGOs have in fact been invited to several other special sessions since then.[19]

As far as the Security Council (SC) is concerned, a legal basis for indirect consultations with NGOs can be found in Article 39 of the Council's Rules of Procedure according to which 'the Council may invite [. . .] other persons, whom it considers competent for the purpose, to supply it with information or to give other assistance in examining matters within its competence'.[20] However, the letter of the norm has been largely overstepped in practice. In February 1997, four NGO representatives briefed the SC on two occasions regarding humanitarian issues in the Great Lakes Region: rather than invoking rule 39,[21] the Council preferred to meet the NGOs' representative informally, in a general room at the UN headquarters.[22] This form of consultation, named an 'Arria meeting' after the Venezuelan Ambassador who pioneered the approach, has developed into a formal practice: an NGO working group on the Council Activities meets on a regular basis with Council members in order to provide briefing on issues of upcoming importance to the SC.

---

   [16]   Ibid., p. 197; see *UN System and Civil Society: an Inventory and Analysis of Practices*, Background Paper for the UN Secretary General's Panel of Eminent Persons on United Nations' Relationship with Civil Society, May 2003, http://www.un-ngls.org/ UNreform.htm, p. 10 (last visited December 2006).

   [17]   According to a Secretary General's Report presented at the start of the post-UNCED review, 'a number of Main Committees have devised informal arrangements which have allowed NGO representatives to make oral statements'. UN Doc. E/AC.70/1994/5, 26 May 1994, p. 42.

   [18]   UN Doc. A/51/864, 7 April 1997; A/51/L.70, 18 April 1997.

   [19]   Willets, 'From consultative arrangements . . .', *supra* note 15, p. 201.

   [20]   S/96/Rev.7, *Provisional Rules of Procedure of the Security Council*, 1983.

   [21]   Under article 39, meetings with experts take place within the official SC activity and minutes are regularly written. Moreover art. 39 provides for the SC input, while in the 'Arria Formula' meetings are held on a regular basis.

   [22]   See Willets, 'From Consultative Arrangements . . .' *supra* note 15, p. 200; see *UN System and Civil Society*, quoted *supra* note 16, p. 10.

Even outside the UN system, the establishment of informal means of consultation seems to be the rule when mechanisms of formal participation are not provided for. During the EUI workshop the Amnesty International (AI) representative stressed that this organization held regular consultations with both the Organisation of American States and the Organisation of African Union before the latter adopted a procedure for accreditation of civil society organizations. In addition to this, AI enjoys an informal relationship with those IGOs which lack arrangements for NGOs' participation (EU, OSCE).

However, even when the relationship with an organ is formally regulated by a normative device, NGOs often keep on participating in other forms. This way they circumvent both the requirements and the selection procedure qualifying the relationship with the IGO.

In some cases, a pre-existing informal arrangement is preferred to formal accreditation according to a new procedure. When the African Union proposed a brand new observer status for civil society organizations, Amnesty International preferred continuing the practice of informal consultations, since it probably perceived the accreditation procedures as time-consuming and the admission requirements as excessively cumbersome.[23]

In other situations, informal participation through already accredited NGOs expressly seeks to circumvent the admissions requirements or the control exercised by the body responsible for monitoring the conduct of NGOs with formal status. Good examples of this practice come again from the UN system. Since the adoption of the first set of rules on NGOs' participation in ECOSOC activities,[24] the tasks of considering applications from NGOs, supervising their activity and proposing the adoption of the consequential measures to the ECOSOC have been entrusted to a specific Committee on Non-Governmental Organisations composed of 19 member states. Given its composition, it is not surprising that, in a number of cases, the Committee appeared to be led more by political than by technical considerations and that proposals for the denial or withdrawal of the status to a given NGO were advanced by the states directly affected by the NGO activity.[25] One of these

---

[23]   According to an AI representative: 'AI has no formal observer status with the African Union . . . Among the requirements for NGOs to obtain observer status are being an African NGO, having the support of five African Union members and no member objecting to the NGO's application. Nevertheless, AI enjoys an informal arrangement with the AU, and was invited to some meetings of the Organisation of African Unity, including OAU Council of Ministers meetings. AI hopes that this arrangement will continue with the AU.' (Answer to the questionnaire circulated at the EUI Workshop.)

[24]   E/43/Rev. 2, *Arrangements for consultation with non-governmental organizations*, 21 June 1946.

[25]   See Aston, *supra* at 12, pp. 943–62.

cases occurred in 1999, when the Commission discussed the application of Human Rights in China.[26]

Human Rights in China (HRC) is an organization devoted to promoting and advancing institutional protection of universally recognized human rights in China. Its action is carried out through research and monitoring activities, advocacy and education initiatives.[27] When the Committee discussed HRC's application for consultative status with ECOSOC at its 693rd meeting, the Chinese representative strongly advocated that the Committee should not recommend the conferral of the status. He stressed that the organization was totally unqualified to make any comments on the human rights situation in China since the overwhelming majority of its members had never set foot on Chinese soil. Moreover he observed that, in the HRC Board of Directors there were criminals, already condemned by Chinese judiciary and that the organization entertained a close relationship with secessionist Tibet organizations. He finally concluded that

> Human Rights in China is not a non-governmental organisation [. . .] but a politically motivated organisation with the purpose of overthrowing the legitimate Government of a Member State of the United Nations and therefore that it did not match the requirements set forth in ECOSOC Resolution 1996/31 according to which NGOs should not engage in activities 'contrary to the purpose and principles of the UN Charter, including unsubstantiated or politically motivated acts against Member States'.[28]

The Chinese representative was able to gather a majority consensus and won the vote both in the Committee and in the ECOSOC.[29] HRC was not granted consultative status but this did not prove enough to block its activities within the UN: Human Rights in China became part of an 'umbrella' organization[30] enjoying consultative status with ECOSOC, and thus was able to keep on providing information on human rights violation in China.[31]

---

26   Reported by Lindblom, *supra* note 3, p. 355.
27   See http://www.hrichina.org/public/index (last visited December 2006).
28   UN Doc. E/1999/109, *Report of the Committee on Non-Governmental Organizations on its 1999 session*, 15 July 1999.
29   Aston defines as 'horse trading', the decision making within the Committee, stressing that the fact of dealing with several complaints at the same time generates political bargains at the expenses of the NGOs concerned. Aston *supra* note 12, p. 955.
30   The Fédération Internationale des Droits de l'Homme.
31   Another similar case has been recorded in 2001, when the representative of Sri Lanka deplored the fact that, at the 57th session of the Commission on Human Rights, members of the Tamil Center for Human Rights (TCHR) had distributed material regarding Sri Lanka. As a matter of fact, while TCHR was refused consultative

More generally, the protean nature of civil society movements multiplies the chances of informal participation in IGOs' activities and significantly reduces the impact of the constraints imposed by formal status. Leaving aside the case of organizations whose peculiar composition ensures indirect forms of participation in IGOs' activities,[32] reference can be made to the cases in which NGOs' activists take part in national delegations or provide national delegations with information then filed to IGO organs as part of the delegation's official documentation.[33]

Consultative Status as an Inadequate Means of Facilitating Participation

A gap between the factual and the legal dimensions of the NGO–IGOs relationship is also reported when it comes to the modalities of NGOs' participation in the activity of intergovernmental organizations. The gap was clearly demonstrated at the EUI workshop when, despite declaring general satisfaction with the status they enjoyed, NGOs reported patterns of interaction with IGOs which departed significantly from the one embodied in a formal relationship. It is submitted that the development of new patterns of NGO–IGO interaction reveals that a consultative relationship cannot satisfactorily channel the claim for increased non-governmental participation or effectively answer the problems that such an increased participation creates.

To start with, the new quantitative levels of non-governmental involvement

---

status in 2000, its members succeeded in obtaining accreditation from another organization and thus in taking part in ECOSOC Human Rights Commission activities. UN Doc. E/2001/86, *Report of the Committee on Non-Governmental Organisations on its 2001 regular session*, 15/June/2001, para. 114.

[32]   At the EUI workshop a representative described the peculiar status of Parliamentarians for Global Action (PGA), a Non Governmental Organisation made up of about 1350 MPs sitting in 103 parliaments in all regions of the world. Because of its unusual constituency, the PGA does not require consultative status with most regional organizations as it already participates indirectly in their activities through its members (for example, PGA has its own parliamentary group in the European Parliament and enjoys the individual membership of its associates in the Parliamentary Assemblies of the CoE, NATO, OCSE, ECOWAS and other organizations). However, Donat-Cattin stressed that 'indirect' participation is not always possible according to the rules on the composition of the IGOs' organs. In such cases the PGA requests formal status. Thus, the PGA has consultative status with ECOSOC ('general consultative status' according to para. 22 ECOSOC Resolution 96/31) and it has been allowed to attend the first session of the Assembly of States Parties of the Rome Statute of the ICC (art.93 Rule of Procedure of the Assembly of States Parties) with the status of 'other participant'.

[33]   See the contribution by Vierucci, in Chapter 5 of this book, 'NGOs before international courts and tribunals'.

in IGO activities has enhanced the relevance of the informal dimension of the NGO–IGO relationship and aggravated its drawbacks.

At the EUI workshop, NGOs' representatives were unanimous in recalling that formal participatory rights are not relevant *in se* but in that they give them the opportunity to lobby governmental organizations. As far as the UN system is concerned, the 'practical dimension' of ECOSOC consultative status was underlined:[34] NGOs are provided with a certain number of permanent or temporary badges which allow access to ECOSOC and other UN organs' open meetings and, in particular, to corridors, cafeteria and other sites at various UN headquarters. These are indeed the most important tools for advocacy and public relations with governmental delegates and IGO officials.[35]

The gap between the actual means of action (lobbying) and the legal framework of the NGO–IGO relationship is made clear by the cases in which, despite the formal respect for their legal status, advocacy NGOs are prevented from having direct access to governmental delegations. In this respect, reference can be made to the firm reaction of some prominent NGOs[36] when they realized that non-governmental organizations were prevented from gaining access to the floor of the plenary of the UN Commission on Human Rights in its 2004 session: they immediately addressed an open letter to the President of the Commission on Human Rights and other high-level UN officials stressing that, by relegating NGOs to the stalls,

> civil society is prevented from interacting with governmental delegates, which is crucial to the advocacy role. Furthermore this is a distressing departure from the long established practice of interaction between the functional commission of ECOSOC and non-governmental organizations in consultative status.[37]

They concluded by urging reconsideration of the 'unfortunate' decision.[38] Another example of the impact of space allocation on NGOs' activity was

---

[34]   Statement by the representative of Parliamentarians for Global Action.

[35]   PGA representative, at note 32.

[36]   Among others: Association for the Prevention of Torture; International Human Rights Watch; International Commission of Jurists; International Federation for Human Rights; World Organisation Against Torture.

[37]   See the open letter addressed to the Director-General of the UN Office at Geneva, the UN Acting High Commissioner for Human Rights and the President of the Commission on Human Rights, 16 March 2004. (Filed at www.fidh.org/article.php.)

[38]   A similar case has been reported by the representative of Amnesty International at the EUI workshop. He recalled that at the 2002 ECOSOC session in Geneva, the high number of NGOs taking part in the meetings made it necessary to change the venue. In the new room, states' delegates sat in the stalls while NGOs' representatives sat on the balcony and were thus prevented from exercising direct lobbying. According to the AI representative, NGOs' contribution to the session was greatly affected.

reported at the Florence workshop. A participant stressed that access to the third floor of the New York UN building is allowed to NGOs as far as the main corridor is concerned; as a consequence, only some of the offices of accredited media may be reached by NGO representatives and this has sometimes proved to be detrimental to their action.[39] More generally, the improved security measures adopted after 11 September 2001 have raised concerns in the NGO community: while NGO representatives acknowledge that security is of paramount importance, they also stress that restrictions are often discriminatory and implemented at their expense. Finally, since the most important part of NGOs' advocacy role is carried out informally, the danger exists that extrinsic circumstances may undermine the effectiveness of their action.

It is worth noting that the mentioned 'extrinsic circumstances' can obviously lie in the diverse political weight, financial resources, dimensions or professional skills of civil society organizations. As a matter of fact, despite being vested with the same set of privileges, certain NGOs or NGOs' categories lack the material means to use them fruitfully and to have a real possibility of affecting the intergovernmental processes. Thus it is not surprising that representatives from small and highly specialized organizations do not perceive consultative status as an effective way to influence the work of non-governmental organizations[40] and rely mostly on other instruments (participation in international conferences, technical advice providing before international courts and participation in civil society networks) which offer more chances to exert influence at a lower cost.[41] More generally, the prevalence of informality risks working to the disadvantage of the smallest, less resourced and less networked organizations and thus, in general, of southern-based NGOs, as revealed by the answers to a questionnaire submitted to almost 150 NGOs within the framework of the process of review of the consultative status promoted by the UN Secretary General in 2003:[42] 'if . . . lobbying is to be a primary means for civil society participation, a greater effort to increase capacity building to develop

---

[39] Statement by the representative of Parliamentarians for Global Action.

[40] As reported during the EUI Workshop by the representatives of the Instituto Internacional de Derecho y Medio Ambiente (IIDMA) and of the AIRE Center. IIDMA is a small environmental law centre providing technical support on environmental matters. The AIRE Center is an association providing individuals with legal assistance before international human rights jurisdictions.

[41] Thus the paradox is apparent: while for influential NGOs the formal status is strictly speaking useless since their action is mainly carried out through informal means such as lobbying, for smaller organizations it is equally useless since they have not enough political weight to make use of those informal means.

[42] See *infra* the third section of this chapter at p. 46.

the necessary skills among civil society representatives from developing countries is needed'.[43]

The inadequacy of existing participatory rights to deal with the growing influence of civil society in IGOs' decision making can also be inferred by the proliferation of new modalities of NGO–IGO interaction which make the 'privileges' of traditional accreditation largely redundant. In this regard the UN system provides us with some interesting examples.

As part of the initiatives taken within the International Decade of the World's Indigenous People,[44] ECOSOC has established a Permanent Forum on Indigenous Issues.[45] The Forum serves as an advisory body of the Council with a mandate to provide expert advice and recommendations on indigenous issues relating to economic and social development, culture, the environment, education, health and human rights. The Forum is a body of experts sitting in their personal capacity; however, while half of the 16 members are traditionally nominated by governments and elected by the Council, the other half is appointed by the President of the Council on the basis of nominations made by indigenous organizations. The forum is a first in recognizing a formal advisory role for a specific sector of civil society on an equal footing with governmental experts. As a matter of fact, if organizations of indigenous people have already taken part in different ECOSOC working groups, they formally did so as observers under the existing consultative arrangements.

Other innovative patterns of interaction between NGOs and the UN have been developed within the Commission on Sustainable Development (CSD). The CSD was established in 1993 as an ECOSOC functional commission,[46] with the mandate to ensure effective follow-up to the 1992 UN Conference on Environment and Development (UNCED) and in particular to examine progress in the implementation of sustainable development principles agreed by governments in the *Agenda for the Twenty-first century* (Agenda 21).[47] Agenda 21 acknowledges that the sustainable development objectives cannot

---

[43]   See *Survey of Civil Society: UN and Civil Society Relationship – Questionnaire on NGO Opinion* – background paper for the Cardoso panel, October 2003, at http://www.un.org/reform/relateddocs.html (accessed December 2006).

[44]   See UN Doc. A/50/157.

[45]   See ECOSOC Resolution 2000/22, *Establishment of a Permanent Forum on Indigenous Issues*, 28 July 2000.

[46]   The General Assembly requested ECOSOC to establish the Commission on Sustainable Development following a recommendation included in Agenda 21 (UN Doc. A/RES/47/191, *Institutional arrangements to follow up the United Nations Conference on Environment and Development*, 29 January 1993). The Commission was finally established by ECOSOC decision 1993/207.

[47]   See UN Doc. A/RES/47/191, *Institutional arrangements . . . supra* note 46, paras 2 and 3.

be achieved without a genuine involvement of societal actors. It identifies the nine constituencies[48] which can, and are requested to, make their contribution and stresses that broad public participation in decision making is a fundamental prerequisite for the achievement of sustainable development.[49]

Driven by these principles, the Commission on Sustainable Development has represented a veritable laboratory of new patterns of interaction with civil society.[50] The most innovative practice is represented by the so-called 'multi-stakeholder dialogues', introduced in 1998 following a recommendation of the 19th Special Session of the General Assembly ('Earth Summit+5').[51] According to the new practice, two-day multi-stakeholder segments are introduced into the official programme of the CSD annual session. During these days major groups' representatives and governmental delegates gather together to discuss specific topics falling within the agenda of the session, with parliamentary rules put aside in favour of an interactive discussion.[52] The outcomes of the dialogue are reported in the Chair's Summary, which is included in the official documentation of the session and is meant to serve as reference material for government delegates negotiating the final decisions to be adopted by the CSD. Recent studies seem to confirm that multi-stakeholder dialogues exert a significant influence on CSD decision making:[53] for example, according to a background paper drafted for the Secretary General's Panel

---

[48]   Women, children and youth, indigenous people, NGOs, local authorities, workers and trade unions, farmers, business and industry, and the scientific and technology community.

[49]   See Agenda 21, chapter 23, UN Doc. A/CONF.151/26/Rev.1, *Report of the United Nations Conference on Environment and Development* held in Rio de Janeiro 3–14 June 1992, Vol. I – Resolutions adopted by the Conference, Annex II, at p. 9.

[50]   As an ECOSOC functional Commission, CSD should be subject to the Council's rules and procedure, including the arrangements for NGOs' participation. However it is clear that existing formal relationships do not meet the requirement set out in Agenda 21 since it allows civil society to observe and not to shape the decision-making process and since it excludes from participation constituencies which are expressly recognized by the Agenda. Hence the need to conceive new patterns of inter-action.

[51]   See UN Doc. A/RES/S-19/2, para. 133e).

[52]   The preparation of the multi-stakeholder dialogue is itself a multi-stakeholder process. The Bureau of the Commission invites representative networks from each major group (defined as 'organizing partners') to form a steering group which coordinates the preparations and facilitates the engagement of the stakeholders. Each organizing partner is called upon to draft, in consultation with its major group, a 'dialogue starter paper' and to appoint a representative for the dialogue. The dialogue papers are part of the official CSD documentation.

[53]   See *Multi-stakeholder Dialogues: Learning from the UNCSD Experience*, background paper n°4 submitted by the Consensus Building Institute, UN Doc. DESA/DSD/PC3/BP4.

on UN relations with Civil Society, up to 80 per cent of the work programme on sustainable tourism development adopted by CSD in 1999 came from proposals made and discussed by the multi-stakeholder dialogue on tourism.[54] It is worth noting that, following the 2002 Johannesburg World Summit on Sustainable Development (WSSD), the CSD has reorganized its work and further enhanced the dialogue with civil society. The multi-stakeholder dialogues have been supplemented by 'interactive dialogues' held during, and not before, the intergovernmental negotiations, with major groups' representatives taking part in the meetings side-by-side with governmental delegates.

These recent developments within the UN Economic and Social Council seem to mark a trend rather than an exception since institutional arrangements allowing for a greater involvement of civil society in IGO decision-making processes have progressively spread beyond the ECOSOC framework.

This is the case with the Joint United Nations Programme on HIV/AIDS, UNAIDS. The Programme was established in 1996 as a joint and co-sponsored initiative of six UN Specialised Agencies[55] to give an urgent, coordinated and comprehensive response to the alarming outbreak of the AIDS epidemic and to its impact on human lives and on social and economic development. UNAIDS is reported to be the first UN Programme to include NGOs representatives on its governing body as full participants rather than observers.[56] The Program Coordinating Board (PCB) comprises 22 government delegates elected by ECOSOC as full-rights members while representatives of the co-sponsor organizations and five NGOs participate in the works of the board without voting rights. It is worth noting that, although the legal instrument defining the arrangements for the participation of NGOs in the PCB attempts to differentiate their status from that accorded to co-sponsor governmental organizations,[57] UNAIDS documentation and official UN

---

[54]   See *UN System and Civil Society – An Inventory and an Analysis of Practices*, background Paper for the Secretary General's Panel of Eminent Persons on UN Relation with Civil Society, May 2003, http://www.un-ngls.org/UNreform.htm.

[55]   UNDP, UNICEF, UNPF, WHO, UNESCO and the World Bank. In the following years other UN Agencies joined: the United Nations Office on Drugs and Crimes (UNODC), ILO, WFP and UNCHR.

[56]   See UN Doc. A/53/170, *Arrangements and the Practices for the Interaction of Non-governmental Organisations in all Activities of the UN System. Report of the Secretary General*, 18 July 1998, para. 30.

[57]   ECOSOC Resolution 1995/2 gives a firm definition of co-sponsors' status in PCB: 'co-sponsors will participate in the work of the PCB and have full rights, except the right to vote'. To the contrary, the Annex to the same resolution (*Arrangements for the participation of NGOs in the work of the Programme Coordination Board: report on the informal consultation of the ECOSOC*) makes every effort to avoid terms that would legally qualify NGOs' participation in the Board. The result is a set of provisions materially describing NGOs' position: NGOs 'will be invited to take part in the work

reports generally do not make any distinction and refer to both categories as 'non voting members' [58]

FROM A NEW POLITICAL ROLE TO A NEW LEGAL RELATIONSHIP? RETHINKING NON-GOVERNMENTAL PARTICIPATION BETWEEN FORMALIZATION AND SELF-REGULATION

The analysis carried out in the previous section has shown that the existing formal arrangements and statuses do not provide a realistic picture of NGO–IGO interaction. The significant gap between the legal status and the factual dimension of NGOs' role evidences a paradigm shift in NGOs' relationship with IGOs. Originally conceived as passive observers of the intergovernmental process within the limited field of economic and social cooperation, NGOs have gradually engaged in much more complicated patterns of interaction with international organizations.

The broader role played by civil society organizations is reflected by the evolution of the terminology employed in official IGO documentation and international legal instruments. Since the early 1990s, new sets of concepts have been progressively introduced, at first within limited domains of UN activity and progressively in a growing number of international fora, in order to describe the interaction with NGOs. Civil society organizations have started to be qualified as 'partners' of governments and IGOs in the pursuit of global goals and 'active participants' of intergovernmental processes. The relationships between NGOs and international organizations have been qualified as 'partnerships' or 'dialogues'. The debates on the need to strengthen and increase the participation of civil society in IGOs' activities have multiplied.

---

of the PCB'; they will have 'seat at the table with the representatives . . . of the Co-sponsoring organisations and of the Member States' and 'would be able to speak'. However NGOs 'would have no negotiating role' and 'would not participate in any part of the formal decision-making process, including the right to vote'. In practice it is difficult to draw a distinction between NGOs' and co-sponsors' positions. The 'invitation' of NGOs to PCB meetings is not discretional and is regulated by provisions excluding any interference of state representatives in the choice of the 'invited' NGOs. Moreover, the prohibition to take part in negotiations meets with the problem of drawing a clear line between what is and what is not a contribution to negotiations.

[58]   See, for example, the information reported on the UNAIDS website, and UNAIDS publications (for example, *A Joint Response to HIV/AIDS: Joint UN Programme on HIV/AIDS*) at www.unaids.org, (accessed December 2006).

While it can be argued that rhetoric plays its part in the new terminology and that a certain ambiguity on the use of concepts exists, a redefinition of the relationship between civil society and international organizations is under way and the concept of participation seems to be at the core of the process.

From a political standpoint, the partnership language reflects the neoliberal idea that intergovernmental action is ineffective or even unable to face alone the challenges of a globalized world. In order to achieve more effectively and more promptly their objectives and to overcome the barriers to their action, IGOs should engage in a closer cooperation with civil society. In this perspective, rather than suggesting an equality of roles or of status, the concept of partnership underlines that, in the pursuit of their respective missions, non-state actors and IGOs may have an interest in bringing together their strengths and capacities; thus IGOs' policies and their implementation should be designed to create synergies with all the relevant actors. Of course, the official discourse on the complementary roles of IGOs, states and civil society organizations does not exclude the possibility that the new 'partnership policy' may also have other (and more controversial) objectives. For instance, a direct involvement of local non-governmental actors could be seen as a way to bypass the resistance and the inaction of states to implement the policies they have endorsed at the international level. Conversely, states may favour a closer relationship with civil society in specific fields (such as environment) to avoid assuming binding commitments. Finally some authors reconnect the new attitude towards NGOs to the debate on the legitimacy of IGOs' action: a stronger engagement with NGOs would aim at compensating the democratic deficit of IGOs and at providing them with a greater legitimacy at a time of increased activism.[59]

Whatever the (political) rationale underpinning the new concept may be, it is crucial to ascertain whether the semantics of partnerships is consolidating into a new legal regime for the NGO–IGO relationship.

In a recent report,[60] the UN Secretary General has defined partnerships in

---

[59]   See for instance M.A. Cameron (1998), 'Democratization of foreign policy: the Ottawa Process as a model', in M.A. Cameron, R.J. Lawson and B.W. Tomlin (eds), *To Walk Without Fear: The Global Movement to Ban Landmines*, Oxford: Oxford University Press, p. 441. See also 'Introduction', ibid., at 10. For a sharp criticism of the idea that an increased role for NGOs in intergovernmental processes could contribute to the democratization and therefore to the legitimacy of international law, see A. Kenneth (2000), 'The Ottawa Convention Banning Landmines, the Role of International Non-governmental Organizations and the Idea of International Civil Society', *European Journal of International Law*, **11**(1), 91–120.

[60]   UN doc. A/58/227 *Enhanced cooperation between the United Nations and all relevant partners, in particular the private sector. Report of the Secretary General*, 18 August 2003.

UN as 'voluntary and collaborative relationships between various parties, both state and non-state, in which all participants agree to work together to achieve a common purpose or undertake a specific task and to share risks, responsibilities, resources, competencies and benefits'. He then added:

> Partnerships between the United Nations and non-State actors work on many levels, address many different issues and serve different purposes. They range from participation in the intergovernmental process, as in the tripartite structure of the International Labour Organisation, to the consultative status of business associations with the Economic and Social Council, to more recent arrangements such as the Global Environment Facility, the Information and Communication Technology Task Force, global initiatives on specific health issues and the Global Compact.

It is clear that the definition proposed by the Secretary General lacks specific legal significance. The aims of partnerships are not defined and may range from policy dialogue and advocacy to fund raising and operational delivery. The addressees of the 'partnership policy' are heterogeneous actors including states, the UN itself, non-governmental organizations, business enterprises and the private sector in general. Most of all, no distinction is made according to the legal framework underpinning the different forms of partnership or the legal positions recognized by the non-state actors: a political concept (cooperation) is preferred to a legal definition of the engagement with the organization (voluntary commitments, bilateral agreements or institutional arrangements providing for a formal status).

In conclusion, the partnership discourse aims at introducing a new political paradigm in the NGO–IGO relationship but leaves unaffected the problem of the legal status of civil society within IGOs: it is recognized that global goals may be achieved only by a greater cooperation with civil society at the international level, but nothing is said about the forms and the degree of formalization that this cooperation should assume.

The Reasons for a Higher Degree of Formalization

We could argue that the recognition of an enhanced participation of civil society in the activity of international organizations should logically be reflected in a new formal status replacing the consultative one: legal regulation would represent the final step of a social and political change which is occurring in practice. A forerunner of this development may be considered to be the Council of Europe (CoE) which, in November 2003, reformed its arrangement for civil society participation by establishing a new 'participatory' status for international non-governmental organizations. According to the preamble of the resolution which has introduced the new framework, it 'is indispensable that the rules governing the relations between the Council of

Europe and NGOs evolve to reflect the active participation of international non-governmental organizations (INGOs) in the organization's policy and work programme'.[61]

In support of this argument we could also invoke a growing IGO practice. Once consolidated, informal participatory mechanisms are often reproduced in formal arrangements, as is shown by the experiences of the Organisation of American States, the Council of Europe and UN ECOSOC.[62] The trend is reflected in the current debates on the reform of the existing consultative arrangements where the formal recognition of a participatory role for civil society is generally associated with proposals on the way institutional arrangements should be reshaped. However, what would make 'indispensable', to use the words of the CoE resolution (2003)8, the formalization of the new role played by civil society in a new legal regime is hardly spelled out in explicit terms.

A first set of reasons is certainly connected to a growing demand for legal certainty and uniformity in the interaction between civil society and international organizations. The experience has shown that the plethora of ad hoc arrangements and informal practices so far developed has fragmented participation and created incoherencies. In a number of cases, organizations or organs which have complementary competence and cooperate in their activities have developed diverging policies towards NGOs' participation, thus threatening the effectiveness of civil society's contribution. The problem is particularly apparent within the UN system whose institutional architecture contemplates a coordinated action of Specialised Agencies, the UN itself and, more generally, the different organs involved in decision making. For instance it has been noted that, owing to the lack of coordination in the accreditation requirements, NGOs which are in a consultative relationship with ECOSOC

---

[61]   See the Preamble of the Resolution Res(2003)8, *Participatory status for international non-governmental organizations with the Council of Europe*, adopted by the CoE Committee of Ministers on 19 November 2003.

[62]   The informal dialogue that used to take place between state delegates in the OAS General Assembly and representatives of civil society organizations has recently been formalized in an official activity of the organization (see General Assembly Resolution, *Increasing and strengthening civil society participation in OAS activities*, 10 June 2003, AG/RES 1915 (XXXIII-O/03), para. 2, which adopted the Permanent Council Resolution, *Strategies for increasing and strengthening participation by civil society organizations in OAS activities*, 26 March 2003, CP/RES 840 (1361/03)). In a similar way, the major innovations introduced by the 1996 reform of the ECOSOC arrangements (general accreditation procedure for international conferences; easier access to consultative status for national NGOs) formalized trends and practices which had already been established informally (see ECOSOC Resolution, *Consultative Relationship between the UN and Non-Governmental Organisations*, 25 July 1996, E/RES/1996/31.

and work on specific cross-institutional issues such as food or health are sometimes prevented from getting access to the relevant specialized agency, even if
that agency actively participates in ECOSOC and its functional commissions.[63] Similarly, one of the reasons most frequently invoked in support of
NGO participation in the works of the General Assembly is precisely the fact
that it is incoherent to prevent NGOs from making their contribution when the
GA has to consider reports from ECOSOC or has to formulate policy on
follow-up conferences in which civil society organizations have played an
active role. To put it in the terms used by the UN Secretary General, 'there
exists a great variety of accreditation processes. Despite a substantial body of
practice, nongovernmental organizations wishing to attend and participate in
United Nations conferences and meetings often encounter uneven standards
and confusing procedures'.[64]

Thus the harmonization of accreditation procedures and participatory privileges through a formal regulation is seen as a necessary condition to enhance
civil society's contribution to IGOs' activities. As has been pointed out by the
Secretary General of the Organisation of American States in a recent review of
the rules of procedure for civil society participation within the OAS, 'it is clear
that there are several proper mechanisms established that have allowed for
increased involvement and partnership; however, for civil society organizations (CSO) participation to reach its most productive potential will require
harmonizing these existing mechanisms and regulation to promote inclusive
participation from CSO'.[65]

A second and solid argument in favour of a more formalized relationship
between civil society and IGOs is generally found in the need to face the problems arising from the new quantitative and qualitative dimensions of NGO
participation.

On the one hand, the multiplication of NGOs seeking participation in
IGOs' activities requires facing an 'openness dilemma': the more IGOs
are open to civil society, the more difficult it is to select the information

---

[63]   The concern was reported during the informal meeting of NGO Focal Points
from the UN System and International Organisations convened in March 2003 by the
United Nations Non-Governmental Liaison Service (NGLS). In particular it was underlined that some specialized agencies' requirements exclude the candidature of national
NGOs which is conversely admitted under the ECOSOC Resolution 1996/31. See
*Summary Report of the Meeting of NGO and Civil Society Focal Points from the UN
System and International Organisations*, 6–7 March 2003, Geneva, www.un-ngls.org/
focalpointmtg.doc.
[64]   See *Strengthening of the United Nations: an agenda for further change*, report
of the Secretary General, A/57/387, 09/10/2002, para. 139.
[65]   *Review of the Rules of Procedure for Civil Society Participation with the
Organisation of American States*, 31 March 2004, CP/CISC-106/04, page 2.

channelled by NGOs and to benefit from their potential contribution.[66] The dilemma is in the first place a challenge for the intergovernmental process: since any engagement with civil society has an 'opportunity cost', the process is strengthened only if the added value of participation exceeds the cost. As a consequence, there is a growing IGO interest in adopting the necessary measures to make sure that the 'appropriate' actors are involved. But over-crowding is equally a concern for NGOs, since more participants imply less participation. As Bettati pointed out as early as 1986, 'le péril majeur qui menace finalement les ONG réside davantage dans l'inflation de leur nombre, dans leur rivalités et dans leurs bureaucraties qui dévalorisent leur action'.[67] And in fact, practice shows that, in some 'high demand' bodies, like the Commission on Human Rights, the increase in the number of civil society organizations asking to participate has already had drastic effects.[68]

On the other hand, a higher degree of regulation is also seen as the neces-sary response to the drawbacks of the informal patterns of relationship so far developed. We have already shown that informality, and in particular the prac-tice of lobbying, is a source of inequalities among different categories of non-governmental organizations and it can be itself a barrier to participation. Even worse, the murky corners of informal relationships allows the so-called 'uncivil society'[69] to push forward its interests in the intergovernmental process.

In broader terms, informal participation affects the transparency of IGO func-tioning since it prevents tracing to what extent and by which specific interest IGOs' decision making is affected. While these distortions raise limited concerns as long as civil society participation has a moderate impact on the outcomes of the intergovernmental processes, they become more and more problematic as NGOs gain political weight and are formally recognized as 'participants' in those processes. As has been pointed out by the High Level Panel established by the UN Secretary General to review the relationship between the UN and civil society:[70] 'as civil society has become more powerful, it is being called upon to

---

66   The dilemma was illustrated by Prof. O. de Schutter at the EUI Workshop.

67   M. Bettati (1986), 'La contribution des organisations non gouvernementales à la formation et à l'application du droit international', in M. Bettati and P.-M. Dupuy (eds), *Les ONG et le Droit International*, Paris: Economica, p. 21.

68   In 2003, speaking time for NGOs on some agenda items of the UN Commission on Human Rights was reduced to 1.30 minutes per speaker. However, over-crowding seems to be a problem affecting only some bodies according to the function performed and their procedural arrangements. See *Summary Report, supra* note 63, p. 6.

69   See, in this volume, the contribution by O. de Frouville, 'Domesticating civil society at the United Nations'.

70   The proposals advanced by the Panel and the following debate which took place in the UN General Assembly will be analysed in the third section of the present chapter, at p. 46.

justify its new status and influence'.[71] Thus the recognition of an enhanced involvement of civil society in IGO decision making seems to imply a more transparent specification of their role and to require a more careful consideration of their legitimacy and accountability. To use again the words of the Panel, 'Member States can reasonably expect the Secretariat to ensure that actors engaging in their deliberative processes meet at least some basic standards of governance and demonstrate their credentials, whether they are based on experience, expertise, membership or a base of support.'[72]

In this framework, a higher degree of regulation both in the selection of civil society interlocutors, in the definition of the modalities of interaction and in the supervision of NGO activity, seems highly desirable.

The Dangers of Formalization and the Option of Self-regulation

As soon as we move on from the enunciation of general principles to devise concrete proposals of formal regulation, serious problems do emerge. To start with, the legitimacy of civil society involvement in the IGO decision-making process is difficult to define and even more difficult to assess. Recent academic and political debates have warned against the danger of simplistic solutions.

On the one hand, it has been underlined that it would be misleading to confuse legitimacy to voice an opinion with representativity. Most organizations make their voice heard on the grounds of their technical expertise, ability to mobilize people, operational effectiveness, track record of working for the public interest and more generally for the values they embody. Thus any selecting criterion or participatory device aiming at enhancing the representativity of these civil society organizations by way, for instance, of fixed quotas for different constituencies or of membership requirements would finally end in a loss of information and policy inputs and would perhaps raise the danger of 'corporatist mechanisms' among civil society.[73] The opposite could also be true. Civil society includes organizations genuinely representative of social and professional groups which claim to speak for the people whose interest they reflect and it goes without saying that such organizations should be asked to give an account of their representativity.[74] More broadly, practice seems to

---

[71]   UN Doc. A/58/817, *We the people: civil society, the United Nations and global governance. Report of the Panel of Eminent Persons on United Nations-Civil Society Relations*, 11 June 2004, para. 16.

[72]   Ibid., para. 18.

[73]   See *Summary Report, supra* note 63, p. 11.

[74]   See for instance the ECOSOC resolution establishing the UN Permanent Forum on Indigenous Issues which expressly prescribes that the indigenous nominated members should be selected according to the 'principles of transparency, representativity and equal

suggest that representative NGOs are more suitable for engaging in institutionalized forms of participation, such as the establishment of a specific body made of selected NGOs' representatives (see, for instance, the cases of the International Labour Organisation and of the UN Permanent Forum for Indigenous Issues). Thus an argument could be made for regulating differently the participation of different categories of civil society. However such an approach would inevitably raise the problem of defining such categories.

Secondly, it could be argued that a single legal regime would not sufficiently take into account that civil society participation is highly differentiated according to the domain concerned. Far from indicating a general evolution of the NGO role within international organizations, the specific ad hoc arrangements introduced by some UN organs, UN Programmes and the OAS General Assembly would evidence that only in some sectors of IGO activity is there a factual or political need for a more formalized relationship with civil society. Thus the fragmentation of participatory means would simply reflect the variety of the NGO–IGO relationship in different domains and would not raise the need for a normative standardization.

Finally, it could also be questioned whether any legal regulation is suitable at all. The effectiveness of a legal regime of participation is far from being proved: a set of formal rules would not necessarily prevent NGOs from acting as informally as they already do today and therefore it would likely fail in addressing the problems raised by informal relationship.[75] Moreover, a higher degree of institutionalization is perceived as a threat by a significant part of civil society, and in particular by the most influential organizations. One of the arguments put forward at the time of the League of Nations not to adopt formal arrangements for NGO participation was precisely that 'it is not desirable to risk diminishing the activity of these voluntary international organisations . . . by even the appearance of an official supervision'.[76]

In more recent times, the experience of the ECOSOC Committee on NGOs has shown that, when the task of selecting and supervising NGOs is entrusted to a governmental body, considerations of political nature are likely to interfere with the assessment of the established parameters if not to make it the battleground of the traditional struggle among states for international advantage. Similarly, the conversion of informal practices into more formal mechanisms

---

opportunity for all indigenous people, including internal processes, where appropriate, and local indigenous consultation processes'. (ECOSOC Res. 2000/22, para. 1.)

[75]   Statement by Prof. O. de Schutter at the EUI Workshop.

[76]   See quotation in B. Seary (1996), 'The early history – from the Congress of Vienna to the San Francisco conference', in P. Willetts (ed.), *The Conscience of the World – The Influence of Non-Governmental Organisations in the UN System*, London: Hurst.

implies the opening of governmental negotiations which could finally result in more restrictive arrangements. In a broader sense, there is a creeping concern that any proposal to tailor a formal participatory status for civil society may actually hide the attempt by IGO member states to hamper the enhanced role that civil society has been playing in the intergovernmental process: bound by the constraints of an institutional function and deprived of the most effective informal means of pressure, NGOs would finally be prevented from playing their role effectively.[77]

Thus we wonder whether the challenges raised by civil society participation could not be faced in a radically different way. Some authors have already asserted that the traditional legal framework should be abandoned as the point of reference for the assessment of civil society position in the international law order. In wondering 'who needs article 71 [of the UN Charter]?', Noortmann suggests that a formal relationship responds more to the needs of IGOs than to the aims of non-governmental organizations. From this perspective, the fact that NGOs are co-opted in international governmental institutions through accreditation procedures stands in contrast to their basic raison d'être, that is, to provide an independent opposition to governmental power and therefore to help establish a system of checks and balances at the international level.[78] Thus, other than urging a reform of the existing legal regime, the gap would require devising a new set of tools to describe better and finally regulate the role played by civil society.

According to this perspective, self-regulation is proposed as the best answer to the problems raised by NGO participation in intergovernmental processes. Other than introducing disputed criteria on NGO selection, IGO should push civil society to organize itself into coalitions and networks in

---

[77]   Hence it is not surprising that on a number of occasions influential NGOs have taken a stance against a more formalized relationship with IGOs. A clear example is provided by the reaction of Amnesty International, Human Rights Watch, FIDH and other organizations to a discussion paper issued by the Commission of European Communities on the relationship between the Commission and NGOs: in a joint letter the NGOs opposed the establishment of a formal mechanism of consultation, since it 'will entail a predetermined selection of the NGOs which might be consulted, and thereby make the dialogue less open'. Between the lines we read the aversion of NGOs towards any formal limit to their action. See *Some Reactions to the Discussion Paper Issued by the European Commission: 'the Commission and NGOs, Building a Stronger Partnership'*, open letter from a number of NGOs, 27 April 2000.

[78]   M. Noortmann (2004), 'Who really needs article 71? A critical approach to the relationship between NGOs and the UN', in W.P. Heere (ed.), *From Government to Governance: the growing impact of non-state actors on the international and European legal system. Proceedings of the sixth Hague Joint Conference held in The Hague, the Netherlands, 3–5 July 2003*, The Hague: T.M.C. Asser Press, p. 118.

order to meet the challenges raised by overcrowding and fragmented participation. Informal participation should be recognized as an inherent pattern of
IGO–civil society interaction and its drawbacks should be addressed by exert-
ing pressure on NGOs to engage in self-commitments such as the compliance
with 'codes of conduct' jointly drafted by NGO and IGO representatives.

The issues of legitimacy and accountability could be significantly played
down by encouraging a voluntary engagement by NGOs to be more transparent about who they are and what they do. In this framework, the scope
of legal regulation should be limited to establish some form of supervisory
mechanism that would guarantee the respecting of self-assumed obligations
and more generally to provide an NGO-friendly environment within
IGOs by removing practical obstacles to participation and increasing IGO
transparency.[79]

MULTIPLYING THE PATTERNS OF NON-GOVERNMENTAL PARTICIPATION

In recent years, the debate on the need to revise the forms of the NGO–IGO
relationship has spread beyond the domain of academic speculation to enter
with force the political agenda of intergovernmental organizations. In a short
lapse of time, official initiatives aimed at reframing the relationship with civil
society have multiplied. In November 2003, the Council of Europe reformed
the arrangements for NGOs' participation in its activities and introduced a new
participatory status;[80] in June 2004, a Panel of Eminent Persons established by
the UN Secretary General with the task to review the relationship between the
UN and civil society[81] submitted a report which advanced concrete proposals
for improved modalities of interaction and suggested a major rethinking of the
UN role; in June 2004, the member states of the African Union approved the
Statutes of the Economic, Social and Cultural Council (ECOSOCC) of the
Union, proposing a new approach to deal with civil society's demands for
participation in intergovernmental activities;[82] in March 2004 and in March
2005, comprehensive studies on the existing procedures for civil society participation were issued by the Secretariat of the Organisation of American States[83]

---

[79]   As proposed by the representative of Parliamentarians for Global Action at the
EUI workshop.
[80]   See *infra* in the text.
[81]   See *infra* in the text.
[82]   See *infra* in the text.
[83]   *Review of the Rules of Procedure for Civil Society Participation with the
Organisation of American States*, 31 March 2004, CP/CISC-106/04, p. 2.

and by the World Bank Vice Presidency[84] with the declared purpose of provid-ing a framework for the continuing internal debates on the way to improve the engagement with civil society organizations.

This unprecedented attention paid by governmental institutions to the mechanisms of cooperation with non-state actors shows a change in the polit-ical climate. Unlike what happened in the early 1990s, when only partial responses were given to the growing claim for civil society participation,[85] a comprehensive reconsideration of the NGO–IGO relationship appears today at the core of the debate. The new approach reveals a generalized need to combine the recognition of the role played by civil society in the intergov-ernmental processes with the definition of a clear framework for their action: in order best to enjoy the advantages and to minimize the shortcomings of a closer relationship with civil society organizations, it is necessary to ratio-nalize and coordinate procedures, improve transparency and define the respective responsibilities. In short, a higher degree of regulation is deemed necessary.

Here the political debate meets the academic speculation. The scholarly alternative between a model of relationship grounded on institutionalization and a different one grounded on informality and self-regulation does not seem to find confirmation in the reforms so far proposed or already adopted. In prac-tice, the two approaches are not necessarily exclusive, since varying degrees of self-regulation and legal formalism may be effectively combined to provide tailored solutions to the problems raised by the interaction with civil society. Thus, instead of a single framework, a plurality of models of interaction are emerging which can be classified according to a decreasing degree of legal formalization. In this order I deal with them hereinafter, with the express warning that the following classification does not aim at being either final or exhaustive.

---

[84] *Issues and Options for Improving Engagement Between the World Bank and Civil Society Organisations*, paper issued by the External Affairs, Communications and United Nations Vice Presidency, the Environmentally and Socially Sustainable Development Network Vice Presidency and the Operations Policy and Country Services Network Vice Presidency in March 2005, http://www.worldbank.org/civilsociety.

[85] The demands for more participation pushed forward by civil society organi-zations in the aftermath of the UN conferences of the early 1990s were met both with the refusal of any general reform of the existing formal relationships and with the establishment of innovative mechanisms of cooperation in specific fields of IGO action; the idea prevailed that informality and the multiplication of the patterns of inter-action would have represented viable solutions to the instances of civil society. We have already pointed out the problems stemming from such an approach.

The Institutionalization of Civil Society Participation

The complete integration of civil society in the institutional machinery of an intergovernmental organization is illustrated by the newly-established Economic, Social and Cultural Council (ECOSOCC) of the African Union (AU). According to article 3.1 of the ECOSOCC Statutes, the interaction with civil society is put in place through membership of an official organ which is statutorily vested with a role in the decision-making process of the organization: 'ECOSOCC shall be an advisory organ of the African Union composed of different social and professional groups of the Member States of the African Union.'

It is worth noting that the ECOSOCC model for civil society participation is not unprecedented. The idea of allowing CSOs to participate as members of an official IGO organ dates back to the establishment of the International Labour Organisation (ILO) in 1919. As is known, ILO is characterized by a so-called 'tripartite structure' which informs the composition of its collegial organs: the national delegations to the ILO shall be composed of four representatives of whom two shall be Government delegates and the other two delegates representing, respectively, the employers and the workpeople;[86] the non-governmental delegates are nominated by member states in agreement with the national organizations which are most representative of the two social categories;[87] every member of the delegation, either governmental or non-governmental, has a right to vote in its personal capacity.

Despite its long-standing tradition and its operational success, the ILO has not represented a viable precedent. Its tripartite structure has always been regarded as a product of the peculiar mandate of the organization. Lindblom recalls that 'it was the focus on labour legislation rather than general considerations on the participation of civil society which opened the doors of the ILO';[88] and in fact, any attempt to reproduce the model in other intergovernmental frameworks has generally failed.[89]

It is only in the late 1990s that forms of institutionalized CSO participation appeared in other sectors of intergovernmental cooperation, as is shown by the establishment of the ECOSOC Permanent Forum on Indigenous Issues and, to a lesser extent, of the UNAIDS Coordination Board.[90] Unlike the previous

---

[86] ILO Constitution, art. 3.1.
[87] ILO Constitution, art. 3.5.
[88] Lindblom, *supra* note 3, p. 411.
[89] At the San Francisco Conference proposals were advanced to inform the ECOSOC structure on the ILO example, but they were not accorded serious consideration either by governmental delegates or by NGOs.
[90] See above at p. 23ff.

ILO experience, CSO participation in the new bodies is not mediated by governmental delegations; non-state members are formally appointed following consultation procedures which rely to a certain extent on NGOs' self-organization, provided that some basic requirements are respected.[91] However, like the ILO precedent, the balance with governments' representatives is still guaranteed by the mixed composition (governmental/non-governmental) of the organs;[92] more generally, the role and the features of the new organs seem to confirm that 'institutionalized participation' is reserved for cooperation with very specific categories of NGOs in restricted domains of activity.

The new African Union ECOSOCC calls into question this basic assumption by proposing a comprehensive interface between the broad complex of civil society and the Union in all its fields of action. The establishment of the new organ is meant to build 'a partnership between governments and all segments of civil society',[93] thus realizing a new 'social contract between African Governments and their people'.[94]

In coherence with this aim, articles 3 and 4 of the ECOSOCC Statutes make clear that ECOSOCC membership will be exclusively non-governmental and will, in particular, consist of 150 representatives of civil society organizations including, but not limited to, the following:

a. social groups such as those representing women, children, the youth, the elderly and people with disability and special needs;
b. professional groups such as associations of artists, engineers, health practitioners, social workers, media, teachers, sport associations, legal professionals, social scientists, academia, business organizations, national chambers of commerce, workers, employers, industry and agriculture as well as other private sector interest groups;
c. non-governmental organizations (NGOs), community-based organizations (CBOs) and voluntary organizations;
d. cultural organizations.

---

91   See ECOSOC Resolution 2002/22, *Establishment of a Permanent Forum on Indigenous Issues*, 28 July 2000, para. 1; ECOSOC Resolution 1995/2, *Joint and Co-Sponsored United Nations Programme on HIV*, 3 July 1995, and its Annex *Arrangements for the participation of NGOs in the work of the Programme Coordination Board: report on the informal consultation of the ECOSOC*, para. 2.

92   See above, paragraph 1.

93   See Preamble, ECOSOCC Statutes, adopted by the African Union General Assembly with decision Assembly/AU/Dec.42 (III), *Decision on the Economic, Social and Cultural Council*, 8 July 2004.

94   See C. Mutasa (2004), 'The African Union – Civil Society Contract. An act of Democracy?', *Civil Society Observer*, **1**(5), on-line publication by the UN Non-Governmental Liaison Service (NGLS), http://www.un-ngls.org/cso/cso5/cso5.htm.

ECOSOCC will also include social and professional groups in the African Diaspora organizations in accordance with the definition approved by the Executive Council.

Such a vast and heterogeneous constituency competing for a limited number of seats raises the usual problem of how to ensure the correct balance among the different components of civil society.[95] The answer provided by the ECOSOCC Statutes to the problem is institutional: quotas are established in order to seek an even representation from a geographical, gender and age point of view. Thus, according to article 4 of the Statutes, ECOSOCC shall include two member organizations from each member state (for a total of 106), ten member organizations operating at regional level and eight at continental level while 20 more member organizations will come from the African Diaspora.[96] Furthermore 50 per cent of ECOSOCC members will consist of persons between the ages of 18 and 35 and genders will have to be equally represented.

A softer approach is preferred, however, when it comes to balancing the heterogeneous interests represented by the different categories of CSOs enlisted in article 3. Thus article 4.1 simply spells out that the Council 'shall include different social and professional groups' but avoids making any references not only to fixed percentages but also to a general principle of equal representation among the different categories of civil society.

Whether or not these devices are suitable to ensure a balanced composition of the ECOSOCC remains to be demonstrated. First of all, the complex mechanism of overlapping quotas and representation criteria does not seem easy to handle and will likely lead to lengthy (and political) negotiations. Secondly, while fixed quotas threaten to have distorting effects and political underpinning reasons, the general clause contained in article 4.1 does not seem to provide sufficient guarantees for an even representation of the different CSO groups; what is more, it seems almost impossible to define what is an even representation of groups which have completely different natures, compositions and grounds of legitimacy.

In this scenario, a crucial role in adjusting the composition of the Council will be played by the procedures established to select the ECOSOCC members. Confirming the trend set by the precedents of the Permanent Forum on Indigenous Issues and UNAIDS Advisory Board, article 5 of the Statutes relies on self-regulation and refers the election of ECOSOCC members to 'consultation processes' to be organized by the CSOs themselves at national, regional and continental level, provided that some eligibility requirements are

---

[95]   See above in the second section at p. 37ff.

[96]   The remaining ten members will be nominated ex officio for special considerations by the Commission of the Union in consultation with the member states.

met.[97] But, especially at national level, it can be questioned whether the procedure will be really out of the reach of governmental authorities. As a matter of
fact, the authoritarian tendencies of a number of African governments and the
reported practice of some of them to use private associations for political
purposes leave few doubts about the possibility of having really transparent
and independent national selection procedures.[98]

As has already been explained, the ECOSOCC aims at promoting the participation of African peoples in their economic and social articulations in all the
activities of the Union. Thus, unlike the ILO tripartite organs or the UN
Permanent Forum on Indigenous Issues which have specialized functions, the
Council is vested with a general mandate, namely to 'contribute, through
advice, to the effective translation of the objectives, principles and policies of
the Union into concrete programmes as well as the evaluation of these
programmes' (art.7). In order to perform this task, the ECOSOCC undertakes
the studies that it deems necessary or that are recommended by other organs of
the Union and submits recommendations as appropriate (article 7.2 and 7.3).

We could wonder whether the composition of the Council fits its general
advisory function. Unlike the structures of traditional representative democracy which guarantee representation across the full set of political issues, civil
society organizations promote defined sets of values or aim at representing
specific economic or social interests. Thus they do not appear suitable, competent or even legitimate to express their views on the whole spectrum of themes
falling within the competence of the Council.

An answer to this problem is provided by article 11 of the Statutes which
establishes a number of Sectoral Cluster Committees organized on the basis of
thematic groupings.[99] The Cluster Committees are qualified as the 'key operational mechanisms' of ECOSOCC and it is likely that they will act as the real
policy makers within the Council. Their composition is not spelled out by the

---

[97]   Article 6 ECOSOCC Statutes.

[98]   Other doubts come from the wording of Article 5.1 which reads: 'Competent
CSO authorities in each member state shall establish a consultation process . . .'. The
ambiguous notion of 'competent CSO authorities' could perhaps provide the pretext for
governmental interference in the selection procedure of national ECOSOCC members.

[99]   Thus we have a 'Peace and Security Committee' dealing with conflict antici-
pation, prevention, management and resolution, reconstruction and peace building,
prevention and combating of terrorism, use of child soldiers, drug trafficking etc.; a
'Political Affairs Committee' focusing on human rights, rule of law, democratic and
constitutional rule, good governance, humanitarian affaire etc.; an 'Economic Affairs
Committee' competent in economic integration issues, monetary and financial affairs,
private sector development etc. The remaining Committees are: Infrastructure and
Energy; Social Affairs and Health; Human Resources, Science and Technology; Trade
and Industry; Rural Economy and Agriculture; Women and Gender.

Statute in explicit terms but it is made clear that they will operate as sub-organs of the Council, submitting reports and opinions to the plenum. Needless to say, the effective functioning of this institutional machinery will be strongly influenced by the voting system provided by article 16, according to which 'each member of the ECOSOCC shall have one vote and decision making shall be by consensus, failing which it shall be by 2/3 majority of those present and voting. However questions of procedure shall require a simple majority'.

Formalized but not Institutionalized Participation

In the UN and the Council of Europe, the crisis of the consultative model of relationship has not prompted discussion on the preference for a formalized, yet not institutionalized, pattern of interaction with civil society. Rather than exploring the possibility of incorporating CSOs into the institutional machinery of the IGO, the debate has focused on how to reform the legal status already recognized in NGOs and how to reshape the working method of the organization in order to face the challenges raised by the new role played by civil society organizations at the global level.

In the United Nations, it was up to the Secretary General to revive the debate on the relationship with civil society as part of the actions proposed in 2002 to achieve the Millenium Declaration goals.[100] In his report, *Strengthening of the United Nations: an agenda for further change*, the Secretary General announced the intention to establish a Panel of Eminent Persons on United Nations–Civil Society Relations with the task of reviewing existing guidelines for NGOs' access and participation in UN deliberations and processes and to identify best practices and better ways of interaction with civil society actors.[101] The Panel was established in February 2003 under the chairmanship of Fernando Henrique Cardoso[102] and, after three meetings and an intense consultation with NGOs, released its final report in June 2004 (the so called 'Cardoso Report').[103]

The Cardoso Report advanced a set of proposals which start from the basic assumption that an enhanced engagement with civil society is a terrific opportunity to make the UN more effective:

---

[100]   See *supra* note 14 on the outcome of previous attempts to reform the status of NGOs in the UN system.

[101]   See UN Doc. A/57/387, 09/10/2002, at para. 141. For Terms of Reference and composition of the Panel, see Un Doc. A/58/817, 11/07/2004, annex I.

[102]   Un Doc. A/58/817, 11/07/2004, annex I.

[103]   UN Doc. A/58/817, *We the people: civil society, the United Nations and global governance. Report of the Panel of Eminent Persons on United Nations–Civil Society Relations*, 11/06/2004, http://www.un-ngls.org/UNreform.htm.

The growing influence of civil society in global policy does not diminish the relevance of intergovernmental processes – it enhances it. Nor does it lessen the authority of Governments within them. [. . .] This is not about sharing power in a zero-sum game. On the contrary, the constructive engagement of civil society can strengthen intergovernmental deliberations by informing them, sensitizing them to public opinion and grass-roots realities, increasing public understanding of their decisions and enhancing their accountability. This makes such forums more relevant, reducing the democratic deficits to which they are prone. Civil society can also promote actions to advance globally agreed priorities, advancing the causes of the United Nations and multilateralism.[104]

In order to fully seize this opportunity, the Panel proposed a change in the working method of the organization. The UN should become more outward-looking, making more of its role as a global convenor of diverse constituencies relevant to an issue: 'the changing nature of multilateralism to mean multiple constituencies entails the United Nations giving more emphasis to convening and facilitating rather than "doing" and putting the issues, not the institution, at the centre'.[105]

Thus in the Panel's vision, interaction with civil society extends far beyond the participation of NGOs in intergovernmental official processes: the UN is called upon to play a new role in global governance by promoting the establishment of a plurality of forums tailored to specific tasks and open to the contributions of every relevant actor, including non-governmental organizations, the private sector, local authorities and parliamentarians.[106]

The Panel recognized, however, that a direct NGO relationship with UN organs will remain important and that it should be kept formal. Therefore it advanced some concrete proposals to improve the existing legal status and accreditation procedures according to three different guidelines: participation in UN governmental bodies should be extended; the accreditation procedures should be streamlined and depoliticized; a new role should be recognized for self-regulation and self-organization in defining the set of rights and responsibilities pertaining to the legal status.

---

[104]   See ibid., para. 19.
[105]   See ibid., Executive Summary, p. 8.
[106]   In the Panel's view, different forums should be used at different stages of an issue's life cycle in the global debate. Each would have a different style of work and degree of formality, with participation determined accordingly: high-level round tables made up of selected governmental and non-governmental participants should tackle emerging issues; once the issue becomes familiar, global conferences open to all the interested constituencies should be convened to define norms and targets; in the implementation phase, cooperation with NGOs and the private sector should be sought to monitor compliance and to ensure implementation through self-commitments and on-field actions.

Extended participation in UN organs. The Panel acknowledged that a number of participatory practices have been developed outside the framework of existing consultative status either on an informal or formal ad hoc basis. It suggested that the time has come for these practices to be extended and standardized so that they become part of the regular component of UN organs' work.

As far as the Security Council is concerned, it proposed that the Arria formula meetings be improved, in particular by lengthening lead times and covering travel costs to increase the participation of southern organizations and actors from the fields. But the Panel also supported the introduction of two more formal modalities of NGOs' interaction with the SC, namely Security Council's seminars and independent commissions of inquiry for Council-mandated operation.[107]

More far-reaching were the proposals advanced to improve the relationship between civil society and the General Assembly. According to the Panel's report, there is nothing in article 71 of the Charter that would preclude the General Assembly from inviting NGOs to participate in its work. Thus the existing informal and ad hoc patterns of interaction between civil society and the General Assembly could be generalized by establishing an accreditation procedure to grant NGOs a consultative status on the model of the ECOSOC relationship.[108]

Streamlined and depoliticized accreditation procedure. In the Panel's view, the set of accreditation procedures currently in use within the UN system is, to a considerable extent, duplicative and time consuming. Thus it proposes to establish a single system of accreditation for all UN forums and notably for ECOSOC, its sub-organs, international conferences and their follow-up and, possibly, the General Assembly.

The new system should overcome some of the major flaws which have so far characterized the work of the existing Committee on Non-Governmental Organisations. In particular, the Panel strongly challenged political use of the accreditation being a proper answer to the problems raised by the growth of civil society participation:

---

[107]   The seminars would consist of meetings between the SC members, other interested governmental representatives and civil society organizations and would provide a forum to discuss issues of emerging importance to the Council. No decision would be taken at the seminar, but the Council would be provided with direct information and a clear representation of the interests at stake before a position is negotiated. The commissions of inquiry should be convened to provide independent assessment of UN operations under SC mandates. The commissions would include the participation of and take evidence from civil society specialists and would assess operations from the perspective of the citizens concerned. (See Panel Report, proposal 12.)

[108]   See *Panel Report*, proposal 6 and para. 122.

The Panel believes it is essential to depoliticize the accreditation process. Accreditation decisions made for political rather than technical reasons effectively reduce the access of the United Nations to independent expertise and knowledge. The Panel is also concerned about the growing phenomenon of accrediting non-governmental organizations that are sponsored and controlled by Governments. Not independent, these 'government-organised NGOs' reflect their Government's position. The speaking opportunities they use in United Nations forums would be better used by others – in keeping with the original principle of accreditation.[109]

In order to depoliticize and to speed up the accreditation process, the Panel suggested recognizing a greater role for the UN administration. Thus the UN Secretariat would pre-screen the applications for accreditation according to a clear set of criteria determined by governments; the Secretariat would consequently draft lists of the NGOs which are recommended or not recommended for the accreditation; finally, such lists would be presented to an appropriate Committee of the General Assembly,[110] which would decide on the accreditation on a no-objection basis. To avoid the current practice of endless deferral of controversial decisions, strict time-limits would be imposed on the Committee.[111]

The success of the procedure proposed by the Panel probably rests with a clear definition of the 'technical criteria' according to which non-governmental organizations should be selected. The report lacks detailed indication on this point, but the generic references made to NGOs' 'expertise, competence and skills' seem to overlook the complexity of non-governmental legitimacy and the difficulties of assessing it univocally.[112]

New role for self-regulation and self-organization. The Panel acknowledged that formal regulation cannot always provide the best answer to the problems raised by the increased participation of civil society in intergovernmental processes. While it is in the interests of UN organs to have fewer, more representative and more professional civil society interlocutors, any formal selection procedure is potentially arbitrary, may be subject to political interference and entails a loss of information. Thus the Panel suggested supplementing formal regulation with the recourse to self-organization and self-regulation. NGOs should be motivated to organize themselves and to gather in coordinated networks by defining categories of relevant actors, rewarding and publicizing good practices, offering incentives.

---

[109]   See *Panel Report*, para. 127.
[110]   As an ECOSOC sub-organ, the existing Committee on Non-Governmental Organisation would not be competent to decide on the accreditation with the General Assembly.
[111]   See *Panel Report*, proposals 6, 19 and 20.
[112]   See above, in the second section at p. 37ff.

In order to reach this goal, the Panel proposed a complete revision of the existing ECOSOC categories of NGO Status (general, special and roster). The new categories should focus on organizational features rather than on the scope of their interaction with the UN. Thus the Panel suggested according the highest accreditation status to 'network partners' which should consist of transnational networks and caucuses including a significant number of organizations either active on a given issue or from a particular constituency. They would be vested with an enhanced right to speak, to distribute statements and to influence the agenda. The category of 'consultative partners' would replace the existing ECOSOC categories and would include individual organizations, either international or national, focusing on advocacy, research or representation of peculiar sectors of society. The participation of consultative partners in a given UN body would be decided according to their expertise and competence in the relevant fields. Finally, the Panel proposed the establishment of a third NGO category including all the organizations engaged in operational cooperation with the UN programmes ('programme support partners').[113]

In the Panel's view, self-regulation could also help to improve the accountability of non-governmental organizations. NGOs should be encouraged to draft a code of conduct which clearly defines their commitment to the principles of good governance (transparency, democratic structure, etc.) and their undertaking to act in coherence with the aims of the Charter and the intergovernmental character of the UN. However the Panel recognized that a positive action is needed to face some of the traditional imbalances which affect NGOs participation. In particular the establishment of a trust fund to promote the participation of NGOs from developing countries was strongly supported.[114]

The proposals advanced by the Cardoso Panel have not found in the General Assembly the necessary political consensus to be endorsed. The attempt made by the Secretary General to pass over the more visionary and politically sensitive parts of the report and to focus on its operational and more concrete suggestions[115] has not succeeded in surmounting the diffidence of member states vis-à-vis a generalized recognition (and uniform regulation) of the participatory role of NGOs in the UN intergovernmental process. As a matter of fact in the debate which took place in the plenary meeting of the General Assembly on 4 and 5 October 2004, the general recognition by

---

113   See *Panel Report*, proposals 22 and 23.
114   See *Panel Report*, proposal 27.
115   See the Report submitted by the Secretary General in response to the Cardoso Report: *Report of the Secretary General in response to the report of the Panel of Eminent Persons on United Nations–Civil Society Relations*, 13 September 2004, UN Doc. A/59/354.

member states of the 'vital' role of NGOs in pursuing the goals of the organization[116] matched a widespread concern to preserve the intergovernmental character of the UN organs and decision making processes.[117]

While we may discuss whether an extended and streamlined non-governmental participation in UN activities could really endanger the intergovernmental character of the organization, it is clear that, in the current UN political context, a fragmented and flexible approach to civil society participation still appears preferable, irrespective of its drawbacks.[118] On the one hand, flexibility allows states to take advantage of a greater cooperation with civil society when it is in their interest, without binding themselves to a general regulation. On the other, advanced practices for non-governmental participation so far developed in specific sectors are preserved from the adoption of a uniform discipline.[119]

Unlike the UN system, in the Council of Europe a political consensus was gathered to establish a new participatory status for NGOs, which is

---

[116] See for instance the declaration of Pakistan (Official Records of the 18th GA Meeting, UN Doc. A/59/PV.18, at page 19), Bangladesh (ibid. at 12), Vietnam (ibid. at 25), Jamaica (Official Records of the 19th GA Meeting, UN Doc. A/59/PV.19).

[117] Inter alia see declaration by Pakistan (Official Records of the 18th GA Meeting, UN Doc. A/59/PV.18, at page 19), Namibia (ibid. at 14), Fiji (Official Records of the 20th GA Meeting, UN Doc. A/59/PV.20, at page 11) and India (Official Records of the 19th GA Meeting, UN Doc. A/59/PV.20, at page 18).

[118] For a more detailed analysis of the different views expressed by member states on Cardoso's and the Secretary General's proposals, see T. Treves (2007), 'Etats et organisations non-gouvernementales' in *Mélanges offerts à Jean Salmon – Droit du pouvoir, pouvoir du droit*, Brussels: Bruylant.

[119] On the agenda of the current process of UN Reform (see *infra* notes 141 and 145) no specific item is expressly devoted to a comprehensive reconsideration of the UN–civil society relationship. However, the issue of non-governmental participation has been specifically addressed when dealing with reform proposals in specific sectors (e.g. establishment of a new Human Right Council – see *infra* note 138), thus confirming the preference for a case-by-case approach. It is interesting to note that the reform process itself has been an opportunity to experience new practices of interaction with civil society and to confirm the role played by NGOs in intergovernmental negotiations at the highest level. For instance, in the preparatory process leading to the 2005 World Summit, the General Assembly organized two days of informal interactive hearings with civil society (*Preparation of the Informal Interactive Hearings*, UN Doc. A/RES/59/291, 25 April 2005, Annex III), in line with the consolidating practice of NGO involvement in GA work (see *supra* at pp. 27 and 28). More generally, NGOs are proving to be crucial in ensuring public participation throughout the process of reform, by disseminating information and key documents on the ongoing negotiations and by mobilizing public opinion on specific issues (see for instance the campaign launched by Amnesty International and other human rights associations for the election of 'clean hands' states in the newly established Human Right Council). However the impact (if any) of non-governmental action on the UN reform still remains to be fully assessed.

characterized by greater reliance on self-regulation.[120] The new system increases the interaction with civil society by attributing a specific role to the Liaison Committee and Thematic Groupings, self-organized bodies which are officially recognized by the Council, respectively, 'as the democratically elected representative body of all of the NGOs enjoying participatory status with the Council of Europe' and as 'their collective voice and, thus, of millions of European citizens, working in each of the fields represented by them'.[121]

Both the Liaison Committee and the Thematic Groupings have been established by an autonomous initiative of the NGOs participating in CoE activities in order to ensure a proper representation of their common interests. Their composition, mandate and function are defined by the Conference of NGOs, which once a year brings together, on a voluntary basis, the NGOs which enjoy formal status with CoE. In particular, the Liaison Committee currently consists of 36 members, 25 directly elected by the Conference and 11 by the Thematic Groupings, in the attempt to balance the principle of equality among NGOs and the need to ensure a correct representation among the different components of civil society. The Committee is entrusted with a general coordination role: it prepares the annual Conference of NGOs, follows the progress of the sectoral NGO meetings and arranges for the NGOs to be consulted by developing close and permanent relations with the CoE organs and the Secretariat. The Thematic Groupings gather all the organizations which are active in a specific area of interests. They aim at coordinating the action of their members and therefore at providing a common interlocutor for all Council of Europe bodies on a specific theme.[122]

The new participatory status established by Resolution (2003)8 mainly relies on an enhanced cooperation with the Liaison Committee and Thematic Groupings to foster the dialogue with civil society as a whole. Thus the major innovations introduced by the resolution consist of specific attributions recognized by the two bodies in view of their peculiar representative character.

---

[120]   Resolution Res(2003)8, *Participatory status for international non-governmental organizations with the Council of Europe*, adopted by the CoE Committee of Ministers on 19/11/2003.

[121]   See Preamble, Res (2003)8.

[122]   See *Rules of Procedure of the Liaison Committee and of the Thematic Groupings of INGOs enjoying participatory status with the Council of Europe* and *Rules of Procedure of the Conference of INGOs* adopted by the Conference of INGOs on 25 January 2005, http://www.coe.int/T/E/NGO/public/Liaison_Committee/Rules_of_Procedure/Rules_of_Procedure_of_Liaison_Committee_2005.asp and http://www.coe.int/t/e/ngo/public/plenary_conference/Rules _of_Procedure/index.asp.

To start with, the Liaison Committee is vested with a consultative role in the procedures leading to the granting and withdrawal of the formal status to individual NGOs. In particular, the Committee is called upon to give its opinion on the proposals which the Secretary General submits on accreditation to the Council of Ministers for tacit approval. This advisory function is certainly meant to increase the transparency of the admission process but it remains to be seen whether self-regulation will avoid the danger of corporatist practices which accredited NGOs could put in place to hamper the access of potential competitors.[123]

Secondly, the Resolution promotes the involvement of the Liaison Committee and Thematic Groupings in those CoE organs which so far have been excluded from the scope of the participatory status:[124]

4. The steering committees, committees of governmental experts and other bodies of the Committee of Ministers, may involve the INGOs enjoying participatory status in the definition of Council of Europe policies, programmes and actions in particular *by granting observer status to the Liaison Committee and to the INGO thematic groupings, in accordance with the terms of Committee of Ministers' Resolution (76) 3.*
5. The committees of the Parliamentary Assembly and of the Congress of Local and Regional Authorities of Europe are invited to study ways of intensifying co-operation with and facilitating INGO participation in their work, for example *by granting observer status or by inviting the Liaison Committee or INGO thematic groupings to provide their expertise.* (Emphasis added)[125]

Thus the new participatory status does not strengthen the legal position of single NGOs by adding new rights or privileges to the ones already recognized in the previous consultative relationship. Rather it reveals a paradigm shift in the working method of the Council which promotes popular participation in its activities through an enhanced dialogue between civil society and CoE organs:

(the) co-operation between INGOs and the Committee of Ministers and its subsidiary bodies, as well as with the Parliamentary Assembly and the Congress of Local and Regional Authorities of Europe has led to the 'Quadrilogue' which is,

---

[123]   The Rules of procedure of the Liaison Committee expressly provides at rule 9.6 that the Committee 'may intervene in relations concerning participation by individual INGOs . . . only at the specific request of the INGOs concerned'.

[124]   The participation in the Steering Committees and the other bodies of the Committees of Ministers does not follow from the rules on consultative (now participatory) status but is granted on an ad hoc basis according to the Rules of Procedures of the Committee of Ministers. See Resolution (76)3 on *Committee Structures, Terms of Reference and Working Methods*, 18 February 1976.

[125]   See Res. (2003) 8.

within the Council of Europe, an expression of democratic pluralism and an essential element for the further development of a citizens' Europe.[126]

The Liaison Committee and the Thematic Groupings are seen as the facilitators and catalysts of the 'quadrilogue' among CoE organs and civil society organizations. The official recognition of their role represents a sort of institutionalization of informal (because self-organized) NGO structures. Thus, despite the profound structural differences, an interesting comparison may be drawn with the role played by the African Union ECOSOCC and its Sectoral Cluster Committees.

Informal Participation and Administrative Facilitation

Finally, it has to be recalled that the dialogue with civil society can be fostered beyond any formal and comprehensive mechanism of accreditation or institutionalization.

A clear example is provided by the European Communities. In the EC, the participation of civil society in the intergovernmental decision making is fully institutionalized in the activity of the Economic and Social Committee, an advisory organ composed of representatives of the various economic and social components of the 'organized civil society'.[127] However, the existence of an institutional channel for non-governmental participation does not exhaust the need for a greater consultation with those civil society actors which have a say or may be affected by a given Community action.[128] In practice, EC institutions,

---

[126]   Ibid., Preamble.

[127]   See art. 257 and ff. of the TEC. At its origin, the Committee was conceived as an assembly of the representatives of workers and employers organizations and of other professional and social categories. The Treaty of Nice has modified article 257 to open the membership to a wider constituency by focusing on the general concept of 'organized civil society' and introducing a reference to the organizations of general interest. However, the members of the committee are still appointed on a de facto binding proposal from the member states: in practice, member states aim to seat in the Committee the representatives of the major national trade unions, employers' organizations and other professional associations.

[128]   The reasons which prompt the coexistence in the EC of different forms of civil society participation (direct democratic representation in the European Parliament; institutionalized civil society participation in the Economic and Social Committee, informal ad hoc participation and administrative facilitation in the relationship with the Commission – see infra in the text) deserve further reflection. However, as far as the Economic and Social Committee is concerned, it is possible to identify in its composition and in the timing of its intervention in the decision-making process (after and not before proposals have been transmitted to the legislature) two key factors which contribute to reducing its effective capacity to channel exhaustively the view of civil society at large.

and notably the Commission, recognize that involvement with social actors is one of the principles of good governance which should inform European policy making.[129]

As for the forms that such an involvement should take, the debate that has followed the launch of the Commission White Paper on European Governance has led to discarding

> the option of a Commission-wide NGO accreditation scheme along the lines of the current systems of the UN or the Council of Europe. Apart from corresponding to requests by only a limited number of NGOs, such a mechanism was regarded as being too exclusive and potentially jeopardising open access to consultation processes.[130]

In this framework, alternative tools are proposed to tackle the problems traditionally connected with the informal NGO–IGO relationship. To start with, the Commission has elaborated a set of minimum standards for the conduct of consultation with NGOs and interested parties. The standards define the basic principles and guidelines which should be applied throughout the Commission department when interacting with civil society. In particular the consultation processes shall be designed in order to have a clear object; the definition of the subject involved in the consultation should be carefully addressed in order to ensure that all the relevant parties have the opportunity to express their views; adequate publication should be ensured to reach all the interested parties; finally, adequate feedback should be provided to the contributors. The minimum standards are not meant to introduce legal obligations for the Commission.[131]

Secondly, mutual arrangements could be concluded with specific NGOs' networks or umbrella organizations in order to provide a more stable framework for consultation. Such arrangements will not be legally binding agreements, subject to legal review, but rather political commitments for cooperation. They will provide NGOs with a more formal recognition of their role and the Commission with better guarantees on NGOs' representativity, accountability and transparency. Moreover the Commission could use this tool

---

[129]   See European Commission, *European Governance: A White Paper*, COM(2001) 428 final.

[130]   Report of Working Group *Consultation and Participation of Civil Society*, June 2001, p. 18, http://www.europa.eu.int/comm/governance/areas/group3/report_en.pdf.

[131]   Communication from the Commission, *Towards a reinforced culture of consultation and dialogue – General principles and minimum standards for consultation of interested parties by the Commission*, 11 December 2002, COM (2002)704. For a more detailed analysis, see Lindblom, *supra* note 3, at 428ff.

to incentivize civil society self-organization and thus streamline and simplify the consultation process.[132]

Finally, administrative practices have been put in place to facilitate and rationalize the relationship with civil society. A clear example is represented by the project to establish a comprehensive database on European civil–society organizations. When registering with the database, NGOs will be invited to supply the Commission with information about their objectives, membership structures, source of financing and the way they involve their members in the decision-making process. Such a database will eventually help the Commission in identifying the civil society organizations which may be interested and/or affected by a specific proposal and therefore which shall be involved in the consultation process.[133]

In conclusion, consultation with civil society is considered a crucial element to complement decision making by the European institutions and is conceived as a parameter of good governance in the assessment of their action. With respect to other models of interaction, the focus is shifted from the status of non-governmental actors to the working method of the organization.

CONCLUSIONS: SAFETY IN FLEXIBILITY?

The profound transformations which have affected the international system in the last decade have placed non-governmental actors in a position to play a broader role and have pushed IGOs to look for an enhanced engagement with civil society. The new quantitative and qualitative dimensions of civil society's participation in the inter-governmental processes open the door to new opportunities and possible synergies, but also create new problems and enhance existing ones. The analysis carried out in the first section of this chapter has shown that the existing participatory devices designed around the outdated paradigm of 'consultative relationship' neither exercise effective control over civil society participation nor answer the needs arising from an enhanced

---

[132]   Report of Working Group *Consultation and Participation of Civil Society*, *supra* note 130, at 17. For an interesting critique of the recourse to measures aimed at encouraging self-organization and self-regulation, in the sense of pushing civil society actors to reorganize themselves in order to be more accountable, open and representative, see K.A. Armstrong (2001), 'Civil society and the white paper – bridging or jumping the gaps?', in C. Joerges, Y. Mény, and J.H.H. Weiler (2001), *Symposium: Mountain or Molehill? A Critical Appraisal of the Commission White Paper on Governance*, Jean Monnet Working Paper n°6/01, Robert Schuman Centre for Advanced Studies – EUI and Jean Monnet Program – NYU, retrievable at http://www.iue.it/RSCAS/research/OnlineSymposia/Walker.pdf.

[133]   Ibid., p. 18.

IGO–NGO engagement. However, while a higher level of regulation is increasingly deemed necessary, no single regulatory model is emerging. Rather, the analysis of the present reforms of the arrangements for civil society participation in IGOs' activities has shown that the opposing approaches of informality and self-regulation and institutionalization of civil society can be combined differently. Flexibility in the design of the forms of NGO–IGO interaction therefore appears a characteristic feature.

Different IGOs develop forms of interaction with NGOs which variously combine informal and formal devices as a consequence of their different degrees of integration, fields of activity and need to rely on non-governmental participation to support and implement their own policies. Within a single IGO, arrangements for non-governmental participation may range from full institutionalization to an informal relationship depending on the activity or the stage of the decision-making process in which the non-governmental contribution takes place.

The multiplication of participatory schemes is also the result of the variety and progressive expansion of the typology of non-state actors engaging in cooperation with intergovernmental organizations. For instance, the notion of an IGO–civil society partnership promoted by the UN Secretary General extends to entities such as profit-making organizations (business companies), public organizations (local authorities) or private organizations performing public functions (political parties, associations representing professional categories and so on). And, indeed, general expressions like 'civil society organizations' and 'civil society' are replacing the classic and narrower notion of non-governmental organizations both in official IGO discourses and in academic writings. Clearly enough, a differentiation of participatory schemes is required in order to accommodate the variety of NGOs whose heterogeneous composition, representativeness, finalities and means of action lead to differentiated contributions to IGOs' activity. Quite interestingly, differentiation is promoted both by IGOs, which may have an interest in establishing a more formal relationship with those organizations which have a representative character or may offer the best expertise, and by civil society organizations themselves. In particular, non-profit organizations have voiced a growing concern for the involvement of companies and profit-making entities in the activities of IGOs,[134] while representative associations of economic or social categories have emphasized the specificity of their role if compared to general advocacy

---

[134]   See, for instance, the reactions of a number of NGOs to the Cardoso Report. See, in particular, the statements by Global Policy Forum (GPF), Amnesty International and CONGO (Conference of Non-Governmental Organizations in Consultative Relationship with the United Nations) published at http://www.un-ngls.org/UNreform.htm (last visited December 2006).

organizations;[135] in both cases NGOs called for a diversified relationship according to the characteristics of the non-governmental organizations involved.

Despite this increasing complexity, it is nonetheless possible to identify some relevant trends in the evolution of NGO–IGO relationship. To start with, most IGOs now formally recognize, if not encourage, the expanded role that civil society has come to play in their policy-making processes. In official documents of an important number of organizations, NGOs are defined as 'participants' or 'partners' rather than mere 'observers' and the initiatives aimed at reforming the existing arrangements for NGOs' involvement multiply. Remarkably, also organizations that are traditionally reluctant to engage with NGOs and resistant to establishing formal statuses or accreditation procedures, have set up administrative structures dedicated to the relationship with civil society (this is, for instance, the case of the World Bank and of the WTO).

Secondly, the recognition of a participatory role for civil society is coupled with a certain degree of formalization of the NGO–IGO relationship. In particular, the adoption of formal rules on participation is often the final step in a process of consolidation of pre-existing and informal participatory mechanisms as is illustrated by the cases of the Organisation of American States, the UN and the Council of Europe. From this perspective, a formal framework for participation appears beneficial both to IGOs, which see in accreditation procedures a tool to control and exert pressure on non-governmental partners, and to NGOs, that aim at a formal recognition of their role. However, the level of formalization adopted by IGOs may vary greatly, from full institutionalization to ad hoc accreditation procedures for cooperation in specific fields of activity. Moreover, formal relationships raise the problem of how to select the relevant non-governmental actors without impairing their potential contribution to IGOs' activities and how to avoid a political (mis)use by states of accreditation mechanisms.

These growing concerns have led to a greater attention to self-regulation as an alternative to direct governmental control. There is an emerging trend to include mechanisms of self-regulation in formal participatory schemes in order to select and organize the participation of civil society. These mechanisms may consist of incentives and enhanced participatory rights for non-governmental organizations that group themselves in coalitions (as in the UN reform proposals), but may also include granting self-organized bodies a

---

[135]   A similar debate occurred in the ILO, where workers and employers' associations enjoy full membership (see *supra* at p. 48) and seek to preserve their peculiar status with respect to other NGOs which are progressively involved in the ILO's activity.

formal role in the management of non-governmental participation (as in the case of the NGO Liaison Committee established within the Council of Europe). Thus practice shows that there is no contradiction between the choice of a formalized pattern of relationship with civil society and the promotion of self-regulation; indeed, self-regulation is encouraged within the most institutionalized forms of IGO–NGO cooperation. For instance, in the cases of UNAIDS, the UN ECOSOC Permanent Forum on Indigenous Issues and of African Union ECOSOCC, the selection of non-governmental members of these official organs is left to NGOs themselves, while IGOs retain control over formal appointments, non-governmental candidates are selected through 'internal selection processes' which should be guided by the principles of representativity, transparency and competence.[136]

Concerns similar to those which have led IGOs to promote non-governmental self-regulation underpin the attempt to shift control over NGO accreditation procedures from state representatives (or rather from IGOs' organs made of state representatives, such as the UN ECOSOC NGO Committee) to IGOs' Secretariats.[137] These proposals to depoliticize NGO selection procedures undoubtedly reflect the need to reduce the unbearable workload of the political organs so far entrusted with the task of managing accreditation, but they also reveal that dialogue with civil society may be crucial for the attainment of IGOs' objectives and conditions the correct exercise of IGOs' power; as a consequence, the need arises to protect such a dialogue from political manipulation.

So far, the emerging concept used to define the new course in the NGO–IGO relationship appears to be the one of 'partnership'. However, the notion is ambiguous and problematic. From a political point of view, the idea of partnership seems to suggest an equality of roles between civil society, IGOs and states. As has been rightly stressed by some commentators, a greater involvement of civil society in IGO activities should not imply a transfer of the ultimate responsibility for decision making from governments (or governmental *fora*) to vague coalitions of actors nor allow states to escape binding

---

[136]   See *supra* third section at p. 46ff.

[137]   See Cardoso Report, proposals 6, 19 and 20 discussed *supra* at p. 52ff). See also the procedure for the granting of participatory status to NGOs in the Council of Europe which vest the CoE Secretary General with the power to confer the status and assign to the political organ (Committee of Ministers) a residual power of control: the Secretary General's decision is submitted to the tacit approval of the Committee of Ministers and, if no specific objection is raised within a time limit of three months, the status is conferred. See Resolution Res(2003)8, *Participatory status for international non-governmental organizations with the Council of Europe*, adopted by the CoE Committee of Ministers on 19 November 2003, arts 12, 14 and 15.

commitments.[138] Only states may be held accountable internally, towards their citizens, and externally, towards the other members of the international community.

From a legal point of view, the equality of roles suggested by the notion of partnership has led an author to draw general conclusions on the legal personality of NGOs in international law.[139] However, we should not confuse the statuses that non-governmental organizations enjoy in IGOs' internal law orders with their subjectivity in international law. Of course, the former ones may be taken into account as elements in assessing the latter, but no straightforward conclusion is possible. This is all the more so because, as we have shown, the concept of 'partnership' is far from providing a univocal legal qualification of the status of NGOs and of their relationship with IGOs; rather it merely introduces a new political paradigm in the way IGOs should deal with civil society. Thus it appears more fruitful to draw from the analysed practice some general conclusions on the functioning of IGOs themselves.

We argue that non-governmental participation is strongly emerging as a parameter of good governance for IGOs.

As a matter of fact, an opinion on the need for IGOs to engage with civil society is consolidating. The focus of the current debate is no longer on whether civil society should be involved in the intergovernmental process but rather on how the participation should take place. Whatever the level of institutionalization of the NGO–IGO relationship, the relationship itself is increasingly described in IGOs' documents as 'indispensable' or 'necessary'. The concrete reasons which are invoked by IGOs to justify such a 'necessary' participation may be the most diverse (achieving more effectively the goals of the organization, overcoming the resistance and opposition of single member states to IGOs' policies through a direct engagement with local actors; strengthening the legitimacy of the organization through participation; allowing the representation of values and interests which are not expressed by states), but they all share the view that a correct functioning of the organization and the effective attainment of its statutory objectives – in short, good

---

[138]   See, for instance, the statements by Global Policy Forum (GPF) and CONGO (Conference of Non-Governmental Organizations in Consultative Relationship with the United Nations), *supra* note 126.

[139]   According to Willetts, 'the changes in UN resolutions and UN practice, particularly those occurring in the 1990s, are so extensive that the international NGOs recognized by ECOSOC may be considered to have acquired a legal personality. (. . .) The new language of the 1990s, with the concept of social partners, is revolutionary because it implies an equality of status between governments and NGOs. The partners are equal in the sense that each has legal personality, but not in the sense that they have the same rights and obligations'. Willetts, 'From Consultative Arrangements to Partnership . . .', *supra* note 15.

administration – require the opening of the intergovernmental process to civil society In such a perspective, the lack of express provisions on non-governmental participation in IGOs' statutes is hardly an obstacle to the involvement of civil society in the intergovernmental process. When this is the case, the power to adopt participatory arrangements is traced back to the power of self-organization which is implied in the attribution of specific competence and which has its reciprocal in the duty of exercising properly that competence.

Of course it can be maintained that the 'necessity' to involve civil society has a merely political and not normative character. As a matter of fact, IGOs and their member states pay serious attention to underlining that civil society participation in the intergovernmental process is allowed on merely voluntary grounds. However, these formal statements often contrast with divergent declarations and more significantly with subsequent conduct.[140] Official declarations aiming at excluding any force of precedent to participatory practices are contradicted by the progressive consolidation of these practices in formal arrangements. The assertion that arrangements for participation are voluntary ad hoc concessions contrasts with the general trend towards an increased involvement of NGOs, as is shown by the number of reforms and proposed reforms launched by IGOs in recent years. Finally, attempts by some states to withdraw or reduce participatory rights recognized in civil society regularly meet fierce opposition from other member states which justify the defence of NGOs' prerogatives with the need to preserve the effectiveness of intergovernmental action.[141]

---

[140]   For an interesting analysis of the varying – and often contradictory – aptitude of states *vis-à-vis* non-governmental organizations, see Treves, 'Etats et Organisations Non-Gouvernementales', *supra* note 118.

[141]   A good example is provided by the debate on the participation of NGOs in the activities of the newly established Human Rights Council (HRC). The launch of the HRC is one of the major achievements of the current process of reform of the United Nations (more on the UN reform process *infra* at note 145) and is aimed at giving a greater centrality to human rights issues in the UN action by replacing the discredited ECOSOCC Commission on Human Rights with a new subsidiary organ of the General Assembly (Resolution A/60/251, 3 April 2006). However during the negotiations leading to the adoption of Resolution 60/251, some states advanced proposals that, if endorsed, would have affected the arrangements and practices for NGO participation developed by the Commission. For instance it was suggested that the new Council should have exclusively applied the rules of procedure of the subsidiary organs of the GA (which do not provide for NGOs participation: Pakistan and Singapore's proposals) or should have adopted (and therefore renegotiated) its own arrangements for NGOs participation. These proposals met with the firm opposition of the great majority of states which stressed the crucial role that NGOs had played in the functioning of the Commission and proposed to preserve the existing 'participatory *acquis*' as one of the strengths of the UN human rights' system. This position was finally endorsed by

The emergence of civil society participation as a parameter of good governance reflects the greater interest paid to the issue of IGOs' accountability within the international community.[142] The transferral of a wide array of regulatory functions to intergovernmental organizations and their increased institutional and operational authority have raised relevant issues of legitimacy of and responsibility for IGOs' actions. The problem is at the core of the academic debate[143] and of the work of international institutions;[144] but it is also

---

Resolution 60/251 in para. 11. It is important to stress that, in extending to a subsidiary organ of the General Assembly the ECOSOCC regime for NGO participation, para. 11 de facto rebuts the allegation advanced by some NGO-opposers according to which article 71 of the UN Charter, by expressly empowering the sole ECOSOC to make arrangements for consultation with NGOs, would implicitly deny a similar power to the General Assembly.

[142]   Accountability can be defined as the need for power holders to account for the exercise of their powers in order to provide legitimacy to their action. Accountability may present itself in different forms – political, legal, administrative, financial – according to the actors involved, to the structure of the social order in which the power is exercised and to the nature of the power itself. Different forms of accountability may combine and overlap. In the case of IGOs, three levels of accountability can be envisaged according to a recent report of the International Law Association: (1) internal and external scrutiny of the acts performed by IGOs in the fulfilment of their functions as established in the constituent instrument, irrespective of potential subsequent liability and responsibility; (2) tortuous liability for injurious consequences arising out of acts or omissions not involving a breach of any rule of international and/or institutional law; (3) responsibility arising out of acts or omissions which constitute a breach of a rule of international and/or institutional law. At each of these levels, the different forms of accountability (political, legal, administrative, financial) combine differently. See International Law Association (2004), 'Final Report on Accountability of International Organisations', in *Report of the 71st Conference held in Berlin, 16–21 August 2004*, pp. 164ff.

[143]   As an example we can quote the growing literature on the problematic lack of effective review of Security Council's decisions affecting individual rights. See, for instance, A. Reinisch (2001), 'Developing human rights and humanitarian law accountability of the Security Council for the imposition of economic sanctions', *American Journal of International Law*, **95**(4), 851–72; E. De Wet (2002), 'Review of Security Council decisions by national courts', *German Yearbook of International Law*, **45**, 166–202; E. Cannizzaro (2006), 'A Machiavellian moment? The Security Council and the rule of law', *International Organizations Law Review*, **3**, 189–224.

144   In the first place, reference has to be made to the work of the International Law Commission on the Responsibility of International Organizations. The subject has been recommended for study by the General Assembly in 2001 and the Commission has so far considered the first four reports presented by the Special Rapporteur Giorgio Gaja. Moving on to the work of Law Societies, we can refer to the International Law Association which in 1996 established a Committee on Accountability of International Organisation. The Committee has submitted at the 2004 Berlin Conference its final report which advances a series of recommended rules and practices. It is interesting to note that the Report devotes a specific section,

reshaping the practice of IGOs. Most organizations have advanced proposals, developed best practices or undertaken reforms to provide an answer to the demand for a greater internal and external accountability.[145]

Principles elaborated in domestic administrative law, such as those of transparency, access to information, public participation and so on, are increasingly invoked as parameters of IGOs' normative and operative action. Internal procedural mechanisms, such as the World Bank Inspection Panel or the limited UN Security Council procedure to list and de-list individuals targeted by UN sanctions, have been established to provide some early forms of remedy against IGOs' acts.

In this quest for IGOs' accountability, arrangements for civil society participation play a crucial role. From a substantive point of view, they give effect to the principles of participation and access to information by allowing affected interests to be represented in international fora and to influence the decision-making process; from a remedial point of view, they offer a political alternative to the lack of internal legality review mechanisms by providing a formal framework to exert public control over intergovernmental action. Thus the attribution of a formal status to civil society appears to strengthen the accountability of international organizations by compensating for the lack of

and some recommended rules of practice, to the relationship between IGOs and NGOs thus endorsing the idea that non-governmental participation plays a role in triggering IGOs' accountability. See International Law Association, 'Final Report . . .' quoted supra at note 142, at 184.

[145] For instance, the issue of internal accountability is expressly addressed in the current process of reform of the UN launched by the Secretary General in 2005. Following the 'Oil for Food Program' scandal, a number of states and notably the US pressed to include the agenda of the 2005 World Summit the reform of UN management. The Outcome Document of the Summit, endorsed by General Assembly Resolution 60/1, devotes a section to the issue (para. 161 to 167) and calls the Secretary General to advance specific proposals to improve the UN oversight and management processes in the light of the principles of organizational accountability, transparency and integrity. Following the indications of the GA, the Secretary General submitted a first set of proposals for management reform in March 2006 (*Investing in the UN: for a stronger Organisation worldwide – Report of the Secretary General*, 7 March 2006, UN Doc. A/60/692). In August 2006 the independent Steering Committee appointed under para. 164 of the Outcome Document to review the UN system of governance and oversight delivered its final report (*Comprehensive Review of Governance and Oversight within the United Nations, Funds, Programmes and Specialized Agencies*, 28 August 2006, UN Doc. A/60/883/Add.1). Finally, in July 2006, another Panel submitted its proposals for a comprehensive reform of the UN internal system of administration of justice (*Report of the Redesign Panel on the United Nations System of Administration of Justice*, 28 July 2006, UN Doc. A/61/205). While no final decisions have so far been adopted by the GA, it is clear that the issue of internal good governance and accountability is perceived as a priority.

procedural rules and review mechanisms of IGOs' action. On the contrary, where such rules and procedures do exist, as in the case of the European Communities, the need or opportunity for an institutionalized or even formalized relationship with NGOs is significantly reduced.

Of course, many questions remain to be addressed. The hypothesis that civil society participation is emerging as a parameter of good governance has to be further verified by extending the research to a greater number of IGOs. The legal nature and content of the principle of good governance itself is far from being ascertained: whether it will evolve in a parameter of legitimacy for intergovernmental acts, or rather will remain a 'best practice' with mere political implications remains to be seen. More generally, the role that civil society participation can play in supporting the legitimacy of intergovernmental action and its relationship with the (lack of) democratic legitimacy at the international level requires further study.

As we have shown with reference to the level of institutionalization of the relationship with civil society, the diversity among IGOs, among their aims and their functions, is likely to justify different solutions to specific questions. However, such a diversity does not bring into question the need for a global approach to the common problems raised by the increased scope and reach of intergovernmental cooperation in a time of globalized interdependence. Academic research in the emerging discipline of global administrative law is just beginning.[146]

---

[146]   See B. Kingsbury, N. Krisch and R.B. Stewart (2005), 'The emergence of global administrative law', *Law and Contemporary Problems*, **68**(15), also available at http://law.duke.edu/journals/lcp.

2. Domesticating civil society at the United Nations

Olivier de Frouville[*]

For a number of years, the actors and the observers of the United Nations' Human Rights Protection System have confirmed the ever-increasing presence of Non-Governmental Organizations (NGOs) with similar views to those of the States. These organizations are often referred to as GONGOs – that stands for Governmental Non Governmental Organizations or Government Orientated NGOs[1] – a term that expresses well the ambiguity of the phenomenon. The aim of this study is not to lead an inquiry or to expose anybody. Based on a factual assessment of the situation, it will define and identify a non-legal category of NGOs. This factual assessment results from a careful reading of the summary records from the sessions of the United Nations Commission on Human Rights and of the new Human Rights Council,[2] from

[*] The author would like to thank Eric Goldstein, who kindly reviewed the English translation of the text.

[1] See N. Ravi (2000), 'Le problème des organisations pro-gouvernementales', *Moniteur des droits de l'homme*, **49**(50), 8–9. The author relates the fact that at the Committee's 56th session, he 'noticed pro-governmental organizations from the US, China, Cuba, Egypt, Algeria, Iran, Bangladesh and even from Nepal'. In this study, we will not be looking into the other categories of 'problematic' NGOs such as the 'BINGOs', Business Initiated NGOs, run by businesses and which are particularly present at the World Trade Organization (cf. FIDH (2001), *L'OMC et les droits de l'Homme. Pour la primauté des droits de l'Homme. Pour la création d'un statut consultatif des ONG*, 320, 11–14). The Commission on Human Rights and the UN are not the exclusive fields of action of this type of NGOs, but the ones that have been chosen for this study. The problem of NGOs with a pro-governmental view has been raised at several UN World Conferences and in particular at the Durban Conference against Racism; cf. D. El Yazami and A. Madelin (spring 2002), 'Durban et les ONG', *Projet*, **269**, 25–32 or more recently at the World Summit on the Information Society. See for example the press release from Human Rights Watch, 'Dispatch from Tunis: The Civil Society Summit that Wasn't', 14 November 2005, and the one by the International Federation of Human Rights Leagues/Human Rights in China, 'China blocks open discussion at WSIS with procedural manoeuvring', 20 September 2005.

[2] Following the proposal made the Secretary General of the United Nations in its report on the reform of the Organization, the General Assembly adopted resolution

1996 to 2006, with the goal of identifying NGOs whose statements are exclusively or almost exclusively aimed at defending a governmental point of view.[3]

The non-legal category is the 'servile society'. For the purpose of this study, all NGOs which, on reading their statements, appear to be exclusively 'serving' the state, with which they generally share the same nationality, are part of this servile society.[4]

The phenomenon, albeit limited, leading to the introduction of servile NGOs in the UN must be analysed together with actions led by certain states against independent human rights NGOs. Increasing attacks are directed towards NGOs within the Commission on Human Rights and the Human Rights Council. They are successfully relayed by these same states within the Committee on NGOs of the Economic and Social Council (ECOSOC), an intergovernmental body in charge of making recommendations to the Council that can grant, suspend or withdraw the consultative status which the NGOs can claim.[5]

60/251 of 15 March 2006, creating a new Human Rights Council. The Council is replacing the Commission on Human Rights, which thus held its last session (the 62nd) in March–April 2006. As of this writing, the Council had convened three ordinary sessions and four extraordinary sessions. Unfortunately, only a few of the summary records had already been published. The situation as regards participation of NGOs is not substantially modified, as resolution 60/251 stipulates that 'participation of and consultation with observers including [. . .] non-governmental organizations, shall be based on arrangements, including Economic and Social Council resolution 1996/31 of 25 July 1996 and practices observed by the Commission on Human Rights, while ensuring the most effective contribution of these entities'. Thus NGOs that had access to the UN Human Rights Commission now have access to the Human Rights Council.

3   The same attentiveness was not given to all the Sub-Commission's reports but a quick read-through enables us to say the phenomenon is broadly the same.

4   An organization that can be considered prima facie servile is one that systematically adopts a laudatory view of its own government or which never criticizes it. An organization can be considered servile *prima facie* if it concentrates its interventions on a country, or on one of a government's major issues regarding foreign affairs, and/or that limits itself to repeating a view held by a government on this given country and issue. By using this approach we are looking to avoid any misunderstanding on the nature of the organizations considered. But by doing so we are probably omitting a number of organizations that, either because of their behaviour at the Commission, their origin, their way of functioning or their financing, would qualify, in the eyes of other observers, as 'GONGOs'.

5   The study is based on the annual reports of the Committee in charge of NGOs from 1990 to 2006.

Thus (1) the strategy tending to the creation of a servile society comes with (2) a vigorous policy of bringing civil society into line.

1.　THE CREATION OF A SERVILE SOCIETY

It is necessary to assess the situation that has prevailed in the last ten years at the Commission on Human Rights, before attempting to explain how servile NGOs gained access to this forum and are now present in the Human Rights Council. We will then ask ourselves about the validity of an initiative of the United Nations' Secretariat: the NGO Informal Regional Network (UN-IRENE). It looks as though this network's activity tends to facilitate the institutionalization of the servile society at the UN.

The Situation: a Servile Society in Action at the Commission on Human Rights

A detailed analysis of the summary records from the sessions of the Commission on Human Rights allows us to define precisely the phenomenon and distinguish two scenarios.

In two instances, the selected NGOs operate in a situation of conflict between states. Their position tends to discredit the other state by attributing to it human rights violations and, conversely, to improve the reputation of the state they serve by tirelessly emphasizing its successes in the field of human rights. This refers to the relationships between the USA and Cuba and the conflict between India and Pakistan over Kashmir.

In two other instances, the function of servile NGOs is limited to a laudatory and imitative role: they relay governmental views while attributing every virtue to their government. The reproduction of governmental views can eventually lead to attacks on 'enemy' states. This mainly concerns two countries: China and Tunisia.

Only organizations that are regularly active at the Commission on Human Rights or at the Sub-Commission on Human Rights are mentioned in this study. But it is to be remembered that there are many other servile NGOs benefiting from a consultative status which are not mentioned, simply because they have not revealed themselves until now through these UN bodies.

A: NGOs that intervene in conflicts between States

The US-Cuba conflict　In recent years, numerous Cuban NGOs have been granted a consultative status. The United States of America has been, within the Committee on NGOs, the only State to oppose this type of infiltration by Cuba.

Freedom of association is very limited in Cuba as no NGO can be created without the consent of the Cuban Government and Communist Party.[6]

There is no doubt that the Cuban government is willing to have its diplomatic orientations backed up by so-called national NGOs, which are, in practice, either direct offshoots of the state and Party, or organizations with very little leeway, tightly watched and controlled, especially when on the international scene.

Thus Cuban NGOs' views combine defence and attack vis-à-vis a sole enemy: the United States of America. Each intervention includes a laudatory element aimed at demonstrating the legitimacy of the Cuban authorities: the welfare of the Cuban women and youth, the justification for such-and-such repressive legislation presented as a measure of 'self-defence', 'heroic resistance of the Cuban people' against imperialism, and so on.[7]

The interventions denounce first and foremost the blockade imposed by the US, which is presented as being the only true source of human rights violations on Cuban soil; secondly, US practices at Guantanamo military base and the denial of Puerto Rico's independence; thirdly, the use, by the US, of weapons containing depleted uranium in Iraq and Kosovo; fourthly, US support for Israel's 'terrorist' policy towards the Palestinians; fifthly, the fact that the debates at the Commission on Human Rights are politically biased, particularly regarding the Cuban case, and the appointment by the

---

6   See M. Doucin (ed.) (2000), *Guide de la liberté associative dans le monde. Les législations des sociétés civiles dans 138 pays*, Paris: La documentation française, pp. 166–7.

7   Centro de Estudios de la Juventud, E/CN.4/2000/SR.38, E/CN.4/2001/SR.29, p. 35, E/CN.4/2003/SR.35, E/CN.4/2004/SR.25, pp. 29, 37, 41, 43. Centro de Estudios Europeos, E/CN.4/1997/SR.51, E/CN.4/1999/SR.19, p. 29, E/CN.4/2000/SR.20, E/CN.4/2001/SR.35, E/CN.4/2002/SR.32, E/CN.4/2003/SR.19, pp. 28 and 38 (joint statement), E/CN.4/2004/SR.18, pp. 19, 25 and 28 (joint statement); Felix Varela Center, E/CN.4/1998/SR.46; Federation of Cuban Women, E/CN.4/2000/SR.17, pp. 27 and 38, E/CN.4/2003/SR.22, pp. 26, 34, 38 and 42 (joint statement), E/CN.4/2004/SR.14, pp. 18, 29, 33, 38 and 41 (joint statement) and written intervention, E/CN.4/2002/NGO/119; Movimiento Cubano por la Paz y la Soberania de los pueblos, E/CN.4/1997/SR.51, p. 39, 51 and 52, E/CN.4/1998/SR.46, E/CN.4/2001/SR.29, E/CN.4/2002/SR.19, p. 34, E/CN.4/2003/SR.17, p. 22, 26, 34, 38 and 42 (joint statement), E/CN.4/2004/SR.19, p. 28 (joint statement) and written interventions, E/CN.4/2002/NGO/113, pp. 114, 115, 117, 175, 176 and 177; Organization of Solidarity of the Peoples of Africa, Asia and Latin America (OPSAAAL), E/CN.4/1999/SR.19, p. 29, E/CN.4/2000/SR.26, p. 35, E/CN.4/2001/SR.29, E/CN.4/2002/SR.40 (joint statement), E/CN.4/2003/SR.34, pp. 38 and 42 (joint statement), E/CN.4/2004/SR.22 (joint statement), p. 29; National Union of Jurists of Cuba, E/CN.4/1998/46, E/CN.4/1999/SR.19, E/CN.4/2000/SR.26, p. 35, E/CN.4/2002/SR.40 (joint statement), E/CN.4/2003/SR.34, pp. 38 and 42 (joint statement), E/CN.4/2004/SR.25, pp. 28, 34, 38 and 41.

Commission of a Special Rapporteur on the human rights situation in Cuba, who is accused of serving American imperialism. More generally, Cuban NGOs criticize the oppression by Western countries of developing countries, which is carried out under US leadership with the complicity of the international financial institutions.

In the US, governmental-originating NGOs do not exist as such and the freedom of association is on the whole respected, even if numerous associations are de facto dependent on the government, as their financing largely depends on governmental sources. For instance, an organization such as the Freedom House – often challenged by Cuba as we will see later – draws the major part of its finances from governmental sources and, in a way, as far as human rights are concerned, behaves as an auxiliary of US foreign policy.

In addition, the US government sometimes very actively supports NGOs formed in their great majority by exiled Cubans who oppose their government. These American NGOs are not present in international bodies. On the other hand, their members are frequently seen integrated in delegations of international NGOs at the sessions of the Commission and the Sub-Commission on Human Rights.

Thus, at the session of the Commission on Human Rights in 2000, the Executive Director of the Centre for a Free Cuba, based in Washington D.C., was the only representative of the NGO called Liberal International.[8] He was also present in 2001, working for the same NGO, but this time in a delegation of three.[9] In 2002 and 2003, the delegation of this NGO was back to being solely made up of Cubans.[10]

A Franciscan priest called Miguel Loredo and Jesús Permuy, both members of the Centre for Human Rights based in Miami, were members of the Freedom House delegation at the Commission on Human Rights in 2000 (only Loredo), 2001, 2002, 2003 and 2004.[11]

Miguel Loredo had previously presented himself before the Commission on Human Rights in 1993 and 1997, under the wing of the International

---

8   See the list of attendance for this session, E/CN.4/2000/INF.1, p. 53.
9   See the list of attendance for this session, E/CN.4/2001/INF.1, p. 103.
10   See the lists of attendance for these sessions: E/CN.4/2002/INF.1, p. 47 and E/CN.4/2003/INF.1, p. 50.
11   See Cuba's report before the Committee of NGOs at the session of 2001, doc. E/2001/86, p. 28: '. . . Freedom House accredited as its representatives members of terrorist organizations, such as Jesús Permuy, Miguel Loredo and Janisset Rivero, persons of Cuban origin, who engage in a wide range of activities under the orders of the National Cuban American Foundation, a terrorist organization based in Miami'.

Association of Educators for World Peace,[12] and in 1994 with the International Association for the Defence of Religious Liberty.[13]

In 1999, the International Council of the Association for Peace in the Continents (ASOPAZCO), an organization made up of Cuban opponents exiled in Madrid, Spain, was granted special consultative status at the ECOSOC. This organization participated in the session of the Commission on Human Rights in 2000, represented by its president and 15 other members.

This all-too-obvious presence of Cubans caused the Cuban government to lodge a complaint before the Committee on NGOs, to obtain the suspension (in 2000), then finally the definitive withdrawal (in 2005) of the consultative status of ASOPAZCO.[14] Even if all these people are not members of servile NGOs in the strict sense of the definition of our category, there is no doubt that a very strong bond exists between US exiled anti-Castro movements and the US government.

The Kashmir conflict   For many years, India and Pakistan have turned UN bodies into a symbolic battleground over Kashmir. Each year, governmental and non-governmental delegations have to endure both the invective of states and mutual accusations under every item on the agenda. As if this were not enough, these same accusations are echoed by Pakistani and Indian NGOs. These NGOs are well known to the Commission's and Sub-Commission on Human Rights' participants: they are, because of their multiple and repetitive intervention, a source of stress and congestion. When one reads the debates, it is easy to recognize the NGOs that support the Pakistani or the Indian causes.

THE NGOS SUPPORTING THE PAKISTANI CAUSE   The first organization is purely national, since it is the 'official' mass organization of the women from Pakistan: the All Pakistan Women's Association.[15] As for the two other active organizations within the Commission, the World Muslim Congress[16] and the

---

    12   See E/CN.4/1993/SR.62, para. 5, and E/CN.4/1997/SR.23, para. 18 and following (in both cases, the speaker was interrupted by a motion of order from Cuba).
    13   E/CN.4/1994/SR.53, para. 30.
    14   See *infra*.
    15   See oral presentations, E/CN.4/1996/SR.26, 44; E/CN.4/2003/SR.35, p. 39.
    16   See oral presentations, E/CN.4/1996/SR.5, pp. 17, 22, 27, 41, 44 and 47; E/CN.4/1997/SR.6, pp. 17, 21, 30, 39 and 52; E/CN.4/1998/SR.31; E/CN.4/1999/SR.11, pp. 19, 24, 34 and 41; E/CN.4/2000/SR.6, pp. 9 and 39; E/CN.4/2001/SR.47; E/CN.4/2002/SR.8, 14, 22, 42, E/CN.4/2003/SR.12, pp. 19, 28, 39 and 44; E/CN.4/2004/SR.14, pp. 25, 29, 35 and 38.

International Islamic Federation of Students Organisations (IIFSO),[17] they are evidently Islamic organizations, probably mainly financed by private funding and whose position coincides with Pakistan's because of obvious common interests The available information makes it impossible to ascertain that organic, legal, financial or de facto links exist between these organizations and the Pakistani government or administration.

Officially, these organizations defend worldwide Muslim interests and benefit from 'relays' throughout the Muslim world. In fact, their role at the Commission is almost exclusively devoted to defending the Pakistani position over Kashmir.[18]

The position of these three organizations is identical. They denounce not only the Indian 'occupation' of Kashmir, but also the 'massive and blatant' violations of human rights, not to say 'genocide' of the population of Kashmir by India. The same position is recycled with a few adjustments on numerous items of the agenda of the Commission.

THE NGOS SUPPORTING THE INDIAN CAUSE   These Indian organizations also intervene on numerous agenda items at the Commission on Human Rights to denounce the human rights violations by Pakistan.[19] These denunciations are

---

[17]   See oral presentations, E/CN.4/1995/SR.46; E/CN.4/1996/SR.41, p. 44; E/CN.4/1997/SR.9, pp. 18, 23, 30, 46 and 54; E/CN.4/1999/SR.46; E/CN.4/2001/SR.35; E/CN.4/2002/SR.14, pp. 34, 41 and 46; E/CN.4/2003/SR.12, pp. 29, 35, 39 and 44; E/CN.4/2004/SR.13, pp. 19, 25, 29, 35 and 38.

[18]   Only the first of the two organizations has a web site. It indicates that the Congress 'resolved that a permanent international Islamic organization be set up to promote solidarity and cooperation among the global Islamic community (Ummah)'. In addition '[s]ince its establishment in 1926, the Motamar Al-Alam Al-Islami has championed Muslim causes such as Palestine, Kashmir, the Filipino Muslims' struggle, freedom of Muslim people from European colonial rule, and the economic emancipation of the Muslim Ummah'. The Congress's correspondent for Africa is none other than Dr Hasan Abdullah Al-Turabi, former Islamic ideologist of Sudan's President Al-Bashir's regime, and today leader of the Popular National Congress, considered as an opposition party (http://www.motamaralalamalislami.org/).

[19]   International Institute for Peace, E/CN.4/1996/SR.8, pp. 11, 18, 19, 23, 41, 44 and 56, E/CN.4/1997/SR.20, pp. 27 and 39, E/CN.4/1998/SR.29, pp. 33, 46 and 54, E/CN.4/1999/SR.11, pp. 19, 41, 46 and 48, E/CN.4/2000/SR.5, p. 26, E/CN.4/2001/SR.14, p. 42, E/CN.4/2002/SR.11, pp. 14, 32 and 46, E/CN.4/2003/SR.12, pp. 15, 38 and 44, E/CN.4/2004/SR.16, p. 29 and 38; European Union of Public Relations, E/CN.4/1999/SR.11, E/CN.4/2002/SR.14, pp. 32, 42 and 46, E/CN.4/2003/SR.12, pp. 19, 28, 39 and 42, E/CN.4/2004/SR.14, pp. 16, 25, 29 and 34; Himalayan Research and Cultural Foundation, E/CN.4/1996/SR.11, pp. 14, 19, 41, 44 and 54, E/CN.4/1997/SR.7, pp. 13, 21, 27 and 39, E/CN.4/1998/SR.29, p. 41, E/CN.4/1999/SR.41, E/CN.4/2001/SR.42, p. 47, E/CN.4/2002/SR.42, p. 46, E/CN.4/2003/SR.19, pp. 35, 39, 46 and 55, E/CN.4/2004/SR.25, pp. 29, 34 and 38; Indian Council of Education,

mainly focused on the situation in Kashmir, whether they concern the part 'occupied by Pakistan since 1947' or the Indian part where Islamic terrorists conduct incursions. But the denunciations are also about the situation in Pakistan itself, in particular owing to the discrimination against ethnic and religious minorities, and the Pakistani support given to terrorist groups throughout the world, such as the *Taliban* in Afghanistan or Abu Sayyaf in the Philippines. The discourse can sometimes become flattering, acclaiming India's wisdom which, unlike Pakistan for example, 'had wisely enshrined the fundamental principle of secularism in [its] Constitution and taken measures to ensure that all religions were treated on an equal footing [. . .]'.[20]

B: The laudatory and imitative NGOs

These are mainly Tunisian and Chinese NGOs. These organizations are not in the middle of any conflict in particular, even if, from time to time, they do take sides. When this happens, they always support the position of the State with which they share nationality. In reality, their main role is to praise and defend their government for its actions and to relay its concerns on foreign affairs at the Commission on Human Rights.

China   Four Chinese NGOs are particularly involved at the Commission on Human Rights. Even if some observers agree that, on the domestic level, these organizations are progressively gaining a sort of autonomy from their authority, their interventions at the Commission on Human Rights show they remain intrinsically tied to the state and Party. The first two are Chinese para-state 'mass' organizations.[21]

Created in 1949, the All-China Women's Federation undertakes numerous activities for the protection of women in China.[22] Its special status regarding the government and the Party is specified from the outset in the general principles of its governing charter:

> The All-China Women's Federation is a mass organization of society which links together women across the country of all minority nationalities and from all walks

---

E/CN.4/1996/SR.14, pp. 23, 19, 29, 36, 47 and 56, E/CN.4/1997/SR.12, pp. 17, 39, 51, 61 and 62, E/CN.4/1998/SR.46, E/CN.4/1999/SR.11, p. 34, E/CN.4/2002/SR.42, E/CN.4/2003/SR.35, p. 55.

20   Indian Council of Education, E/CN.4/1996/SR.23.

21   About Chinese NGOs and their evolution, see China Development Brief (August 2001), *250 Chinese NGOs. Civil Society in the Making*.

22   See E/CN.4/1996/SR.41; E/CN.4/1997/SR.39, pp. 54 and 60, E/CN.4/1999/ SR.19; E/CN.4/2001/SR.47; E/CN.4/2002/SR.34, p. 38 (joint interventions); E/CN.4/ 2003/SR.2; E/CN.4/2004/SR.38, p. 41.

of life under the leadership of the Chinese Communist Party to achieve further liberation, and a bridge and a transmission belt linking the masses of women with the CCP and the government. It is one of the most important pillars of the state power.

The Federation's employees have an official status and receive their salaries from the state. A majority of them are Party members. Because of its close links with the country's governing body, the Federation benefits from opportunities to access international fora. Even though it is a national organization, it was granted consultative status to the ECOSOC in 1995, before resolution 1996/31[23] was adopted. It is true that, in the same year, Beijing hosted the World Conference on Women. Similarly, in 1998, at the Symposium on Human Rights organized in Vancouver as part of the bilateral talks between the People's Republic of China and Canada, some representatives of the Federation were part of the Chinese official delegation even though Canadian NGOs were neither invited nor authorized to participate at the meeting.

The China Disabled Persons Federation is another 'mass' organization[24] created by one of Deng Xiaoping's sons and set up by the government in 1998 to promote disabled people's rights. This organization makes itself much scarcer than the previous one at the Commission on Human Rights.

The very official United Nations Association of China[25] and the China Society for Human Rights Studies[26] are also present. The latter was created in 1993, on the occasion of the World Conference on Human Rights in Vienna. Although its representatives were accredited as NGOs, its status remains ambiguous and the Chinese government contributes to this confusion. Along these lines, in 1997, the year when the European Union and China re-established bilateral talks on human rights, a delegation led by the Secretary General of the China Society visited several European capitals to defend the state of human rights in China, advocating 'constructive dialogue' rather than 'confrontation'.

The oral presentations of these NGOs are essentially aimed at answering accusations directed at China concerning human rights violations. Several presentations are specifically devoted to the 'heretical sect' Falun Gong.[27]

---

23   The resolution has opened up the consultative status to national NGOs, as we will see further on, *infra*, in the section entitled 'The introduction of service NGOs into the United Nations system'.

24   See E/CN.4/2002/SR.38 (joint intervention).

25   See E/CN.4/2002/SR.34, p. 38 (joint intervention), E/CN.4/2003/SR.26 (joint statement); E/CN.4/2004/SR.29, p. 35.

26   See E/CN.4/2000/SR.38, E/CN.4/2002/SR.34, 42, E/CN.4/2003/SR.26 (joint statement), E/CN.4/2004/SR.29, p. 33.

27   Among others, Association de la Chine pour les Nations Unies, E/CN.4/2002/SR.34.

Others are aimed at (1) defending the Chinese human rights track record and at pointing out that 'States accusing China of violating human rights are those who have committed massive violations of the rights of Chinese people during armed conflicts';[28] (2) convincing the Japanese government to solve the 'comfort women' issue;[29] (3) expressing indignation that, within the Commission, the Western States use the issue of human rights as a pretext 'for interfering in the internal affairs of sovereign States';[30] and (4) denouncing human rights violations in the USA, in particular concerning women's rights.[31]

Tunisia   Tunisia is probably the state that, on an international level, resorts most to the use of servile NGOs. The 'servile society' is particularly well developed in Tunisian society, controlled by President Zine el-Abidine Ben Ali's party, whether it is small local associations, shiny façade organizations, or public service supplementary associations. These NGOs spread the presidential word even within international organizations and rail against all the 'other' NGOs which, with patent insincerity, blame the regime for not respecting human rights.

The talk is always mostly laudatory, in that it acclaims, in all fields, the politics adopted by the country's regime.[32] It is also imitative, in the sense that it takes up the essence of the Tunisian interventions before the Commission and brings to mind President Ben Ali's proposals on different subjects. The Tunisian servile NGOs also defend the regime: they denounce the 'slanderous' comments made by the NGOs that dare accuse Tunisia of violating human rights.[33]

---

28   Société chinoise d'étude des droits de l'homme, E/CN.4/2002/SR.42.
29   All China Women's Federation, E/CN.4/1996/SR.41.
30   All China Women's Federation, E/CN.4/1997/SR.39.
31   All China Women's Federation, E/CN.4/1999/SR.19.
32   Association to Defend Tunisians Abroad – ADTE, E/CN.4/Sub.2/1999/SR.10; Association Tunisienne des Mères, E/CN.4/Sub.2/1998/SR.28; Association Tunisienne des Droits de l'Enfant: E/CN.4/2001/SR.31, E/CN.4/2004/SR.25; Association Tunisienne pour l'Autodéveloppement et la Solidarité (ATLAS), E/CN.4/2000/SR.27, E/CN.4/2001/SR.35, E/CN.4/Sub.2/1999/SR.13, E/CN.4/2003/SR.35, E/CN.4/2004/SR.29; Organisation Tunisienne de l'Éducation et de la Famille, E/CN.4/2000/SR.17; Organisation Tunisienne des Jeunes Médecins sans Frontières, E/CN.4/1999/SR.29, E/CN.4/2001/SR.42, E/CN.4/2002/SR.42, E/CN.4/2003/SR.39, E/CN.4/2004/SR.35; Union Nationale de la Femme Tunisienne, E/CN.4/2000/SR.38, E/CN.4/2002/SR.42, E/CN.4/2002/SR.46, E/CN.4/2003/SR.42, E/CN.4/2004/SR.38, p. 41.
33   Association Tunisienne des Mères, E/CN.4/Sub.2/1998/SR.28. See also Organisation Tunisienne des Jeunes Médecins sans Frontières, E/CN.4/2001/SR.42.

Even if it is limited to a few situations or to a few States, the presence of the servile society can be widely felt within the United Nations' Commission on Human Rights and now within the new Human Rights Council. We are left with the question of how these NGOs gained access to these fora.

The Introduction of Servile NGOs into the United Nations System

Resolution 1996/31, adopted by the Economic and Social Council on 25 July 1996, is entitled 'Consultative Relationship between the United Nations and Non-Governmental Organizations'. It replaces resolution 1296 (XLIV) dated 23 May 1968, which used to govern these relations.[34]

The main innovation in resolution 1996/31 is the possibility for national NGOs to apply for consultative status to ECOSOC. But this innovation is crippled by the obligation of having to ask for the recommendation of the 'member State concerned' which, in effect, in the instance of certain states, grants access to servile NGOs and denies access to truly independent ones. Furthermore, the body in charge of recommending consultative status to the ECOSOC – the Committee on Non Governmental Organizations – remains an intergovernmental body, a set-up that makes it incapable of making objective decisions, based on the criteria established by resolution 1996/31. On the contrary, the Committee turns out to be hostage of its members' own interests.

Together, these two factors enable servile NGOs to join the United Nations' system.

A: The condition for consultation of the 'member State concerned' for national NGOs

Paragraph 4 of resolution 1996/31 of the ECOSOC stipulates: 'Except where expressly stated otherwise, the term "organization" shall refer to non-governmental organizations at the national, subregional, regional or international levels.' The major innovation of the 1996 reform is that national NGOs can now be granted consultative status to the ECOSOC in the same capacity as international NGOs.[35] Under resolution 1296 (XLIV), this was accepted but as a strictly defined exception to the general rule.[36]

---

[34]   See Sara Guillet (1995), *Nous peuples des Nations Unies. L'action des ONG au sein du système de protection internationale des droits de l'homme*, Paris: Montchrestien.

[35]   About the reform, cf. S. Guillet (winter 1999), 'Les relations entre les ONG et l'ONU dans le domaine des droits de l'Homme: un partenariat en mutation', *L'Observateur des Nations Unies* (7).

[36]   ECOSOC Resolution 1296 (XLIV) of 23 May 1968, para. 9: 'National organizations shall normally present their views through international non-governmental

Following the collapse of the Berlin Wall, this reform was necessary to take into account the massive development of NGOs in the East and the South. In a number of formerly closed states, the transition processes towards democracy have led to the creation of dynamic non-governmental sectors which are legitimately demanding direct access to the UN, instead of having to go through an 'umbrella' organization within which their distinctiveness and concerns cannot be fully expressed.

This reform was mainly created for the NGOs coming from the developing countries as well as from countries with 'economies in transition' – a euphemism to describe the transition from a communist economy to a market economy. It is therefore logical that resolution 1996/31 encourages the Committee on NGOs to give them priority of attention to ensure their participation, to 'help achieve a just, balanced, effective and genuine involvement of non-governmental organizations from all regions and areas of the world'.

But this commendable concern for balance and openness is contradicted by maintaining an institution which was already present in resolution 1296: indeed, according to resolution 1996/31, 'national organizations [. . .] may be admitted [. . .] after consultation with the Member State concerned. The views expressed by the Member State, if any, shall be communicated to the non-governmental organization concerned, which shall have the opportunity to respond to those views through the Committee on Non-Governmental Organizations'.

This advisory procedure was in coherence with resolution 1296 which set up a system whereby national NGOs could exceptionally gain consultative status. But it can no longer be justified in the widely open system established by resolution 1996/31.

In this new context, maintaining this condition has the effect of conferring on the 'concerned State' a quasi-right of veto to prevent the admission of NGOs of which it disapproves. The principle of openness for national NGOs, combined with the condition of consultation of the concerned state, results in the admission of servile NGOs and the exclusion of independent ones. In dictatorial countries or in countries with prolonged 'democratic transitions' only servile NGOs are likely to receive a favourable recommendation from the

---

organizations to which they belong. It would not, save in exceptional cases, be appropriate to admit national organizations which are affiliated to an international non-governmental organization covering the same subjects on an international basis. National organizations, however, may be admitted after consultation with the Member State concerned in order to help achieve a balanced and effective representation of non-governmental organizations reflecting major interests of all regions and areas of the world or where they have special experience upon which the Council may wish to draw.'

concerned state, whereas independent NGOs – often made illegal or even criminalized when they exile their headquarters to a foreign country – will inevitably be vetoed. In fact, most of the national NGOs confronted by this type of reaction simply avoid applying to the Committee on NGOs, knowing full well that the game is not worth the candle.

But some NGOs have agreed to take the test. This is the case of Human Rights in China (HRIC), which is based in New York, comes from the Tian An Men Square student movement and is probably the most important exiled Chinese NGO defending human rights. Noticing that an increasing number of China-based NGOs were being granted consultative status, they decided to try their luck.

The committee reviewed HRIC's application at its substantive session on 4 June 1999, the day of the tenth anniversary of the Tian An Men Square massacre.[37] First, a discussion began to determine whether the NGO was Chinese, as its headquarters was in New York. For Algeria, there was no doubt that HRIC was a Chinese NGO, which made the consultation of the Chinese delegation 'necessary' and even 'compulsory'. Cuba, Ethiopia and Pakistan agreed: to them, the NGO was undoubtedly Chinese, even though it was based in the US.

The session's chairperson organized a debate based on a half-hour presentation by the Chinese representative, who explained that HRIC was in reality a group of criminals wanted in China who, spurred on by their personal resentment against the country, were trying to overthrow its government. The Committee's report only reflects the Chinese declarations, but makes no mention of the answers given by HRIC.[38]

China, while giving itself a decisive role in the decision the Committee on NGOs was to take – implicitly designating itself as the only 'concerned State' with the exception of the United States, where HRIC has its headquarters – referred continuously to the fact that the members of HRIC were all living outside China and had no regular contact with the country.

The French delegate offered to defer the review of the case. But China asked for the question of the attribution of status to be voted on immediately. The Chinese request not to recommend the status of HRIC to the ECOSOC was adopted by 13 votes to three, with two abstentions.[39]

---

[37]   See B. Laroche (Fall 1999), 'Maligned & Excluded in a Politicized Process. HRIC Denied Consultative Status', *China Rights Forum (publication de HRIC)*, pp. 24–9.

[38]   See the report of the Committee on NGOs, doc. E/1999/109.

[39]   France, Ireland, US voted in favour; Algeria, Bolivia, China, Colombia, Cuba, Ethiopia, India, Lebanon, Pakistan, Russia, Sudan, Tunisia, Turkey voted against; Chile and Romania abstained.

This case is particularly revealing because of the reputation of HRIC and the quality of its work, but in 1996–97[40] and 2004[41] there were other examples of status refusals based on the 'consultation' of the 'concerned State' for organizations of lesser importance.

B: The Committee on NGOs: an inappropriate body

The procedures relating to the consultative status of the ECOSOC involve a subsidiary organ of the Economic and Social Council: the Committee on NGOs. This Committee is made up of 19 States: five African, four Asian, two Eastern European, four Latin American and Caribbean and four from Western Europe and others.[42] It convenes annually in May–June, before the Economic and Social Council's substantive session in July. Even if the final decision belongs to the latter, the Committee on NGOs plays a fundamental role in the sense that, in nearly all cases, the Council ratifies its recommendations.

The Committee rules on status applications and on requests for reclassification from one category to another.[43] It reviews the quadrennial reports

---

[40]   The case of the South Korean organization Centre for the Advancement of North Korean Human Rights because of the opposition of North Korea. See doc. E/1996/102, para. 6; E/1996/SR.55, pp. 4–5; E/1997/90, para. 38.

[41]   For two organizations coming from Nigeria, African Hebrew Organization and the Fédération des communautés Ijaw; an organization working on Viet Nam, Alliance Vietnam Liberté which, according to the delegate of Viet Nam, 'had committed acts of sabotage in her country and was featured in a 1992 United States Federal Bureau of Investigation (FBI) list of criminal organizations'; an organization from Ghana, Thirty-First December Women's Movement which had, according to the observer delegate of Ghana, 'been involved in activities against her Government' and of functioning as 'the women's wing and an integral part of the National Democratic Congress, one of the political parties in Ghana'; an organization allegedly from Cameroon, African Network of Grassroots Democracy which had, according to the representative of Cameroon, 'never been registered in Cameroon' and 'had criticized her Government in its application'; finally the International Association Promoting Human Rights, accused by Cuba of 'being created in Mexico by the Miami-based anti-Cuban terrorist organization Cuban Democratic Directory and of having links with the Cuban American National Foundation. Cf. doc. E/2004/32, pp. 11–14.

[42]   In 2006, the members of the Committee were Cameroon, Chile, China, Colombia, Côte d'Ivoire, Cuba, France, Germany, India, Iran, Pakistan, Peru, Romania, Russian Federation, Senegal, Sudan, Turkey, United States of America, Zimbabwe.

[43]   Resolution 1996/31 creates two categories of status: 1) 'general' for the organizations 'that are concerned with most of the activities of the Council and its subsidiary bodies and can demonstrate to the satisfaction of the Council that they have substantive and sustained contributions to make to the achievement of the objectives of the United Nations in fields set out in paragraph 1 above, and are closely involved with the economic and social life of the peoples of the areas they represent and whose membership, which should be considerable, is broadly representative of major segments of society in a large number of countries in different regions of the world'

NGOs are required to hand in. Then, depending on the review given to the report, the Committee can advise on the NGOs' reclassification, status suspension or withdrawal.

The role of the Committee on NGOs is therefore fundamental to the system set up by resolution 1996/31, and yet the governmental structure of the Committee makes it impossible for it to fulfil its missions.[44] A detailed analysis of this body's day-to-day functioning makes this clear and highlights three phenomena. First, a majority of the members of the Committee pronounce themselves in favour of granting consultative status to servile NGOs; conversely, the minority that might dissent is often very passive: when the question is not raised by a state, generally the US, this minority lets things run their course or just dissociates itself from the consensus without necessarily calling for a vote; finally, the only active state to prevent servile NGOs from being granted the status, the US, is selective in its indignation, insofar as its own objections mainly concern Cuban NGOs.

A majority of the members of the Committee support the applications presented by servile NGOs　All the votes that have taken place at the Committee on NGOs regarding servile NGOs were called for by the US. Each time, the US was defeated by an overwhelming majority and the Committee adopted a decision to recommend the NGO in question for consultative status in the ECOSOC. In 1996,[45] the following NGOs were granted consultative status after the US called for a vote: the Centro de Estudios sobre Asia y Oceania,[46] the Centro de Estudios

---

(para. 22) (corresponding to category I under resolution 1296 (XLIV)); 2) and 'special' for the organizations 'that have a special competence in, and are concerned specifically with, only a few of the fields of activity covered by the Council and its subsidiary bodies, and that are known within the fields for which they have or seek consultative status' (para. 23) (corresponding to category II under resolution 1296). Furthermore, an organization which has no general or special status can be included on a *roster* when it can 'make occasional and useful contributions to the work of the Council or its subsidiary bodies or other United Nations bodies within their competence' (para. 24) (this possibility already existed in resolution 1296).

44　J. Aston (2001), 'The United Nations Committee on Non-governmental Organizations: guarding the entrance to a politically divided house', *European Journal of International Law*, **12**(5), 943–62.

45　Report of the Committee on Non-Governmental Organizations for the session of 1996, doc. E/1996/102.

46　The vote was requested by Cuba on the USA's proposal to defer the examination of the request at the second part of the session. The American proposal was rejected by 11 votes to five with one abstention. Subsequently, a vote (not recorded) was requested by the USA on the recommendation made to the ECOSOC to put this NGO on the Roster. The recommendation was adopted by 12 votes to one with four abstentions.

Europeos,[47] the Movimiento Cubano por la Paz y la Soberania de los Pueblos.[48] The United States expressed reservations about these NGOs before the Economic and Social Council. Cuba replied that it 'did not accept statements from other countries on its legal system and domestic political activities, or on its civil society'.[49]

In 1997, five new organizations were granted status.[50]

At the ECOSOC, the delegation of the United States publicly dissented from 'the Council's approval of consultative status for five Cuba-based organizations [. . .] since his Government believed that those groups did not meet the definition of an independent NGO. Moreover, it had doubts regarding the contribution they could make to furthering the goals and principles of the United Nations. It had opposed granting them consultative status in the Committee on Non-Governmental Organizations and it opposed the decision just taken by the Council'.

To which Cuba replied that the five NGOs in question, whose headquarters are in Cuba, are NGOs that 'were all legitimate and independent organizations having their own statutes and financial arrangements. They all enjoyed the status of national NGOs under Cuban law, apart from OCLAE, which was an international organization whose activities were not contrary to the principles and purposes of Cuban social policy [. . .] the organizations cited represented the interests of the Cuban people and giving them special consultative status would enable them to work effectively with the Council and within the United Nations system'.[51]

In 1998, the penetration of the system by Cuban organizations continued with the entry of three new NGOs.[52] Finally, in 1999, the status was granted

---

47   The vote (not recorded) was requested by the United States on the proposal to recommend to the ECOSOC to grant the Status category II. Proposal approved by 11 votes in favour, one against with five abstentions.

48   The vote was requested by Cuba on the proposal by the USA to defer the application's review. The proposal was rejected by nine votes to two with seven abstentions. Subsequently, a vote was requested by the USA on the proposal to recommend to the ECOSOC the attribution of a status category II. The proposal was approved with seven votes in favour, two against and nine abstentions.

49   E/1996/SR.55.

50   The National Association of Cuban Economists; the Félix Varela Center, the National Union of Jurists of Cuba, the Federation of Cuban Women and the Latin American and Caribbean Continental Organization of Students (OCLAE). See the report of the Committee on NGOs, doc. E/1997/90.

51   E/1997/SR.40, 23 July 1997, pp. 16–17.

52   Organization for the Solidarity of the Peoples of Asia, Africa and Latin America (OSPAAL), Unión de Escritores y Artistas de Cuba, et le Centro de Estudios sobre la Juventud. Cf. doc. E/1998/72 and Add.1. For the debate before the ECOSOC, see E/1998/SR.45, 29 July 1998, p. 2.

to the Asociación Cubana de las Naciones Unidas, once again by a majority vote.[53] The United States have always been the only State to vote against granting the status to Cuban NGOs, except in the instance of the Movimiento Cubano por la Paz y la Soberania de los Pueblos, when the United Kingdom joined it.

The passivity of a minority of the members of the Committee and the selective indignation of the USA A strong minority of member states of the Committee appear to vote passively by taking refuge in abstentions or even, sometimes, by agreeing to vote in favour of the servile NGOs. This remains true, even if in recent years we have noticed that, in certain cases, certain European states, particularly France and Germany, show a greater resolve in their interventions.

This passivity becomes obvious when a state requests a vote, but it is more often invisible: among all the servile NGOs whom the Committee recommended for observer status, only Cuban NGOs were subjected to a vote. States in the Committee have never raised problems that the admission of mass Chinese NGOs might cause. At no time has the Committee questioned the independence of Tunisian NGOs that have appeared before it.

In 1995, following the Srebrenica massacre and the seizure of Zepa in Bosnia-Herzegovina, Croatia and Albania asked the ECOSOC to send back before the Committee an organization (the International Committee of Peace and Human Rights) they suspected was covering up for the World Serbian Union. They received the support of Austria, Egypt, the United States, Libya and the United Kingdom on the grounds that new facts had emerged between the Committee's decision to grant consultative status to the International Committee and the session of the ECOSOC.[54] In 1999, after many deferrals, the Committee ended the application's review without reaching a verdict on whether to grant consultative status.[55] The Council ratified this 'conclusion' in resolution 2000/214.[56]

But at the same session of the ECOSOC in 1995, the same states refused to treat in the same way an Indian NGO denounced by Pakistan, the Himalayan Research and Cultural Foundation, on the pretext that Pakistan had not introduced 'any new facts' since the review of the application by the Committee.

---

[53] Proposal adopted by 15 votes to one, with three abstentions. Report of the Committee on Non-Governmental Organizations for the session of 1999, E/1999/109, para. 32.

[54] See E/1995/SR.54, 26 July 1995, pp. 8ff.

[55] See E/1999/109/Add.2 (Part I), p. 4 & Corr.1.

[56] Decision 2000/214 in E/2000/INF/2/Add.1, p. 29.

On a purely procedural basis, the members were probably right to want to avoid a challenge by the ECOSOC to a recommendation made by one of its subsidiary bodies. The fact remains that they were fundamentally wrong to override the serious allegations expressed by Pakistan when it declared in a session that the organization in question 'is undoubtedly an offshoot of the Indian intelligence services whose aim is to undertake subversive activities in Pakistan'.[57]

The attitude of the Europeans remains ambivalent. For nearly ten years, they expressed no reservations about granting status to NGOs for which it was fairly easy to demonstrate close links with their government. In recent years, they made two interventions of unequal value, which illustrates the absence of a clear position with regard to the question.[58]

As for the United States, their indignation is selective: in addition to the Cuban NGOs it was also directed at an Iraqi,[59] a Sudanese[60] and several Islamic NGOs.[61] In other words, servile NGOs bother the US because the state they are associated with is in the crosshairs of American foreign policy rather than because they are servile and their admission would violate resolution 1996/31.

Servile NGOs enter the United Nations system because of the politicized selection process within a body dominated by states that have an interest in

---

[57]   E/1995/SR.54, p. 12. Only in French, translation from the author.

[58]   In 1998, Ireland dissociated itself from the decision taken by the Committee to recommend to the ECOSOC the Iranian NGO called the 'Organization for defending victims of violence'. In 2004, France, supported by Germany, 'while joining in the consensus on the granting of consultative status to the organization' China Care and Compassion Society, 'questioned the organization to ensure that it was truly a nongovernmental organization, that it was transparent and democratic, and that it operated in conformity with the principles stipulated in Economic and Social Council resolution 1996/31. (. . .) He also said that his delegation [France] will follow attentively the organization's activities in the future and its contribution to the work of the Council.' Doc. E/2004/32, pp. 10–11.

[59]   The General Federation of Iraqi Women. See the report of the Committee on its resumed 1998 session, doc. E/1999/10, para. 12.

[60]   See the decision of the United States to dissociate itself from the decision taken by the Committee regarding the International Women's Muslim Union. Doc. E/1999/109, para. 35.

[61]   As to 1997, see the comments by the US and the UK on the Islamic World Studies Centre and the Qatar Charitable Society. On the latter, the United States stated they wished to dissociate themselves as this organization 'might be involved in activities inconsistent with the Charter of the United Nations'. Doc. E/1997/90, respectively paras 62 and 66. In 1998, see the decision by the United States and the United Kingdom to dissociate themselves from the decision regarding the Africa Muslims Agency. Doc. E/1998/8, para. 34.

seeing these NGOs participate in the sessions of the Commission and Sub-Commission on Human Rights. But most worrying is the fact that, once inside the system, these NGOs act as representatives of their country's civil society and become the United Nations' prime contacts. One wonders to what extent the UN Secretariat encourages this tendency to institutionalize these servile NGOs.

Towards the Institutionalization of a Servile Society?

In November 1999, a report from the Secretary-General at the General Assembly announced that, in the future, 'The Section [in charge of NGOs within the Economic and Social Department of the UN] will work to improve the exchange of information through informal networks of country or regionally based NGOs in consultative status with the Council, which will serve as links between the NGO Section and NGOs in each region.'[62]

This is the basis on which the Informal Regional NGO network (UN-IRENE) was launched at a meeting in Arcaju, Brazil in April 2001. Six 'representative organizations' from North Africa, West Africa, Asia and the Pacific, Eastern Europe and Latin America were invited. The criteria for selection and 'representativeness' of these organizations are unknown, but one thing is certain: there were no independent human rights NGOs among them. In the final session of the meeting, five organizations were designated as the network's 'regional coordinators'.[63]

UN-IRENE's first official meeting for Africa took place on 8–11 January 2002 in Hammamet, Tunisia, under the patronage of Tunisian President M. Zine el-Abidine Ben Ali. The meeting was jointly organized by the United Nations' Section of NGOs and the Association féminine Tunisie 21, the network's 'regional coordinator'.

Fifteen 'representative' NGOs of the five African Sub-regions as well as several senior civil servants from the United Nations, the President of the Economic and Social Council, some informal partners such as the Conference of NGOs in consultative relationship with the United Nations (CONGO), the

---

[62]   UN Secretary-General, Analysis of the organizational structure and technical resources of the non-governmental section of the UN Secretariat, A/54/520, 11 November 1999.

[63]   North Africa, Association Féminine Tunisie 21 (Tunisia); West Africa, Conseil Économique et Social de l'Afrique de l'Ouest (Senegal); Asia and Pacific, Organization for Industrial, Spiritual, and Cultural Advancement (OISCA) (Japan); Eastern Europe, International Scientific and Educational 'ZNANIE' Association (Russia); Latin America and Caribbean, World Family Organization (Brazil).

World Federation of United Nations Associations and others, were present.[64] The talks led to the designation of five sub-regional coordinators.[65]

The Network's activities need to find financing. The Committee on NGOs appears to be the appropriate body to handle this issue. The head of the NGO Section introduced the informal regional network at the session of the Committee in 2002.[66] Following this intervention, and 'as evidence of the support of the Section for its outreach programme', the Sudanese delegate introduced a request to the Committee for 'the establishment of a voluntary trust fund to support the informal regional network IRENE in assisting NGOs worldwide with equally distributed financial support'.[67] The Committee on NGOs adopted this decision by consensus; [68] the ECOSOC then endorsed it.

In decision 2002/225 concerning the 'Establishment of the general voluntary trust fund in support of the United Nations NGO Informal Regional Network',[69] the ECOSOC reaffirms 'the important role of the United Nations NGO Informal Regional Network in achieving NGO capacity-building to take part in United Nations work, support the coalition of NGOs and disseminate the work of the Council'. From then on it considers 'recognizing the need for human and financial resources and technical assistance in order to ensure increased participation of NGOs from developing countries and countries with economies in transition in the work of the Council and its subsidiary bodies, and to work to ensure parity and an equitable and representative NGO

---

[64]   See press release, AFR/374, DEV/2366, NGO/356, January 2002.
[65]   North Africa: Association Féminine Tunisie 21 (Tunisia); West Africa, Coalition des Familles pour la Lutte contre le SIDA et la Pauvreté (Burkina Faso); Central Africa, Ligue pour l'Education de la Femme et de l'Enfant (Cameroon); East Africa, Association des Nations Unies Ethiopie (Ethiopia); Afrique méridionale: Angola Network for Poverty Reduction (Angola).
[66]   See E/2002/71 (Part II), para. 6. A few months before the publication of the report by the Secretary General announcing the creation of the Network (see *supra* note 62), at the substantive session of 1999 of the ECOSOC, the Algerian Ambassador, Mr Dembri mentioned 'the sensitive issue of financing of NGOs', judging 'it was inappropriate for certain NGOs to be heavily subsidized by Governments with no observance of the precautionary rule set forth in paragraph 13' of resolution 1996/31, on the financing of NGOs. To face up to this situation, Mr Dembri felt 'it was urgent to ensure that Government financing did not go directly to NGOs but to a United Nations fund, to be managed by a governing body made up of figures of high moral probity, such as winners of the Nobel Peace Prize and independent experts. The governing body would apportion the contents of the entire fund on the basis of well-defined criteria, including geographical distribution. The experts should be remunerated to protect them from any suspicion of partiality'. E/1999/SR.44, 28 July 1999, p. 5.
[67]   Ibid., para. 10.
[68]   See E/2002/71 (Part I), Draft decision IV 'Establishment of the general voluntary trust fund in support of the United Nations NGO Informal Regional Network'.
[69]   Cf. E/2002/INF/2/Add.2, p. 133.

presence and contributions to United Nations goals, including development goals as set out in the United Nations Millennium Declaration [. . .]'.

In order to achieve this, the ECOSOC requests 'the Secretary-General to establish a general voluntary trust fund [. . .] in order to achieve those aims and ensure an equal development of activities for NGOs in consultative status with the Council in all regions through the equitable division of available resources'.

The Global Informal Regional Network's mandate is then described in the appendix, in 12 points that do little to clarify the mission with which the ECOSOC is planning to entrust the new institution. It is about enabling 'interactive exchange among NGOs regionally and interregionally, and between NGOs worldwide and the United Nations, through the Non-Governmental Organizations Section of the Department of Economic and Social Affairs of the Secretariat', by implementing 'an ongoing, regularly updated technology-based system' and 'capacity-building workshops, seminars and training programmes' in order to 'strengthen NGO capabilities for effective contribution, at both operational and policy levels', and to facilitate and enable 'an environment conducive to the development of an active and effective NGO sector', or to create 'opportunities for NGOs to interact by, for example, convening meetings, organizing exchange visits or study tours in order to promote cooperation, sharing of resources and collaborative action among network participants'.

It is thus a good opportunity for a few NGOs selected on the basis of unknown criteria and whose ranks include no 'embarrassing' NGOs, such as independent human rights NGOs. After five years, the Network's results are significant.[70] Admittedly, the voluntary fund is not a success – the only contribution being 10 000 dollars from Turkey.[71] Nevertheless, UN-IRENE is progressively managing to assert its existence in several regions and countries of the world.[72]

---

[70]   See the Network's website, http://www.unpan.org/NGO-Africa.asp and the regular 'updates' on the Network's activity in particular.

[71]   See the 'update' n° 7, April 2004, p. 1.

[72]   Africa, Regional Coordinator, Association des Mères Tunisiennes (Tunisia). Mauritania, Association Mauritanienne pour le Bien-Etre et le Secours de l'Enfant et de la Mère. Arab States (in fact limited to the United Arab Emirates), Zayed International Prize for the Environnment (United Arab Emirates). Latin America, Reg. Coord., World Family Organization (Brazil). 'North America' (in fact limited to Canada), Hope for the Nations (Canada). Eastern Europe, Reg. Coord.: Fondation Université de la Mer Noire (Roumanie). Sub-Reg. Coord. I (South-Eastern Europe), Association for Democratic Initiatives (Macedonia). Sub-Reg. Coord. II (Central Europe), Federation for Women and Family Planning (Pologne). Caucasus-Central Asia, Reg. Coord., Fund of Aid for Youth (Azerbaïdjan). Azerbaïdjan: National

Even though the Network is supposed to be informal, the designation of regional or national coordinators amounts to an institutionalization of the relationship between the Secretariat of the ECOSOC and NGOs that define themselves as 'representatives' of civil society, with the blessing of the concerned states. Such a selection process is problematic, especially in countries where freedom of association is not respected, such as Tunisia, Mauritania and China. In any case, UN-IRENE is undoubtedly in a position to support the control of civil society in these countries by choosing non-governmental focal points for the UN, who will be its main reference during the preparation of key events such as the World Summit on Information Society in Tunisia.[73]

Servile NGOs who do not yet have consultative status with the ECOSOC are strongly encouraged to apply during regional or national seminars, as was the case when the Network was launched in China.[74] Is this one more of the United Nations' 'energy wasters' or is it a UN–GONGOS Network? Whatever the intentions of its founders, UN-IRENE has worked in favour of institutionalizing servile society at the UN. While the servile NGOs are establishing themselves within the world organization, other NGOs that are more critical of the states, particularly with regard to human rights, see their freedom of action and expression becoming increasingly limited.

2.   PUTTING CIVIL SOCIETY IN LINE

The progressive introduction of servile NGOs into the United Nations bodies is accompanied by attacks on NGOs considered too critical of the concerned

---

Assembly of Youth Organizations of Republic of Azerbaijan. Japan: Organization for Industrial, Spiritual, and Cultural Advancement. China, The Chinese People's Association for Peace and Disarmament. India, All India Women's Education Fund Association. Pakistan, All Pakistan Women's Association. Inside the Pakistani Coordination, as well as All Pakistan, there is the World Muslim Congress. Also indicated is an organization representative for Western Europe, World for World Organization (Italy), but we have not been able to find any reference for a launch meeting of the Network in this region.

[73]   The Secretariat of the UN-IRENE initiated, in January 2005, a mission of assistance to the 'two leading NGOs' (L'Association des Mères Tunisiennes et l'Association Tunisienne des Droits de l'Enfant) in charge of organizing the Forum for Civil Society which was held in April, notably to prepare the 'contribution of the NGOs' at the Tunis Summit.

[74]   V. Mission Report, Capacity Building for NGOs in China (Beijing, Shanghai 10–18 October 2002), para. 26: 'All of the NGOs which the UN delegation met have expressed their interest to participate in the UN NGOs-IRENE/UNPAN Network, and have shown their willingness to apply for the ECOSOC/NGO Consultative Status. They have taken note of the fact that, although China is the biggest developing country, there are so far only 14 NGOs in China with the ECOSOC consultative status.'

states. Some states within the Committee on NGOs use every excuse to try and intimidate what they believe are hostile NGOs. In some cases they even try to have their status suspended or withdrawn. It starts with simple warnings, graduates to requests for 'special reports', and culminates in the adoption of strong disciplinary sanctions.

The Warnings

These oral attacks are not followed by requests for special reports, status suspension or withdrawal. They are carried out by way of warning or intimidation. The intervening state very often declares that it reserves to itself the right to request status suspension or withdrawal if necessary. This sort of attack generally happens during the review of the organization's quadrennial report by the Committee on NGOs.

Paragraph 55 of Resolution 1996/31 states that in 'periodically reviewing the activities of non-governmental organizations on the basis of the reports submitted under paragraph 61 (c) below[75] and other relevant information, the Council Committee on Non-Governmental Organizations shall determine the extent to which the organizations have complied with the principles governing consultative status and have contributed to the work of the Council'. On this basis, NGOs have to submit to a session of 'question time'. In their absence, the questions are addressed to them by the Secretariat and the examination of the report is deferred to the subsequent session. The review of the quadrennial report can therefore be put off for several years if a state deems the answers 'unsatisfactory' and it requests clarifications.[76]

In 1991, Cuba reproached the Confédération internationale des syndicats libres for having the AFL-CIO as an affiliate. Cuba accused the latter of being 'implicated in activities directed against its government and of having a

---

[75] Quote in note 87, *infra*.

[76] During the 2006 session of the Committee, the delegate from Germany 'voiced strong concern over the protracted treatment of the report [of an NGO called Centrist Democrat International], which had been before the Committee since 2002. He explained that, by not taking note of the report, the Committee was not doing its job. The examination of quadrennial reports should be a routine exercise, not a form of harassment. The inability by the Committee to take note of the report owing to the objections of one delegation [Cuba], despite numerous questions posed and answers given over the years, was detrimental to the Committee's reputation' E/2006/32 (Part I), para. 74. So, funny as it may seem, Cuba explained that it was pointing out its concerns regarding the activities of the organization because 'it had never really been clarified how an organization which was made up of political parties, [. . .] preserves its independence from government when these parties become the ruling parties in power'.

[political] agenda', of having 'launched an international campaign to discredit' the government of Cuba, of having 'encouraged subversive and terrorist activities on Cuban soil' and of having 'used vulgar and insulting language with respect to Cuba's head of state'. Costa Rica defended the Confederation, noting with satisfaction its ongoing collaboration with United Nations bodies.[77]

Cuba then took aim at the International League of Human Rights whose observers, at the eighth United Nations Congress on crime prevention and the treatment of offenders in Havana, appeared to have pursued 'a political agenda' and acted as 'provocateurs'. Cuba reserved the right to raise the issue of the League's consultative status when it so chooses. Chile, Greece, Costa Rica and Ireland supported the League, declaring, 'during the 45th session of the General Assembly, several delegations voiced their concern at the restrictions imposed on observers from certain nongovernmental organizations at the Havana Congress'.[78]

In 1995, China and India set their sights on the International League for the Rights and Liberation of Peoples (LIDLIP).[79] China sought clarifications on statements made to the Commission on Human Rights on Tibet's right to self-determination. India sought clarifications on the idea that only 'peoples' can be members of the association. Ireland and Russia supported the organization. After a session break, China declared it had received assurances from the organization that its activities were in no way intended to call into question China's territorial integrity.

At the same session, China and Cuba attacked the International Federation of Free Trade Unions (IFTU).[80] Cuba declared that the organization was 'politically biased' and noted the lack of information on the organization's contribution to the ILO. China regarded this absence as a violation of resolution 1296. These two delegations expressed strong reservations about the IFTU's quadrennial report and said that, in the future, it should be more detailed. In the end, the Committee took note of the report.

In 1999, the requests filed by certain members of the committee were tantamount to outright attacks. Thus, at the examination of the quadrennial report of the Robert F. Kennedy Memorial, China asked the memorial to clarify the accreditation of a member of the Human Rights in China organization, while Sudan sought to know the names of the recipients of the RFK Human Rights Award in Sudan.[81]

---

77   E/1991/20, paras 26–7.
78   Ibid., paras 28–33.
79   E/1995/108, paras 43–53.
80   Ibid., paras 57–65.
81   E/1999/109, para. 47.

The Society for Threatened Peoples was criticized for accrediting 20 to 30 people at the last Commission on Human Rights. Russia requested clarification on the way the organization reached its conclusions on Chechnya and sought to know who their contacts were and the sources of information they had used.[82]

A request, addressed to the International Federation of Human Rights Leagues (FIDH) regarding 'its policy and modalities of accreditation of its representatives to the Commission on Human Rights, particularly at the fifty-fourth session of the Commission' announced Algeria's complaint, which was to be lodged later on in the session and which led the Committee to request a 'special report' from the FIDH.[83]

The Special Reports

In 1993, Iraq, China and Cuba attacked the organization Pax Christi International (PCI). The criticisms expressed by the first two states were respectively based on the use of the terms 'Kurdistan' and 'Tibet' in the organization's report. Iraq requested the suspension of PCI's status. Cuba noted the seriousness of the allegations formulated by the representatives of the two states and called for the organization to be reclassified from category II to the Roster.[84] In the end of this 1995 session, the Committee decided to request from PCI a report on its activities from 1992 to 1993.[85] The legal basis of the decision is not stated in the report.

By doing this, the Committee created a precedent that would be formalized in 1997, when a complaint was lodged by Cuba before the Committee against the International Association of Educators for World Peace organization.[86] In 1997, Cuba tells of 'an incident at the United Nations' office at Geneva' involving this organization. It requested a special report from the association, pursuant to paragraph 61 c) of resolution 1996/31. The United States requested

---

[82] E/1999/109, para. 48.

[83] Ibid., para. 55. In 2002, at the examination of the quadrennial report of Human Rights Watch, the same states pushed this logic further: Cuba and Zimbabwe 'questioned the criteria selected by the organization in its country studies' whilst 'one delegation believed that the organization should be more balanced in its views and judgements and not lead the campaign against African countries as the organization has done recently in the Sudan and Zimbabwe'. Iran also gave HRW a lecture on the evolution of human rights in the world, advising the organization to have a 'balanced approach' in order to 'to address all human rights issues and dynamics at the national and international level'. Cf. doc E/2003/32 (Part II), p. 9.

[84] Regarding the different consultative status categories, see *supra* note 43.

[85] E/1993/63, paras 37–41.

[86] E/1997/90, paras 94–97.

a vote on this proposal which was adopted by nine votes to four. Thus, the Committee seems to have found a 'legal basis' for the use of 'special reports'.[87]

There followed a series of complaints expressed in the same manner. In 1998, a complaint was lodged by a 'state representative' against Libération and the Society for Threatened Peoples regarding incidents that took place at the 49th session of the Sub-Commission on Human Rights and the 53rd session of the Commission: some 'individuals with a criminal past' had allegedly been accredited by two organizations.[88] The same year, a special report was requested from four organizations, on the grounds that Iran had filed a complaint.[89] In 1999, it was the International Federation of Human Rights Leagues' turn, on the grounds of an Algerian complaint.[90]

In 2000, the presence of members of the Cuban opposition in exile within three International NGOs, the International Council of the Association for Peace in the Continents (ASOPAZCO), the Agence des cités unies pour la coopération Nord-Sud and Freedom House, angered Cuba, which tried, with

---

[87]   Paragraph 61 c) of resolution 1996/31 is the exact transposition of paragraph 39(b) of resolution 1296 (XLIV), 23 May 1968, which governed the consultative status up until 1996. It is drafted as follows (only the last sentence is relevant to the 'special reports'): 'Organizations in general consultative status and special consultative status shall submit to the Council Committee on Non-Governmental Organizations through the Secretary-General every fourth year a brief report of their activities, specifically as regards the support they have given to the work of the United Nations. Based on findings of the Committee's examination of the report and other relevant information, the Committee may recommend to the Council any reclassification in status of the organization concerned as it deems appropriate. *However, under exceptional circumstances, the Committee may ask for such a report from an individual organization in general consultative status or special consultative status or on the Roster, between the regular reporting dates'* (emphasis added).

[88]   E/1998/8, para. 45.

[89]   Cf. E/1998/72/Add.1, paras 33–4. The organizations in question are the World Confederation of Labor, Pax Christi International, the International Federation of Women in Legal Careers and the Movement Against Racism and for Friendship Among Peoples (MRAP). In 2001, Iran lodged a new complaint against five organizations, the International Association for Democratic Lawyers (IADL), the International Federation of Human Rights Leagues, New Human Rights, Women's Human Rights International Association, the Movement Against Racism and for Friendship Among Peoples (MRAP). See doc. E/2001/86, paras 111–12; E/2002/10, para. 92; E/2002/71 (Part II), paras 108–12.

[90]   E/1999/109, para. 82. See report by the International Federation of Human Rights Leagues reproduced in E/C.2/1999/3/Add.1. On this basis, Algeria decided to withdraw its complaint but requested that 'in the future, if such situations reoccur, the Committee will take the appropriate measures'. Cf. E/1999/109/Add.2 (Part II), para. 78.

very long statements, to establish links between these organizations and Cuban 'terrorist' organizations.

The first of the two organizations was suspended for three years after summary proceedings.[91] The second was required to hand in a special report to clarify its activities and the links they share with the ASOPAZCO.[92] The third organization, Freedom House, entered a long justification process, perpetuated not only by Cuba, but also by China, Sudan and Iran: each year, the four states demanded that Freedom House furnish written answers to their very detailed questions.

In 2001, the complaint procedure became common law but also broadened its reach. Thus Mauritius, Bahrain and China strengthened the grounds for a *délit d'opinion* at the Commission on Human Rights, by basing their complaints and requests for special reports on the mere distribution of 'subversive' documents by NGOs. Mauritius passed a request for a special report from the World Confederation of Labour for the circulation of a document by its representative at the 56th Session of the Commission on Human Rights.[93]

Bahrain made a long statement to complain regarding the 'activities' of one of the representatives of the 'International Confederation of Human Rights' (which is in fact the International Federation of Human Rights) who had 'circulated materials detrimental to the Government of Bahrain', at the 56th session of the Commission on Human Rights. The content of the documents circulated by the delegate was 'detrimental to the Government of Bahrain, in violation of the rules and regulations established by the Economic and Social Council for the enjoyment of consultative status by non-governmental organizations'. Bahrain then called 'upon the Committee to take action to prevent this type of person from engaging in such behaviour' and stated its openness to take into account all the requests it had received concerning human rights, in order to stop 'persons like [the delegate of the International Federation of Human Rights] and his cohorts, who represent no one but themselves, to sully the reputation of States Members of the United Nations and the organizations through which they operate'. Even if the Committee ended up closing the case, Bahrain succeeded in pushing forward the idea that circulating documents 'detrimental' to the states' reputation was an infringement of the ECOSOC regulations! The Chair of the Committee himself – Levent Bilman (Turkey),

---

[91]   See *infra*.

[92]   The case of the complaint was finally closed by the Committee. Cuba took note with satisfaction, as 'an example to be followed of good practices and willingness to respect and comply with the provisions of Council resolution 1996/31', the fact that the NGO withdrew, at the 58th session of the Commission, their accreditation from the two people affected by the Cuban complaint. See E/2002/71 (Part II), paras 103–7.

[93]   E/2001/8, para. 93.

seemed satisfied with this specious interpretation by concluding that the Secretariat of the Commission on Human Rights in Geneva 'should be informed once again that necessary precautions should be taken to avoid such incidents recurring during future sessions of the Commission'.[94]

China complained of 'abuses in violation of Economic and Social Council resolution 1996/31' committed by the Society for Threatened Peoples and the Transnational Radical Party at the 57th session of the Commission on Human Rights: 'Such misconduct included distribution of materials in violation of the rules, making statements disregarding the topic under discussion, and vile behaviour of representatives.'[95] In 2002, at the review of the quadrennial report by the France-Libertés – Fondation Danielle Mitterrand organization, China won a double victory when it got the Committee to require that the French organization submit a 'special report' to 'correct' its comments regarding 'China's relationship with Tibet'.[96]

A first victory: it is now possible to require a 'special report' merely for a *délit d'opinion*. France-Libertés – Fondation Danielle Mitterrand was told to 'think properly' by being made to state that Tibet has always been a Chinese province. Formerly, complaints for délits d'opinion were always accompanied by reproaches, such as regarding the behaviour or the identity of representatives of the organization at the Commission on Human Rights.

A second victory: this special report was required following consideration of a quadrennial report. It did not, as in the previous cases, originate in an 'incident' at the Commission on Human Rights.[97] The France-Libertés – Fondation Danielle Mitterrand special report was considered by the Committee at its ordinary session in 2002. China made a long statement to express its dissatisfaction regarding the organization's report, in particular the statement that China 'has invaded and occupied Tibet', which is, for China, a serious attack on the 'United Nations Charter' and 'represents an open challenge and contempt for China's sovereignty and territorial integrity, as well as violating article 2 of the resolution 1996/31 of the ECOSOC . . . China was asking the Committee to put its President in charge of sending a letter to the organization reminding it 'to correct its erroneous position on Tibet'. The Committee only acceded to the second request which was for France-Libertés – Fondation Danielle Mitterrand to hand in a supplementary special report on the matter at the resumption of its 2002 session in January 2003.[98]

At the report's consideration, the Chinese representative 'stated that she

94   Ibid., paras 94–8.
95   E/2001/86, para. 116.
96   E/2002/10, paras 80 and 95.
97   E/2002/10, para. 80.
98   E/2002/71 (Part II), paras 113 and ff.

regretted that the organization had clung to its erroneous position on the question of Tibet and that Tibet had been an inalienable part of Chinese territory since the thirteenth century'. She also stressed that China could have asked for the suspension of the organization's status, but instead it wanted to 'show flexibility' by giving France-Libertés – Fondation Danielle Mitterrand 'another opportunity to reconsider its position on Tibet in a further special report'. The proposal was ratified by the Committee.[99] Finally, in 2003, the organization backed out: Danielle Mitterrand met the Chinese Ambassador in Paris to tell him 'she was sorry for the misunderstanding the statement provided in the special report may have caused' and that she was delighted to be able to dissipate it as 'the organization had never intended to question the territorial integrity of China'. At the Committee, China took note that 'the organization had expressed its respect for the sovereignty of China and its territorial integrity and also its intention to abide by the principles and purposes of the Charter' and there the story ended.[100]

In the meantime, new complaints were lodged by Vietnam (against the Transnational Radical Party), Sri Lanka (against the Asian Legal Resource Centre), Turkey (against the International League for the Rights and Liberation of Peoples) and Colombia (against Agir ensemble pour les droits de l'homme).[101] The complaints by Turkey and Sri Lanka were for the circulation of 'offensive' documents at the last session of the Commission on Human Rights.

Finally, in 2003, Libya made its contribution by lodging a complaint to the Committee against the Simon Wiesenthal Centre. The latter was accused of having 'distributed a letter urging Member States to oppose the candidacy of the Libyan Arab Jamahiriya for the chairmanship of the fifty-eighth session of the Commission on Human Rights', which amounted, according to Libya, to interfering 'in the affairs of a Member State, thus violating the rules of conduct as stipulated in Council resolution 1996/31'.[102]

The special reports have been distorted from their original purpose, which was to have NGOs provide explanations of specific incidents that, generally, took place at the annual session of the Commission on Human Rights. The reports had been turned into a sanction, wielded arbitrarily by a number of states within the same Commission, against independent thinking. Henceforth, the slightest criticism of the human rights situation, the slightest protest

---

[99]   Cf. E/2003/11, pp. 27–8.
[100] E/2003/32 (Part. II), p. 18, para. 64.
[101] E/2002/71 (Part II), paras 117ff. and E/2003/11.
[102] E/2003/32 (Part II), p. 20, para. 79. In the end, because the members could not come to an agreement on the follow-up of the case, the Committee decided to end its examination on 27 May 2004, doc. E/2004/32, p. 37.

against history's official version, the slightest comment 'detrimental to the reputation of a State', can lead to disciplinary action that starts with the request for a special report and can end with a sanction being issued.

The Sanctions

The sanctions against NGOs are (A) status suspension, or (B) the withdrawal of the NGOs' consultative status.

A: Status suspension

Status suspension is the most commonly used sanction, probably because it lies in between requesting a special report and revoking status. Out of the seven suspension cases, four deserved some sort of sanction from the Committee, even though the appropriate sanction, in light of the criteria established by resolution 1996/31, might not have been suspension.[103]

In 1994, the International Lesbian and Gay Association (ILGA) was challenged by the USA because one or several of its affiliated associations supported paedophilia.[104] In 2003, nearly ten years later, the US requested suspension for the Indian movement Tupaj Amaru, whose representatives at the Commission on Human Rights 'rushed towards the United States delegation carrying a large cylindrical object' and had – which is less serious – unfurled a banner with 'Peace' written on it while chanting anti-American slogans in front of a Cuban television crew.[105]

In 2004, Cuba requested a three-year suspension for the organization Reporters without Borders based on three points: the incidents that took place in France at the demonstrations organized by the association in front of the Cuban Embassy in Paris and the peaceful occupation of the Cuban tourism information office; the interruption at the opening of the 59th session of the Commission on Human Rights in Geneva, when the representatives of

---

[103]　The resolution makes provision for the Committee to either suspend or withdraw the status of an NGO in the following cases: '(a) If an organization, either directly or through its affiliates or representatives acting on its behalf, clearly abuses its status by engaging in a pattern of acts contrary to the purposes and principles of the Charter of the United Nations including unsubstantiated or politically motivated acts against Member States of the United Nations incompatible with those purposes and principles; (b) If there exists substantiated evidence of influence from proceeds resulting from internationally recognized criminal activities such as the illicit drugs trade, money-laundering or the illegal arms trade; (c) If, within the preceding three years, an organization did not make any positive or effective contribution to the work of the United Nations and, in particular, of the Council or its commissions or other subsidiary organs.'

[104]　See *infra*.

[105]　See *infra*.

Reporters without Borders threw flyers from the top of the public gallery to denounce the election of Libya as the Commission's chair; the fact that the organization had not submitted any quadrennial report since it had been granted consultative status to the council in 1993.[106]

Finally, in 2005, China lodged a complaint against A Woman's Voice International, because one of its representatives at the 61st session of the Commission on Human Rights 'had introduced an illegal weapon into the meeting room'.[107]

The other cases are based on purely political motives. In 2000, Cuba had requested a three-year suspension for the International Council of the Association for Peace in the Continents (ASOPAZCO), an NGO made up of Cuban exiles founded in Madrid, for having 'distributed information published by Miami-based organizations that organized, supported and financed subversive activities both inside and outside Cuba for the purpose of overthrowing the constitutionally elected government'.[108] As for the Transnational Radical Party (TRP), it was twice confronted with demands for its suspension: the first time by Russia in 2000, for accrediting one of Chechen President Aslan Maskhadov's representatives so that he could address the Commission on Human Rights;[109] and the second time in 2002, by Vietnam because it had accredited a member of a 'terrorist' organization called the Montagnard Foundation based in Carolina, in the United States.[110]

---

[106]　See E/2003/32 (Part II), pp. 21–3.

[107]　See E/2005/32 (Part II), pp. 26–9. A recommendation of a one-year suspension of the consultative status was adopted by 15 votes to one with one abstention. At the ECOSOC, the decision was adopted by consensus (decision 2005/238) but the United States made an intervention to say they dissociated themselves from the consensus and to express their support towards the organization that had 'spoken about government persecution of Chinese Christians and the leaders of unregistered Christian churches'. E/2005/SR.35, pp. 5–6.

[108]　See *infra*.

[109]　The request for suspension was adopted by consensus by the Committee; the United States dissociated themselves from it. The TRP then transmitted a letter of explanation to the Secretariat, which became the organization's ground of defence before the ECOSOC. In the end, the request for suspension was rejected by 23 votes to 20 with nine abstentions. Cf. E/2000/SR.46, para. 55.

[110]　The report requested from the TRP by Viet Nam was examined in 2004. China proposed a three-year suspension of the status. The Committee adopted the proposal by nine votes to eight with two abstentions. Viet Nam led a campaign at the ECOSOC for the ratification of the recommendation: two letters were sent to the members and delivered as official documents. The first letter contained a series of documents which were supposed to establish MFI's guilt. The European Union answered back with a letter also with enclosed documents pleading in favour of the organization. On 23 July 2004, the Committee of NGO's recommendation was finally rejected by 22 votes to 20 with

Beyond the causes which led to these suspension requests, all these cases highlight the extreme politicization of the sanction procedure. The positions of the States, within the Committee on NGOs, are dictated purely or solely by their national interests.

First, the ASOPAZCO and Tupaj Amaru cases show the USA and Cuba fighting each other through the intermediary of NGOs. The United States, supported by the Europeans, came to the ASOPAZCO's rescue, while Cuba and its allies of the moment (China, Russia, Zimbabwe) tried to save Tupaj Amaru.

In 2000, Cuba refused to defer the vote on its suspension request to enable the representatives of the ASOPAZCO to answer their questions.[111] The United States was able to get a hearing at the ECOSOC for the organization in exchange for acquiescing in the suspension of its provisional consultative status.[112]

In 2003, a representative of Tupaj Amaru was invited to appear before the Committee in New York, but, for controversial reasons, was absent. According to Tupaj Amaru and Cuba, he was not granted a visa to enter the United States. According to the latter, no application for a visa was ever made. The US requested a one-year suspension. Cuba considered such a sanction unjustified, since the NGO had apologized and withdrawn their accreditation from the two representatives concerned: to decide to suspend in these conditions 'by taking action in this way, the Committee would pursue a policy totally different from the practice followed during the past 10 years.'[113] Finally, the request by the US was adopted with ten votes in favour, four against and five abstentions.[114] For Cuba, such a decision established a precedent: 'where recognition of mistakes and apologies will no longer be seen as being sufficient in considering similar cases'.

Second, the International Lesbian and Gay Association (ILGA) case highlights well the risks that a state assumes when it wants to use 'objectively' the suspension procedure. Following the United States' accusations, the

---

11 abstentions. In the name of the European Union, the Dutch Ambassador declared that an NGO should not have its consultative status suspended on the sole basis that it had denounced human rights violations.

[111]   The proposal for deferral presented by the United States was rejected by five votes to 12 with two abstentions. Cf. E/2000/88 (Part II), para. 83. The Cuban proposal for a three-year suspension was then adopted by 11 votes to five with two abstentions.

[112]   Cf. E/2000/SR.45, para. 126 for the American proposal and para. 143 for the vote on the proposal (rejected by 21 votes to 17 with seven abstentions).

[113]   E/2004/32, para. 120.

[114]   E/2004/32, pp. 34–7 and, for the vote, p. 36, para. 125. In favour: Cameroon, Chile, Colombia, France, Germany, Ivory Coast, Peru, Romania, Turkey and US; against: China, Cuba, Russian Federation, Zimbabwe; abstentions: India, Iran, Pakistan, Senegal, Sudan.

organization decided, at its annual conference in June 1994, to ban member organizations supporting paedophilia and to adopt a resolution stating that groups or associations 'whose "predominant aim" was to support or promote paedophilia were incompatible with the future development of ILGA'. But this was not sufficient for the US, because it considered that the wording of the resolution allowed other groups whose 'predominant aim' was not paedophilia to retain their membership. The organization replied that 'they did not have the means or capacity to screen all affiliated members or to determine the goals and objectives in every case'. The United States' delegation proposed that 'the Association's consultative status with the Council should be suspended until such time as ILGA could provide such assurances' that 'there were no other organizations in its membership which promoted, condoned or supported the legalization of paedophilia'.[115] Resolution 1994/50, 'status of the International Lesbian and Gay Association with the Council', takes up this proposal.

Although it has no legal basis in resolution 1996/31 of the ECOSOC, this new mechanism invented by the United States enabled prima facie softening the suspension procedure's rigour, by providing an option to terminate the procedure in response to 'assurances' provided by the organization. In reality, this mechanism had a pernicious effect: by leaving it to the Committee to decide on the reinstatement of the status, it gave certain states the power to make the suspension permanent, whereas, according to resolution 1996/31 (paragraph 57) the sanction cannot exceed three years. This is what happened to the ILGA.

In 1998, the organization submitted a request to regain its status. The request was only reviewed in 2001. A number of delegations questioned the ILGA regarding the means put into place to assure none of its affiliates supported paedophilia. The discussion went on at the 2001 resumed session of the Committee where several states, such as Senegal, Sudan, Lebanon and Pakistan, launched attacks. Sudan pointed out that it is the NGO's responsibility to give evidence that it does not maintain any ties with organizations encouraging paedophilia. As there was no evidence, Sudan proposed to the Committee not to recommend status for the Association. Sudan's proposal was adopted by eight votes to six with five abstentions.[116]

According to one of the voting states in favour of the proposal, 'there was a clear congruence between homosexuality and paedophilia'.[117] In the end, not

---

[115] See E/1994/SR.50, pp. 2–11.

[116] E/2002/10, paras 12 and ff; and regarding the vote, para. 7. Voted in favour of the proposal by Sudan: China, Ethiopia, Lebanon, Pakistan, Russian Federation, Senegal, Sudan, Tunisia; against: Bolivia, Chile, France, Germany, Romania and US; abstained: Algeria, Colombia, Cuba, India, Turkey.

[117] Ibid., para. 29.

only was the procedure initiated against the ILGA by the Committee illegal for having no basis in resolution 1996/31, but it was also dangerous, as it finally ended with a disguised withdrawal.

In 2004, the mechanics of restoring status once it had been suspended were somewhat different for Reporters Without Borders (RWB) and the ASOPAZCO. For RWB, Cuba presented a draft decision that would require the organization reporting to the Committee on its compliance with the Council's resolution 1996/31 that year. The Committee would then pronounce itself on status restoration 'in the light of the answer'. For the ASOPAZCO, Cuba proposed that the Committee ask the organization to submit a 'special report' that would be consulted at the following session. France went on to seek advice from the United Nations legal affairs department. The latter concluded that status should be reinstated automatically upon the expiration of the suspension period, which can last for 'up to three years' in accordance with paragraph 57 of resolution 1996/31. According to France, the ILGA case did not constitute a precedent as consultative status had been suspended in 1994, before resolution 1996/31 had been adopted. But still, both cases had to be put to a vote. The decision to restore RWB's status was adopted by 13 votes to five, with one abstention,[118] whereas the Cuban proposal regarding the ASOPAZCO won a majority of ten votes to three with six abstentions.[119]

B: Status withdrawal
In this section, we will examine the cases of two organizations that had their status withdrawn following the recommendations from the Committee on NGOs: Christian Solidarity International (CSI), on a Sudanese initiative, and the ASOPAZCO, whose status had already been suspended following a complaint from Cuba.[120]

---

[118] Cf. E/2004/32, pp. 26–8. In favour: Cameroon, Chile, Colombia, France, Germany, India, Ivory Coast, Peru, Romania, Senegal, Sudan, Turkey and US; against: China, Cuba, Pakistan, Russian Federation, Zimbabwe; abstention: Iran.

[119] Cf. E/2004/32, pp. 28–30. In favour: China, Cuba, Colombia, Iran, Ivory Coast, Pakistan, Russian Federation, Senegal, Zimbabwe; against: Chile, Turkey, USA. Abstentions: Cameroon, France, Germany, India, Peru, Romania.

[120] As of this writing, a third organization had its status withdrawn, on the initiative of the US, the Islamic African Relief Agency, based in Sudan. In the Committee, the US 'stated that the organization had been placed on the list of terrorist organizations by the United States Department of the Treasury for its involvement in terrorist financing, specifically of Al-Qaida and Hamas. The Agency is formerly affiliated with Maktab Al-Khidamat, which was co-founded and financed by Osama bin Laden and is the precursor organization of Al-Qaida'. The Organization was defended by the Ambassador of the Sudan. As no answer had been received from the organization, the Committee took the decision to withdraw its status. See E/2006/32 (Part I), paras 90

First, on 28 April 1999, Sudan wrote a letter to the Committee on NGOs to lodge a complaint against CSI because the organization had accredited 'and given the floor to speak' to John Garang, 'the Commander of the terrorist separatist group of Southern Sudan'. Sudan stated that this action by the NGOs constituted a 'flagrant breach and abuse of status'[121] and asked the Committee for the status to be withdrawn. The complaint was passed on to the Committee on 3 May 1999 and sent, through the post, to CSI on 2 June 1999. CSI was requested by the Committee to hand in a special report on the incident. On 7 June 1999, the organization answered that it did not have sufficient time to prepare the report. On 9 June, the Secretariat requested a written account of the incident for the Committee in lieu of a special report. It also suggested that the organization dispatch a representative before the Committee to answer its members' questions.

On 17 June, the Committee considered CSI's answers dated 7 and 15 June. Several members of the Committee found them 'unsatisfactory'. The representative of the United States introduced a motion of order to ask for the adjournment of the debates, on the ground that the consideration of the complaint from Sudan was not part of the meeting's agenda. The motion was rejected by 13 to one with four abstentions.[122] A second motion was then introduced by the United States to determine whether the Committee was competent to propose the withdrawal of CSI's consultative status, on the basis that it had not handed in a special report, as provided in paragraph 55 of resolution 1996/31.[123] The motion was rejected by 11 votes to one with four

---

and ff. But at the resumed session in May, an answer had been received. Thus Sudan proposed to reverse the decision previously taken. The motion was rejected by a vote of nine against to eight in favour and two abstentions. Sudan regretted the decision, India and Pakistan stated that the organization 'had the right to be heard and provide all information on its activities'. In addition, Pakistan said that 'the Committee did not have the authority to look at the alleged accusation of terrorist activities lodged by the United States', while Cuba 'would have liked to have the information on the activities implemented by the organization before a decision was taken in January. His delegation condemned all terrorist activities'. See E/2006/32 (Part II), paras 74–86.

[121]   E/1999/109, para. 69.

[122]   Ibid., para. 72.

[123]   Paragraph 55 of the resolution, in the eighth section on the 'suspension' and the 'withdrawal' of the status, on the role of the Committee: 'In periodically reviewing the activities of non-governmental organizations on the basis of the reports submitted under paragraph 61(c) below and other relevant information, the Council Committee on Non-Governmental Organizations shall determine the extent to which the organizations have complied with the principles governing consultative status and have contributed to the work of the Council.' It therefore clearly appears, that a decision of the Committee regarding the suspension or the withdrawal of the status of an organization can only apply following the examination of a report submitted in accordance with paragraph 61(c) of the resolution.

abstentions.[124] Finally, Sudan's proposal for status withdrawal was put to a vote and won by 12 votes to one with four abstentions.[125]

On 28 July 1999, the general debate regarding NGOs at the ECOSOC was very tense. Finland intervened on behalf of the European Union and associated countries of central and eastern European states, as well as Cyprus, Malta and other states, to denounce the drift in the Committee on NGOs' work. It was of course alluding to the CSI's status withdrawal 'incident':

> All NGOs applying for consultative status with the Council should be given the same treatment, strictly based on an evaluation in conformity with Council resolution 1996/31. There was a disturbing tendency to set aside those criteria and to take up politically motivated considerations. It had become far too easy for Governments which felt uncomfortable with the accreditation of a particular NGO to block that NGO's participation in the Council's work. The European Union was also of the view that any NGO facing withdrawal or suspension of consultative status, regardless of its possible merits or alleged misconduct, was entitled to have its case considered with fairness, impartiality and mature reflection, in accordance with due process.[126]

In the same way, Canada called for an 'urgent review' of the Committee's procedures.[127] The NGOs' Conference on consultative status with the ECOSOC (CONGO) also made a long intervention to say that it 'was deeply concerned at the manner in which Council resolution 1996/31 was being applied, in particular regarding the granting and withdrawal of NGOs' consultative status'. It denounced the fact that 'NGO Committee decisions appeared to be increasingly politically motivated. It might even be wondered whether some NGOs which had obtained consultative status actually met all the criteria set forth in paragraphs 9 to 13 of resolution 1996/31, regarding their goals, and, especially, their independence vis-à-vis their Governments.'[128]

Conversely, India, Cuba, Pakistan (the latter in the name of the member states of the Organization of the Islamic Conference) and Comoros, intervened to denounce 'misuses' of the consultative status by certain NGOs, such as 'the representation of several NGOs by the same individual' (India, Cuba), untimely remarks (Cuba) and NGOs that 'misrepresent Islam' (Pakistan).[129]

On 30 July 1999, Indonesia presented a new draft decision aiming at

---

[124]   Ibid., para. 74.
[125]   Ibid., para. 76. Voted in favour: Algeria, China, Cuba, Ethiopia, India, Lebanon, Pakistan, Russian Federation, Senegal, Sudan, Tunisia, Turkey; voted against: US; abstentions: Chile, France, Ireland, Romania.
[126]   E/1999/SR.44, p. 3.
[127]   Ibid., p. 6.
[128]   Ibid., pp. 6–7.
[129]   Ibid., pp. 3–4 for India; p. 4 for Cuba; pp. 5–6 for Pakistan; p. 7 for Comoros.

replacing the draft decision written up by the Committee on NGOs on CSI's status withdrawal. The draft decision, which grew out of extensive consultations, was adopted by consensus. Sudan immediately pointed out its flexibility. The decision requested the Committee to convene in order to consider Sudan's complaint. In order to do this, CSI was given until 31 August 1999 to submit a written report addressing the Committee's concerns. The latter would therefore meet to consider the answers in order to make a recommendation to the Council on the decision to make before it resumed its session on 16 September 1999. In the meantime, the privileges CSI benefited from thanks to its status were temporarily suspended.[130]

For Canada, '[h]uman rights NGOs must be free to speak out, even when their message might cause discomfort to Governments. Any deliberations concerning them by the Council or its subsidiary bodies, therefore, must meet the highest standards of transparency and due process. Those standards had not been met in the case in question'.[131]

Finland, for its part, on behalf of the European Union and the countries associated with it, pointed out that the provisional suspension procedure was not part of resolution 1996/31 and that the Council's decision must not, in this respect, be considered as a precedent.[132]

The Committee on NGOs met on 7 September to 'resume and complete its consideration of the question of the consultative status' of CSI. The Committee was to consider a document that the NGO had submitted and could ask questions of its representative. Sudan made a long statement to denounce CSI and all 'such rebellious and terrorist organizations, which are involved in activities against sovereign States'.[133]

The United States proposed to change the withdrawal measure to a three-year suspension, but Sudan's request for withdrawal was adopted by 14 votes to one, with four abstentions.[134] Sudan's motion to vote on CSI's status withdrawal, even though the question was not on the agenda and the organization was not given a chance to submit its report, appears flagrantly to violate the spirit and the letter of resolution 1996/31 and the general principle of respecting the rights of the 'defendant'.

Second, in 2004, the Committee on NGOs had decided, upon Cuba's request, to ask ASOPAZCO to submit a special report, as a prerequisite for all

---

130   E/1999/SR.46, p. 13 and Decision 1999/268, in E/1999/INF/2/Add.2.
131   Ibid., p. 14.
132   Ibid., p. 15.
133   E/1999/109/Add.1, para. 5.
134   Ibid., para. 32. Voted in favour: Algeria, Bolivia, China, Colombia, Cuba, Ethiopia, India, Lebanon, Pakistan, Russian Federation, Senegal, Sudan, Tunisia, Turkey; against: US; abstentions: Chile, France, Ireland, Romania.

decisions concerning the restoration of consultative status.[135] The report was considered in January 2005 and Cuba, deeming the report unsatisfactory, requested that the organization 'submit a new application' to the Committee. The proposal led to an animated debate, with Cuba, China, Sudan, the Russian Federation, Iran and Pakistan drawing on the ILGA precedent, and Germany, France and the United States responding that this case could not serve as a precedent because it had occurred before the 1996 reform. The United States introduced a motion of adjournment that was dismissed by eight votes to five with five abstentions. The United States then proposed to amend the Cuban request: the ASOPAZCO was asked to present an *updated* application instead of a new one, which would be considered at a later session.[136] It was conceding too much with regard to resolution 1996/31, which stipulates that a suspension can last no more than three years and only plans a 'new application' in the case of status withdrawal.[137]

The Committee did examine the application when it resumed its session in May 2005. On 11 May, Cuba, of course, sought to throw out the organization's application as it was 'trying to misinform the Committee on matters that it had hidden, misrepresented or omitted' and ended by agreeing 'reluctantly [. . .] that the organization would be notified by the Secretariat of the Committee's intention to act on a proposal to withdraw its status during the current session'. The ASOPAZCO was granted an extension of five working days to answer Cuba's questions. On 19 May, Cuba reformulated its request by asking for the withdrawal of the organization's consultative status. This proposal was put to the vote after an animated debate and won a majority of eight votes to four with six abstentions.

The Europeans (Germany, France, and Romania) pointed out that the procedure was flawed for two reasons: because the organization was not given enough time to prepare its defence and, most importantly, it had already been punished for the same facts; that is, that the withdrawal followed the suspension without a new complaint being officially lodged.[138]

---

135   See *supra*.
136   E/2005/32 (Part I), pp. 16–19.
137   Res. 1996/31, para. 59: 'An organization whose consultative status or whose listing on the Roster is withdrawn may be entitled to reapply for consultative status or for inclusion on the Roster not sooner than three years after the effective date of such withdrawal.'
138   E/2005/32 (Part II), pp. 15–18. Voted in favour of the Cuban proposal: Cameroon, China, Cuba, Iran, Russian Federation, Senegal, Sudan, Zimbabwe; against: France, Germany, Romania, US; abstentions: Chile, Colombia, India, Pakistan Peru, Turkey.

Recommendation to Deny the Consultative Status to NGOs

This should logically be the first step taken in order to put NGOs in line, but, chronologically, this type of recommendation (applied to NGOs that cannot be suspected of not respecting the terms of resolution 1996/31) has appeared only recently. It happened in a rather spectacular way, as four gay and lesbian NGOs applied for consultative status at the same time and saw their application altogether rejected by the Committee. If it was meant to be a test in order to show how much the Committee is biased, one could say the test had been totally successful.

At its 2006 session, the Committee had to examine the applications of the five following NGOs: International Lesbian and Gay Association, which had already been subject to the Committee's sanctions (see *supra*); the Danish National Association for Gays and Lesbians; the International Lesbian and Gay Association – Europe; the Lesbian and Gay Federation in Germany; and the Coalition Gaie et Lesbienne du Québec.

The latter was given some time, as the answer it had provided to the questions put by some Committee members was in French, and not translated into English yet.[139] But the other four could not escape: Germany led the fight in their defence, by proposing the adjournment of the debate on each organization. Each time the adjournment was refused. Then the Committee went to vote on a decision not to grant the status, and each time the decision was adopted.[140] After the votes on the ILGA and the Danish Association, the representative of Germany stated that 'the Committee had taken two decisions that would haunt them for a long time'. He continued as follows:

> The Committee had committed an act of discrimination against two organizations whose sole purpose was to combat discrimination. These decisions reflected badly on a Committee that had been criticized in the past for introducing partisan political considerations into its work in a manner that was inappropriate for an administrative Committee of the Economic and Social Council. However, he was convinced that those who hoped to stifle the debate on human rights and sexual orientation had achieved the exact opposite. He was convinced that member States will live to see the day when it would be universally accepted that discrimination on the grounds of sexual orientation was impermissible.[141]

---

[139] E/2006/32 (Part II), para. 20.
[140] For the ILGA, see E/2006/32 (Part I), paras 35ff; for the Danish National Association for Gays and Lesbian, see E/2006/32, paras 51ff; for International Lesbian and Gay Association – Europe, see E/2006/32 (Part II), paras 39ff; and for Lesbian and Gay Federation in Germany, see E/2006/32 (Part II), paras 22ff.
[141] E/2006/32 (Part I), para. 64.

In the ECOSOC, the debate went on, and Germany led the defence of the five NGOs. About ILGA and the Danish Association, it proposed to amend the draft decision in order to replace 'the Council decides *not* to grant consultative status' with 'the Council decides *to grant* consultative status'. Russia, invoking rule 67.2 of the Council's rules of procedure, required that the Council take no decision on the proposal put forward by Germany. This no-action motion was put to a vote: in the first case (ILGA) the motion was adopted.[142] Germany then asked for a vote to be taken on the draft decision and lost.[143] In the second case, the majority turned out to be different and, though the no-action motion was adopted,[144] the draft decision not to grant consultative status to the Danish Association was rejected.[145]

This debate found an unexpected follow-up, as the Special Representative on the Situation of Human Rights Defender, Hina Jilani, took up the cases of those NGOs and sent a communication to ECOSOC members drawing their attention to the refusal to grant consultative status to NGOs working on human rights for Lesbian and Gay persons. This action provoked a debate during the second session of the Human Rights Council where Algeria, on behalf of the African group, along with Ghana, Tanzania and China, attacked the Special Representative for having taken such an initiative it regarded as going beyond her mandate. As the 'Council Monitor' of the International Service for Human Rights reports, 'They used the incident to call for the adoption of a code of conduct for special procedures to avoid such "erratic action".'[146] The Special Representative tried to explain that she had withdrawn that communication from her report, but it seemed that this would not satisfy the complaining states.

CONCLUSION

Judging by its reports, the Committee on NGOs has never engaged in collective deliberation about the phenomenon of servile NGOs. The question was only mentioned once and all that remains of it is an enigmatic passage in the

---

[142]   By 25 votes to 21, with five abstentions. See E/2006/SR.34, p. 7.
[143]   By 22 votes to 19, with nine abstentions. Ibid., p. 8.
[144]   By 23 votes to 23, with six abstentions. Ibid., p. 9.
[145]   By 22 votes to 19, with nine abstentions. What happened is that the United States and Australia, who had voted against the granting of consultative status to ILGA, voted in favour of the Danish Association. At the same time, the Republic of Korea who had abstained in the first case, also voted in favour of the Danish Association. The majority was thus reversed.
[146]   See Human Rights Council, 2nd session, Preliminary Overview, *Council Monitor (ISHR)*, 6–7, http://www.ishr.ch/hrm/council.

Committee's 1999 report under the heading 'Independence from Government Influence':

> In the course of the Committee's review of new applications, it encountered several instances of small and large organizations, predominantly from the South, that had significant ties to government. After serious discussion during which several delegations expressed concern regarding the ability of such organizations to retain their independence from undue influence and freedom of expression, it was recognized that at times *such organizations required government assistance in order to function*, particularly in such matters as the sharing of expertise in the areas of technology and project management.[147]

It is more important than ever to understand the servile society phenomenon. At stake are both the future of the United Nation's protection of the Human Rights system – since, as we have seen, the problem mainly concerns this domain – and the principle of letting NGOs contribute to the works of international organizations. The 'rationalizing' processes of the Commission on Human Rights at the UN multiplied during the last years of this body, leading to an erosion of the rights initially granted to the NGOs. Using the excuse of the increase in the numbers of NGOs benefiting from consultative status of the ECOSOC in the last ten years,[148] a number of states tried to impose restricted access and limited speaking time.

In this unfavourable context, the United Nations Secretary-General, Kofi Annan, decided to 'assemble a group of eminent persons representing a variety of perspectives and experiences to review past and current practices and recommend improvements for the future in order to make the interaction between civil society and the United Nations more meaningful'.[149] This decision probably reflects the realization of the new role played by the NGOs at the United Nations. At the same time, it is risky, as all the reform processes that were started in recent years at the United Nations resulted in a decrease in the rights of the NGOs without compensation elsewhere, such as in the level of participation.

The group of eminent persons handed in its final report in June 2004.[150] The Secretary-General answered it in a report in September 2004, by highlighting several suggestions.[151] The two reports were transmitted to the

---

147   E/1999/109/Add.2 (Part II), pp. 11–12, para. 45 (emphasis added).
148   The number of NGOs endowed with the status has quadrupled in a little more than 30 years: 500 NGOs were endowed with the status in 1968; around 1600 in 1995; 2613 in 2005.
149   A/57/387, para. 141.
150   A/58/817.
151   A/59/354.

General Assembly to be considered. The latter has not, for the time being, followed it up, even for the United Nations global reform process ratified by resolution 60/1 of 16 September 2005, '2005 World Summit Outcome'.[152]

The proposals regarding the reform of the consultative status are, on the face of it, heading the right way, in the sense that they plan to extend the consultative status to all the United Nations' systems – no longer only to the ECOSOC and its subsidiary bodies – and to establish the accreditation procedure at the General Assembly level.[153] But if the Committee on NGOs future seems over, there is no certainty that its replacement will be better, as a political organ will continue to hold the power to rule on granting, suspending or withdrawing status.[154] A study of the conduct of the Committee on NGOs over 15 years pleads against this solution. The stakes in a possible reform to come are important. Beyond the United Nations, the evolution of the consultative status to the ECOSOC can be used as a reference for all the other international organizations working with NGOs. Indeed many international organizations already have a definite consultation status, more or less inspired by the ECOSOC's system, and are also trying, because of the increasing numbers of NGOS, to reform the status.[155] Other organizations maintain

---

[152]   The World Summit contents itself with a minimal reference to civil society, at the end of the document, which tends to show that this question is no longer a priority: '172. We welcome the positive contributions of the private sector and civil society, including non-governmental organizations, in the promotion and implementation of development and human rights programmes and stress the importance of their continued engagement with Governments, the United Nations and other international organizations in these key areas. 173. We welcome the dialogue between those organizations and Member States, as reflected in the first informal interactive hearings of the General Assembly with representatives of non-governmental organizations, civil society and the private sector.' Regarding the 'interactive hearings', see the note of the President of the General Assembly H.E. Jean Ping, 'the informal interactive hearings of the General Assembly with representatives of non-governmental organizations, civil society organizations and the private sector'. A/60/331.

[153]   Proposal 19 of the Panel of Eminent Persons, transmitted by the Secretary General.

[154]   Proposal 20 of the Panel consists in setting up a two step procedure: first, the examination of the applications for accreditations is left to an 'Accreditation Unit' created within the General Assembly Secretariat. This Unit would be in charge of setting up an advisory body that would help decide 'whether applications should be recommended or not'. Subsequently, a General Assembly Committee would come to a decision based on this organ's recommendations. In his report A/59/354, the Secretary General transmits the idea of a 'pre-screening' by the Secretariat, but is less specific about the terms of the examinations by the governments as he only proposes that '[m]ember States should be provided with consolidated lists of applications for consideration'.

[155]   Several organizations are thinking of ways to reform their relations with the NGOs: see the comments from the working groups of the NGOs of the World Bank:

informal relationships with NGOs and are studying the option to set up a definitive status.[156]

In both cases, the precedents of the past years within the framework of the ECOSOC, as well as a possible reviewing exercise in the future, will certainly have a determining influence on the processes used by other international organizations. In the present state of affairs, the criteria established by resolution 1996/31 seem insufficient to enable an organ to dismiss on an objective basis the applications of servile NGOs. Paragraph 12 of the resolution imposes two conditions: the organization must not have been formed by 'a governmental entity or intergovernmental agreement'; and, regarding its formation, the organization can accept 'members designated by governmental authorities, provided that such membership does not interfere with the free expression of views of the organization'. Another condition that can be added is the obligation of financial openness, stipulated in paragraph 13 of the resolution: 'Any financial contribution or other support, direct or indirect, from a Government to the organization shall be openly declared to the Committee through the Secretary-General and fully recorded in the financial and other records of the organization and shall be devoted to purposes in accordance with the aims of the United Nations.' This last condition is a way of implicitly recognizing that if, on principle, an NGO must be mainly financed by private funding, the presence, even in the majority, of public funds, cannot be considered in itself as a distinctive criterion for a governmental NGO.

The autonomous highlighting of the principle of freedom of expression mentioned in paragraph 12 is missing from this list of criteria. Thus, an amendment of resolution 1996/31 should be adopted so that national NGOs should be able to prove, through their views and behaviour, their independence vis-à-vis the government they come under. But the legal criteria do not count for much so long as the process remains in the hands of the Committee on NGOs in its present composition. Indeed, as long as this organ remains purely

---

'Enhancing Civil Society Capacity to Influence the Emergence of Participatory Socio-Economic Policy Formulation in the World Bank. Re-Invigorating the Global Agenda of the NGO Working Group on the World Bank' (http://www.worldbank.org/devforum/files/ngowg.pdf). But also within the framework of the FAO, 'FAO Policy and Strategy for cooperation with non-governmental and civil society organizations', http://www.fao.org/documents.

[156]   This organization is the case with World Trade. For a summary, see G. Marceau and P. Pedersen (1999), 'Is the WTO open and transparent? A discussion of the relationship of the WTO with non-governmental organisations and civil society's claims for more transparency and public participation', *Journal of World Trade*, **33**(1), 5–49 and the International Federation of Human Rights League, report quoted in note 1. This is also the case for the Organization for Security and Cooperation in Europe (OSCE).

intergovernmental, these decisions will facilitate the entry of servile NGOs in the United Nations' system and will enable the use of the procedure, by certain states, to repress criticism of them within the Commission on Human Rights. Consequently, it appears urgent to modify the present system by adopting two measures:

1. Suppression of the advice procedure of paragraph 8, which gives de facto a right of veto to the 'concerned State', in other words to the state being criticized by the national NGO at issue. This procedure became meaningless when, in 1996, the ECOSOC decided to open the status to national NGOs.
2. Ending the intergovernmental nature of the Committee of NGOs. Its present set-up makes it a political organ, incapable of making decisions using the objective criteria defined in resolution 1996/31. Several alternatives can be considered. The Committee could, for example, be made up only of independent experts or even at parity of experts and of NGOs representatives appointed by the Secretary General by sectors.

Until the adoption of this type of reform, provisional measures have to be taken by the ECOSOC and the Committee in charge of the NGOs under the ECOSOC's instructions, in order to stop the development of the servile society at the UN and to end the unjustified attacks against independent NGOs. Such measures may consist of the following:

1. No 'request for explanations' expressed by a state towards the application or the quadrennial report from an NGO should have any effect if it is not officially ratified by the whole Committee. At the moment, one member state of the Committee can stop the review of the application or of the report of an NGO for years by a unilateral formulation of a request for explanations.[157]
2. Precise regulation should be carried out of the mechanism by which the Committee requests an NGO to produce a 'special report' on an incident

---

[157]   The French and the English version of the last sentence of para.15 of resolution 1996/31 may seem contradictory on this issue. The French version is: 'Une organisation non gouvernementale qui demande le statut consultatif général ou spécial ou son inscription sur la Liste doit avoir la possibilité de répondre à toute objection *que peut soulever le Comité* avant de prendre sa décision' (emphasis added). Whereas, according to the English version: 'A non-governmental organization applying for general or special consultative status or a listing on the Roster shall have the opportunity to respond to any objections being *raised in the Committee* before the Committee takes its decision' (emphasis added).

or a period of time shorter than the period covered by the quadrennial report. At present, the 'special reports' are used in the context of a disciplinary procedure that can constitute a preliminary step toward the withdrawal or the suspension of the status. This procedure, despite its gravity, is based merely on an elliptical sentence of resolution 1996/31 (paragraph 61-c), which gives no guarantee to the NGOs submitted to it.

3. The Economic and Social Council should declare illegal the procedure of conditional suspension it has adopted in its resolution 1994/50 against the ILGA. This procedure is against paragraph 57 of resolution 1996/31, which limits the suspension of the status to a duration of three years. At the same time as recognizing its illegality, the ECOSOC should commit itself not to use it again and to restore the status (Roster) of the ILGA, without conditions beyond those stipulated in resolution 1996/31.

4. The ECOSOC should also declare illegal the procedure of 'provisional suspension' of an organization's status, pending a definite decision from the Committee. This procedure has no legal basis in resolution 1996/31.

5. It must be clearly stated that resolution 1996/31 allows suspension for a period of three years maximum and that, beyond that deadline, the status of the organization must be automatically restored.

6. The case of an organization of whom the Committee is considering the withdrawal or the suspension should be on the Committee's agenda. In addition, the Committee should make sure this examination always takes place with a representative of the target NGO present. In order to achieve this, it is up to the Committee to get to the NGO a summons specifying the date on which the hearing will be held. Finally, the NGO should be given sufficient time to defend itself, by means of a report answering the accusations brought against it. In any case, the examination should never take place solely on the basis of the allegations of the state, as happened for Christian Solidarity International.

7. The Committee must respect the general principle *non bis in idem*, applicable in criminal and disciplinary matters, by virtue of which no one can be put on trial twice for the same deed.

3. NGOs and the development policy of the European Union

Valentina Bettin

INTRODUCTION

The relationship between NGOs and the European Union (EU) has been the subject of a long and intense debate since the Commission's publication of the White Paper on European Governance in 2000.[1] This debate has focused on the role that civil society should play at the EU level and how the EU should make its decision-making process more democratic. This issue is without doubt an important one. However, the current work limits itself to a question that is associated but that has been somewhat neglected,[2] namely the evolution of the status of NGOs in a specific area of EU action, that is development policy. The international order being the legal system of reference, the EU becomes relevant in this context, not as a state-oriented organization, but rather as an international organization. From this point of view, the sector of development is particularly interesting for two reasons. First of all, it is one of the few areas left where the European Union is entitled only to complement

---

[1] According to the Commission, the aims are to focus on getting 'people and organizations more centrally involved in both shaping and delivering EU policy', *European Governance – A White Paper*, COM (2001) 428.
[2] Most of the scientific contributions focus on the role that NGOs can play at the European level to make the EU decision-making process more participative. See, for instance, Peter Hermmann (ed.) (1998), *European Integration between Institution Building and Social Process: Contributions to a Theory of Modernisation and NGOs in the Context of the Development of the EU*, New York: Nova Science; Carlo Ruzza (2004), *Europe and Civil Society: Movement Coalitions and European Governance*, Manchester, UK and New York: Manchester University Press; M.A.Wilkinson (2003), 'Civil society and the re-imagination of European constitutionalism', *European Law Journal*, **9**(4), 451–72; Stijn Smismans (2006), *Civil Society and Legitimate European Governance*, Cheltenham, UK and Northampton, MA: Edward Elgar. The only exception, to the best of the present author's knowledge, is Marjorge Lister and Maurizio Carbone (2006), *New Pathways in International Development: Gender and Civil Society in EU Policy*, Aldershot, Hants, England, and Burlington, VT: Ashgate. This work was published too recently for inclusion in the notes below.

the actions of the member states and cannot legislate in their place;[3] in this field, therefore, the EU may be more easily studied through international law, in so far as it safeguards some fundamental features of a traditional international organization. Second, in the development sector, interaction between EU organs and NGOs is extensive and various. Hence, development policy is a fruitful field of analysis for tracing the whole spectrum of relations existing de facto and de iure between the EU and NGOs in general.

The present contribution is organized into two parts: the first part deals with the relationship between the EU and NGOs in implementing development policy; the second part, instead, focuses on the role of NGOs in policy formulation.

THE EVOLUTION OF THE ROLE OF NGOS IN THE IMPLEMENTATION OF EU DEVELOPMENT POLICY: FROM AID IMPLEMENTERS TO DEVELOPMENT PARTNERS

EC development policy was one of the first areas where EC institutions understood the added value of involving non-state actors (NSAs) in the implementation of their programmes. This section tries to identify the main steps that allowed for the establishment of the earliest contacts between EC and NGOs. It is organized into two subsections so as to help underline the main differences existing between the two forms of the implementation of developing projects: EC projects, elaborated by the EC, supervised by EC institutions and executed by NGOs; and NGOs projects elaborated by NGOs, supervised by

---

3   According to arts 180 and 181 of the EC Treaty: 'The Community and the Member States shall coordinate their policies on development cooperation and shall consult each other on their aid programmes, including in international organizations and during international conferences.' Moreover, 'within their respective spheres of competence, the Community and the Member States shall cooperate with third countries and with the competent international organizations. [. . .] The previous paragraph shall be without prejudice to Member States' competence to negotiate in international bodies and to conclude international agreements.' These two articles have been interpreted by the doctrine as attributing to the EC a concurrent competence *sui generis*, that is a concurrent competence which is not submitted to the principle of pre-emption. See F. Martines, 'Alcuni problemi relativi alla politica di cooperazione allo sviluppo della Comunità europea', *Diritto dell'Unione europea*, **8**, 891–4. This interpretation has been confirmed by art. I-14 of the Treaty establishing a Constitution for Europe according to which, 'in the areas of development cooperation and humanitarian aid, the Union shall have competence to carry out activities and conduct a common policy; however, the exercise of that competence shall not result in Member States being prevented from exercising theirs'.

NGOs but largely financed by the EC. In the former, NGOs play merely the role of executive arms of the EC institutional framework. In the latter, instead, it is already possible to attest an evolution of the relationship between EC and NGOs from aid implementers to development partners.

NGOs as Aid Implementers

The first contacts between the EC and NGOs[4] go back to the end of the 1960s when the EC adopted a programme on food aid.[5] This programme, which is still in place, provides for the gathering and distribution of food in third world countries in order to improve the nutritional level of their populations. According to the regulation in question, Member States are required to store food for the Commission, which is then responsible for the distribution and administration of the aid. When the programme was first put into place, the Commission did not have enough resources to manage the aid properly. First of all, it did not have delegations on the ground in many third world countries because of the interruption of diplomatic relations caused by the Cold War. Second, it did not have an expertise in the area of development, which, at that time, was outside its competences.[6] Finally, it lacked the necessary human and

---

[4]   As far as the notion of NGOs is concerned, EC law does not provide for a binding definition. However, some EC documents offer a definition of non-state actors for practical purposes. See, for example, the Communication from the Commission to the Council, the European Parliament and the Economic and Social Committee on *Participation of Non-State Actors in EC Development Policy*, where it is said: 'The term NSA is used to describe a range of organizations that bring together the principal, existing or emerging, structures of the society outside the government and public administration. NSAs are created voluntarily by citizens, their aim being to promote an issue or an interest, either general or specific. They are independent of the state and can be profit or non-profit-making organizations. The following are examples of NSAs: Non-Governmental Organisations/Community Based Organisations (NGO/CBO) and their representative platforms in different sectors, social partners (trade unions, employers associations), private sector associations and business organizations, associations of churches and confessional movements, universities, cultural associations, media', COM(2002) 598 final, 7.11.2002, p. 5.

[5]   For an historical analysis of the relationship between EU and NGOs active in the field of development co-operation, see Andrea Lapucci, *Partners in sviluppo: ONG e Unione europea da Lomé a Cotonou*, Università di Firenze, unpublished final dissertation, pp. 21–38.

[6]   The EC was provided with an explicit competence in the area of development co-operation (Title XX of the EC Treaty) only from entry into force of the Treaty of Maastricht. Before 1992, EC institutions adopted acts in this field using art. 308 on implicit powers, art. 133 on trade policy and art. 310 on association agreements. See F. Martines (1991), 'La politica di cooperazione allo sviluppo e la CEE. Rassegna delle attività principali', *Rivista italiana di diritto pubblico comunitario*, **1**, 403–21.

infrastructural resources able to cope with all the challenges raised by this type of intervention. The experience of NGOs in the field being substantial, the Commission concluded private agreements with three big NGOs: the World Council of Churches, the Catholic Group of European Caritas Agencies and Oxfam. These agreements set out that NGOs were entitled to transport and distribute food in third countries on behalf of the Commission.

That solution proved so effective that the Commission decided to extend this model of co-operation to other areas, including humanitarian aid; the protection and promotion of democracy, the rule of law and human rights in third countries; North–South co-operation in the fight against drug abuse; aid for poverty-related diseases; gender integration in development and, environment and tropical forests protection.

Even if the mandate is different, the nature of relations between the EC and NGOs in all these fields is always the same. The Commission selects NGOs on the basis of their capacity to achieve the purpose established by EC regulations in a specific area and concludes with them a grant agreement by which NGOs are entrusted with EC financial resources to execute a specific project.

In principle, all NGOs are admitted to the screening process.[7] The only sector where NGOs are required to submit themselves to an accreditation procedure is humanitarian aid. In fact, if NGOs want to work over the long term with the Humanitarian Aid Office of the European Community (ECHO), they have to conclude with this office a Framework Partnership Agreement (FPA), which is an administrative instrument for selecting in advance NGOs on the basis of their operational, administrative and financial capacities, as well as their specialization and experience in the field of humanitarian emergencies.[8] The first ECHO FPA scheme was adopted in 1993, the second in

---

[7]   All the regulations on financial aid, no matter what the sector, require only that the entities be non-profit-making autonomous organizations in a Member State of the Community under the laws in force in that Member State of the European Union, and have their main headquarters in a Member State of the European Union or in the third countries in receipt of the aid.

[8]   The European Commission Framework Partnership Agreement (FPA) with Humanitarian Organisations for the Financing of Humanitarian Aid Operations is based on Article 16.2 of Council Regulation (EC) No 1257/96 concerning humanitarian aid of 20 June 1996, published in the OJ L 163 of 2 July 1996. Pursuant to Article 7.1 of this regulation, 'organisations must be non-profit-making autonomous organizations in a Member State of the Community under the laws in force in that Member State of the European Union, and have their main headquarters in a Member State of the European Union or in the third countries in receipt of the aid. This headquarters must be the effective decision-making centre for all Operations financed by the Community. Exceptionally, the headquarters may be in a third donor country'. Moreover, according to art. 8 of the Framework Partnership Agreement with Humanitarian Organisations in force at the moment, 'to determine an organization's suitability to

1998. The third FPA has been in force since 1 January 2004. Despite FPA describing the relationship between the European Community and NGOs as a 'partnership',[9] NGOs act as de facto agencies of the EC rather than as autonomous actors. Indeed, the activities of NGOs are strictly monitored by ECHO from the moment an NGO project is approved, which is done on the basis of the EC list of priorities and strategies, to the implementing phase, which is checked rigorously.[10]

If this is true for humanitarian aid where the use of the term 'partnership' shows at least an effort on the EC's part to reduce its pervasive control over the conduct of NGOs, it is *a fortiori* truer for the other areas of co-operation mentioned above, where NGOs are used simply as aid implementers. In both cases, the freedom of action of NGOs is so reduced that, from the international-public-law point of view, they could be assimilated to organs of the EC, while they are acting to execute projects approved by the latter.[11]

However, the FPA, and the grant agreements for NGO projects aimed at implementing the regulations cited above, do not exhaust the panoply of relations at present existing between EC and NSAs. In particular, the awareness by the EC of the importance of safeguarding the independence of NGOs in order not to jeopardize their mandate has, since the mid-1970s, induced the

---

[sic] ECHO partnership, account shall be taken of the following factors: (a) its administrative and financial management capacities; (b) its technical and logistical capacity; (c) its experience in the field of humanitarian aid; (d) the results of previous operations carried out by the organization concerned, and in particular those financed by the Community; (e) its readiness to take part in [sic] co-ordination system set up for humanitarian Operations; (f) its ability and readiness to work with humanitarian actors and communities in third countries; (g) its impartiality in the implementation of humanitarian aid; (h) its previous experience in third countries'.

    9   See the Preamble: 'The partnership, which is set up by the Framework Partnership Agreement, is based on trust and on respect for the objectives, principles and values set out in this Preamble. The signatory Parties undertake to promote and consolidate their relationship and their co-operation by ensuring that each one knows and respects the mandates, charters or statutes of the other and by recognizing the specificity of each other's contribution to the humanitarian action. Signatory Parties carry out their roles in the execution of Operations funded by the European Community preserving their freedom and autonomy and assuming their responsibilities.'

    10   This is what emerged from some interviews with the officers of One World, an NGO who had concluded a FPA with ECHO and benefited from EC financial resources for humanitarian actions in Bosnia.

    11   See art. 8 of the text on the Responsibility of State for Internationally Wrongful Acts, approved by the International Law Commission in December 2001, according to which 'The conduct of a person or group of persons shall be considered an act of a State under international law if the person or group of persons is in fact acting on the instructions of, or under the direction or control of, that State in carrying out the conduct.'

Commission to search out a more balanced relationship with these organizations.

NGOs as Development Partners

The first document that shows an effort by the Commission to co-operate with NGOs without imperilling their autonomy is the Communication addressed to the Council on 6 October 1975. In this Communication, the Commission set out its thinking on the topic of relationships with NGOs active in the field of development co-operation. It suggested general criteria to finance development actions elaborated by NGOs and, for the first time, it advanced a proposal to co-finance projects carried out by the latter.

In 1976, these suggestions were translated into concrete measures. The budget authority, in fact, set a financial line[12] for co-financing NGOs' projects in developing countries. These resources were meant to finance NGOs acting *on their own* in geographical and thematic areas where EC interventions were officially absent. The co-financing strategy was not new. The Netherlands, Germany, the United Kingdom, Italy and Belgium had already adopted similar co-financing schemes as early as the 1960s,[13] and the autonomous actions carried out by NGOs, though small, proved, in fact, very effective in assisting African countries.

The EC conditions for co-financing were made explicit in a binding regulation only in 1988.[14] This regulation assigned EC financial resources to NGOs active in the food aid sector. The selection of the projects had to take into account the needs of beneficiary countries, the quality of the project itself and the capacity of NGOs to carry it out. The EC financial contribution had to be bigger than the NGO's one. At the same time, the NGO's own resources had to cover at least 25 per cent of the global cost. The choice of not supporting the entire amount of NGO project costs was intended to help preserve the

---

[12] Budget article 941 replaced by financial line B7-6000 that has now become 21 02 03.

[13] The Netherlands and Germany endorsed this form of co-operation with NSAs from the 1960s, Italy at the beginning of the 1970s, the United Kingdom in 1975 and Belgium in 1976. France following the other European governments as well as the EC Commission, adopted a co-financing scheme in 1977. See Lapucci, *supra* note 5, p. 31.

[14] Council Regulation (EEC) No 2508/88 of 4 August 1988 on the implementation of co-financing operations for the purchase of food products or seeds by international bodies or non-governmental organizations, OJ L 220, 11/08/1988, p. 4–5. Before, these conditions were set up by the Commission in an internal administrative document: General Conditions for co-financing NGOs actions in developing countries. See European Commission, Doc. T/997/1/77 (GCD).

autonomy of such organizations vis-à-vis financial contributors. As far as subjective requirements were concerned, the co-financing scheme did not provide for an accreditation procedure. All NGOs could immediately apply for a co-funding provided that they were non-profit-making autonomous organizations in a Member State of the Community, under the laws in force in that Member State, and provided that they had their main headquarters in a Member State of the EC, where headquarters meant an effective decision-making centre for all operations financed by the Community.

The co-financing scheme is still in force and continues to attract interest – one might even say extraordinary interest – from NGOs, demonstrating the strong desire of these organizations to be independent in conceiving and carrying out their own development programmes, no matter the responsibilities and difficulties that this choice involves.[15] The co-funding regulation in force at present was adopted in 1998.[16] The criteria of selections and funding for NGOs projects are identical.[17] At the same time, the meaning that this financial instrument has assumed for EC development policy has changed. In 1976, in fact, the EC Commission saw co-funding as a way to associate its name with initiatives all around the world that, for various reasons, it was not able to accomplish itself. In 1998, instead, the adoption of the co-funding regulation was meant to provide EC development policy with an instrument to *decentralize* its co-operation.

Since the beginning of the 1990s, the European Community has looked at decentralized co-operation as the new strategy to endorse, to allow civil society to fully participate in the taking of decisions and the management of co-operation.[18] But only in 1998, on exactly the same day as the approval of the regulation on co-funding, did it adopt regulation n.1659/98 on decentralized co-operation.[19] This regulation, designed to promote a more participative approach in development co-operation closer to the needs of Third World

---

[15]   In 1979 an Annual Assembly of European NGOs and a Liaison Committee of NGOs (CLONG) were established to develop an institutional dialogue with the EC Commission and the European Parliament. One of the aims of these bodies was to increase the financial endowment assigned to co-funding actions.

[16]   Council Regulation (EC) No 1658/98 of 17 July 1998 on co-financing operations with European non-governmental development organizations (NGOs) in fields of interest to the developing countries, OJ L 213, 30 July 1998, p. 1–5.

[17]   See art. 3 and art. 6 of the Regulation.

[18]   See the Fourth Lomé Convention and Council Regulation (EEC) No 443/92 of 25 February 1992 on financial and technical assistance to, and economic cooperation with, the developing countries in Asia and Latin America, OJ L 052, 27 February 1992, p. 1–6.

[19]   Council Regulation (EC) No 1659/98 of 17 July 1998 on decentralised cooperation OJ L 213, 30 July1998, pp. 6–8.

populations, has been associated with regulation n.1658 on co-funding in so far as this regulation is, at the moment, the most effective EC instrument in allowing civil society agents to develop their own strategies without EC interference.[20]

From that point of view, in the case of co-financing, the term 'partnership' is not inappropriate for describing the relationship between EC and NGOs, even though it concerns only the phase of the *implementation* of EC development policy. Both EC and NGOs, in fact, need each other to fulfil their mandate. On the one hand, NGOs need EC financial resources to accomplish their development programmes. On the other, the EC needs NGOs to make its co-operation more participative and open to stimuli from below. The special feature of this co-funding system is precisely that it generates a synergy without putting in danger the independence and autonomy of either the NGO or the EC. This is also the reason why, in the case of co-financing, unlike the other EC initiatives mentioned above, it is almost impossible to consider NGOs as organs of the EC. Under international public law, in fact, to attribute to the EC the actions accomplished by NGOs, the former should constrain the liberty of the choice of the latter while executing its own project.[21] That is not at all the situation with co-funding where NGOs, albeit depending largely on EC financial support, are not monitored by this entity as far as their course of action is concerned.

Having said that, it is also important to note that the contribution of civil society in setting out the content of EC development co-operation through co-founded projects is still indirectly conditioned by the EC's power of selection of NGO projects. In fact, even if this selection is made on the grounds of the quality of the project presented, the Commission inevitably also takes into account the compatibility of the strategies pursued by NGOs with those carried out by the Community.[22] Bearing this in mind, the only way for the EC to trace a development policy that is authentically participatory is to allow civil society not only to take an active part in the phase of the implementation of the policy but also to take part in its formulation. This is the reason why,

---

[20] At the moment, the two instruments (regulation on decentralized co-operation and regulation on co-funding) are provided with two separate financial lines (budget line 21 02 03 [ex B7-6000] for co-funding and budget line 21 02 13 [ex-B7-6002] for decentralized co-operation). The EC Commission, to be more consistent, is studying the elaboration of a unique legal act to finance non-state actors for the two budget lines.

[21] See art. 8 of the Responsibility of State for Internationally Wrongful Acts, *supra* note 11.

[22] A study of the annual reports of the Commission on the projects co-funded and those financed by the Lomé Convention shows that most of the NGOs' projects in Africa co-funded by the EC were complementary to actions carried out by the EC under the European Development Fund. See Lapucci, *supra* note 5, pp. 37–8.

from the early 1990s, European institutions began to reflect on the possibility of opening up the EC decision-making process to NSAs.

THE EVOLUTION OF THE ROLE OF NGOS IN THE FORMULATION OF EU DEVELOPMENT POLICY: FROM INFORMAL TO FORMAL CONSULTATION

Since the entry into force of the Treaty of Rome the main reference to the involvement of civil society for the formulation of European Community policies has consisted in arts 257–61 (previously 193–7). These articles provide for the establishment of a consultative body, the European Economic and Social Committee (EESC), which brings together representatives of employers' organizations, including public-sector corporations (Group I), employees (Group II) and representatives of various interest groups, such as consumers, traders and farmers (Group III).[23] These members (whose number has now risen to 317) are appointed by the Council of Ministers on the basis of lists prepared by each Member State. The EESC must be consulted by European institutions in a wide range of areas covered by the EC Treaty[24] and, while it is mandatory to take account of its opinions, these are not binding.

The EESC, because of its composition and its advisory powers, is the expression of an institution-based dialogue between the European Union and NSAs. Unfortunately NGOs active in the development sector benefit only remotely from the presence of this consultative body, for the EESC is not

---

[23]   According to art. 193 (now 257) of the Treaty of Rome, 'An Economic and Social Committee is hereby established. It shall have advisory status. The Committee shall consist of representatives of the various categories of economic and social activity, in particular, representatives of producers, farmers, carriers, workers, dealers, craftsmen, professional occupations and representatives of the general public.' This article has been recently modified by the Treaty of Nice to include a specific reference to 'organised civil society'. Accordingly, 'The Committee shall consist of representatives of the various economic and social components of *organised civil society*, and in particular representatives of producers, farmers, carriers, workers, dealers, craftsmen, professional occupations, consumers and the general interest' (emphasis added).

[24]   The areas where European institutions are required to ask for an opinion of the EESC are the following: agriculture, freedom of movement of workers, freedom of establishment, freedom to provide services, transport, harmonisation of legislation concerning taxes, approximation of national laws, regulations or administrative provisions directly affecting the establishment or functioning of the common market, asylum and immigration, employment, social policy, education, vocational training and youth, public health, trans-European networks, research and technological development, economic and social cohesion, consumers protection and environment.

competent to give mandatory opinions in the field of development co-opera-tion;[25] nor does it have representatives from NGOs operating above national level. In fact its members, being appointed by the Council on the basis of a proposal from Member State governments, represent organizations concerned with *national* issues only.[26]

This deficiency has obliged NGOs working in the development field to establish their own channels of communication with European institutions. These contacts, from being completely informal have become more and more structured and, in the case of the Cotonou agreement, are now, if not institu-tionalized, at least formalized. The purpose of the present section is to illus-trate the evolution of the role played by NGOs in the formulation of development policy, taking into account the main steps that marked the passage from informal to formal consultation.

Informal Consultation

Since the beginning of the 1990s the Commission has underlined the impor-tance of involving national and European civil society in EC decision making through an open and direct dialogue. In its 1992 Communication, for instance, it urged all EC institutions to remain open and accessible to a wide variety of organizations, including NGOs.[27] In the area of development these indications had already been put into place long before the adoption of the 1992 Communication, through a series of ad hoc meetings organized by the Commission and the European Parliament with NGOs competent in the field.[28]

---

[25]   According to art. 179 of the EC Treaty the Council shall adopt the measures necessary to further the objectives of the development policy, following the co-decision procedure (that is, through the involvement of the European Parliament but without asking any opinion of the EESC).

[26]   See the EESC Final Report of the *ad hoc* group on structured cooperation with European civil society organizations and networks, Rapporteur Mr Bloch-Lainé, 17 February 2004, http://www.esc.eu.int, p. 2.

[27]   Commission Communication of 2 December 1992, *An Open and Structured Dialogue between the Commission and Special Interest Groups*, JO C63 of 5 March 1993.

[28]   Since the end of the 1970s, European NGOs benefiting from a financial aid from the EEC, established an Annual Assembly and an executive body, democratically elected, representing national NGOs (the Liaison Committee). This body was orga-nized in working groups covering the main areas of co-operation between European NGOs and EEC in the field of development (co-financing, food and humanitarian aid). The Development Directorate of the Commission and the Development and Co-opera-tion Commissions of the European Parliament have held, since then, a stable and constant relationship with these groups. See, Lapucci, *supra* note 5, pp. 34–6. See, also,

Notwithstanding the positive value of these contacts, the informal dialogue established between EC institutions and NSAs in the area of development suffered from two limitations. First of all, only European NGOs were consulted, while NGOs from third countries, namely from those developing countries benefiting from the EC aid, were neglected. This disregard by EC institutions was the result of the institutional weakness of non-European NGOs and the lack of an umbrella organization capable of representing their interests in Brussels. Also consultation with NGOs did not touch on one of the crucial elements of EC development policy: the planning of financial aid.

After the entry into force of Lomé I, the Community planned its financial aid in favour of African, Caribbean and Pacific countries (ACP) through the elaboration of the so-called National Indicative Programmes (NIP). These Programmes were meant to identify priorities and purposes to achieve in each ACP for a period of five years. The NIPs were elaborated by the Commission on the basis of consultations between EC delegations and governmental authorities of the country that was supposed to benefit.[29] Despite NIPs being the crucial element which defined the content of EC development policy in a specific geographic area and despite the important suggestions that NGOs active on the ground could have made to clarify the principal needs of the territory, NSAs, European as well as non-European, were not involved in the drafting of these documents.

The affirmation of a new conception of development aid based on the principles of decentralization (or ownership) and deconcentration[30] encouraged the Commission to solve these two difficulties. In fact, both the lack of dialogue with non-European NGOs and the exclusion of NSAs from the elaboration of the NIPs worked against the idea of the transfer of power from EC central quarters to those benefiting from the aid, that is governments, local authorities and, last but not least, the civil society of developing countries.

Commission Discussion Paper on *The Commission and Non-Governmental Organisations: Building a Stronger Partnership*, presented by then President Prodi and Vice-President Kinnock, p. 8, http://www.europa.eu.int/comm/development/body/theme/ngo/ngo_useful-docs_en.htm.

[29]   For a detailed description of the programming of EC aid in favour of ACP countries under the Lomé Conventions, see Pietro Romano Orlando, *La cooperazione dell'Europa comunitaria allo sviluppo dei Paesi ACP*, Napoli: Edizioni Scientifiche Italiane, pp. 29–31.

[30]   See the joint Council/Commission Policy Statement on *The EC's Development Policy* (10.11.2000) where the importance of the ownership of strategies by the partner countries and the encouragement of the most wide-ranging participation of all segments of society are recognized, Conseil/00/421, Brussels, 10 November 200012929/00 (Presse 421), 2304th Council meeting – DEVELOPMENT – Brussels, http://europa.eu.int/rapid/pressReleasesAction.do?reference=PRES/00/421&format=HTML&aged=1&language=EN&guiLanguage=it.

The need for a dialogue with non-European NGOs and for the involvement of NSAs in general in the elaboration of development strategies for each country has been the main object of reflection by the Commission in its Communication of 2002 on *Participation of Non-State Actors in EC Development Policy.*[31] In this Communication, the Commission, first of all, underlines the importance of involving NSAs in the preparation of the new instruments in force at EC and national level to plan development aid, that is, the Country Strategy Papers and the National Development Strategies.[32] The former are elaborated by the Commission, after consultation with the national authorities of the developing country. The latter are prepared exclusively by the national government. The involvement of NGOs, local and European, in the preparation of both these documents is considered by the Commission to be the best way to enhance dialogue with NSAs. At the same time, to enable NSAs to play a constructive role in the programming process, NGOs, it is said, should be provided with capacity building support.[33]

The Commission especially encourages European NSAs to pass on their know-how to their partners in developing countries. Co-operation and transfer of knowledge between Northern and Southern NSAs is, in fact, a crucial element for attaining ownership and a participatory approach.[34] Finally, the Heads of the EC Delegations in developing countries can play a central role in strengthening Southern civil society, by promoting and facilitating the dialogue between NSAs and the national governments.[35]

The importance of these directives has been pointed out also in the 2003

---

[31] Communication from the Commission to the Council, the European Parliament and the Economic and Social Committee, *Participation of Non-State Actors in EC Development Policy*, Brussels, COM(2002) 598 final, 7 November 2002.

[32] 'The programming model that is now being applied to all geographical regions is based on Country Strategy Papers (CSPs), which are the instrument for guiding, managing and reviewing EC assistance programmes. The purpose of CSPs is to provide a framework for EU assistance programmes based on EU/EC objectives, the Partner Country Government policy agenda, an analysis of the partner country's situation, and the activities of other major partners. The CSP points to where Community assistance will be directed and how it integrates with what other donors are doing. CSPs thus contribute to better planning of co-operation activities, improved donor co-ordination/complementarity, and greater overall coherence of external assistance policy with other EU policies', see the Commission Communication, COM(2002) 598 final, p. 6. The Country Strategy Papers and the National Development Strategies (NDS) do not replace the National Indicative Programmes. They simply precede them. The NIPs in fact, are more specific documents drafted to precise the ways to achieve the general purposes identified in the CSP and the NDS.

[33] COM(2002) 598 final, p. 15.

[34] Ibid., p. 19.

[35] Ibid., p. 18.

Commission Communication on *Governance and Development*[36] and they have been implemented in the document drafted by the Development Directorate: *Guidelines on Principles and Good Practices for the Participation of Non-State Actors in Development Dialogues and Consultations.*[37] This document is addressed to the Development Directorate and to EC Delegations in developing countries in order to provide guidance on good practices in the context of the planning process. Besides reaffirming most of the advice made by the Commission in the documents that have already been mentioned, it gives suggestions on how to make the involvement of NGOs in the planning process possible. Among these suggestions are some that are especially worth mentioning: the identification of all existing NSA networks and organizations (including national/international NGOs, media, economic and social partners, research organizations, associations for women, other organizations with special status such as the Red Cross and so on), through a mapping study; the dissemination of information on the different possibilities for NSA involvement as well as on the preparation and the follow-up of consultations by EC institutions; the adoption of EC programmes on capacity building of NSA; and, finally, the elaboration of a monitoring system to assess the quality of the process of participation and an NSA's added value for policy formulation.

It is interesting to observe that in none of the Communications adopted by the Commission is the *formalization* of the relationship of consultation between EC institutions and NGOs desired. Despite a request by NGOs to work in this direction,[38] the Commission, since the adoption of the White Paper on *European Governance*, has always rejected the establishment of a formal mechanism of accreditation and consultation similar to that provided by the Council of Europe.[39] According to the Commission, in fact, the European Union already has an institutional arena that allows for this kind of

---

[36]   Communication from the Commission to the Council, the European Parliament and the European Economic and Social Committee on *Governance and Development*, COM(2003) 615 final, 20 October 2003, p. 6.

[37]   European Commission, DG Development, Development Policy and Sector Issues, Development Policy, Coherence and Forward Studies, *Guidelines on Principles and Good Practices for the Participation of Non-State Actors in the Development Dialogues and Consultations*, November 2004, http://www.europa.eu.int/comm/development/body/theme/ngo/index_en.htm

[38]   See the Commission Discussion Paper, *The Commission and Non-Governmental Organisations: Building a Stronger Partnership*, *supra* note 28, where it is said that 'Some NGOs have raised the issue of having an official consultative status for NGOs along the lines of existing systems in the United Nations and Council of Europe', p. 12.

[39]   See the White Paper on *European Governance*, *supra* note 1, where it is said that: 'Creating a culture of consultation cannot be achieved by legal rules which would create excessive rigidity and risk slowing the adoption of particular policies', p. 17.

interaction, and that is the European Economic and Social Committee. To add new formal opportunities for consultation, rather than favouring the dialogue between EC and NSAs, risks paralysing it.[40] Hence the choice of supporting exclusively the adoption of codes of conduct which, even if these create some constraints on the Commission and its delegations, do not give NGOs true guarantees of being heard, or at least not of being heard well.

Formal Consultation

In the quest for more guarantees and transparency, NGOs have tried to protect their right to be heard, asking for the inclusion, in the EC Treaty, of, at least, a generic article on civil-society dialogue.

Their request had a weak echo in the Treaty of Nice where art. 257 on the European Economic and Social Committee was modified in order to include an explicit reference to 'organised civil society'.[41] Despite the Economic and Social Committee representing national organizations only, NGOs active in the development sector have indirectly benefited from this change. EESC, in fact, pointing to this new reference, has tried to make much of its role as an institutional mediator between EC institutions and European civil society. So, in February 2003, it decided to set up an ad hoc group with the following mandate: 'to explore arrangements and procedures for potential structured cooperation with European civil society organisations and networks'. The option chosen in the final report of the ad hoc group, adopted in February 2004, has been to establish 'a mechanism more pragmatic than institutional but nonetheless permanent, (...) a liaison body and forum for political dialogue',[42] made up of the EESC and European organizations and networks representing, as much as possible, the various areas of organized civil society (including, clearly, the development sector).

The need for the formalization of the dialogue with civil society was also

---

[40] See the Commission's Communication on *An Open and Structured Dialogue between the Commission and Interested Groups*, where it is pointed out that 'the Commission has always wanted to maintain a dialogue which is as open as possible without having to enforce an accreditation system', JO C **63**, 5 March 1993.

[41] According to art. 257: 'An Economic and Social Committee is hereby established. It shall have advisory status. The Committee shall consist of representatives of the various economic and social components *of organised civil society*, and in particular representatives of producers, farmers, carriers, workers, dealers, craftsmen, professional occupations, consumers and the general interest' (emphasis added).

[42] European Economic and Social Committee, Final Report of the *ad hoc* group on *Structured Cooperation with European Civil Society Organizations and Networks*, Rapporteur: Mr Bloch-Lainé, CESE 1498/2003 fin FR/CD/ET/ht, 17 February 2004, p. 6.

insisted upon by NGOs during the European Convention. The result was the inclusion in the Constitutional Treaty of art. I-46 providing for the principle of participatory democracy.[43] Even though the Constitutional Treaty is unlikely to enter into force, the mere drafting of this article is meaningful in as much as it shows the existence, at the European level, of a general understanding of the importance of the involvement of civil society in the EC decision-making process and of the need to formalize this principle.[44]

The main achievement attained so far by NGOs has, though, been the insertion in the Cotonou Agreement of art. 4.[45] This article, in fact, imposes a general duty of consultation with NSAs for the drafting of policies and strategies: ACP countries, European States and European Union being responsible. This provision (we must remember that it is an agreement and now mandatory) is particularly significant because it gives NGOs a veritable right to be heard by EU and ACP institutions. Unfortunately the immediate compulsory nature of art. 4 is undermined by the presence of the phrase 'where appropriate' which, implicitly, refers to art. 6 of the same agreement.[46] In particular,

---

[43]   According to art. I-46: '1. The Institutions shall, by appropriate means, give citizens and representative associations the opportunity to make known and publicly exchange their views in all areas of Union action. 2. The Institutions shall maintain an open, transparent and regular dialogue with representative associations and civil society. 3. The Commission shall carry out broad consultations with parties concerned in order to ensure that the Union's actions are coherent and transparent. 4. Not less than one million citizens coming from a significant number of Member States may take the initiative of inviting the Commission, within the framework of its powers, to submit any appropriate proposal on matters where citizens consider that a legal act of the Union is required for the purpose of implementing the Constitution. A European law shall determine the provisions for the procedures and conditions required for such a citizens' initiative, including the minimum number of Member States from which they must come.'

[44]   The inclusion of this article has probably been possible because of the special composition of the body that drafted the Constitution. The European Convention being composed not only of representatives of national governments but also of representatives of National Parliaments and of the European Parliament was keener than the traditional IGCs responsible for the previous amendments of the EC treaty, on experimenting at the EU level with new forms of democracy.

[45]   According to art. 4: 'The ACP States shall determine the development principles, strategies and models of their economies and societies in all sovereignty. They shall establish, with the Community, the cooperation programmes provided for under this Agreement. However, the parties recognize the complementary role of and potential for contributions by NSAs to the development process. To this end, under the conditions laid down in this Agreement, NSAs shall, where appropriate, be informed and involved in consultation on cooperation policies and strategies, on priorities for cooperation especially in areas that concern or directly affect them, and on the political dialogue.'

[46]   According to art. 6: 1. The actors of cooperation will include (a) State (local, national and regional); (b) Non-State: Private sector; Economic and social partners,

the latter gives contracting parties the right to screen NGOs eligible to become actors of co-operation, on the basis of their capacity to address the needs of the population, on their specific competencies and on the question of whether they are organized and managed democratically and transparently.[17] However, even if art. 4 of the Cotonou Agreement is not self-executing, its importance must not be underestimated. In fact, once NGOs have been selected according to art. 6, they will be fully entitled to be involved in the formulation of development strategies and, if not, they will be able to go before the European Court of Justice or ACP national courts, in order to enforce their right to be consulted.

This degree of formalization in NGO consultation is absolutely a *unicum* not only in the field of development policy, but also in all the areas covered by the EC Treaty. It might be considered the first example of what some authors call 'committed consultation', that is, the principle that NGOs have the 'right to be heard, to receive an answer, and, if the answer is not satisfactory, to apply for a judicial review of the quality of the grounds given in response to objections made in the course of the consultation procedure'.[48] Such form of involvement has been deemed more promising than participation and mere consultation. Participation, in fact, risks 'depoliticizing further the decision-making mechanisms within the Union, whilst, [sic] what it is required is, instead, their repoliticization'. Consultation, in turn, risks remaining only theoretical, unless NGOs' proposals benefit from 'sufficient political backing'.[49] Notwithstanding the advantages that this form of consultation might bring to the decision-making process in all the areas covered by the EC treaty, it is very unlikely that, in the short term, it will be transposed from Cotonou to all European policies. The Commission Communication 'towards a reinforced culture of consultation and dialogue'

---

including trade union organizations; Civil Society in all its forms according to national characteristics. 2. Recognition by the parties of non-governmental actors shall depend on the extent to which they address the needs of the population, on their specific competencies and whether they are organized and managed democratically and transparently.

[47] The concrete mechanism and entity which should supersede the NGOs screening process are not specified in the Cotonou Agreement. The 'ACP Civil Society Discussion Forum' has suggested the creation of a national/regional Steering Committee to take the final decision on the eligibility criteria in accordance with the guidelines provided in art. 6. This body should comprise the National Authorising Officers /Regional Authorising Officers, the relevant ACP Government authorities, mandated non-state actor representative(s), and the EC.

[48] O. de Schutter, 'Europe in search of its civil society', *European Law Journal*, **8**(2), 214.

[49] Ibid., p. 214.

is quite eloquent on that issue.[50] In this Document, in fact, the Commission declares itself to be

> convinced that a legally-binding approach to consultation is to be avoided, for two reasons: First, a clear dividing line must be drawn between consultations launched on the Commission's own initiative prior to the adoption of a proposal, and the subsequent formalised and compulsory decision making process according to the Treaties. Second, a situation must be avoided in which a Commission proposal could be challenged in the Court on the grounds of alleged lack of consultation of interested parties. Such an over-legalistic approach would be incompatible with the need for timely delivery of policy, and with the expectations of citizens that European Institutions should deliver on substance rather than concentrating on procedures. Moreover, the fear expressed by some participants in the consultation process that the principles and guidelines could remain a dead letter because of their non-legally binding nature is owing to a misunderstanding. It goes without saying that, when the Commission decides to apply the principles and guidelines, its departments have to act accordingly. Finally, the Commission is of the opinion that improvement of its consultation practice should not be based on a 'command and control' approach but rather on providing the appropriate guidance and assistance to Commission officials in charge of running the consultation processes. The general principles and minimum standards should serve as a reference point for a permanent in-house learning process.[51]

In the field of development policy, the EU probably agreed on an exception, because the main responsibility for the involvement of NGOs in the elaboration of strategies reposes in ACP countries rather than in EC institutions. This is the direct consequence of the wording of art. 4 of the Cotonou Agreement, where, before recognizing the complementary role of NGOs in the decision-making process, it is pointed out that 'The *ACP States* shall determine the development principles, strategies and models of their economies and societies in all sovereignty' (italics added). It is surely not a coincidence that,

---

50   Communication from the Commission, *Towards a Reinforced Culture of Consultation and Dialogue – General Principles and Minimum Standards for Consultation of Interested Parties by the Commission*, COM(2002) 704 final, 11 December 2002.

51   Ibid., p. 10. We would suggest that the formalization of NGO consultation in the EU decision-making process is desirable, despite the important arguments raised by the Commission. The risk of an over-legalistic approach, of an overload of work for the EC judicial bodies, of a delay in delivering policy is real. But, at the same time, it is related to the numbers of potential NSAs entitled to be heard. To avoid these problems, rather than denying NGOs the formal right to be consulted, the EC might cut the numbers of interlocutors by, for instance, promoting the creation of NSA networks. A screening mechanism would decrease substantially the inefficiencies related to a formalized consultation and would help the EU in its efforts to reduce its democratic deficit through a participative approach.

during the negotiations for the Agreement, most ACP countries were against the recognition of NGOs as co-operation partners next to EU, European and ACP States.[52] Nevertheless, it is certain that the legalization of consultation provided for in the Cotonou agreement remains a meaningful achievement which, at least, over time, might offer an important precedent for the EU's internal decision-making process.

CONCLUSION

EU development policy is an interesting sector for seeing the recent evolution of the role of NSAs in the international arena. On the one hand, it shows, clearly, a degree of interpenetration of the EU and NGOs, which is absent in other international organizations. The most striking example concerns the implementation of development policy. The formula of co-financing, inherited from European national governments, has allowed both EU institutions and NGOs to be associated together in geographic or thematic areas related to development, benefiting each from the contribution of the other, without jeopardizing their freedom and independence. On the other hand, it reveals a tension between the formalization and non-formalization of the involvement of NGOs in development policy, which in other international organisations, such as the Council of Europe, has already been resolved in favour of the former. The only exception, in this regard, is Cotonou, where art. 4 requires consultation with NGOs deemed representative, transparent and democratic. The legalization of consultation, in the context of the relationship between the EC and ACP countries, has been possible because the formal involvement of NSAs affects an international institutional framework and not the internal decision making of the European Union. In other geographical or thematic areas of development and, more generally, in the other sectors covered by the EC Treaty, the Commission has instead, despite repeated requests from NGOs, shown itself reluctant to undertake a legalized approach. The main worry is related both to an overload of the work of the European Court of Justice and to excessive slowness in the decision-making procedure. The EU, regardless of the fact that it is, more than other international organizations, in need of a participatory decisional mechanism, has failed so far to do so. It has depended, instead, upon informal consultation because it could boast other important forms of civil society involvement, such as institutional participation through the European Economic and Social Committee. Notwithstanding the decisive

---

52   See, O. Elgström (2000), 'Lomé and post-Lomé: asymmetric negotiations and the impact of norms', *European Foreign Affairs Review*, **5**(2), 192.

role that the EESC might play in the future in giving voice to civil society at the European level, it is still desirable that the example set by Cotonou will also be followed in other areas. The EESC alone, in fact, because of its peculiar composition, is not able to represent adequately the entire spectrum of the heterogeneous world of NSAs.

4. Controversial developments in the field of public participation in the international environmental law process

Attila Tanzi[1]

ENVIRONMENTAL GOVERNANCE AND THE ROLE OF NON-STATE ACTORS

The protection and preservation of the environment is certainly one of the areas in which the traditional regulatory power of nation-states faces challenges more difficult than in others. Since environmental issues can hardly be confined within the national borders of one state, domestic legislation, as such, may never tackle appropriately transboundary issues and, even more so, global environmental problems, such as climate change. Furthermore, domestic regulatory constraints in this field may be easily circumvented, particularly in the current context of globalization, by transferring polluting activities to states with lower standards of environmental protection.

Such considerations account for the fact that, since its inception, environmental law has always had a primarily international vocation. Through international environmental law, states create and undertake obligations in relation to issues that may have, not only a transboundary impact (for example in the use, management and protection of international rivers and lakes) but also a global relevance, that is with regard to the atmosphere, or biodiversity. This internationalization of the individual states' regulatory powers has attracted the attention of those actors that for a long time have not been involved in international law making and enforcement, and whose interests are most directly affected by environmental policies. On the one hand, one finds the so-called PINGOs (public interest NGOs), who are supposed to represent the civil

---

[1]   Although the author has been a member of the Italian delegation to diplomatic exercises addressed in the present paper, the opinions expressed below do not necessarily reflect the views of the Italian Government.

society at large, that is, individuals and communities, present and future, who may fall victim of sudden environmental harmful occurrences, as well as of the progressive deterioration, or exhaustion, of natural resources essential to vital human needs. On the other hand, one finds the so-called BINGOs (business interest NGOs) representing precisely the business community, particularly industry, whose activity may be the object of possible regulation. They have claimed a standing with a view to minimizing the impact on their activities of possible regulatory measures in this field. As a result of a process which started virtually with the beginning of the environmental law process itself, at the last UN World Summit in the field of the environment, the Johannesburg World Summit on Sustainable Development (WSSD), the issue of environmental governance was addressed by giving an increased role to the 'private sector', made up of both civil society and the business community. It may be recalled that Secretary-General Kofi Annan, in his opening speech stated that '[a]ction starts with Governments ... [b]ut Governments cannot do alone. Civil society groups have a critical role, as partners, advocates and watchdogs. So do commercial enterprises. Without the private sector, sustainable development will remain only a distant dream'.[2]

This chapter will focus on the status of NGOs in the field of international environmental law against the background of some recent controversial elements of international practice. In doing so, the substantive issue will not be addressed as to whether representation of civil society by NGOs is effective and genuine. For, given the NGOs' low degree of regulatory democratic legitimization, due basically to self-election, their credibility and legitimacy may be tested only by the quality of their action, their expertise and factual transparency.

Firstly, brief consideration will be given to the most significant indications deriving for states from international instruments to the effect that public participation in environmental law making at the domestic level should be promoted as a requirement for the achievement of sustainable development. Secondly, the issue will be addressed of the ground on which to find the basis for public participation in environmental forums at the international level. To that end, the research draws mainly from the basic indications deriving from Rio and from the latest developments within the framework of the Aarhus Convention. Thirdly, the analysis will underscore the recent shift of emphasis in the role of NGOs in the environmental process from decision making to the implementation phase.

---

2 Text available at http://www.un.org/events/wssd/statements/sgE.htm.

THE INTERNATIONAL RECOGNITION OF NGOS ACTING AT THE DOMESTIC LEVEL: THE PRINCIPLE OF PUBLIC PARTICIPATION

International diplomatic instruments of a global scope in the field of environmental protection recognize the role of NGOs and other actors coming from civil society under the principle of public participation. More particularly, the firm conviction has been emphasized of the impossibility that sustainable development and sustainable governance may be achieved if citizens and the public at large are left outside of the relevant decision making process, without access to information and to possible judicial remedies. This concept is spelt out under Principle 10 of the Rio Declaration, in the following terms:

> Environmental issues are best handled with participation of all concerned citizens, at the relevant level. At the national level, each individual shall have appropriate access to information concerning the environment that is held by public authorities, including information on hazardous materials and activities in their communities, and the opportunity to participate in decision-making processes. States shall facilitate and encourage public awareness and participation by making information widely available. Effective access to judicial and administrative proceedings, including redress and remedy, shall be provided.

The principle of public participation in the environmental process has been further confirmed in the Rio document Agenda 21 as a precondition for the achievement of sustainable development.[3] Its Preamble calls for the involvement of NGOs in environmental governance (Ch. 1.3), while Chapter 27 is devoted to NGOs as one of the major groups whose partnership is deemed to be critical in the implementation of the programme. To that end, states are required to adopt within their legal order '[A]ny legislative measures necessary to enable the establishment by non-governmental organizations of consultative groups, and to ensure the right of non-governmental organizations to protect the public interest through legal action'.[4]

---

[3] Agenda 21, ch. 23.2 ('One of the fundamental prerequisites for the achievement of sustainable development is broad public participation in decision-making'). The need for 'effective participation' as an essential element of sustainable development was already identified in the *Bruntland Report* (Bruntland Commission (1987), *Our Common Future*, Oxford: Oxford University Press, at 65). On the same line, Principle 5 of the 2002 ILA *New Delhi Declaration of Principles of International Law on Sustainable Development* (http://www.ila-hq.org/pdf/Sustainable%20Development/ Sus%20Dev%20 Resolution%20+%20Declaration%202002%20English.pdf, accessed 15 January 2006), defines participation as 'essential' to sustainable development.

[4] Paras 27.10 and 27.13.

More recently, this principle has been echoed in para. 16 of the 2000 Malmö Ministerial Declaration, adopted at the first Global Ministerial Environment Forum, to the effect that '[t]he role of civil society at all levels should be strengthened through freedom of access to environmental information to all, broad participation in environmental decision making, as well as access to justice on environmental issues'.[5]

In line with the results reached on the issue under consideration in Rio ten years earlier, the Johannesburg World Summit on Sustainable Development reiterates the substance of Principle 10 quoted above. The Johannesburg Declaration on Sustainable Development affirms that 'sustainable development requires (. . .) broad-based participation in policy formulation, decision-making and implementation at all levels',[6] while the Plan of Implementation provides that states are to

[e]nsure access, at the national level, to environmental information and judicial and administrative proceedings in environmental matters, as well as public participation in decision-making, so as to further principle 10 of the Rio Declaration on Environment and Development, taking into full account principles 5, 7 and 11 of the Declaration.[7]

Moreover, at WSSD the relevance of the principle of public participation in relation to the implementation of international environmental regulation at the national level was strengthened by the conclusion of a 'Partnership for Principle 10', a so-called Type-II initiative, promoted by 'The Access Initiative', a network of NGOs extremely active at the Summit.[8] Similar initiatives of a soft-law nature are to be found also at regional level, such as the Inter-American Strategy for the Promotion of Public Participation in Decision-Making for Sustainable Development.[9]

---

5   Malmö Ministerial Declaration, First Global Ministerial Environment Forum – Sixth Special Session of the Governing Council of the United Nations Environment Programme, 5th plenary meeting, 19–21 May 2000, http://www.unep.org/malmo/malmo_ministerial.htm (accessed 15 January 2006).

6   Johannesburg Declaration on Sustainable Development, doc. A/CONF.199/20, Annex, para. 26.

7   Plan of Implementation, doc. A/CONF.199/20, Annex, para. 123.

8   On Type II initiatives and partnerships see *infra*, text at notes 35ff. For more information on Partnership for Principle 10, see www.pp10.org (accessed 15 January 2006).

9   This strategy was launched within the OAS framework after the 1996 Summit on Sustainable Development, where the Heads of state '[i]n order to support the specific initiatives on public participation contained in the Plan of Action, entrust the OAS with assigning priority to the formulation of an inter-american strategy for the promotion of public participation in decision-making for sustainable development'. The Strategy was

Apart from the significant international soft-law instruments enhancing the principle of public participation, one should also not lose sight of those Multilateral Environmental Agreements (MEAs) containing provisions that translate the principle of public participation into legally binding obligations.[10]

Most importantly, the 1998 Aarhus Convention[11] has gone so far as to provide a comprehensive legal regulation on the matter in hand. It sets out the three pillars making up the principle in point, that is, access to information, participation in decision making and access to justice in environmental matters, also providing for detailed substantive and procedural standards for an advanced system of compliance monitoring.[12] It should be noted that this Convention, adopted within the United Nations Economic Commission for Europe (UNECE) and ratified by a large number of states within the Pan-European region, has potentially a global reach, being open to non UNECE Members.[13] It requires Parties to afford within their domestic systems a number of rights to information in the environmental field to 'the public' in general, that is, any natural or legal person and, subject to domestic law requirements, associations and organizations. Under the Convention, rights relating to participation and access to justice are to be conferred only on 'the public concerned', that is, a range of subjects to be determined in relation to the particular interest that individual members, or sectors, of the public may have in a given controversial situation. However, it may be noted on this point

---

formally adopted by a resolution of the Inter-American Council for Integral Development at its fifth Session in 2000; see CIDI/RES. 98 (V-O/00), doc. OEA/Ser.W/II.5 CIDI/doc. 25/00. For further information see the Strategy's website at http://www.ispnet.org (accessed 15 January 2006).

[10] For an overview, see D. Shelton (2002), 'Human Rights and Environment Issues in Multilateral Treaties Adopted between 1991 and 2001', *Joint UNEP–OHCHR Expert Seminar on Human Rights and the Environment*, http://www.unhchr.ch/environment/bp1.html (accessed 21 January 2006). The provision on access to information under the OSPAR Convention (Convention for the Protection of the Marine Environment of the North-East Atlantic, 22 Sept. 1992 (1992) **2**, *International Legal Material*, p. 1069) has also been the object of a dispute settled by arbitration, see *Dispute Concerning Access to Information under Article 9 of the OSPAR Convention*, Award of 2 July 2003, http://www.pca-cpa.org/ENGLISH/RPC/OSPAR/OSPAR%20final%20award%20revised.pdf (accessed 15 January 2006).

[11] Convention on Access to Information, Public Participation in Decision-making and Access to Justice in Environmental Matters (1999), *International Legal Material* (38), 517.

[12] See the specific contribution on this issue by C. Pitea, Chapter 6 in this volume, *infra* p. 181.

[13] Art. 19 para. 3.

that, under the Convention, public interest NGOs are always deemed to have such a particular interest.[14]

It appears that, by and large, in certain regions more than in others, the existing international legal framework on the subject in hand provides for a fairly well defined legal status for NGOs acting at the domestic level in environmental decision making and enforcement. Accordingly, individuals and the organizations they are members of are entitled, at the domestic level, to be informed, to participate in decision-making processes and to have access to justice in environmental matters. The fact that such rights may be defended before domestic courts adds significantly to the existing body of the international law of human rights relating to the protection of the environment.

Corporate Sector

Among the international instruments setting out standards relevant to our field, one should underscore those – whose adoption has been boosted by the widespread trend towards economic liberalization following the fall of the Berlin Wall – that pay special attention to the role of the corporate sector.[15] They have been adopted both at the intergovernmental level and by the international business community itself. A good example of the latter is to be found in the Business Charter on Sustainable Development, adopted in 1991 by the board of the International Chamber of Commerce.[16] A considerable impetus to the trend under consideration was provided in the year 2000 by the UN Secretary General (S-G) in his 'voluntary corporate citizenship initiative' called Global Compact.[17] Among the nine requirements corporate participants are to commit themselves to under this initiative, one finds the following commitments: (a) to promote the precautionary principle; (b) to engage in initiatives to promote environmental responsibility; and (c) to develop environmentally friendly technologies. Along with the S-G's initiative, the Plan of Implementation adopted at the WSSD calls for states to 'enhance corporate environmental and social responsibility and accountability'.[18]

Within this trend towards an attempt at promoting some kind of 'compassionate' industrial development on a voluntary basis, one should refer to the

---

[14]   Art. 2, para. 5.
[15]   But see Chapter 30 of Agenda 21.
[16]   See L. Thomas (1992), 'The Business Charter for Sustainable Development: Action Beyond UNCED', *Review of European Community and International Environmental Law*, **1**(3), 325–7.
[17]   www.unglobalcompact.org/Portal.
[18]   Para. 17 (a).

2000 update[19] of the 1976 OECD Guidelines for multinational enterprises.[20] Part V of the document in point provides in general terms as follows:

Enterprises should, within the framework of laws, regulations and administrative practices in the countries where they operate, and in consideration of the relevant agreements, principles, objectives and standards, take due account of the need to protect the environment, public health and safety, and generally to conduct their activities in a manner contributing to the wider goal of sustainable development.

More particularly, the Guidelines set out a number of basic standards for the enterprises to follow. They include the obligations to establish an appropriate system of environmental management; to make the environmental impact assessment of their activities and to provide prompt information to those who may be affected by the environmental and health impact thereof; to follow the precautionary principle; to make and maintain contingency plans for preventing and mitigating serious environmental or health damage.

Incidentally, it may be considered that the body of standards addressing the environmental conduct of private operators, though not legally binding per se, may serve a twofold purpose of international and domestic normative relevance. On the one hand, they may provide important substantive legal elements for the development of a uniform domestic legislation in line with Principle 13 of the Rio Declaration providing that 'States shall develop national law regarding liability and compensation for the victims of pollution and other environmental damage (. . .).' At the same time, such standards may enhance the elaboration of the contents of the due diligence obligations for States to prevent the harmful use of their territories, both at the State-to-State level in a transboundary context,[21] and in relation to the obligations owed by

---

[19]   DAFFE/IME (IME) 20, Annex.

[20]   See the 1976 text in (1976), *International Legal Material* (15) 969 and the amendments of 1979, 1982 and 1984 in (1992), *International Legal Material* (31) 494.

[21]   See the following international case-law: *Trail Smelter, United States* v *Canada, RIIA,* III (1905); *Corfù Channel, United Kingdom* v *Albany, ICJ Reports* (1949) 3ff; *Lac Lanoux,* in *UNRIIA,* XII, 281ff; *Advisory Opinion on the Legality of the Threat or Use of Nuclear Weapons,* in ICJ Reports, 1996, p. 226, para. 29. As to the assessment of the contents of the due diligence obligations for States to prevent the occurrence of harm to individuals and/or the environment, see Pierre-Marie Dupuy (1976), *La responsabilité des Etats pour les dommages d'origine technologique et industrielle,* Paris: A. Pedone, at 204; P.-M. Dupuy (1991), 'L'Etat et la réparation des dommages catastrophiques', in Francesco Francioni and Tullio Scovazzi (eds), *International Responsibility for Environmental Harm,* London: Graham & Trotman, Dordrecht [etc.]: Nijhoff, 125–47, at 133ff.; R. Pisillo Mazzeschi (1991), 'Forms of international responsibility for environmental harm', ibid., at 15–35; C. Romano, (2000), 'L'obligaton de prévention des catastrophes industrielles et naturelles', in

States vis-à-vis individuals within their territory, also under the international law of human rights.

Recent case-law of the European Court of Human Rights is exemplary of the latter perspective. In 1994, in *Lopez Ostra* v *Spain* the Court found Spain in breach of art. 8 of the European Convention, as the defendant State did not prove to have taken all appropriate measures to prevent the release by a private operator of emissions harmful to individuals on its territory.[22] The European Court applied the same reasoning in 1998 in *Guerra and Others* v *Italy*[23] and, most recently, in 2005 in *Fadeyeva* v *Russia*.[24]

NGOS IN INTERNATIONAL ENVIRONMENTAL DECISION MAKING: SOME RECENT DEVELOPMENTS

As to the recognition of public participation in environmental governance at the international level, the picture is less clear than the one at the domestic level described above. It is beyond question that NGOs have contributed significantly to the setting of the international environmental law agenda, as well as to the actual elaboration of the basic principles, standards and rules of international environmental law, and also to their implementation and enforcement. However, the modes for their participation in such processes vary considerably from one international forum to the other, and are often extremely informal. In some cases, such as information campaigns and lobbying activities, NGO activity is by definition not suited for regulation. At the same time, international environmental law is characterized by a growing trend of institutionalization.[25] Apart from the large UN diplomatic confer-

---

David D. Caron and Charles Leben (eds), *Les aspects internationaux des catastrophes naturelles et industrielles*, The Hague/Boston/London: Nijhoff, 379–428; A. Garane (2003), 'La responsabilité internationale de l'Etat: un instrument économique de la protection de l'environnement?', in Michael Bothe and Peter H. Sand (eds), *Environmental Policy: From Regulation to Economic Instruments*, The Hague/Boston/London: Nijhoff, 607–48; T. Scovazzi (2005), 'Some remarks on international responsibility in the field of environmental protection', in Maurizio Ragazzi (ed.), *International Responsibility Today. Essays in Memory of Oscar Schachter*, Leiden [etc.]: Brill, 209–22, at 215–17.

22   ECHR, 9 December 1994, in *Publications of the European Court of Human Rights*, series A, v 303-C, 38ff., especially at paras 52–8.

23   ECHR, 19 February 1998, in *Reports of Judgements and Decisions*, 1998-I, 64, especially at paras 58–60.

24   ECHR, 9 June 2005. See http://www.echr.coe.int/echr.

25   See V. Röben, (2000), 'Institutional developments under modern international environmental agreements', *Max Planck Yearbook of United Nations Law*, **4**, 363–443; R. Churchill and G. Ulfstein (2000), 'Autonomous institutional arrangements in multi-

ences, such as the 1992 UNCED and the 2002 WSSD, and from MEAs, environmental law is made through the day-by-day work carried out by the various bodies established precisely under various different MEAs. While Conferences, or Meetings, of the Parties (COP/MOP) of the various MEAs play a crucial role in the environmental governance, as well as their subsidiary bodies, particularly those concerned with compliance monitoring and enforcement, public participation in those forums has taken place on a case-by-case basis, rather informally. This accounts for the fact that there is no general instrument, or set of instruments, setting out the principles and requirements for NGOs' participation in one and all international environmental forums. Indeed, under the scattered institutional environmental law setting, one cannot find a homogeneous regulatory scenario of the kind set out by the resolutions adopted by the UN General Assembly and ECOSOC which have implemented through the years Art. 71 of the Charter, providing for three different degrees for the observer status for NGOs within the ECOSOC.[26]

Even if, more often than not, MEAs are negotiated and adopted within the UN framework, each of them lives an institutional life of its own. Against this background it appears very difficult from a legal perspective to envisage the elaboration of a uniform regulatory setting on public participation that may be applicable to all international environmental forums. Furthermore, in policy terms, states parties are reluctant to make the effort to develop a general framework that may bind them once and for all to accord certain rights of public participation, which they may find acceptable within the context of a given MEA, but not of another one. Similarly NGOs themselves do not seem to be keen on crystallizing regulations that may set out in general terms limitations to their participation in international environmental forums that they may overcome on a case-by-case basis.

Be that as it may, sufficient ground can be found on which to base a flexible approach to NGOs' participation in international environmental forums, precisely on a case-by-case basis, usually under the rules of procedure of each such forum. Under the above-mentioned Principle 10 of the Rio Declaration, participation should be envisaged at any 'relevant level', hence including the international level, where global environmental problems (such as climate

---

lateral environmental agreements: a little noticed phenomenon in international law', *American Journal of International Law*, **94**(4), 623–59.

26   See GA res. 3 (II) of 1946, and ECOSOC res. 288 B (X) of 1950, res. 1296 (XLIV) of 1968, res. 1 and 1996/31 of 1996. On the actual admission process carried out upon recommendation by the United Nations Committee on Non-governmental Organizations, see J. Aston (2001), 'The United Nations Committee on Non-governmental Organizations: guarding the entrance to a politically divided house', *European Journal of International Law*, **12**(5), 943–62.

change, desertification, biodiversity and water issues) find or should find their primary source of regulation. Consistently with this interpretation, Chapter 27.9 of Agenda 21 calls for the UN and other international forums to establish and enhance the involvement of NGOs in their activities.

As a mitigation of the general statement made above, to the effect that states are reluctant to set out standards in the matter under consideration that may apply generally, that is, beyond the framework of a given international forum, note should be taken of Article 3.7 of the Aarhus Convention. It expressly requires Parties to promote the principles of the Convention 'in international environmental decision-making processes and within the framework of international organizations in matters relating to the environment'.[27] Despite its mandatory language, this provision does not contain indications as to how it should be implemented. Therefore, the Final Declaration of the first MOP in Lucca called for the elaboration of some guidance to that effect.[28] An expert group was therefore established to assist the Working Group of the Parties in studying the subject, possibly with a view to submitting operative proposals.[29]

This exercise finally led to the adoption of the 'Almaty Guidelines on Promoting the Application of the Principles of the Aarhus Convention in International Forums'[30] [Almaty Guidelines] at the second MOP held in May 2005 in the Kazak capital. It may be noted that the adoption of this document does not mark the end of the process, for the same decision approving the Guidelines established a task force on the same topic. It was vested with the mandate to consult relevant international forums, mostly secretariats from other MEAs, on the content of the Guidelines and to report back to the Working Group of the Parties with a view to reviewing the Guidelines at the next MOP.

The genetic process of the Almaty Guidelines has highlighted the basic distance between the different views about the principle of public participation at the international level held by the various actors involved. One could say that this exercise was in itself a case of 'good practice' in the implementation of the principle of public participation. The expert group had a tripartite composition, consisting of representatives from the NGO community and academia, sitting on a par with representatives from states and from secretariats of international organizations. The result of the work of the expert

---

27   Article 3 para. 7 of the Aarhus Convention.
28   See Lucca Declaration, doc. ECE/MP.PP/2/Add.1, para. 31.
29   As to the workings of the expert group, see http://www.unece.org/env/pp/ppif.htm (accessed 15 January 2006).
30   The text is annexed to Decision II/4 of the MOP, doc. ECE/MP.PP/2005/2/Add.5.

group, that is, the original draft-guidelines, was met with some resistance by the governmental representatives sitting at the MOP. The latter finally approved a text which modified the one submitted by the expert group, which already in its original version was far from being an extravagantly innovative text.[31]

Be that as it may, the language of the Guidelines reflects their non-binding nature and their flexibility, as well as the will of states to retain a large margin of discretion in their application, on a case-by-case basis. This feature does not undermine their importance, for they represent the first official accomplished attempt to deal comprehensively with the issue of public participation at the international level. It is also important to note the scope of the Guidelines, which is not confined to one particular international organization or process. Their purpose is precisely to 'provide general guidance to Parties on promoting the application of the principles of the Convention in international forums in matters relating to the environment' (para. 1), as well as in the contents of any rules that such forum may produce (para. 2). The notion of an international forum is fairly wide in the document under consideration, for it encompasses the negotiation and management of international agreements, intergovernmental conferences at any stage, policy development forums and the decision making within international organizations.[32] Therefore, if applied by Parties, the Guidelines may 'positively influence the way in which international access is secured in international forums in which Parties to the Convention participate' (para. 6), so long as these forums deal with environmental issues, even if they are not primarily environmental forums.

Furthermore, the document recognizes the importance of public participation in environmental matters at the international level by stressing its close relation to the principle of sustainable development. This interlinkage appears as a requisite for good governance and as a tool for the improvement of the

---

[31] See doc. ECE/MP.PP/2005/8.

[32] Para. 4 indicates that the latter sentence includes '(a) The negotiation and implementation at the international level of MEAs, including decisions and actions taken under their auspices; (b) The negotiation and implementation at the international level of other relevant agreements, if decisions or actions undertaken at that level pursuant to such agreements relate to the environment or may have a significant effect on the environment; (c) Intergovernmental conferences focusing on the environment or having a strong environmental component, and their respective preparatory and follow-up processes at the international level; (d) International environmental and development policy forums; and (e) Decision-making processes within the framework of other international organizations in matters relating to the environment.' However, para. 9 specifies that '[t]his does not include any regional economic integration organization or forums exclusively comprising all member states of a regional economic integration organization', thus excluding European Union processes from its scope.

quality of international decision-making processes (paras 11 and 12). The cornerstone of the Guidelines lies in the idea that international forums should each develop clear internal rules and standards for access to information (para. 19) and public participation (paras 29, 31, 35 and 36), as well as mechanisms for reviewing their application (para. 40). Transparency of participation policies appears throughout the text as the main guarantee against abusive restrictions, while a number of substantive standards – even though of a rather general character – are provided with regard to public access to information and participation in international decision making.[33]

When considering the actual role of NGOs in the Guidelines, one should place the issue in hand against the background of the general language contained in the document under consideration to the effect that 'in any structuring of international access, care should be taken to render, or keep, the processes open to the public at large', as a general rule (para. 14). While this objective is perfectly reasonable in relation to the principle of access to information, particularly through the use of modern information technologies, this is less so where actual participation is concerned. Here, two sets of limitations come into play. On the one hand, as provided for in the Aarhus Convention, only the 'public concerned' enjoys participation rights. On the other, at the international level it would be impossible, or very difficult in practice, to meet participation demands coming from all interested members of the public. This would be particularly the case with regard to bodies with restricted membership. On that score, the Guidelines provide that 'the number of members of the public concerned participating in the meetings may be restricted if this is necessary and unavoidable for practical reasons' (para. 31).

The peculiar position of NGOs in representing different sectors of the public when selection is needed has also been addressed by the Guidelines. They draw on this point from the Aarhus Convention under which public interest NGOs are deemed to be part of the 'public concerned' for the purpose of affording participation rights. Accordingly, the Guidelines provide that 'representatives of public-interest organizations, such as environmental citizens' organizations, are included among the relevant stakeholders whose participation may be sought or recognized' (para. 30). While the fact of promoting public interests amounts in itself to a selection criterion among NGOs, it has been felt that appropriate selection for effective representation called for further criteria. As a first step in that direction, and in line with the basic principle of transparency, the Guidelines provide that accreditation 'should be based on clear and objec-

---

[33]   It may be noted that the 'access to justice' pillar of the Convention has been deemed not to be suitable at the international level. This was a decision motivated more by considerations of policy than of technical and legal feasibility.

tive criteria, and the public should be informed accordingly' and that 'procedures [for selection] should be transparent, fair, timely, accountable and accessible, and aimed at securing meaningful and equitable participation, while avoiding excessive formalization' (para. 31).

The expert group had engaged in a long discussion on whether substantive selection criteria should be set out in the Guidelines. Transparency, legitimacy, breadth of representation, co-ordination, preparation for meetings, consultation with constituencies and the need for funding were some of the issues raised in this respect. Eventually, a consensus was reached that this was a matter of self-organization by NGOs, which fell outside the scope of the Guidelines, which would avoid endorsing, or even encouraging, in any way governmental interference with the internal organization of NGOs. The Draft submitted to the second MOP contained a provision stressing that '[s]elf-organization and self-selection processes among members of the public concerned sharing common goals could, if appropriate, be encouraged', but even this language was found too 'interventionist' into the internal affairs of NGOs. Therefore, this sentence was deleted in the text finally approved.[34] Only a number of very general criteria were mentioned in the document, namely 'field of expertise, representation in geographic, sectoral, professional and other relevant contexts, and knowledge of the working language' (para. 31).

Be that as it may, the Guidelines aim to promote the achievement of balanced participation through the representation of possibly all relevant interests, taking into consideration that NGOs do not enjoy exclusive rights of representation. Accordingly, the document adds two categories of stakeholders among those specially entitled to participate in international forums. Namely, '[t]he members of the public who are, or are likely to be, most directly affected' and '[r]epresentatives of other interests that might cause, contribute to, be affected by or be in a position to alleviate the problems under discussion'. Since different stakeholders may find themselves in significantly different positions as to their actual capacity to participate in international forums, the Guidelines recognize that an effort should be made to balance the differences concerning the financial capacity to participate between environmental NGOs and business organizations (para. 15). At the same time, the instrument in hand expresses the need to involve persons most directly affected in any given case, also paying special attention to the difficulties in taking advantage of the opportunities of participation for NGOs from disadvantaged countries, with a view to avoiding the risk that NGOs' participation may become a tool for the promotion of universalized western values (para. 17).

---

[34] See doc. ECE/MP.PP/WG.1/2005/8/Add.1, para. 43.

The Guidelines and their *travaux préparatoires* have certainly furthered the present international process which affords NGOs significant participatory opportunities in international forums when the latter are dealing with environmental issues. To a certain extent, the recognition emerging from the document under review of the role of NGOs appears to be differentiated with respect to that of other stakeholders, without implying a governmental intrusion in the NGOs' internal affairs. After all, the impact of this instrument on the status of NGOs in international environmental law seems to be quite limited, despite the fact that it has been approved by a restricted number of countries belonging to the Pan-european region. Moreover, apart from its non-legally binding format, one may wonder whether its contents, because of its very soft character, will bear significantly on the conduct of UNECE state members (even only the Parties to the Aarhus Convention) when attending international forums.

THE SHIFT OF FOCUS FROM PARTICIPATION IN DECISION MAKING TO PARTNERSHIP IN IMPLEMENTATION: EMPOWERING OR WEAKENING NGOS?

The process within the Aarhus Convention just described testifies to the continuing relevance in the international agenda of the issue of public participation in international decision-making processes. At the same time, one cannot ignore that the WSSD has marked a shift of attention from the role of civil society in the making of environmental law, both international and domestic, to the notion of partnership in the implementation of international environmental principles.[35] The outcome of the Summit on this point is twofold. The so-called 'Type I' outcomes are those of a traditional intergovernmental nature, including the political Declaration and the Plan of Action. On the other hand, Type II outcomes refer to the so-called 'partnerships for sustainable development'. Such partnerships consist of multi-stakeholder

---

[35]   This may be considered as a direct consequence of the more general shift of focus, currently undergoing in the international environmental law process, from law-making to law-implementation, as witnessed by the very outcomes of the Johannesburg Summit. See U. Beyerlin and M. Reichard (2003), 'The Johannesburg Summit: Outcome and Overall Assessment', *Zeitschrift für ausländisches öffentliches Recht und Völkerrecht*, **63**(2), 213–37, at 233–4 and M. H. Ivanova (2003), 'Partnerships, international organizations, and global environmental governance', in Thorsten Benner, Charlotte Streck and Jan Martin Witte (eds), *Progress or Peril? Networks and Partnerships in Global Environmental Governance. The Post-Johannesburg Agenda*, Berlin/Washington D.C.: Global Public Policy Institute, 9–36, at 17.

activities, projects and actions that are agreed upon by governments, intergovernmental organizations and corporate actors with the aim of furthering sustainable development through the implementation of the objectives set out in Type I documents.[36]

Further to the adoption at the intergovernmental level of the 'guiding principles' for the establishment of such partnerships,[37] more than 300 partnerships have been registered with the Commission on Sustainable Development.[38] Nonetheless, the linkage between Type-I and Type-II outcomes appears to be weak. One should not lose sight of the fact that the latter have been agreed upon on the side of, and independently from, the mainstream negotiations.[39] As a consequence, they are not always in line with the targets set out at the intergovernmental level under Type I documents. Furthermore, the 'guiding principles' for partnerships are vague and their official registration has no clear legal relevance, while mechanisms enhancing their accountability through review are poor.[40]

Partnerships may well be a new factor in environmental global governance,[41] where NGOs partner public and business sectors in implementing sustainable development goals. However, while the effectiveness of such formulas has been subject to differing views, their relevance on the status of NGOs in international environmental law is also controversial. Despite the commendable complementary function of partnerships vis-à-vis governmental action, one has the impression that the emphasis placed on Type II outcomes at the WSSD is due to the substantive weakness of Type I outcomes, as well

---

[36]   On this distinction, see Ivanova, *supra* note 35, at 14–17. See also J. Gupta (2003), 'The role of non-state actors in international environmental affairs', *Zeitschrift für ausländisches öffentliches Recht und Völkerrecht*, **63**(2), 459–46.

[37]   The 'guiding principles for partnerships for sustainable development' were initially agreed upon at the Fourth Session of the PrepCom in Bali (Indonesia) (available at http://www.un.org/esa/sustdev/partnerships/bali_guiding_principles.htm, accessed 15 January 2006). Subsequently, the Commission on Sustainable Development, at its 11th session, developed a new set of principles for partnerships, see doc. E/CN.17/2003/6, at 9–10 (also available at http://www.un.org/esa/sustdev/ partnerships/csd11_partnerships_decision.htm, accessed 15 January 2006).

[38]   See the list at http://webapps01.un.org/dsd/partnerships/public/browse.do (accessed 15 January 2006).

[39]   J. M. Witte, C. Streck, and T. Benner (2003), 'The road from Johannesburg: what future for partnerships in global environmental governance?', in Thorsten Benner, Charlotte Streck and Jan Martin Witte (eds), *Progress or Peril? Networks and Partnerships in Global Environmental Governance. The Post-Johannesburg Agenda*, Berlin/Washington D.C.: Global Public Policy Institute, 59–84, at 70.

[40]   See Beyerlin and Reichard, *supra* note 35, at 228.

[41]   For a thorough discussion on partnerships in this perspective, see Witte, Streck and Benner (2003), *supra* note 39.

as to the scant governmental willingness to commit itself to them, as has been highlighted especially by NGOs.[42] The case has been made that the focus on partnerships is nothing more than the 'greenwashing' of the states' (and corporations') unwillingness to set up an international legal framework in which binding targets are agreed upon and clear mechanisms for ensuring accountability and compliance established.[43] It may seem as if this non-committal attitude by governments has been tentatively made up for by devising some kind of 'privatization' of the actions to be taken with a view to achieving sustainable development, hence using tools, such as partnerships, which escape the international law accountability test.

While the 'abdication' by states of their responsibilities in the field of the international protection of the environment in favour of the private sector may result in a legal framework increasingly governed by private transnational regulation,[44] the role of NGOs in global environmental governance risks being placed increasingly on the side of the rule of international law. However, the inclusion of partnerships among the outcomes of an intergovernmental summit, and their inclusion within a legal and institutional framework, although rudimentary and non-binding, could also be seen as the starting point of a process of 'appropriation' by international law of this special phenomenon of co-operation between states and non-state actors. It has been suggested that possible improvements in the system of partnerships could include the creation of a regulatory framework that may itself include those arrangements within the overall system of global environmental governance, which might eventually provide for generally accepted ground rules for partnerships and mechanisms for their monitoring and evaluation.[45] In the long run, this regulatory framework could well be provided for by international law, through the will of states. This would require (a) linking partnerships to the binding targets set out by MEAs; (b) a general treaty on corporate accountability and rules for partnerships, or a consistent set of soft-law instruments to that effect that may be generally acceptable; (c) developing a special role in this area for inter-

---

[42]   R. Parmentier (2002), 'Type 1 versus Type 2 outcomes: explaining the jargon, exposing the trap', available at http://archive.greenpeace.org/earthsummit/docs/jargon.pdf (accessed 21 January 2006).

[43]   See Gupta (2003), *supra* note 36, at 481.

[44]   Gupta rightly observes that '[i]t is not so much that non-state actors are now equal partners within the process of interstate negotiation on legally binding agreements, but rather the nature of the agreements have changed to allow non-state actors to become partners', ibid., at 483.

[45]   See in that direction Witte, Streck and Benner (2003), *supra* note 39, at 69. The authors, however, make the case that the process of elaboration of such a framework should be truly participatory, involving all stakeholders, in particular the constituencies of partnerships, and that its outcome should take fully into account the

governmental organizations (the UN in particular) as 'managers' of partnerships;[46] and (d) setting up special mechanisms of compliance and accountability review.

Were the scenario just depicted ever to materialize, it would constitute a prominent example in which the international legal order would encompass transnational legal relationships between an array of actors, beyond states, including NGOs. In this case, international law would adjust to the challenges of the developments under way in the international society, enhancing global governance through international public legal consistency, rather than by simply relinquishing its prerogatives.

CONCLUDING REMARKS

From the above analysis, one may draw a few concluding considerations. Firstly, it appears from international practice that the principle of public participation through NGOs in environmental law processes is fairly well established with regard to such processes taking place at the domestic level. The regulatory standards set out in the Aarhus Convention are most exemplary of that – all the more so, in view of the fact that, despite its adoption within the UNECE Pan-european framework, this Convention is open to non-UNECE members.

Secondly, the above research shows that the principle of public participation in environmental matters is significantly weaker with regard to the international level. This conclusion is drawn from the very general character of the few authoritative statements in that area and from the highly informal and case-by-case approach followed in the various international environmental forums. This seems inherent precisely in the scattered setting of the international environmental institutional scenario, in which both states and NGOs seem to have, for opposite reasons, a strong interest in avoiding the formalization of a regulatory framework for public participation in international forums generally applicable. On the one hand, states are wary about binding themselves for the future to afford certain rights of public participation which they may have found acceptable within the context of a given MEA, but might

---

need to preserve flexibility of partnerships (ibid., at 74). To that end, the need has been stressed (Ivanova (2003), *supra* note 35, at 19–20) to tie the outcomes of partnerships into the intergovernmental environmental agenda, clarifying the future role of states and intergovernmental organizations in promoting sustainable development and environmental governance.

46   On the possible role of IGOs in this area, see Ivanova (2003), *supra* note 35, at 20ff.

not agree to in another one at another time. For their part, NGOs appear not to be keen on freezing at some point in time regulations that may set out in general terms constraints on their participation in international environmental forums that they may overcome in the future on a case-by-case basis.

The recently increased focus on the role of NGOs, particularly from the corporate sector, in the implementation of environmental principles seems to be pointing in the same direction, towards some kind of deregulation of their status under international law, let alone the fact that the whole focus on implementation appears to have occurred as a consequence of the diminished inter-governmental drive towards the making and developing of international environmental standards altogether. This trend is not regarded as irreversible, however; if any change is ever to occur it will depend on the general will of states and the good practice of NGOs, rather than on legal theory.

PART II

NGOs, international courts and compliance
review mechanisms

5. NGOs before international courts and tribunals

Luisa Vierucci

INTRODUCTION

Access to justice may be seen as one of the major components, together with access to information and access to decision making, of the relations between intergovernmental organizations (IGOs) and civil society.[1] This element of the relationship has become increasingly crucial by reason of the proliferation of international courts and tribunals that we have been witnessing in the last 15 years. While international justice was until recently a prerogative of states, with the limited exception of some human rights treaties granting legal status to individuals, the last decade of the twentieth century saw not only the establishment of new international jurisdictions of a universal character (such as the International Tribunal for the Law of the Sea and the International Criminal Court (ICC)), but also tribunals with limited *ratione temporis* jurisdiction (such as the International Criminal Tribunals for the former Yugoslavia (ICTY) and for Rwanda (ICTR)) as well as experimental hybrid courts such as the Special Court for Sierra Leone.

Judicial proliferation coupled with enhanced international public participation calls for a re-assessment of the interrelationship between international judicial bodies and that part of civil society which is represented by NGOs.[2] The chapter starts with a pragmatic approach, namely, enquiring whether NGOs are satisfied with the access to justice they are currently experiencing, and only after such a *démarche* does it elaborate on the desirability eventually

---

[1]   These are the three areas in which the rights of individuals and associations in the environmental field shall be protected according to the Aahrus Convention (Access to Information, Public Participation in Decision-Making and Access to Justice in Environmental Matters, 25 June 1998).

[2]   For the purpose of this chapter, the word NGO will be used in an a non-technical sense so as to indicate private associations which carry out non-lucrative activities at the international level with the aim of defending interests of common concern.

to suggest changes *de lege ferenda* in order to make NGOs' participation in international justice more fruitful for the interests that NGOs purport to represent and defend.

To this end, the chapter will focus on the role of NGOs before international courts and tribunals or quasi-tribunals, in particular within the regional systems of human rights protection, the WTO dispute settlement mechanism and the ICSID system of state/investor dispute settlement. Notwithstanding the significant practice relating to treaty monitoring bodies and non-compliance mechanisms, especially in relation to human rights, several thorough studies are available,[3] and discussion on those bodies will therefore only be marginal.

NGOS IN INTERNATIONAL ADJUDICATION: NOT A UNIFORM PICTURE

The opposition of states towards participation of other actors in international judicial proceedings commenced faltering not only with the right granted in 1950 to individual persons or groups to have recourse to a regional body such as the European Commission on Human Rights, but also with the right of private investors to sue states within the ICSID system since 1965. Needless to say, the possibility that individuals and groups today have a right of action before a few pre-established international courts, such as the European Court of Human Rights (ECHR), constitutes a ground-breaking change in the traditional inter-state system of litigation.[4] Only recently the examples set by the ECHR and the ICSID system have started to produce a domino effect also in non-Western areas of the world (Africa) and new fields of international law regulation (environment and trade).

In this respect, it is remarkable that NGOs appear to be generally convinced that their participation before international courts and tribunals is fruitful.[5] This fruitfulness seems mainly to take two forms. Firstly, the technical expertise

---

3   See, for example, Philip Alston (2005), *Non-State Actors and Human Rights*, Oxford: OUP and Andrew Clapham (2006), *Human Rights Obligations of Non-State Actors*, Oxford: OUP.

4   With the entry into force of Protocol n. 11 to the European Convention on the Protection of Human Rights and Fundamental Freedoms on 1 November 1998, individuals, NGOs or private groups have acquired the right to submit claims directly to the ECHR.

5   This is the view expressed by the majority of NGOs participating in the workshop concerning 'A legal status for NGOs in contemporary international law?', held in November 2002 at the European University Institute (Florence).

which NGOs are able to offer may help the complainants/defendants prepare their briefs, or else may enlighten the international judge on highly specialized issues. Such expertise is more and more crucial with the increasing workload and variety of matters that adjudicators are called upon to address. Secondly, thanks to their subject-matter competence and specific knowledge of the adjudicatory body they are dealing with, NGOs may help developing jurisprudence and, in particular, clarifying the scope and content of individual or collective rights.

By and large, international adjudicatory bodies are well aware of the crucial contribution that NGOs may make to the proceedings and, to a varying degree, tend not to evade the general question of their relations with NGOs.[6]

Against this background of general satisfaction which is expressed by NGOs, on closer scrutiny major differences emerge as to the role (hence contribution) that different types of NGOs are currently able to play in international proceedings. Procedural issues related to the modalities of participation of NGOs in the litigation are the unavoidable departure point of the analysis as they may have an impact not only on the ability of the organization to voice its interests and concerns, but also on the outcome of the case.

Direct v Indirect Participation of NGOs in International Adjudication

For the purposes of this chapter, NGOs' direct participation in proceedings will be examined, namely the question of legal standing. This choice is linked to the fact that the degree of openness of judicial bodies to such a form of NGO participation is one of the clearest indicators of the retreat of a legal order based exclusively on inter-state relations as well as of the advance of an international order where individual values and claims may be firmly defended. As to forms of indirect participation, the focus will be placed exclusively on *amicus curiae* interventions submitted by NGOs. This modality of third party participation, that is most recently developing before international judicial bodies, is susceptible of influencing also legal standing with time.[7]

Direct participation: legal standing
An analysis of the constitutive instruments or internal regulations of international judicial and quasi-judicial bodies shows that almost all of them allow access to entities other than states. However, only five of them, the European

---

6 N. Vajic (2004), 'Some concluding remarks on NGOs and the European Court of Human Rights', in Tullio Treves et al. (eds), *Civil Society, International Courts and Compliance Bodies*, The Hague: T.M.C. Asser Press, p. 104.

7 This thought will be expanded upon in the concluding remarks.

Court of Human Rights, the Inter-American Commission of Human Rights (IAmComHR), the African Commission for Human and Peoples' Rights (AfrComHR)) and the recently established African Court as well as, to some extent, the European Court of Justice (ECJ), can be considered as granting legal standing to NGOs, although to varying degrees.

The ECHR authorizes an application by a 'non-governmental organization or group of individuals' provided that the applicant claims 'to be the victim of a violation by one of the High Contracting Parties of the rights set forth in the Convention or the protocols thereto'.[8] Although the jurisprudence of this court is not lacking in cases submitted by NGOs, there are also examples of NGOs which were refused standing on account of a restrictive interpretation of the victim requirement.[9]

Similarly, the ECJ (and the Court of First Instance) has admitted applications by NGOs also in the absence of explicit standing on condition that they satisfied the extremely stringent test for recourse by individuals.[10] As a consequence the liability of NGOs complaints to rejection is very high, as evidenced in *Stichting Greenpeace Council* v *Commission*, where the NGO was found both by the Court of First Instance and the ECJ not to be 'individually' affected by the decision constituting the cause for action. On this basis the NGO claim, though relating to a public interest action, was dismissed.[11]

It is noticeable that judicial and quasi-judicial bodies outside the European continent appear to be more open towards NGOs direct participation in their proceedings. The IAmComHR, the AfrComHR and the African Court on Human and Peoples' Rights give right of standing to NGOs regardless of proof of direct violation of one of their rights. The IAmComHR is explicitly empowered to act upon petitions concerning alleged violations of a human right contained in the relevant international instruments that are submitted by NGOs 'on their own behalf or on behalf of third persons'.[12] The only condition

---

8   Art. 34 of the 1950 European Convention for the Protection of Human Rights and Fundamental Freedoms as amended by Protocol No. 11.

9   For example, in *Conka* v *Belgium*, 13 March 2001 (decision on admissibility), the FIDH was not recognized legal standing as the applicants could represent themselves.

10   Pursuant to art. 230, par. 4, of the EC treaty, only those individuals who are 'directly and individually concerned' by an act of the institutions may seek EC judicial protection. For the interpretation of those conditions by the Community courts see J. Almqvist, 'The Accessibility of European Integration Courts from an NGO Perspective', in Treves et al. (eds), *supra* note 6, pp. 280ff.

11   *Stichting Greenpeace Council* v *Commission*, Case T-585/93, [1995] ECR II-2205, judgment of the Court of First Instance; and Case C-321/95 (2 April 1998) ECR [1998] I-1651, judgment of the ECJ.

12   Art. 23 of the Rules of Procedure and Evidence.

attached to this right is the recognition of the applicant NGO in one or more member states of the Organization of American States, albeit not necessarily in the respondent State.[13] Moreover, the Rules of Procedure and Evidence of the IAmComHR do not even require that the petition contain the name of the victim.[14]

Also the AfrComHR has broad competence as it may hear communications coming from other than state parties.[15] This provision has been interpreted in practice to give a blanket right to NGOs to submit communications on behalf of the victim without any restriction.[16] It is further to be observed that the newly established African Court of Human Rights has the discretion to 'entitle' NGOs to institute cases directly before it, the only fulfilling conditions being that the NGO be 'relevant' to the case and that it enjoy observer status before the Commission.[17] An NGO may also file requests for advisory opinions with the Court, provided that the former is recognized by the African Union.

However both the IAmComHR and the AfrComHR can only issue reports or defer the case to the respective courts and, although practice shows that in some instances a Commission deferred to the competent court cases which originated in a petition submitted by an NGO,[18] such occurrences are rare and cannot be assimilated to a proper *actio popularis*. An *actio popularis* power, whereby NGOs are entitled to represent the 'public interest' before a judge,

---

[13]   According to art. 44 of the American Convention on Human Rights, 'Any person or group of persons, or any nongovernmental entity legally recognized in one or more member states of the Organization, may lodge petitions with the Commission containing denunciations or complaints of violation of this Convention by a State Party.'

[14]   According to art. 28 (e), the name of the victim shall be provided 'if possible'.

[15]   The 1981 African Charter on Human and Peoples' Rights generically recognizes that the Commission may consider communications 'other than those of States parties' (art. 55).

[16]   Interestingly, no limitations as to the *locus standi* of NGOs are set either in terms of the complainant's citizenship, or of the registration of the NGO in a state member of the African Union, with the consequence that a number of communications have been filed by NGOs which were not based in Africa; Anna-Karin Lindblom (2005), *Non-Governmental Organisations in International Law*, Cambridge: Cambridge University Press, p. 281.

[17]   Cf. Art. 5(3) of the 1998 Protocol to the African Charter on Human and Peoples' Rights on the Establishment of an African Court on Human and Peoples' Rights, which entered into force on 15 January 2004. Yet such standing is subject to the acceptance declaration of such competence by states parties. On this point, see N. Udombana (2000), 'Toward the African Court on Human and Peoples' Rights: better late than never', *Yale Human Rights and Development Law Journal*, pp. 88–9.

[18]   Lindblom, *supra* note 16, p. 277.

can be said to exist today only with respect to the African Court of Human Rights.[19]

With the fast-increasing role that civil society is playing in practically all areas regulated by international law, from treaty making to law enforcement, and the widespread outcry of NGOs' representatives claiming more room for manoeuvre in the international arena, it is remarkable that the degree of NGOs' access to international justice is not subject to opening, especially in those areas, such as the environment, where agreements on dispute settlement solutions have been widely accepted. As has been observed with reference to the environment, 'While the role of MEAs [multilateral environmental agreements] in international environmental disputes has without doubt increased over the last two decades, the opportunities for participation of NGOs and other civil society actors in international decision-making and dispute resolution has not kept pace. The primary avenues of NGOs for legal enforcement are still domestic tribunals and NGOs in international dispute enforcement are still largely relegated to advisory and publicity roles.'[20]

Given that the right to *locus standi* is the form of participation in judicial proceedings par excellence, and on account of the extremely limited number of jurisdictions providing for such a right, the fact that NGOs perceive their participation in international proceedings as being fruitful warrants reflecting about the opportunity to relax the *locus standi* requirements in those courts which do not grant the right to civil society representatives. Moreover, the strict provisions on standing contained in the instruments establishing the European courts, coupled with restrictive interpretation of those rules, are susceptible to restraining the ability of NGOs to assert rights or represent an interest before the international judge.

---

[19]   See *supra* note 17. It is to be noted that the human rights supervisory system elaborated within the Council of Europe allows, in art. 33 of the European Convention on Human Rights, *actio popularis* on the part of member States to the Convention, although such a right has been exercised only seldom. As specified by the ECHR in *Ireland* v *United Kingdom* (1978), 'Unlike international treaties of the classic kind, the Convention comprises more than mere reciprocal engagements between contracting States. It creates, over and above a network of mutual, bilateral undertakings, objective obligations which, in the words of the Preamble, benefit from a "collective enforcement". By virtue of Article 24 [current art. 33], the Convention allows Contracting States to require the observance of those obligations without having to justify an interest deriving, for example, from the fact that a measure they complain of has prejudiced one of their own nationals'; on this point, cf. O. de Schutter, (1996), 'Sur l'émergence de la société civile en droit international: le rôle des associations devant la Cour européenne des droits de l'homme', *European Journal of International Law*, **7**(3), 375.

[20]   D. Currie, 'The experience of Greenpeace International', in Treves et al. (eds), *supra* note 6, p. 151. See also the contribution by C. Pitea, Chapter 6 in this volume.

In this regard it is interesting to record a great variety of opinions concerning the need for NGOs to acquire legal standing before those international jurisdictions – an outstanding percentage – which are currently closed to them. One might think that the position would depend on the specific function/activity carried out by each NGO. Service-delivery NGOs, whose main objective is to ensure the respect for certain rights by taking concrete actions mainly in the field, would presumably be more concerned about their enhanced or formalized participation in international adjudication compared to advocacy NGOs, whose primary function is to sensitize governments and public opinion to the promotion of and respect for treaty rules.

The empirical data indeed tend to indicate that advocacy NGOs, such as Amnesty International (AI), view the question of enhanced participation of NGOs before judicial bodies as fairly marginal.[21] The reason appears to be that these NGOs are able to influence the outcome of judicial bodies, mainly treaty-monitoring bodies, through informal mechanisms, for example by submitting a written document directly to the judge, or speaking directly with a treaty-body member in advance. Given such a state of affairs, it is feared that, by giving NGOs the right to file complaints, this would limit their ability to lobby and paradoxically restrict their margin of manoeuvre. In addition cost-related considerations are inescapable constraints also for big international NGOs such as AI,[22] let alone for Southern NGOs which are not membership-based.

Interestingly, service-providing NGOs (mainly those representing individuals or groups before the ECHR) display conflicting views. On the one hand, the argument is ventilated whereby the possibility for NGOs to submit complaints to international judicial bodies is the most useful tool in the hands of the civil society and should therefore be enhanced. This is because only NGOs are in a position to represent and defend certain public goods, such as the rights of future generations, in which an individual or a state does not necessarily have a vested interest. NGOs are best placed also to represent the collective dimension of some rights, for instance economic or social rights, and therefore capable of defending broad categories of persons in the same litigation.[23] In

---

[21] It is to be stressed, however, that the AI position relates primarily to its experience before treaty-monitoring bodies, especially those linked to the UN, as it does not normally intervene directly before judicial bodies to represent individual cases. AI does arouse international awareness about individual cases and occasionally it gives support to other NGOs in representing individuals before judicial bodies.

[22] See the remarks made by D. Zagorac, 'International courts and compliance bodies: the experience of Amnesty International', in Treves et al. (eds), *supra* note 6, at 38.

[23] This would be a proceeding similar to the 'class action' in the US system.

addition, allowing NGOs to be a party as a matter of procedure enables a more correct use of *amicus curiae* briefs, as the latter type of intervention is often relied upon by NGOs in order to overcome the lack of standing in contentious cases, with the risks of abuse that will be analysed below. As a consequence, according to some service-providing NGOs, it would be desirable to devise mechanisms to enhance the direct participation of NGOs in international proceedings not only by granting standing in a wider number of international jurisdictions but also by eliminating the victim requirement before those courts that currently entertain it.

On the other hand, some service-providing NGOs align themselves with the view of advocacy NGOs, though on totally different grounds. These NGOs claim that an *actio popularis* power entrusted to them, especially to those organizations active within the European human rights enforcement system, would have a dramatic impact upon the workload of regional human rights courts, which is already considerable, and hence negatively affect the individual's right of recourse.[24] Moreover, only individuals with access to vocal NGOs would benefit from this opportunity, thus creating an unfair divide between categories of victims. It should also be emphasized that the perspective of applications submitted by NGOs without the need for the victim requirement to be satisfied would most probably cause a reduction in the number of individual applications, thus threatening the guarantee system established by the European Convention on Human Rights and Fundamental Freedoms.[25]

It seems that most concerns expressed above about enhancing direct participation of NGOs in international adjudication relate to the negative impact that participation may have on the principle of the fair administration of justice or the rights of the parties involved in the dispute. In other terms, some NGOs fear that their increased legal standing before international courts and tribunals would generate more problems than it solves.

However, albeit such concerns are certainly legitimate, as shown for instance by the *Pinochet* case, where the linking of one judge with an NGO led to delays in the proceedings, they do not seem to constitute an insurmountable obstacle, especially for those adjudicative bodies that are by vocation more open to instances coming from non-state actors. Nor does the floodgates argument pose questions which cannot be successfully addressed. In this respect, the reform of the ECHR as drawn up in Protocol 14 introduces

---

24   This would mainly concern delays in the proceedings.

25   Also some scholars agree that an unrestricted *actio popularis* for NGOs contrasts with the personal character of the human rights safeguards included in the European Convention; see e.g. M. Frigessi di Rattalma, 'NGOs' participation before the European Court of Human Rights: beyond *amicus curiae* participation?', in Treves et al. (eds), *supra* note 6, p. 63.

important changes which are aimed at improving the efficiency of the Court faced with an overwhelming increase in the number of complaints lodged.[26]

Another issue, the representation of NGOs acting before international courts and tribunals, is a cause for major concern especially outside NGOs' circles. The question is complex, suffice it here briefly to note that the issue bears tremendous weight with reference to the *locus standi* of NGOs claiming to defend the 'public interest'. Clearly, judicial decisions in public interest cases have a bearing not so much on the rights of the NGO itself but on those of the people (or the international community as a whole) on behalf of whom the organization purports to be acting. Actually the position advanced by authoritative scholars, whereby 'the glory of organizations of civil society is not democratic legitimacy but the ability to be a pressure group' because such organizations 'are by their nature peculiar, and lack the ability to confer general legitimacy'[27] has undisputable merits. However, blindly embracing such an approach seems not to be appropriate when it comes to legal standing. The decision to restrict *locus standi* to those NGOs that have consultative or similar status with an international body, as is the case of the African Court for Human and Peoples' Rights, appears to be addressing this specific concern. In addition other solutions may be explored and successfully adopted (we will come back to this question in the conclusions) to overcome this legitimate concern.

Indirect participation: *amicus curiae* intervention

Amicus curiae (friend of the court) submissions are a form of third-party intervention which consists in the presentation of a technical view of a party not represented before the judge on points of law or fact. This type of intervention in judicial proceedings has rapidly expanded, not only from common law systems, where it originated, to countries with civil law tradition, but also from national to international adjudication fora. Indeed its role is increasing in parallel with the expansion of international litigation.[28] Several judicial

---

[26]   For example, new procedures have been introduced at the level of the Court's Committees and Chambers so that they may issue joint decisions on admissibility and merits of individual cases; see articles 28 and 29 of Protocol No. 14 to the European Convention for Human Rights and Fundamental Freedoms Amending the Control System of the Convention, 13 May 2004.

[27]   Cf. K. Anderson (2000), 'The Ottawa Convention banning landmines: the role of international non-governmental organizations and the idea of international civil society', *European Journal of International Law*, **11**(1), 92.

[28]   The literature on *amici curiae* in international law is abundant. See, in particular, H. Ascensio (2001) 'L'*amicus curiae* devant les juridictions internationales', *Revue Générale de Droit International Public*, **105** (4), 897–929 and C. Chinkin and R. Mackenzie 'Intergovernmental organizations as "friends of the court"', in Laurence

bodies allow for such third-party intervention on the basis either of the constitutive treaty (such as the ECHR),[29] or internal rules (ICTY, ICTR[30] and ICC[31]).

This type of intervention is meant to constitute an impartial aide to the judge in cases of a highly technical nature.[32] Several considerations are as of late pushing even those jurisdictions that are traditionally opposed to non-parties intervention, especially arbitral tribunals, to consider opening their proceedings to the public through various ways, including by accepting *amicus* submissions. In 2003, the NAFTA Free Trade Commission, which is the body competent to issue binding interpretations on the agreement, stated that 'No provision of the North American Free Trade Agreement ('NAFTA') limits a Tribunal's discretion to accept written submissions from a person or entity that is not a disputing party.'[33] Along the same lines, in 2006, the ICSID Arbitration Rules where amended to allow, inter alia, third party interventions

---

Boisson de Chazournes, Cesare Romano and Ruth Mackenzie (eds) (2002), *International Organizations and International Dispute Settlement: Trends and Prospects*, Ardsley, NY: Transnational Publishers, pp. 135–62.

[29]   With the adoption in 1998 of Protocol no. 11 the possibility for *amicus* submission has been included in the European Convention on Human Rights at art. 36(2), but has to be solicited by the President of the Court, who has the discretion to decide whether such intervention is 'in the interest of the proper administration of justice'. It should be noted that, despite the fact that art. 34(2) of the Statute of the International Court of Justice, concerning the faculty of the Court to request and receive 'information relevant to cases before it' by 'public international organizations', could be interpreted so as to grant NGOs the right to submit *amicus* briefs, the International Court of Justice has so far limited such competence to intergovernmental organizations (see P.M. Dupuy, 'Article 34', in Andreas Zimmermann, Christian Tomuschat and Karin Oellers-Frahms (eds) (2006), *The Statute of the International Court of Justice: A Commentary*, Oxford: OUP, p. 548).

[30]   Art. 74 of the Rules of Procedure and Evidence of both the ICTY and ICTR.

[31]   Rule 103 of the Rules of Procedure and Evidence of the ICC.

[32]   There is a danger that friends of the court increasingly shift towards representation of either party interest or a direct legal interest of the intervener itself. Such a degeneration of this type of participation has already taken place in the US: (S. Krislov (1962), 'The *Amicus Curiae* briefs: from friendship to advocacy', *Yale Law Journal*, **72**, 694; E. Angell (1967), 'The *Amicus Curiae* American development of English institutions', *International and Comparative Law Quarterly*, **16**, 1017; M. Lowman (1992), 'The litigating *Amicus Curiae*: when does the party begin after the friends leave?', *American University Law Review*, **41**, 1243, and could be detrimental to proceedings should a similar practice extend to the international level.

[33]   NAFTA, Statement by the Free Trade Commission on the Participation of Non-Disputing Parties, 7 October 2003, http://www.ustr.gov/assets/Trade_Agreements/Regional/NAFTA/asset_upload_file660_6893.pdf (accessed 17 December 2006).

by interested parties.[34] Following the amendments, the authority to accept friends of the court's written submissions rests with the tribunal and not with the parties to the dispute.

It is to be noted that such regulatory developments crystallize, and to some extent advance, the practice that had been followed in the previous years by NAFTA panels concerning non-disputing parties interventions. In a few well known cases, absent an express provision in the constitutive act and rules of procedure, friends of the court had nonetheless been allowed to submit their views on the basis of an extensive interpretation of the treaty. For instance, two NAFTA tribunals in the well known cases *Methanex Corporation* v *United States of America*[35] and *United Parcel Service of America Inc.* v *Government of Canada*,[36] grounded their power to accept *amici* briefs on art. 15, par. 1, of the Arbitration Rules of the UN Commission on International Trade Law, which empowers arbitrators to conduct the proceedings 'in such a manner as they consider appropriate'. In those cases it was not clear what role the parties could play with respect to *amici* written submissions. According to the new rules, the parties have to be 'consulted' on the appropriateness of the briefs' submission, but retain no veto power upon the tribunal decision concerning acceptance of the brief.[37]

The right to participate as *amicus curiae* may be given to individuals, organizations or governments either through oral or written submissions. The main aim and advantages of a similar intervention are very diversified as *amici* may acquire specific features following the context in which they operate. In general terms, the main purpose and also positive aspects of this type of intervention can be summarized as follows. An *amicus* brief reinforces the individual application with external technical support that is more and more needed considering the variety of technical issues upon which the international

---

[34]   ICSID Arbitration Rules (as amended and effective on 10 April 2006), Rule 37. Such amendments will have effect also on NAFTA tribunals by way of art. 41 of the ICSID Additional Facility Rules, as the latter apply to certain classes of proceedings, including dispute between investor and a state brought under Chapter 11, that fall outside the scope of the ICSID Convention. Art. 41 of the ICSID Additional Facility Rules repeats *verbatim* art. 37 of the ICSID Arbitration Rules.

[35]   *Methanex Corporation* v *United States of America*, Decision of the Tribunal on Petitions from Third Persons to Intervene as 'Amici Curiae', 15 January 2001, http://naftaclaims.com/Disputes/USA/ Methanex/MethanexDecisionReAuthorityAmicus.pdf.

[36]   *United Parcel Service of America Inc.* v *Government of Canada*, Decision of the Tribunal on Petitions for Intervention and Participation as Amici Curiae, 17 October 2001, available at http://naftaclaims.com/Disputes/Canada/UPS/ UPSDecisionReParticipationAmiciCuriae.pdf (last visited 18 December 2006).

[37]   However, according to rule 37(2), the parties 'are given an opportunity to present their observations on the non-disputing party submission'.

judge is required to adjudicate. Furthermore, it may put forward unrepresented public interests. It is not rare for either parties, be they states or other entities, to be unwilling to take up issues of general interests before the court, although they may be relevant to the case. Only an impartial third party with an interest in society will then be able to voice those concerns. In addition, *amicus* briefs may contribute to the development of international law by way of jurisprudence.[38] Finally, if duly publicized, an *amicus* brief may contribute to sensitizing public opinion on a specific issue.

An *amicus* submission may therefore give a terrific contribution to the law which is not necessarily confined to the proceeding but may yield effects outside the courtroom. Nevertheless, the shortcomings linked to *amicus* briefs submitted by NGOs will also be underscored. In the case where the *amicus* brief is submitted to support the application of one party to the proceedings or to put forward a public interest, representation issues arise. As has been observed above, questions such as who controls the legitimacy of the organization, and who represents it cannot be easily dismissed. One way of addressing such concerns is that, in the event that an NGO has consultative or similar status with an international body, status ipso facto entitles the organization to present an *amicus* brief before the judicial body of the IGO, because granting status implies the fulfilment of certain requirements, which assures some degree of control over the structure, funding and objectives of the organization.

Some form of control over the legitimacy of the NGO submitting an *amicus* brief before an international judicial body also seems desirable in view of the fact that a defence of 'public interest' might not be the main or only objective pursued through the submission of the brief. Fund raising concerns and opinion sensitizing may constitute the underlying reasons for indirect participation of an NGO before a judicial body. The fact that NGOs' representation issues may have an adverse impact on the ability of those organizations to submit *amicus* briefs is borne out by the unwillingness of some states to accept such a type of contribution in support of their briefs lest that should threaten the objectivity of their legal argument. Some ill-informed campaigns that led to bad publicity for states or international companies, together with the doubt that some NGOs are in fact government supported,[39] or in any case have a hidden agenda, cautioned some states against adopting a liberal approach towards NGOs *amicus* briefs.

---

38   Numerous examples can be given of such contribution, for instance the role played by Interights in the case of *M.C.* v *Bulgaria* before the ECHR, judgment of 4 December 2003, concerning the criminalization of rape in international law. For the acknowledgement of the important contribution made by Amnesty International in a number of ECHR judgments, see Zagorac, *supra* note 22, pp. 21ff.

39   Cf. O. de Frouville, 'Domesticating civil society at the United Nations', present volume, p. 71.

In this respect the recently amended Practice Direction of the International Court of Justice (ICJ) may shed some light. On 30 July 2004, the ICJ formalized the practice thereto followed, whereby in advisory cases a brief or a document submitted by an 'international non-governmental organization' 'is not to be considered as part of the case file', but shall be treated by the parties to the case 'in the same manner as publications in the public domain'. To facilitate consultation of those documents, they will be placed in a 'designated location in the Peace Palace'.[40] The assimilation of written statements or documents presented by NGOs to publications coming from other sources seems a sound way of addressing legitimacy questions while trying to leave open the possibility of non-party submissions. It will be either the already established credibility of the NGO or the correctness and accuracy of the arguments contained in the brief (or both) which will determine the success of the brief, no less than the expertise of an individual or research centre and content will be determinative of the reputation and authority of a publication of scientific value. It is remarkable that no limitations as to the format and timing of the briefs (for example as to the length or the type of contribution) has been set by the ICJ beyond confining the contribution to 'a written statement and/or document'.

The fact that such practice has not been extended also to the contentious jurisdiction of the Court is revealing of the Court's concern for the principle of party autonomy,[41] so that, though it cannot be denied that in the past NGOs have had an influential impact on the very decision of a state to bring a case

---

[40]   Practice Direction XII reads as follows: '1. Where an international non-governmental organization submits a written statement and/or document in an advisory opinion case on its own initiative, such statement and/or document is not to be considered as part of the case file. 2. Such statements and/or documents shall be treated as publications readily available and may accordingly be referred to by States and inter-governmental organizations presenting written and oral statements in the case in the same manner as publications in the public domain. 3. Written statements and/or documents submitted by international non-governmental organizations will be placed in a designated location in the Peace Palace. All States as well as intergovernmental organizations presenting written or oral statements under Article 66 of the Statute will be informed as to the location where statements and/or documents submitted by international non-governmental organizations may be consulted.'

[41]   It has been suggested that the reluctance of the ICJ to entertain *amicus* briefs by NGOs in contentious proceedings mirrors the diffidence of states towards recognizing legal standing of NGOs in inter-state proceedings. See D. Shelton (1994), 'The participation of nongovernmental organizations in international judicial proceedings', *American Journal of International Law*, **88**(4), 626. Such argument is defeated by the very nature of *amicus* participation, which is different from third party (direct) intervention. More convincing is the argument advanced by Christine Chinkin (1993), *Third Parties in International Law*, Oxford: Clarendon Press, p. 250, based on the sacrosanct character of the principle of party autonomy for the ICJ.

before the ICJ and/or the development of the arguments of a case by the Court itself,[42] the type of contribution that still nowadays NGOs may provide to the contentious jurisdiction of the ICJ can be but an indirect one.

Along with representation issues, due process concerns also arise in relation to the presentation of *amicus* briefs by NGOs. In particular, in criminal cases, the question arises of the effect that the *amicus* may have on the outcome of a trial. The choice of arguments to be brought to the attention of the judge, especially when it comes to points of law, may have a significant influence on the judges' determination of the case. In this respect one should not underestimate that the interests defended by the *amicus* might contrast with the defendant's or plaintiff's rights, thus leading to an additional burden placed on the party by a third-party intervention.[43]

Other human rights issues, such as the consequences of the involvement of a judge with an NGO participating as *amicus* would also need to be regulated, though in this case the probability that his or her impartiality would be put at risk is substantially inferior to the case of involvement with an NGO that is participating directly in the proceedings.

The uncontrolled submission of *amicus* briefs is also susceptible to interfering with the rights of the parties in other ways. For example, the submission of unsolicited briefs may limit the right of WTO member states to be present at all the presentations made before the panel as provided for in art. 10(2) of the Dispute Settlement Understanding of the WTO.[44] The way that WTO panels (but the remark might be appropriate also with respect to the human rights courts) dealt with NGOs' submissions also raises evidentiary concerns. Contrary to the parties, the subjects presenting *amicus* briefs do not have to prove the veracity of their statements even when the position they support is clearly detrimental to one of the parties. Although the WTO Appellate Body tried to remedy the situation,[45] the risk remains that the onus of rebuttal falls exclusively on one of the parties, with obvious consequences in terms of equality of arms.

---

[42]   See E. Valencia-Ospina, 'Non-Governmental Organizations and the International Court of Justice', in Treves et al. (eds), *supra* note 6, pp. 227–8. Critically, on this point, see the separate opinion of Judge Guillaume in the Advisory Opinion on the *Legality of the Threat or Use of Nuclear Weapons,* ICJ Reports, 1996, at 287.

[43]   A known example of this is the *Tadic* case which was decided upon by the Appeals Chamber of the ICTY in 1995, *Appeal Chamber's decision of 2 October 1995,* where the judge mentioned an *amicus* brief in support of one party's reasoning.

[44]   This risk has been underlined by B. Stern (2003), 'L'intervention des tiers dans le contentieux de l'OMC', *Revue Générale de Droit International Public,* **107**(2), 290–93.

[45]   Ibid.

IS THERE A NEED FOR A HIGHER DEGREE OF REGULATION?

The question of NGOs' participation in international litigation requires weighing mainly two conflicting interests: on the one side, the need to ensure that those issues that can be put forward or properly dealt with only by NGOs have an avenue for presentation before the international judge; on the other, the necessity to limit the risks that uncontrolled participation of NGOs may constitute for the rights of the parties to the dispute.

The fundamental importance of these conflicting interests and the difficulties inherent in finding a balance between them are arguments in favour of a higher regulation of NGOs' participation in judicial proceedings. Advocating regulation of private participation in international proceedings also conforms to the formalism that is inherent (and necessarily so) in the very nature of international proceedings. Therefore, unlike other areas of NGOs' participation and despite the view of a conspicuous number of NGOs, a more formalized legal status for NGOs' participation, be it direct or indirect, in international adjudication seems unavoidable in order to address the tension between the differing interests at stake.

The problem of the most suitable degree and type of regulation then arises. Clearly such questions are difficult to answer, especially because any solution has to be tailor-made to the type of jurisdiction and modality of intervention. For instance, given the binding nature of the contentious jurisdiction, participation in it needs to be more strictly regulated compared to participation in advisory matters. By the same token, NGOs' participation as *amicus curiae* raises concerns for the safeguards of parties' rights which do not arise in the case of direct intervention. The crucial question then becomes whether informal or formal regulation is best suited to address the above-mentioned concerns.

The Case for Informal Regulation

Informal regulation usually takes the form of self-regulation carried out by NGOs themselves.

NGOs' self-regulation appears to be a developing tool. In particular, voluntary codes of conduct are being increasingly resorted to by NGOs in disparate fields in order to provide standards of behaviour for action. Although no such codes appear to be specifically drafted to guide the behaviour of NGOs acting before international tribunals, most of the principles that they enounce certainly are applicable also to the judicial aspects of NGOs' activity.[46]

---

[46] Principles such as those of transparency towards the members and donors or independence from governments are undoubtedly relevant also for the participation of NGOs in international judicial proceedings.

Nevertheless a code which is specifically designed to address the issues that arise from participation in international proceedings, for example a clear indication that the rights of the parties shall not be affected by the NGO intervention, would be desirable as it would offer unambiguous evidence of NGOs' awareness of the specific problems related to their participation before international tribunals as well as their willingness to defend the public interest rather than a direct one.

Despite their non-binding legal nature, codes of conduct may constitute a useful tool for informal regulation, especially when they are adhered to by a significant number of organizations, because they represent a self-restraint exercise with high moral authority on the part of NGOs. However, in some instances those codes could take on legal effects. For example, the enjoyment of certain rights could be made subject to adherence to a specific code. An IGO may decide that the NGOs enjoying consultative or observer status[47], or aspiring to do so, shall agree to respect a specific code of conduct. A similar type of informal regulation already exists at the national level: in Australia, adherence to the Code of Conduct of the Australian Council for Overseas Aid is a requirement for any NGO seeking funding from the Australian Agency for International Development, a government body that allocates overseas aid.[48] Similarly, an international tribunal may decide that acceptance of a certain code is an element in favour of granting leave to participate before it. The advantage of this solution consists in the ability to accommodate the interests of both NGOs and tribunals: NGOs are able to rely on a self-regulation mechanism which may preserve the multiform nature of the non-governmental planet, while at the same time favouring the identification of standards of behaviour applicable to a number of organizations, whereas tribunals may benefit from a screening mechanism that is carried out outside the courtroom, thus limiting floodgates and dealing with a better known actor. Moreover, different types of tribunals might count on different codes of conduct, so that different codes of conduct might be considered as pertinent in view of the type of participation that is sought by the NGO.

So far codes of conduct have been drawn up by the same subjects to which they were to apply, namely NGOs themselves (for example, the 1994 Code of Conduct for the International Red Cross and Red Crescent Movement and Non-Governmental Organizations in Disaster Relief; and the recently drafted Code of Ethics and Conduct for NGOs of the World Association of Non-Governmental

---

47   See e.g., art. 5(3) of the Protocol establishing the African Court on Human and People's Rights.
48   A. Adair, 'Codes of Conduct, a Necessary Reform', 1 October 1999, http://www.iea.org.uk/record.jsp?type=article&ID=1.

Organisations[49]) and adherence or withdrawal has been voluntary. However it is possible that in the future such codes will be prepared by actors which are external to the non-governmental sector, for example by the states parties to an agreement or by IGOs.[50] Though this sort of 'soft law' instrument started off as a self-regulatory mechanism, with time it might pave the way for the adoption of formal rules.

The Case for Formal Regulation

Formal regulation relating to the modalities of private participation in international proceedings may take two forms: legislative or judicial. The intrinsic value of legislative regulation, which as seen above is rare in the field of NGOs participation in international tribunals,[51] consists in the emanation of rules from an organ that is statutorily competent to perform such a function,[52] so that complaints as to the law-making competence of the emanating body are likely to be kept to the minimum. In addition the constitutive act of the international tribunal or its regulations offer direct answers concerning the possibility and extent of private participation in the proceedings. Lastly, human rights concerns can be specifically addressed in the rules. For example, art. 103(2) of the Rules of Procedure and Evidence of the ICC specifies that both the Prosecutor and the defence shall have the opportunity to respond to *amicus* submissions, thereby offering a chance to the party that may be negatively affected by the submission to voice its concerns.

However, the shortcomings of this type of regulation should not be underestimated. Generally speaking, rules that have been so adopted are difficult to change because the amendments procedure of a treaty usually requires onerous

---

[49]   The Code was drafted in 1994 and is available at http://www.wango.org/ activities/codeofethics/web_ccbook1.pdf. This Code of Conduct has the peculiar feature of being designed to be applicable to the multifaceted variety of existing NGOs.

[50]   At the national level, codes of conduct have been imposed on NGOs, see A. Adair, *supra* note 48, where the author affirms: 'In South Africa legislation was passed in 1998 to facilitate the establishment of non-profit organizations in the post-apartheid era. The legislation provides for a voluntary register of non-profit organizations, and sets out standards of governance, accountability and public access to information. In the United Kingdom the Government has reached agreement with the peak council of national voluntary organizations on a compact "aimed at creating a new approach to partnership between Government and the voluntary and community sector".'

[51]   As has been shown in the first part of the chapter, such rules may be contained in the constitutive charter of the tribunal or its procedural rules.

[52]   Cf. e.g. the remarks of Uruguay, Zimbabwe and Singapore, whereby only the WTO General Council is statutorily empowered to adopt decisions on relations with WTO, WT/GC/M/60, 23 January 2001, respectively at paras 6, 57 and 61 (www.wto.org).

majorities which are not easily attainable. Furthermore, the heteronomous origin of such rules increases dangers that the NGOs interests are not duly safeguarded.

For these reasons, the field under examination is more frequently regulated by the judicial authority than by rules of positive law. Judicial regulation may take a variety of forms, such as providing an extensive interpretation of a rule aimed at filling a gap left in a tribunal's statute, or drafting rules giving more precise content to a statute's provisions. For example, the judges of the ECHR have amended the Rules of Procedure of the Court so as to specify the conditions upon which NGOs may be allowed to take part in the proceedings.[53] By doing this the judges were bound to stick to the general framework for friends of the court submissions designed in the Convention.[54]

As opposed to legislative regulation, the rules laid down by judges have the peculiarity of being valid, not necessarily in each future case, but may limit their effects on the case which is under adjudication. The first hypothesis is typical of the judicial law-making activity which is carried out in the ad hoc international criminal tribunals and the ECHR, while the second is well illustrated by the 2001 Additional Procedure adopted by the WTO Appellate Body for the purposes of the pending appeal only. In the *Asbestos* case the Appellate Body laid down the conditions for the admissibility of unsolicited *amici* briefs and for filing the document once leave had been granted.[55]

The clear advantage of flexibility that judicial regulation affords when its

---

[53]   Pursuant to Art. 44 of the Rules, requests for leave of 'any person concerned who is not the applicant' to 'submit written comments or, in exceptional cases, to take part in a hearing', must be 'duly reasoned and submitted in writing in one of the official languages' not later than twelve weeks after notice of the application has been given to the respondent contracting party. The provision confirms the wide discretionary power of the President by allowing him to set 'any [other] conditions, including time limits', and even deciding 'not to include the comments in the case file or to limit participation in the hearing to the extent that he or she considers appropriate'.

[54]   Such a form of regulation is closer to the legislative rather than the judicial one because, though the performing subject is the judge, he has been delegated such power by a competent body. This is the more so in those cases where the judge has to create new law because of the statute's silence. A case in point is the rule on the participation of NGOs as *amici curiae* which the judges introduced in the rules of procedure and evidence (art. 74 both ICTY and ICTR), despite lack of indication as to friends of the court intervention in the tribunal's statute.

[55]   *European Communities – Measures Affecting Asbestos and Asbestos-Containing Products,* Communication of the Appellate Body, WR/DS/135/9, 8 November 2000. The Appellate Body specified that the legal basis for the Additional Procedure was rule 16(1) of the Working Procedures for Appellate Review, and not Art. 17, par. 9, of the Understanding on Rules and Procedures Governing the Settlement of Disputes, in order to limit the application of the procedure to the case in question.

effects are limited to the case *sub iudice* (which could probably be considered as an instance of informal regulation), is to be contrasted with criticism with respect to the faculty of the judge to perform law-making functions. Without entering into the debate of what the limits of the adjudicatory function are, it is clear that the boundaries between judicial interpretation and regulatory activity on the part of the judge are not easy to define in practice. Especially when courts adopt a teleological approach, the degree of regulation that may be brought about by such exercise is difficult to assess. This suggests that a certain amount of creativity is inherently embedded in the judicial function.[56]

It should be noted that those who conceive of the judicial function as strict application of black-letter law have to accept judicial *non liquet* for all situations which are not specifically regulated in the relevant legal instruments. The potential prejudice for the interests of justice that such a consequence entails appears to be at least as worrisome as the risks of having judges stating what the law is in legally ambiguous situations.

Judicial regulation in the field of third party participation may take place through extensive interpretation of the founding statute. A case in point is the *Shrimp/Turtles* litigation where the WTO Appellate Body affirmed that the 'discretionary authority' enjoyed by the panel to 'seek information and technical advice from any individual or body which it deems appropriate' or from 'any relevant source' pursuant to the Dispute Settlement Understanding (DSU), includes 'the authority to *accept or reject* any information or advice which it may have sought and received, or to *make some other appropriate disposition* thereof' (emphasis in the original).[57] The Appellate Body

---

56   P.M. Dupuy (2000) 'Cours Générale de Droit International Public', *Recueil des cours de l'Academie de droit international de La Haie*, The Hague, p. 297.

57   *United States – Import Prohibition of Certain Shrimp and Shrimp Products*, report of the Appellate Body, WT/DS58/AB/R, adopted by the Dispute Settlement Body on 6 November 1998, paras 104 and 107. This is the first case in which a WTO panel has accepted an unsolicited *amicus* brief (although on condition that it formed part of a party's submission). Later the Appellate Body applied such interpretation of the DSU to its Working Procedures for Appellate Review, which do not contain any provision to consider information other than that presented by the parties; *United States – Imposition of Countervailing Duties on Certain Hot-Rolled Lead and Bismuth Carbon Steel Products Originating in the United Kingdom*, WT/DS138/AB/R, 10 May 2000, para. 42, where the Appellate Body held that '[W]e are of the opinion that we have the legal authority under the DSU to accept and consider *amicus curiae* briefs in an appeal in which we find it pertinent and useful to do so'. Finally, in *European Communities – Measures Affecting Asbestos and Asbestos-Containing Products*, WT/DS135/AB/R, 12 March 2001 (*Asbestos* case), the Appellate Body laid down a set of rules, valid for the purposes of that appeal only, establishing the criteria that 'written communications' submitted by persons other than the parties or third parties should meet in order to be accepted by the Body; cf. Communication of the Appellate Body, *supra* note 55.

explained that 'against this context of broad authority vested in panels by the DSU, and given the object and purpose of the panel's mandate as revealed in art. 11, we do not believe' that a literal interpretation should apply, as it would be 'unnecessary, formal and technical in nature'.[58]

Though stretched to the limit, this approach can be viewed as anchored in the founding treaty. More daring is the position advocating for leave to file *amicus* submissions lacking *any* reference to judicial authority relating to third party intervention in the tribunal's constitutive statute. A similar position had been endorsed in early 2005 by a group of NGOs asking for leave to participate, in various forms, in a pending case which opposed a French company, Aguas Argentinas S.A., to Argentina before an ICSID arbitral tribunal.[59] One of their arguments relied on the general trend towards openness to the public followed by other tribunals and organizations by virtue of the 'public component involved in certain commercial disputes'.[60] The position is substantiated by a review not only of the recent practice of arbitral tribunals that allows for increasing transparency and external participation, but also through reference to the practice of the WTO, the ICJ the ECJ and regional human rights protection mechanisms in order to point out that the trend toward openness 'reflects the democratic values of an international order where fundamental human rights may be exercised'.[61] This argument recalls the debate over the binding force of the interim measures of the ICJ which arose in the *LaGrand* case (*Germany* v *United States*). There the openness of other international judicial bodies towards expressly declaring the binding nature of the measures was successfully advocated by the applicant. The interest of this argument lies in the emergence of a common international procedure for *amici curiae*[62] that may have far-reaching implications if it paves the way to the determination of the leave to file *amicus* briefs as a matter of customary law.[63]

---

[58]   WTO Appellate Body report in *Shrimp/Turtles*, *supra* note 57, para. 107.

[59]   International Centre for Settlement of Investment Disputes, *Aguas Argentinas, S.A., Suez, Sociedad General de Aguas de Barcelona, S.A., and Vivendi Universal, S.A. And the Republic of Argentina*, Case no. ARG/03/19, Petition for Transparency and Participation as Amicus Curiae submitted by a group of six NGOs on 27 January 2005. The document is available at http://www.ciel.org.

[60]   Ibid., p. 15.

[61]   Ibid., p. 19.

[62]   Cf. R. Mackenzie, 'The *Amicus Curiae* in International Courts: towards common procedural approaches?', in Treves et al. (eds), *supra* note 6, pp. 295ff.

[63]   It is too early to affirm that such a customary rule is in formation, but certainly some elements of practice start to emerge. In the case at issue, *Aguas Argentinas, S.A., Suez, Sociedad General de Aguas de Barcelona, S.A., and Vivendi Universal, S.A. and the Argentine Republic*, Order in Response to a Petition for Transparency and Participation as Amicus Curiae, 19 May 2005, the tribunal has decided that its power

It is submitted that judicial regulation offers high guarantees also in terms of respect for the rights of the parties. The judge's role is indeed to be the guarantor of the respect for the rights and duties of the parties as spelt out in the applicable law, and he or she does so exactly by evaluating rights and duties of all parties in each specific case. Such flexibility, which by necessity entails some degree of judicial discretion, in our opinion is the main advantage offered by this type of regulation. Maybe it is on account of such considerations that recent judicial regulation concerning *amici* participation before courts has prompted no reaction.[64]

Clearly, legislative regulation may be induced by the judiciary, as is often the case for the European Court of Justice and the European Community/Union treaties. A legislative process based on the relevant judicial experience is possibly the best instrument available. On the one hand, a legislative regulation based on the experience of the judiciary has the advantage of being carried out by the organ which is formally entrusted with the task of laying down rules; on the other, such a type of regulation does not neglect the concrete necessities evidenced by the experience of the adjudicative organs. A similar modality of regulation seems also to have been pursued by ICSID and is currently ongoing within the WTO, which is in the process of revising some provisions of the Dispute Settlement Agreement also on account of the case-law developed by the panels and the Appellate Body.

CONCLUSIONS: TOWARDS CONDITIONAL PARTICIPATION OF NGOS IN INTERNATIONAL ADJUDICATION

The whole debate on the need to enhance the participation of NGOs in international judicial or quasi-judicial proceedings as well as the question concerning

---

to accept *amicus* submissions was founded in art. 44 of the ICSID Convention, but added that in the present case it 'finds further support for the admission of *amicus* submissions in international arbitral proceedings in the practices of NAFTA, the Iran–United States Claims Tribunal, and the World Trade Organization', para. 15. It made reference to the practice of those tribunals also with respect to the specific conditions for the admission of *amicus* briefs (paras 22 and 25). The same position was reiterated in *Aguas Provinciales de Santa Fe S.A., Suez, Sociedad General de Aguas de Barcelona, S.A., InterAguas Servicios Integrales del Agua S.A. and the Argentine Republic*, Order in Response to a Petition for Participation as *Amicus Curiae*, 17 March 2006, paras 15, 21 and 24.

64   It is remarkable that the 2003 amendment to art. 44 of the Rules of the ECHR carried out by judges led to no reaction on the part of the contracting states of the Convention.

the degree and type of suitable regulation provide evidence of the underpinning ideological positions. At one extreme of the spectrum of possible positions lay value-oriented views whereby participation of NGOs should be enhanced and left without strict regulation. The position held by Joseph Weiler, though only with respect to *amicus curiae* participation, may constitute an example of such an approach. He affirms:

> [. . .] for lawyers, and particularly judges one of whose primary tasks is to preserve and guarantee the integrity of a legal process, the notion of excluding voices affected by one's decision and not hearing arguments by them runs counter not only to the ethic of open and public process but to the very principles of natural justice [. . .]. To reject, imperiously, with no explanation, applications to submit *amici* briefs is indeed a privilege of emperors, not of courts. The legitimacy of courts rests in grand part on their capacity to listen to the parties, to deliberate impartially favouring neither the powerful nor the meek, to have the courage to decide and then, crucially, to motivate and explain the decisions.[65]

Because of the nature of the values it defends, such a position appears to have been first adopted in human rights litigation but it is also expanding in other sectors, such as international trade.

At the other extreme of the spectrum one finds the view that conceives of the right of private participation in dispute settlement only so long as such right has been the object of precise regulation by the body which is statutorily competent to do so. The 'contractarian' vision of international law that has been propounded in relation to the WTO dispute settlement mechanism may be taken as an example of such a position. According to this position, which is based on a utilitarian view of the need to grant right of action to non-state entities, private participation in trade litigation would contribute to strengthening the enforcement of international trade rules,[66] but such participation has to be the object of a specific agreement between the WTO and contracting parties.

In the light of the above, one may wonder whether a middle-spectrum position may be identified. For example, it seems reasonable to suggest a form of NGOs' participation in international adjudication whose degree of formalization varies according to (i) the degree of intrusiveness of the participation; and (ii) the type of jurisdiction. In other words, forms of conditional participation

---

65   J. Weiler (2001), 'The rule of lawyers and the ethos of diplomats: reflections on the internal and external legitimacy of WTO dispute settlement', *Journal of World Trade*, **35**(2) 204.

66   J. Trachtman and P. Moremen (2003), 'Costs and benefits of private participation in WTO dispute settlement: whose right is it anyway?', *Harvard International Law Journal*, **44**(1), 230ff. Cf. also S. Ohlhoff and H. Schloemann (2001), 'Transcending the nation-state? Private parties and the enforcement of international trade law', *Max Planck Yearbook of United Nations Law*, **5**, 675.

may be suggested *de lege ferenda* with the aim of attempting to fill the gaps left open by the positions at the two poles.

Although it is not the purpose of this chapter to devise a new regime for NGOs' participation in international judicial proceedings, given the variety of judicial fora available, some ideas may be brought to the fore with a view to try and address two of the major concerns raised by the above-depicted direct and indirect forms of participation of NGOs before international courts and tribunals: representation issues as well as concerns related to the rights of the parties to the dispute.

Representation Issues

Practice shows that international courts and tribunals have been trying to address representation concerns since the very early days of NGOs' involvement in international adjudication. The solutions adopted by each adjudicative body ranges from reliance on the already established reputation of a certain NGO[67] to adoption of practice followed in the IGOs/NGOs relationship.[68] While the first solution necessarily involves a high degree of judicial discretion, the second technique relies on the selection criteria that are elaborated by the member states of the organization.

Both these types of procedural requirements are devised *outside* the NGOs' circle. However, as anticipated above, also a regulation which takes place *inside* the NGO field itself may successfully address representation concerns. Self-regulation taking place in the form of codes of conduct embracing specific types of NGOs has been analysed above as a case in point.

In an attempt to find a connecting point between external and internal regulation of NGOs' participation in international proceedings, a useful tool is the specification of the nature of the interest which the NGO represents. While showing impairment of a right accruing to the organization would exclude too broad a category of participants in the adjudication proceedings and not necessarily allow for the public interest to be protected, NGOs must clearly state what their interest is in the proceeding. This may be a public interest,[69] or an

---

[67]   This practice is already followed by the ECHR with respect to friends of the court submissions; Lindblom, *supra* note 16, p. 345.

[68]   For example, the African Court for Human Rights makes the *locus standi* of an NGO dependent on the consultative status acquired by the organization within the African Union.

[69]   As seen above, the indisputable existence of a public interest in the arbitration (citizens' access to drinking water), led the Tribunal in *Methanex* to open to *amicus* participation; *Methanex Corporation* v *United States of America*, Decision of the Tribunal, *supra* note 35, para. 49.

interest of a different character, but in any case its nature should be clearly stated by the organization, either when filing an application to an international tribunal or in an *amicus* submission. The affirmation of the nature of the interest is a crucial factor as it provides the adjudicators with an important value element susceptible of guiding their determination to accept or refuse the NGO application or *amicus* submission.

After addressing procedural devices which may help counterbalancing representation concerns, one is led to wonder whether focusing on substantive issues would not yield more satisfactory outcomes than the strictly procedural approach. In other words, a shift from procedure to substance may be conducive to solutions which may help accommodating the parties' conflicting interests. The shift in the substance of the argument brought forward by an NGO implies that the legitimacy of the organization is not determinative of its legal standing so long as its arguments are solid.[70] It is the content of the argument that is primarily evaluated rather than strict procedural requirements.

The application of this perspective is probably not problematic in *amicus* submissions, where participation is already evaluated in light of the concrete contribution it may bring to the proceedings.[71] An illustration of such an exercise is the *Methanex* case which was adjudicated upon by a Chapter 11 NAFTA Tribunal. On 15 January 2001, the Tribunal decided to accept *amicus* submissions, despite the disputable legal basis for such a power in the founding treaty, because the 'undoubtedly public interest'[72] of the case under arbitration raised 'substantive issues [which] extend far beyond those raised by usual transnational arbitration between commercial parties. This is not merely because one of the Disputing Parties is a State [. . .]. The public interest in this arbitration arises from its subject-matter'.[73] Also the new ICJ practice direction XII,[74] allowing NGOs to submit to the Registrar written briefs that may be freely consulted both by the parties and the judges seems to indicate that it is the soundness of the legal reasoning that is privileged rather than formal procedural requirements.

In this perspective, less stringent conditions ought to apply to *amicus*

---

[70]   J. Dunoff, (1998), 'The misguided debate over NGO participation in the WTO', *Journal of International Economic Law*, **1**, 439.

[71]   In this sense also R. Baratta (2002), 'La legittimazione dell'*amicus curiae* dinanzi agli organi giudiziali della Organizzazione mondiale del commercio', *Rivista di diritto internazionale*, **85**(3), 565.

[72]   *Methanex Corporation* v *United States of America*, *supra* note 35, para. 49.

[73]   Ibid.

[74]   Cf. *supra*.

submissions than is currently the case. For example, the recent practice towards reversing the burden of proof that is followed by some tribunals,[75] whereby it is the judge's duty to explain satisfactorily the reasons for rejecting *amicus* briefs rather than for the NGO to show why the brief should be accepted by the court,[76] deserves support and development. Therefore, it is suggested that *amicus* submissions be allowed also in the silence of the tribunal's constitutive act to the extent that it is in the interest of justice, and in particular whenever there are no other ways for the public interest to be articulated and judicially protected.

The application of this approach to *locus standi* is more problematic in view of the principle of the certainty of the law, but the fruits it bears may outweigh the disadvantages, as some practice already shows. For instance, in the *Chernobyl* case adjudicated in 1990 by the ECJ,[77] the Court privileged 'the substantive issue of promoting institutional balance' rather than the application of the formal requirements of art. 230 of the EC Treaty.[78]

Last but not least, conditional openness to *amicus curiae* briefs submitted by NGOs may constitute a way for the judge, and eventually for those drafting rules, to start to know the real nature of the NGOs they are most frequently confronted with. Although this process is inherently infinite, meaning that new NGOs will always be created and old ones transform themselves – circumstances which render it impossible to have a pre-determined and fixed view on each single NGO – *amici* submissions represent a valuable opportunity to get a better insight into the NGOs' environment. This may ultimately lead to knowledgeable regulation not only in respect to access to the court on the part of NGOs acting as true *amici*, but also with regard to NGOs' direct participation to the proceedings. In other words, (formal or informal) rules relating to *amici* submissions that are in the process of being devised by each tribunal according to its features and needs, as well as ensuing practice, might provide information and suggestions for how to best deal with NGOs' direct participation in international proceedings.

---

[75] According to P. De Cesari, 'NGOs and the activities of the ad hoc criminal tribunals for Former Yugoslavia and Rwanda', in Treves et al. (eds), *supra* note 6, this already happens in the ICTY and ICTR, p. 118.

[76] In our opinion an NGO should still indicate its interest in the proceedings.

[77] *European Parliament v Council (Chernobyl)*, Case C-70/88 [1990] ECR I-2041. In that case the Court considered the Parliament as a privileged applicant as the latter had brought an action to protect its own interests.

[78] A. Cygan, (2003), 'Protecting the interests of civil society in community decision-making – the Limits of Article 230 EC', *International and Comparative Law Quarterly*, **52**(4), 1002.

Concerns Relating to the Safeguards of the Rights of the Parties

As shown above, concerns relating to the detriment that NGOs' participation in international proceedings may bring to the rights of the parties are justified. However, the excessive emphasis that tends to be put on those concerns overlooks the fact that a mechanism which should preside over the respect for the rights of the parties exists – and that is the judge himself (or herself). This principle was rightly affirmed by the WTO Appellate Body with reference to a panel's right to seek information and technical advice from non-parties. The appeal organ subjected the authority of a panel to determining '*the need for information and advice* in a specific case, to ascertain the *acceptability* and *relevancy* of information or advice received, and to decide *what weight to ascribe to that information or advice*',[79] and to respect for the procedures laid down in the Dispute Settlement Understanding.[80]

Furthermore, it is not rare that, also on account of the pressure exercised by judges, rules are amended so as to afford further guarantees of respect for the rights of the parties.[81] Obviously, any solution to issues relating to the rights of the parties has to be tailored to the type of jurisdiction and quite a few jurisdictions, such as the arbitral tribunal established within the ICSID system, are already finding their own solution. In this transition process, it may be useful that, whatever the decision taken in each and every case, the judges motivate their determination in an exhaustive way. The motivation not only provides the succumbing party with arguments that may be raised at a later stage of the proceedings or before another jurisdiction, but also serves the purpose of setting standards which (hopefully) would ultimately lead to the best normative solution for that very jurisdiction. In this respect, it is superfluous to remark that normative regulation is often preceded by uniform judicial practice.

---

79   *Shrimp/Turtle* case (Appellate Body report), par. 104.
80   Ibid., para. 107.
81   This is the case for the ECHR rules, as amended on 7 July 2003, cf. *supra* note 53.

6. The legal status of NGOs in environmental non-compliance procedures: an assessment of law and practice

Cesare Pitea

INTRODUCTION

In recent decades, rules of international law, especially treaty law, concerning the environment have proliferated, but the compliance record with them is still poor. In the framework of multilateral environmental agreements this problem is increasingly addressed through the establishment of routine procedures of control based on periodical self-reporting and review thereto and, in a dramatically growing number of cases, of ad hoc procedures to address the circumstances and causes of a given case of non-compliance, often referred to as non-compliance procedures (hereinafter NCPs).[1] While one may find that the large majority of such procedures are basically modelled on the one set up under the Montreal Protocol,[2] they vary considerably from one another. Any attempt to reduce them to unity would lead to oversimplification, blurring, rather than clarifying, their respective features.

Nonetheless, there are several features that are common to all the procedures in question. Firstly, they are all designed to overcome the well known difficulties inherent in the judicial or arbitral assessment of a breach of the law

---

[1]   On the distinction between routine and ad hoc procedures see T. Marauhn (1996), 'Towards a procedural law of compliance control in international environmental relations', *Zeitschrift für ausländisches öffentliches Recht und Völkerrecht*, **56**(3), 696–731, at 698–9 and M. Ehrmann (2002), 'Procedures of compliance control in international environmental treaties', *Colorado Journal of Environmental Law & Policy*, **13**(2), 377–443, at 435–6. For an analysis of routine procedures, see K. Sachariew (1991), 'Promoting compliance with environmental legal standards: reflections on monitoring and reporting mechanisms', *Yearbook of International Environmental Law*, **2**, 31–52. A list, with full references, of NCPs already operational, or under negotiation, is provided for in the annex to this chapter.

[2]   See the Annex to the present chapter for full references.

within the traditional framework of state responsibility.[3] The alternative ratio-nale common to those procedures is precisely that of aiming to enhance compliance in a non-confrontational fashion, through co-operation within treaty regimes, hence avoiding stigmatization of the wrongdoing states.[4] Secondly, they all provide for the setting up, by the Conference or Meeting of the Parties (COP/MOP), of a dedicated body, normally called the Implementation, or Compliance, Committee, composed either of a restricted number of representatives of the Parties, or of independent experts sitting in their personal capacity. Thirdly, the characteristic function of such Committees is to consider individual cases of non-compliance by Parties, while in some cases they are also vested with the general task of monitoring compliance through the review of state reports. Generally, individual cases of non-compli-ance by Parties are brought to the attention of the Committee by a state Party – either the non-complying state itself or another Party – or by the Secretariat, often upon consideration of state reports on implementation. Usually, the Committee proceeds in consultation with the Party concerned (that is, the Party whose non-compliance is at issue) with a view to identifying the causes of non-compliance, as well as possible action to facilitate compliance. The Committee's task is normally to report to the COP/MOP, which retains the power to take action upon recommendation by the Committee. Direct action towards the Party concerned is rarely envisaged and, in those cases, severely limited. Finally, one may note that, generally, measures taken under the proce-dures in point have a facilitative nature. Exceptionally, in serious cases more incisive measures may be envisaged.

This chapter will focus on the legal status of NGOs in non-compliance mechanisms set up by MEAs. Firstly, a few policy considerations introduce

---

    3   M. Koskenniemi (1992), 'Breach of treaty or non-compliance? Reflections on the enforcement of the Montreal Protocol', *Yearbook of International Environmental Law*, **3**, 123–62, at 125–8; R. Wolfrum (1999) 'Means of ensuring compliance with and enforcement of international environmental law', *Recueil des cours de l'Academie du droit international*, **272**, 9–154, at 96–100; Ehrmann, *supra* note 1, at 379–86.

    4   These procedures are based on compliance theories developed by Abraham Chayes and Antonia Chayes (1995), *The New Sovereignty. Compliance with International Regulatory Agreements*, Cambridge: MA and London, UK: Harvard University Press. For a different view, see G. Downs, D. Rocke and P. Barsoom, (1996), 'Is the good news about compliance good news about cooperation?', *International Organization*, **50**(3), 379–406. For an overview of recent theories on compliance with international obligations, see J. Brunnée (2006), 'Enforcement mech-anisms in international law and international environmental law', in Ulrich Beyerlin, Peter-Tobias Stoll and Rüdiger Wolfrum (eds), *Ensuring Compliance with Multilateral Environmental Agreements*, Leiden, NL, Boston, MA: Martinus Nijhoff, 1–23.

the subject. Secondly, the issue is addressed of the informal attitude favoured by states, even where in practice a role is recognized for NGOs in the proce-dures in hand. Thirdly, as a case study, the role of NGOs is analysed in the functioning of the non-compliance procedure under the Aarhus Convention. Finally, the chapter considers the far from encouraging indications emerging on the point at issue from the recent Guidelines on public participation in inter-national forums adopted within the follow-up to the Aarhus Convention.

POLICY CONSIDERATIONS ON THE ROLE OF NGOS IN NON-COMPLIANCE PROCEDURES

NGOs may be called to play a role in different phases and aspects of an NCP. First of all, when public attendance in the meetings is permitted, NGOs may help monitoring the workings of the committees they attend, ensuring that their proceedings are fair and equitable. When allowed to participate as observers, they may contribute to steering the committee's work, by making general suggestions on the method of work and its procedure. This role is obviously more incisive when individuals with an NGO background sit as full members.

While NGOs' participation in the mechanisms under consideration may thus play an important role in ensuring fairness in the proceedings, only excep-tionally are NGOs vested with the power to trigger such mechanisms on indi-vidual cases of non-compliance. Such a possibility is generally regarded with hesitation, if not suspicion, by states. Less controversial is the possibility for a committee to use information coming from non-governmental sources, possi-bly taking advantage of NGOs' expertise, in proceedings already initiated otherwise. Objectively, allowing NGOs to bring individual cases to the atten-tion of the committee and to submit related information and technical advice during the procedure would enhance significantly the effectiveness of the mechanisms in point. It would help identifying cases of non-compliance, and the causes thereof, through factual information and scientific and legal assess-ment. Such a contribution could be desirable in view of the fact that NGOs are usually less constrained than states, if at all, by considerations of 'diplomatic appropriateness' in raising often delicate issues of non-compliance with envi-ronmental standards and rules. Regardless of the specific kind of NGOs' participation and notwithstanding the advantages in terms of fairness and effectiveness, it is met with a fundamental objection by states, namely that it could undermine the non-confrontational and co-operative nature of the mech-anism. The practical concern is also felt that, if the procedure may be triggered also by actors other than states, Committees' agenda could become over-loaded, with the consequent increase of the costs of the procedure.

The above concerns underlie the negotiating attitudes that have led to the different formulas set out in different MEAs on the issue in hand, as will be shown in the following sections.

ATTEMPTS TO FORMALIZE THE POSITION OF NGOS

The majority of compliance procedures do not contain explicit provisions on NGOs' participation. The committees are generally composed of a restricted number of state Parties[5] or individuals sitting in their personal capacity that are elected by states Parties,[6] while they do not contain explicit provisions on observer participation. Moreover, relevant meetings are rarely open to the public, so that public scrutiny is possible only through the examination of reports and documents. The trigger mechanism is often in the hands of states, either as self-trigger or party-to-party trigger,[7] while the triggering role by the secretariat of the relevant MEA[8] tends to be limited to compliance issues emerging from national reports.[9] As far as information gathering is concerned, most existing procedures do not explicitly mention NGOs as a source of information.[10]

In a few instances, the role of NGOs in the procedures under consideration is formally recognized, as illustrated below.

(a) Treaty provisions establishing the procedure. Article 15 of the Aarhus Convention and Article 15 of the Protocol on Water and Health provide that '[the arrangements for reviewing compliance] shall allow for appropriate public involvement'. The Aarhus Convention further indicates that these arrangements 'may include the option of considering communications from the public'. According to the definition given by the Aarhus Convention, 'the public' includes individuals, as well as their associations, organizations or

---

5   See Montreal NCP, para. 5; Basel NCP, para. 5; LRTAP NCP, para. 1; Espoo NCP, para. 1.

6   See Kyoto NCP, section II, para. 6; Cartagena NCP, section II, para. 3; Aarhus NCP, para. 1; Draft Water and Health NCP, para. 4.

7   Virtually all compliance procedures provide for these trigger mechanisms. See Montreal NCP, paras 1 and 4; Basel NCP, paras 9(a) and 9(b); Kyoto NCP, section VI, paras 1(a) and 1(b); LRTAP NCP, paras 4(a) and 4(b); Aarhus NCP, paras 15 and 16; Espoo NCP, paras 4(a) and 4(b). In the Basel NCP, however, only directly involved Parties may invoke non-compliance by another Party (para. 9(b)).

8   See LRTAP NCP, para. 5; Aarhus NCP, para. 17.

9   See Montreal NCP, para. 3; Basel NCP, para. 9(c).

10   See Montreal NCP, paras 7(b) and 7(c); LRTAPT NCP, paras 6(a) and 6(c); Aarhus NCP, paras 25(a) and 25(c); Espoo NCP, paras 7(a) and (c) (former 6(a) and 6(c)).

groups.[11] As will be seen in more detail below, the NCPs elaborated under these two UNECE treaties are the most generous among MEAs in formally recognizing a role for the public and NGOs.

(b) Institutional arrangements. Thus far only three MEAs provide for compliance procedures which explicitly recognize a role for NGOs in their institutional mechanism. The Aarhus NCP contains the most far reaching provision on the point at issue, for it grants those NGOs that are entitled to obtain observer status before the MOP the right to put up candidates for election as a Committee's full members.[12] In the first round of elections at the first MOP of the Aarhus Convention in Lucca, two NGO candidates were eventually elected out of eight members.

The Water and Health NCP contains a slightly weaker version of the same provision, since it provides that Parties shall elect members 'from among candidates nominated by the Parties taking into consideration any proposal for candidates made by NGOs qualified or having an interest in the fields to which the Protocol relates'.[13] This notwithstanding, three out of the nine elected members of the newly established Committee actually have an NGO background.

The Aarhus NCP and the Water and Health NCP do not indicate whether NGOs may also participate in Committees' meetings as observers, and this matter has been left to practice, as explained in the following paragraph. In the Alpine NCP, participation as observers is the tool used to involve NGOs in the working of its Verification (that is, compliance) Committee whose composition differs from that of above-mentioned ones, being made up of representatives of every Party to the Convention. In fact, NGOs represented in the main subsidiary body of the COP, the Standing Committee, are allowed to send up to two representatives to the Verification Committee.[14] According to rule 3 of Rules of Procedure of the Standing Committee,[15] international NGOs may be admitted as observers if they pursue in their Statutes the objectives of the Alpine Convention and they give a substantial contribution to the Committee's workings, they are active in the whole Alpine area, they have their seat in the Alpine area and an organizational structure, and if they fulfil a need or cover a field of activity that is not sufficiently represented by other organizations enjoying observer status.

Observers may participate in the discussion before the Verification Committee, without the right to vote, but they are bound to confidentiality.

---

11   See A. Tanzi in Chapter 4 of this volume, *supra* at 135.
12   Aarhus NCP, para. 4.
13   Water and Health NCP, para. 5.
14   See Alpine NCM, section II, para. 1.1.
15   Available on the Alpine Convention website, www.convenzionedellealpi.org.

However, Parties may decide to exclude observers as a sanction for the infringement of confidentiality, or for other reasons, including the need to discuss confidential information.[16] Quite interestingly, the entitlements of participation are so wide that NGOs are not in a position fully to take advantage of them. In fact, they have decided to send only one representative each[17] and, in practice, very few observers have exercised their right to participate.[18]

(c) Trigger mechanisms. The Aarhus NCP has been the first explicitly to vest non-state actors with the power to set in motion a compliance procedure. Section VI of the Aarhus NCP allows any member of the public, that is 'any natural or legal person', including NGOs, to make communications concerning a Party's non-compliance, without a need to show a specific interest in the matter brought to the Committee's attention. The communication system is applicable after the expiry of a one-year transitional period starting from the entry into force of the Convention for the Party concerned, unless the latter has availed itself of the possibility of opting out. It is remarkable that, until now, no Party has made a declaration to this effect,[19] that in any case would preclude the consideration of communication only for the limited period of time of a maximum four years. This provision is complemented by admissibility requirements designed to offer guarantees against an abusive use of the procedure. The Committee cannot consider anonymous, manifestly ill-founded and abusive communications or those incompatible with the provisions of the Convention or of the decision setting up the procedure; moreover, it shall take into account whether available and effective domestic remedies have been exhausted.[20]

After lengthy discussions,[21] it was agreed that the non-compliance procedure of the Protocol on Water and Health should contain provisions on communications from the public in terms identical to those of the Aarhus NCP. The agreement on such a formula was reached on the understanding that the third MOP will review this arrangement in the light of the experience gained by the committee in its first years of practice.[22]

---

[16]   See Alpine NCP, Section II, para. 3.1.5.
[17]   T. Enderlin (2003), 'Alpine Convention: a different compliance mechanism', *Environmental Policy & Law*, **33**(3–4), 155–62, at 157.
[18]   See Relazione della Presidenza del Gruppo di Verifica (Austria) alla IX Conferenza delle Alpi (Alpbach, Austria, 19 November 2006).
[19]   See Report of the Compliance Committee, doc. ECE/MP.PP/2005/13, 11 March 2005, para. 19.
[20]   For a discussion and further references on this point see V. Koester (2005), 'Review of Compliance under the Aarhus Convention: a Rather Unique Compliance Mechanism', *Journal for European Environmental & Planning Law*, **2**(1), 31–44, at 37.
[21]   See C. Pitea (2004), 'UN/ECE Protocol on water and health – towards the entry into force', *Environmental Policy & Law*, **34**(6), 267–72.
[22]   See Water and Health NCP.

Also with respect to non-state actors' trigger, the Alpine NCP follows a different model. Namely, it does not afford the right to set this procedure in motion to the public in general, but only to those NGOs already enjoying observer status.[23] Therefore, this right may be exercised by a limited number of NGOs, basically those that have participated in the Convention negotiations and that, presumably, appear most reliable to state Parties.

Another formula which has been given serious consideration in some negotiations – such as that carried out within the framework of the Water and Health NCP – is the one which would indirectly allow for NGOs' trigger through the Secretariat. This option is currently under consideration in the draft PIC NCP, to the effect that the Secretariat may refer an issue to the Committee 'when it receives submissions from individuals or organizations having reservations about a Party's compliance with its obligations under the Convention'.[24] However, this solution is also met with the fundamental criticism that entrusting secretariats with such a 'quasi-prosecutorial' role may impair the perception of their neutrality vis-à-vis Parties.[25]

(d) Provisions on sources of information. The explicit reference to NGOs as a possible source of information for compliance committees is a rarity. Thus far, the only example to that effect is to be found in the procedure adopted under the Kyoto Protocol.[26] The Water and Health NCP vests the committee with the power to '[c]onsider any relevant information submitted to it' and '[to s]eek the services of experts and advisers, including representatives of NGOs or members of the public, as appropriate'.[27]

On the other hand, the Basel NCP, by stating that 'a Party may also consider and use relevant and appropriate information provided by civil society on compliance difficulties',[28] seems to imply that NGO information may be considered by the committee only when channelled through a state Party. This is confirmed by a provision according to which information from

---

[23]   Alpine NCP, Section II para. 2.3.

[24]   Establishment of a Compliance Procedure, in Report of the Open-ended Ad Hoc Working Group on Non Compliance on the work of its first session, UNEP/FAO/RC/OEWG.1/3, 28 September 2005, Annex, para. 12(c).

[25]   See M. Goote and R. Lefeber, 'Compliance building under the International Treaty on Plant Genetic Resources for Food and Agriculture', FAO Background Study Paper n. 20 (2003), ftp://ext-ftp.fao.org/ag/cgrfa/BSP/bsp20e.pdf, at 11 and H. Adsett, A. Daniel, M. Husain and T. L. McDorman (2004), 'Compliance committees and recent multilateral environmental agreements: the Canadian experience with their negotiation and operation', *Annuaire Canadien de Droit International*, **42**, 91–142, at 109.

[26]   Kyoto NCP, section VIII, para. 4.

[27]   Water and Health NCP, para. 23(c) and 23(d).

[28]   Basel NCP, para. 17.

non-governmental sources can be considered only 'either with the consent of the Party concerned or as directed by the Conference of the Parties'.[29]

IS THE LACK OF FORMAL RECOGNITION OF NGOS AN INSURMOUNTABLE OBSTACLE FOR THEIR INVOLVEMENT IN COMPLIANCE PROCEDURES?

Recognition of a formal role for NGOs in compliance mechanisms would give legal certainty to their rights and powers in such procedures. However, lack of recognition of such a formal status does not necessarily imply denial of any role for NGOs on the matter under consideration. This is corroborated by the practice relating to sources of information. The majority of existing procedures does not list exhaustively the sources of information a committee can rely upon,[30] while providing for the power to seek experts' and advisers' opinions.[31] Similar provisions give the broadest discretion to the compliance bodies as to the sources from which to acquire information.[32] Accordingly, the inadmissibility of direct information from NGOs requires to be based on specific language. This could consist of an exhaustive list of sources not including NGOs or of language along the lines of that used in the Basel NCP.

As to the participation in the institutional mechanism, it should be noted at the outset that, even in the absence of recognition of formal entitlement for NGOs, nothing prevents Parties from nominating for membership in committees

---

[29]   Basel NCP, para. 22(c).
[30]   Basel NCP, para. 22; Kyoto NCP, section VIII, paras 3–6; Cartagena NCP, section V, paras 2–3; Aarhus NCP, para. 25; Espoo NCP, para. 6; LRTAP NCP, para. 6.
[31]   Basel NCP, para. 19(c) (but see *supra* note 28); Kyoto NCP, section VIII, para. 5; Aarhus NCP, para. 25(d); Espoo NCP, para. 7(d) (former 6(e)) .
[32]   See Goote and Lefeber (2003), *supra* note 25, at 15; Ehrmann, *supra* note 2, at 399. In the Espoo NCP the provision allowing the Committee to seek the services of scientific experts and other technical advice as appropriate had been considered by the Committee as a sufficient legal basis to seek non-governmental information; see doc. MP.EIA/WG.1/2003/8 (2003), para. 10, p. 3. This notwithstanding, the phrase 'and consult other relevant sources' has been added at the first review of the procedure (compare Espoo NCP, para. 7(d) with para. 6(e) of Decision II/4, Review of Compliance, Doc. ECE/MP.EIA/4, Annex IV, p. 75). See also the informal document drawn up by the Aarhus Compliance Committee on 'The NGOs and the compliance committee' (hereinafter NGOs and the Aarhus Compliance Committee), para. 2 (www.unece.org/env/pp/compliance.htm, accessed 12 January 2006), in which it is stressed that 'the Committee is not required to make any distinction between information submitted to it by individuals and States and information submitted by NGOs' under para. 25 of the Aarhus NCP'.

individuals from NGOs, or the private sector,[33] as corroborated practice.[34] However, in these cases these persons would sit either in their personal capacity or as government representatives. Strictly speaking, representation of NGOs may take place through the granting of observer status. The rarity of formal regulation on this issue has prompted a diversified and, in some cases, controversial practice.

The Aarhus Committee has taken the lead in opening its meetings to observers, including those from the non-governmental sector. Through the application *mutatis mutandis* of the Rules of Procedure of the MOP,[35] the Committee held that its meetings should normally be open to the public and that this affords to all the participants 'the right to comment, the right to be heard and the right to have comments taken into account by the Committee'.[36] Thus representatives from, inter alia, NGOs are treated as being 'observers'.[37] This attitude of openness towards civil society, and the NGO community in particular, reflects the principles of the Convention, as implemented, inter alia, in the practice of the MOP.[38] However, the equal treatment accorded to attending public and observers is questionable. In accordance with the Aarhus Convention and the Rules of Procedure of the MOP, NGOs should have two different entitlements of participation before the MOP and subsidiary bodies, with different requirements and, arguably, a different status. Participation as observers is open only to representatives of NGOs 'qualified or having an interest in the fields to which the Convention relates' which have informed the Secretariat of its wish to be represented, unless one-third of present Parties objects.[39] Such limitations do not apply when NGOs are entitled to attend open meetings, as members of the general public. In fact, the Rules of Procedure provide that the MOP, and *mutatis mutandis* the Committee, shall be open to members of the public 'unless the MOP, in exceptional circumstances, decides otherwise especially to protect the confidentiality of information pursuant to

---

[33]   That was noted by the Espoo Committee (Doc. MP.EIA/WG.1/2003/8 (2003), para. 14, p. 3).

[34]   Following the proposal of the Committee (see doc. MP.EIA/WG.1/2004/4 (2004), para. 12, p. 3) the Meeting of the Parties agreed to include Poland among the member Parties. Poland appointed Jerzy Jendroska, who is not a government official.

[35]   Doc. MP.PP/C.1/2003/2, para. 11. The Rules of Procedure were adopted at the first MOP, see Decision I/1 on Rules of Procedure, doc. ECE/MP.PP/2/Add.2.

[36]   Doc. MP.PP/C.1/2003/2 para. 16.

[37]   Ibid., para. 15.

[38]   See J. Wates (2005) 'NGOs and the Aarhus Convention', in Tullio Treves et al. (eds), *Civil Society, International Courts and Compliance Bodies*, The Hague: T.M.C. Asser Press, pp. 167–85, at 167ff.

[39]   Art. 10.5 of the Aarhus Convention and Rule 6.2 of the Rules of Procedures.

the Convention'.[40] Thus, there is a clear differentiation in requirements and this should be reflected in the status accorded: observers actively participate in meetings, having the right to be notified of meetings, to take the floor and to submit documents, while attendance by the public should be merely passive.

The Water and Health NCP explicitly provides for the publicity of meetings, while leaving the participation of observers to a decision by the Committee, on a case-by-case basis.[41] Proposals to the effect of recognizing such status of a close number of NGOs have been rejected out of the consideration that this would have afforded non-state actors with greater entitlement than States (Parties and signatories, for instance) and that the presence of 'institutional' observers made little sense in a body composed of independent experts. However, it was also noted that other provisions, such as those on openness of meetings and powers of the Committee to invite and accept the presence of any person deemed useful for the performance of its tasks, constitutes a basis for NGOs or other actors in participate to the Committee's meetings.[42] It will be interesting to see to what extent the practice of the Aarhus NCP, that in many respects has inspired the Water and Health NCP, will be considered as a precedent.

The opposite view on openness of meetings prevails in the Montreal Committee, where confidentiality is the rule and a number of attempts by NGOs to participate have proved unsuccessful.[43] The Basel NCP, although with some room for flexibility, adopts a similar approach in that it provides for the confidentiality of meetings where individual issues of non-compliance are discussed and the party concerned does not agree otherwise.[44] In practice, none of the Committee's meetings so far have been attended by observers. Similarly, the Rules of Procedure of the Kyoto Committee[45] do not address participation by observers and no such instance is reported.

---

[40]   Rule 7 of the Rules of Procedure. This rule adds that '[w]here it is not feasible to accommodate in the meeting room all the members of the public who have requested to attend the meeting, the proceedings of the meeting shall be relayed to those members of the public using audiovisual equipment wherever possible.'

[41]   See the Rules of procedure for the meetings of the Parties to the Protocol on water and health to the 1992 Convention on the protection and use of transboundary watercourses and international lakes, doc. ECE/MP.WH/2/Add.1-EUR/06/5069385/1/Add.1.

[42]   Doc. MP.WAT/AC.4/2005/2, para. 13.

[43]   See D. Victor (1996), 'The early operation and effectiveness of Montreal Protocol's non-compliance procedure', *IIASA Paper ER-96-2*, www.iiasa.ac.at/Publications/Documents/ER-96-002.pdf, at 6 and Ehrmann, *supra* note 1, at 403–4.

[44]   Basel NCP, para. 16.

[45]   Rules of procedure of the Compliance Committee of the Kyoto Protocol in Report of the Conference of the Parties serving as the meeting of the Parties to the Kyoto Protocol on its second session, Addendum, FCCC/KP/CMP/2006/10/Add.1, p. 19.

The issue of observer participation has been a source of debate. The Espoo Committee, having given long consideration to the possibility of admitting observers representing the public,[46] at its 4th Meeting admitted as an observer an NGO already enjoying observer status before the MOP. However, the Committee made clear that this decision was to be taken on an ad hoc and experimental basis. It was also understood that the view expressed by the NGO representative in point would not be reflected as such in the Report and that the NGO representative was bound by confidentiality.[47]

A similar debate is taking place within the Cartagena Committee, whose rules of procedure leave it with the discretion to decide whether to hold public or closed sessions, with a motivated decision on a case-by-case basis.[48] Furthermore, the Committee has considered that, as a general rule, only Parties could attend open sessions, but it left open the possibility of 'inviting' other observers.[49] Again, there seems to be some confusion on the issue, since participation as an observer should be distinguished from participation upon invitation of the Committee, a possibility explicitly provided for by the Committee's Rules of Procedure.[50] However, a degree of uncertainty or disagreement on the issue emerges from the records of the debate, since the Committee itself has underlined that 'participation of Parties and, as appropriate, observers, could provide information, enrich the deliberations and facilitate the resolution of issues being considered by the Committee'.[51] It is not surprising that the Committee has decided that its third meeting 'will be open for interested observers from Parties, other governments, and relevant international organizations, including non-governmental organizations'.[52]

The question whether non-governmental direct referral to a committee of cases of non-compliance is admissible without an express provision to that

---

[46]   The Committee did not feel it necessary to take an immediate decision on the issue of active participation, deciding that '[t]he need for such a provision would be reviewed in the light of experience and a recommendation might be made to the Parties at their fourth meeting', see Doc. MP.EIA/WG.1/2003/8 (2003), at paras 14–15, p. 3.

[47]   See Report of the Fourth Meeting of the Implementation Committee, Doc. MP.EIA/WG.1/2004/3 (2003), para. 3, p. 1.

[48]   See Decision BS-II/1 on Rules of procedure for meetings of the Compliance Committee, doc. UNEP/CBD/BS/COP-MOP/2/15, Annex I, p. 28ff. (hereinafter Rules of Procedure of the Cartagena Committee), Rule 14.1.

[49]   See Report of the Compliance Committee on the Work of its Second Meeting, doc. UNEP/CBD/BS/COP-MOP/3/2, para. 16, p. 3.

[50]   Rules of Procedure of the Cartagena Committee, *supra* note 48, Rule 14.3.

[51]   See Report of the Compliance Committee on the Work of its Second Meeting, doc. UNEP/CBD/BS/COP-MOP/3/2, para. 17, p. 4.

[52]   Doc. UNEP/CBD/BS/CC/3/INF/1.

effect is even more controversial. As already noted in legal literature,[53] nothing prevents NGOs from bringing an issue informally to the attention of a committee, either when a given committee may act *proprio motu*, or through a state Party, or the Secretariat. However, such possibilities are made subject to a number of limitations. Referrals through the Secretariat are feasible only when the power of referral is not confined to cases emerging from governmental reports.[54] In the case of the Kyoto NCP, reliance on information from a non-governmental source seems implicit. That procedure may in fact be triggered by the Secretariat with regard to problems of implementation emerging from reports made by expert review teams, which in their turn may contain information drawn from non-governmental sources.[55] Apart from this precedent, doubts have been generally cast over the appropriateness of vesting secretariats with 'prosecutorial' tasks, also in consideration of the impact that this role may have on the impartial exercise of the secretarial functions.[56]

One may recall the amount of controversy stirred up by the only case in which NGOs have attempted to use the *proprio motu* triggering powers, within the Espoo Committee. After a lengthy discussion, the Committee under that Convention decided that it could not consider a submission made by *Ecopravo-Lviv*, a Ukrainian NGO, on the project of construction of the Bystroe canal from the Danube River. The Committee, notwithstanding para. 5 of the Espoo NCP,[57] has reached the conclusion that 'considering unsolicited information from NGOs and the public relating to specific cases of non-compliance was not within the Committee's existing mandate'.[58] It found that its mandate covers only action to be taken when the proceedings are initiated by a state. This view was not shared by a minority of the Committee's

---

53   See Ehrmann, *supra* note 1, at 397; M. Goote (1999) 'Non-compliance procedures in international environmental law: the middle way between diplomacy and law', *International Law Forum*, **1**(2), 82–9, at 87.

54   See M. Bothe (1997) 'Compliance control beyond diplomacy: the role of non-governmental actors', *Environmental Policy & Law*, **27**(4), 293–7, at 296.

55   Kyoto NCP, Section VII.1. This linkage has been stressed by S. Urbinati (2003), 'Non-compliance procedure under the Kyoto Protocol', *Baltic Yearbook of International Law*, **3**, 229–51, at 239.

56   Goote and Lefeber, *supra* note 25, at 11.

57   This provision on 'Committee's initiative' provides as follows: 'Where the Committee becomes aware of possible non-compliance by a Party with its obligations, it may request the Party concerned to furnish necessary information about the matter. Any reply and information in support shall be provided to the Committee within three months or such longer period as the circumstances of a particular case may require. The Committee shall consider the matter as soon as possible in the light of any reply that the Party may provide.'

58   See doc. MP.EIA/WG.1/2004/3 (2003), at paras 7–10 and doc. MP.EIA/WG.1/2004/4 (2004), at paras 9–12.

members, who believed that the provision in the Espoo NCP on the 'Committee Initiative' allowed the opening of proceedings *proprio motu,* whenever the Committee became aware of a case of non-compliance, regardless of the source of information.[59] This view seems to be correct, for, according to a contextual reading of para. 5, the power of initiative by the Committee has not been made subject to the request by a state.[60] The Committee seems to have realized the weakness of its original stand, which it reversed in a later report by stating 'that its mandate allowed it to take the initiative when it became aware of possible non-compliance'.[61] Upon a request by the MOP,[62] the Committee further discussed the issue and proposed to the Working Group on Environmental Impact Assessment to consider asking the next MOP for the adoption of an amending decision listing sources of information the Committee may rely upon to initiate the procedure *proprio motu.* The list proposed by the Committee included, although in square brackets, 'the public, including non-governmental organizations'.[63] The Working Group considered the matter and finally endorsed the comments made by the EU to the effect that the Decision already provided the Committee with a discretionary power to initiate the procedure on the basis of information from sources other than Parties and that an amendment of the relevant Decision was unnecessary. It suggested rather that the list could be included in the proposed 'operating rules' (that is, rules of procedure), but that it should not 'formulate the possible sources of information too strictly nor to overemphasize certain sources of information'. Thus the text proposed by the EU and endorsed by the Working Group reads: '[t]he sources of information by which the Committee might become aware of a possible non-compliance can be (i) Parties' work under the Convention and (ii) any other source'.[64] The circularity of this debate is thus evident: the absence of a clear indication that the Espoo Committee may initiate *proprio motu* the procedure on the basis of information provided by NGOs led to a denial of NGOs' role, but also prompted a call for clarification through the enactment of formal rules. The political response to this request was to indicate that it was understood that, under the existing rules, NGOs would be

---

59   Doc. MP.EIA/WG.1/2004/4 (2004), para. 7.

60   According to para. 3(a) of the Espoo NCP the Committee may '[c]onsider any submission made in accordance with paragraph 4 below *or any other possible non-compliance by a Party with its obligations that the Committee decides to consider in accordance with paragraph 5*, with a view to securing a constructive solution' (emphasis added).

61   Doc. MP.EIA/WG.1/2005/3 (2005), para. 13, p. 3.

62   See Decision III/2, para. 7.

63   See doc. ECE/MP.EIA/WG.1/2006/4, para. 5ff.

64   See doc. ECE/ MP.EIA/WG.1/2006/2, p. 10(f) and (g)).

entitled to submit such information, but at the same time that it was better not to formalize this understanding through explicit language.

Be that as it may, it is of interest to note that, shortly after the Espoo Committee refused to entertain the case brought forward by the NGO *Ecopravo-Lviv*, the latter submitted the same case to the Aarhus Committee,[65] which upheld it, as reported below. At the same time, Romania initiated three different proceedings in relation to this case. On the one hand, it made a submission to the Espoo Committee[66] and one to the Aarhus Committee;[67] on the other, it requested the establishment of an enquiry commission pursuant to Article 3, para. 7, of the Espoo Convention.[68] While the compliance procedure under the Espoo Convention has been suspended pending the inquiry procedure,[69] the Aarhus Committee, after joining the cases brought by *Ecopravo-Lviv* and Romania, respectively, has found Ukraine in non-compliance with a number of conventional provisions.[70] One may underline that the first two cases of non-compliance of a Party-to-Party nature were initially raised by an NGO.[71]

---

[65]   Communication ACCC/C/2004/03, http://www.unece.org/env/pp/compliance/C2004-03/communication/communication.doc (accessed 15 January 2006).

[66]   The submission has been made in May 2005, see doc. MP.EIA/WG.1/2005/3 (2005), para. 14.

[67]   Submission ACCC/S/2004/01.

[68]   According to this provision a party who considers to be affected by a proposed activity falling within the scope of the Convention and that has not been notified according to art. 3 para. 1, failing agreement with the party of origin on the likelihood of a significant adverse transboundary impact, may request the establishment of an inquiry commission to determine that question. Romania has so requested by a letter of 19 August 2004. More information is available at http://www.unece.org/env/eia/inquiry.htm (accessed 15 January 2006). Interestingly, a mixed EU–international conventions fact-finding mission on the environmental aspects of the project has also been established (see the Report at http://europa.eu.int/comm/environment/enlarg/bystroe_project_en.htm).

[69]   According to para. 15 of the Espoo NCP, '[w]here a matter is being considered under an inquiry procedure under Article 3, paragraph 7, of the Convention, that matter may not be the subject of a submission under this decision'. The Espoo Committee accordingly decided to suspend the consideration of the submission (see doc. MP.EIA/WG.1/2005/3 (2005), para. 14 and doc. MP.EIA/WG.1/2005/4 (2005), paras 18 and 19).

[70]   See doc. ECE/MP.PP/C.1/2005/2/Add.3 (2005) and doc. ECE/MP.PP/2005/13/Add.3 (2005). The recommendations of the Committee have been upheld by the MOP, see doc. ECE/MP.PP/2005/2/Add.8.

[71]   Ecopravo–Lviv has been particularly active at the national and international levels in relation to the Bystroe canal case. More information on the various actions taken in this respect is available on line at http://epl.org.ua/a_cases_Danube_C.htm (accessed 15 January 2006).

THE PRACTICE OF THE AARHUS COMMITTEE: A TESTING GROUND FOR STATES' RELUCTANCE TOWARD FORMAL RECOGNITION OF THE ROLE OF NGOS IN NCPS

As already indicated,[72] there are two main reasons why states tend to limit access by NGOs to compliance committees, especially with a view to avoiding non-state triggering. On the one hand, there is the fear that a political use may be made of the committee and that this may be prejudicial to the non-confrontational and even co-operative rationale of NCPs. On the other, there are the concerns about the prospective increase of workload for committees and the implications deriving from such an increase on the finance and on the effectiveness of their working. One may say that the first years of experience of the Aarhus Committee seem to provide little justification for these concerns.

As to the membership of individuals sponsored by NGOs, or even affiliated with them, the possibility of a conflict of interest was dealt with by the Committee with the result of requiring its members to submit a statement of disclosure of the facts that could prejudice their impartiality with regard to a specific case of non-compliance. It was decided that, when the Committee finds that in any given case reasons for concern about the impartiality of one its members may be well-founded, the member in question 'would be treated throughout the procedure as an observer and would not take part in formal discussions or participate in the preparation or adoption of findings, measures or recommendations with respect to the case in question'.[73] However, the Chair of the Committee, in its presentation on its work to the second MOP, has confirmed the view that 'the fact that some of the members of the Committee were originally nominated by the NGO community never played any role in our proceedings and deliberations'.[74]

Other forms of NGOs' involvement in the Committee's workings have also proved beneficial to it and have proved the reluctance of states unfounded. The participation as observers of NGO representatives has added value to the work of the Committee.[75] This is corroborated by a number of actions and practices adopted, or suggested, by the Committee with a view to

---

[72] See *supra* section 2 of this chapter.
[73] See doc. MP.PP/C.1/2003/2, para. 22; doc. MP.PP/C.1/2004/6, para. 53; and doc. ECE/MP.PP/2005/13, para. 11.
[74] V. Koester, *Report on the work of the Compliance Committee – Speaking Notes*, 27 May 2005, http://www.unece.org/env/pp/compliance/VKspeakingnotes 270505.doc (accessed 15 January 2006), at 4.
[75] Ibid.

enhancing its relationship with the public, including the holding of a special session for dialogue with NGOs and the consultation with national NGOs on its draft findings, measures or recommendations.[76]

Thus far, the Committee has received 17 communications from the public. All but three were filed by NGOs. Among those, only one has been declared inadmissible, and five out of the seven that have been considered in the merits have led to findings of non-compliance.[77] The MOP has endorsed the conclusions and recommendations of the Committee in all the cases it has considered.[78] As underscored by the Committee's Chair, these figures demonstrate that 'the right of the public to file communications has in no way been misused' and that 'almost all communications were well documented and well founded, so the NGO Community did act in a responsible and disciplined manner'.[79] This seems to confirm the view, already expressed elsewhere,[80] that NGOs, in order to attain full participatory rights, are prepared to exercise a great deal of self-restraint in pursuance of the general interest in enhancing compliance with the various agreements. While this may not provide full guarantee for the future, it remains a matter of fact.

Even though it would be inappropriate to say that the Committee has been flooded with communications, the above figures are significant. The Committee has adapted its procedure (or modus operandi, to put it in the terms used by the Committee itself), by designating a rapporteur (curator in the language used by the Committee) for each communication and by increasing the use of electronic means of communication to speed up the process and to allow the Committee's work to continue in the intersessional periods.[81] The MOP, for its part, has partially responded to this issue by deciding that, starting from its third meeting, it will elect an additional member to the Committee.[82] In the long run, those adjustments could, indeed, prove insufficient to meet the

---

[76]   See doc. MP.PP/C.1/2003/4, paras 27 to 32 and the informal document on *NGOs and the Compliance Committee*, http://www.unece.org/env/pp/compliance/ The%20NGOs%20and%20the%20CC.doc (accessed 15 January 2005).

[77]   Detailed information and figures on the state of communications can be found in the Committee's page in the Convention website at http://www.unece.org/env/pp/pubcom.htm (accessed 15 January 2006).

[78]   See Decision II/5a, *Compliance by Kazakhstan*, doc. ECE/MP.PP/2005/2/Add.7; Decision II/5b, *Compliance by Ukraine*, doc. ECE/MP.PP/2005/2/Add.8; Decision II/5c, *Compliance by Turkmenistan*, doc. ECE/MP.PP/2005/2/Add.9.

[79]   See *supra* note 74, at 4.

[80]   See C. Pitea (2005), 'NGOs in non-compliance mechanisms under multilateral environmental agreements: from tolerance to recognition?', in Tullio Treves et al. (eds), *supra* note 38, 205–24, at 221.

[81]   See doc. MP.PP/C.1/2004/4, paras 39–40 and doc. ECE/MP.PP/2005/13, para. 9.

[82]   Decision II/5, doc. ECE/MP.PP/2005/2/Add.6.

amount of work of the Committee, since the number of communications, particularly those from the public, is expected to grow as the knowledge of the Aarhus Convention and its compliance mechanism is spreading more and more into the NGO community.[83]

At the end of the day, while the non-confrontational rationale underlying compliance procedure may be undermined more easily by the unco-operative attitude of state Parties rather than of NGOs,[84] the prospective increase of the workload for the Committee is certainly one element in the states' hesitation about affording NGOs the power to initiate NCP that may find justification.

PROSPECTS FOR NGOS' PARTICIPATION IN COMPLIANCE PROCEDURES ON THE BASIS OF THE LESSONS LEARNT FROM PAST NEGOTIATIONS AND THE ALMATY GUIDELINES

Notwithstanding the positive experience under the Aarhus NCP described above, the states' attitude towards the recognition of a significant role for NGOs in NCPs remains predominantly negative. This applies not only to developing countries, whose traditional opposition to NGOs is founded on their perceived reliance on 'Western' values by NGOs, but also to states of a liberal tradition. The delegation of the United States as a UNECE member, but not a Party to the Aarhus Convention, has secured that a statement be annexed to the Report of the first MOP, expressing concerns with respect to the compliance mechanism and the negotiating process which had led to it. In particular, this statement expresses concern, inter alia, for the 'variety of unusual procedural roles that may be performed by non-state, non-Party actors, including the nomination of members of the Committee and the ability to trigger certain communication requirements by Parties under these provisions' and 'about the efficacy of such provisions as a general policy matter'. It concludes that the 'United States will not recognize this regime as precedent'.[85]

A cautious approach seems to prevail also in the European region and European States, including EU members, appear to be quite divided on the issue. While some argue in favour of an expanded role for NGOs in NCPs, others are much more cautious on this point. The decision not to apply the Aarhus NCP to the Protocol on Pollutant Release and Transfer Registers

---

[83]   See doc. ECE/MP.PP/2005/13, paras 53–5.
[84]   Lack of cooperation is underlined by the Aarhus Committee; see doc. ECE/MP.PP/2005/13, para. 34.
[85]   See doc. ECE/MP.PP/2, para. 45 and Annex.

(PRTR Protocol) to the Aarhus Convention and to set up a free-standing and separate compliance body and procedure[86] is largely based on the desire of avoiding the automatic extension of its provision on public participation. Precisely on this point, an agreement has not been reached yet, because of the opposition of influential delegations. However, the elaboration of a common position of the EU Member States on compliance mechanisms under MEAs is currently under consideration. In a document of 2001, containing 'horizontal elements for an EU position on compliance mechanisms under MEAs',[87] a preference was expressed for committees composed of independent experts, holding public hearings, with the possibility of trigger by non-state actors through the secretariats. As underscored in a recent document, however,

> [t]he possibility of allowing individuals to trigger directly the mechanism was not identified as a horizontal objective. There seems to be no reason to change the position taken by the EU so far, by which direct triggering by individuals should only be envisaged on MEAs such as the Aarhus Convention, whose objective is to guarantee the rights of access to information, public participation in decisionmaking and access to justice in environmental matters. When allowed, it should be accompanied by specific safeguards in order to avoid the overburden of submissions to the Compliance Committee.[88]

Similarly, one of the most controversial issues during the negotiations of the 'Almaty Guidelines on Promoting the Application of the Principles of the Aarhus Convention in International Forums'[89] (Almaty Guidelines) has been precisely their applicability to non-compliance mechanisms. This issue has both a legal and a political component. From a legal point of view, non-compliance procedures fulfil a preparatory function of the decision-making process to be completed at the COP/MOP. They are administered by a dedicated body, usually composed of states, with the task of collecting the relevant information and addressing recommendations to the COP/MOP, which retains the exclusive power to take action towards the non-complying Party. Compliance committees are usually qualified as subsidiary bodies of the COP/MOP. Only in a few instances, such as the Enforcement Branch of the Kyoto Committee and, to a lesser extent, the Committees established under the Aarhus Convention,

---

[86]   See doc. ECE/MP.PP/AC.1/2005/4.

[87]   See doc. 14811/1/01 REV 1 of 21 December 2001.

[88]   See Commission Staff Working Paper, Compliance Mechanisms in Multilateral Environmental Agreements (MEAs), doc. SEC(2005) 405 of 18 March 2005.

[89]   On the Almaty Guidelines, see in more detail A. Tanzi, in Chapter 4 of this volume. The text of the guidelines is annexed to Decision II/4 of the MOP, doc. ECE/MP.PP/2005/2/Add.5.

the Cartagena Protocol and the Water and Health Protocol, has this model been deviated from, owing to their composition by individuals sitting in their personal capacity. In these cases, the procedures seem to function more as a *sui generis* dispute settlement mechanism, rather than as a preparatory stage of decision making.

Be that as it may, during the negotiations of the Almaty Guidelines it was decided that issues relating to non-compliance mechanisms would not fall under the second pillar of the Aarhus Convention, on participation in decision making, which provides for a fairly extensive entitlement to participation, but under the 'access to justice' pillar. Against this background, language which has remained bracketed until deletion mildly referred to the possible involvement of the public in 'implementation review mechanisms and procedures'.[90] Eventually, when the discussion reached the MOP level in Almaty, compliance procedures and dispute settlement mechanisms were excluded altogether from the scope of the Guidelines.

Practice shows that, when NGOs have been recognized by a significant role in the procedures under consideration, they have discharged with diligence and efficiency the responsibilities entrusted to them, furthering the effectiveness of the compliance review action. One could say that recognition of a formal status for NGOs seems to enhance their transparency and accountability, at least within the area under consideration.

However, this is far from being the prevailing view among governments. Although elements of practice seem to suggest otherwise, the governmental view still prevails that NGOs' participation, with special regard to their power to initiate NCPs, may undermine the non-confrontational functioning of those procedures and bear negatively on their efficiency. There is no doubt that the increased activity that would derive from allowing NGOs' participation in NCPs would have financial implications. Whether the additional costs and prospective negative impact on the efficiency of the procedure would overweigh, or be set off by, the prospective advantages in terms of enhancement of its effectiveness, transparency and accountability depend on political evaluations that may fall outside the scope of a scholarly legal analysis.[91] Nevertheless, it seems that, at least for the Parties to the Aarhus Convention and its Signatories – who, pursuant to Art. 18 of the Vienna Convention on the

---

90   See doc. ECE/MP.PP/WG.1/2005/8/Add.1, para. 54.

91   The Aarhus Committee, on this point has observed that 'Notwithstanding the commitment of time and resources implied in the processing of communications from the public, the Committee remains convinced that this aspect of the mechanism provides a unique and valuable channel of information on matters relevant to compliance, which would otherwise not necessarily come to its attention or to that of the Meeting of the Parties' (doc. ECE/MP.PP/2005/13, para. 56).

Law of Treaties, are under the obligation not to take a stand which frustrates the scope of the signed Convention – compliance with, and promotion of, the principle of 'public participation at all levels' should not be subservient to concerns of the additional costs that its fulfilment involves, unless such an increase became unreasonable.

Even though lack of formal legal status could limit the means by which NGOs may have an impact on the process, it does not imply setting at naught the role of NGOs within non-compliance procedures. As has been shown by practice, thanks to their expertise, professional skills and technical information, NGOs are given the opportunity to be involved in, and may contribute to, the process of existing NCPs through various ways and means. However, the positive impact of the formal involvement of NGOs (including openness of meetings, participation in the institutional mechanism, possibilities to trigger the procedure and to submit factual information, as well as scientific and legal assessments) within non-compliance mechanisms in terms of increased efficiency and transparency is becoming evident. The possibility that the regulation on the point at issue in the Aarhus NCP would remain an isolated example has now been superseded: the Water and Health NCP demonstrates that good arguments and negotiating skills, together with joint efforts between NGOs, the Secretariat and like-minded Parties, can lead to egregious results in promoting public involvement in NCPs. New developments are expected from the negotiations on the establishment of NCPs currently under way.[92]

---

92   See the list annexed.

ANNEX LIST AND REFERENCES OF NCP ALREADY IN OPERATION OR UNDER NEGOTIATION

CRM are operative under the following global or regional treaties:

- 1987 Montreal Protocol on Substances that Deplete the Ozone Layer to the 1985 Vienna Convention on the Protection of the Ozone Layer (1987) 26 ILM 1529 and 1550 ('Montreal Protocol'); see MOP Decision IV/5, doc. UNEP/OzL.Pro.4/15, Annex IV (1992), p. 44, subsequently amended by Decision X/10, doc. UNEP/OzL.Pro.10/9 (1998), p. 23 and consolidated text in Annex II, p. 47 ('Montreal NCP').
- 1989 Basel Convention on the Transboundary Movement of Hazardous Wastes and Their Disposal (1989) 28 ILM 649 ('Basel Convention'); see COP Decision VI/12, doc. UNEP/CHW.6/40, pp. 45–50 ('Basel NCP').
- 1997 Kyoto Protocol to the 1992 Framework Convention on Climate Change (1998) 37 ILM 22 ('Kyoto Protocol'); see Decision 24/CP.7 of the COP of the Convention, doc. FCCC/CP/2001/13/Add.3, pp. 64–77, subsequently adopted at the first COP/MOP of the Kyoto Protocol as decision 27/CMP.1, doc. FCCC/KP/CMP/2005/8/Add.3, pp. 92–103.
- 2000 Cartagena Protocol on Biosafety to the Convention on Biological Diversity (2000) 39 ILM 1027 ('Cartagena Protocol'); see COP/MOP Decision BS-I/7, doc. UNEP/CBD/BS/COP-MOP/1/15 (2004), p. 98 ('Cartagena NCP').
- 1979 Long-Range Transboundary Air Pollution Treaty (1979) 18 ILM 1442 ('LRTAPT'), see Decision 1997/2, Doc. ECE/EB.AIR/53 (1997), Annex III, p. 28, as amended by Decision 1998/3, ECE/EB.AIR/75 (2002), Annex V, p. 35 ('LRTAP NCP'). The mechanism applies to the Convention and its Protocols.
- 1991 Espoo Convention on Environmental Impact Assessment in a Transboundary Context (1991) 30 ILM 802 ('Espoo Convention') and 2003 Kiev Protocol on Strategic Environmental Assessment ('SEA Protocol'), see MOP Decision II/4, doc. ECE/MP.EIA/4 (2001), Annex IV, p. 72 revised by MOP Decision III/2, doc. ECE/MP.EIA/6 (2004), Annex II, p. 49 (consolidated text) ('Espoo NCP').
- 1998 Convention on Access to Information, Public Participation in Decision-making and Access to Justice in Environmental Matters (1999) 38 ILM 517 ('Aarhus Convention'), see MOP Decision I/7, doc. ECE/MP.PP/2/Add.8 (2004), as amended by MOP Decision II/5, doc. ECE/MP.PP/2005/2/Add.6, para. 12 ('Aarhus NCP').
- 1991 Convention on the Protection of the Alps, BU 991:883 ('Alpine Convention'). An unofficial English translation may be found in

T. Treves, L. Pineschi and A. Fodella (eds) (2002), *International Law and Protection of Mountain Areas*, Milan, p. 185). See Alpine Conference Decision VII/4, reprinted in 33 *Environmental Policy and Law* (2003), p. 179 ('Alpine NCP'); the mechanism applies to the Convention and to its Protocols.

- 1999 Protocol on Water and Health to the 1992 Helsinki Convention on the Protection and Use of Transboundary Watercourses and International Lakes, available at www.unece.org/env/documents/ 2000/wat/mp.wat.2000.1.e.pdf ('Water and Health Protocol'); see Decision I/2 on review of compliance, doc. ECE/MP.WH/2/Add.3-EUR/06/5069385/1/Add.3.

NCPs are under negotiation for the following global and regional treaties:

- 1998 Rotterdam Convention on the Prior Informed Consent Procedure for Certain Hazardous Chemicals and Pesticides in International Trade (1999) 38 ILM 1 ('PIC Convention'); see COP Decision RC-2/3, doc. UNEP/FAO/RC/COP.2/19 (2005), Annex, p. 22 ('Draft PIC NCP').
- 2001 Stockholm Convention on Persistent Organic Pollutants (2001) 40 ILM 532 ('POPs Convention'); The COP, at its first meeting convened an Open-ended Ad Hoc Working Group on Compliance (OEWG), to consider the establishment of procedures and institutional mechanisms on non-compliance has been convened. At its first meeting the OEWG considered a Draft prepared by the Secretariat, but did not complete the first reading. The latest version of the Draft is contained in doc. UNEP/POPS/OEWG-NC.1/3 (30 April 2006), Annex, p. 5 ('Draft POP NCP').
- 1996 London Protocol to the 1972 London Convention on the Prevention of Marine Pollution by Dumping of Wastes and Other Matter (not yet in force); the establishment of an NCP is envisaged by article 11 of the consolidated text of the Convention. The Consultative Meetings of the Contracting Parties (MCP) has created an ad hoc Working Group on Reporting and Compliance, whose work has led to an 'Amended Version of the Base Text for Compliance Procedures and Mechanisms, Pursuant to Article 11 of the 1996 Protocol to the London Convention', i.e. a working paper forming the basis for the future final compliance procedure.
- 2001 International Treaty on Plant Genetic Resources for Food And Agriculture ('ITPGRFA'), FAO Conference, Thirty-first Session (November 2001), Resolution 3/2001; at its First Meeting, the Governing body was unable to reach an agreement on the NCP and the text of the 'Draft Procedures and Operational Mechanisms to Promote

Compliance and to Address Issues of Non-Compliance', is still bracketed; see doc. IT/GB-1/06/Report, Appendix I, p. 79. It decided nevertheless to establish a Compliance Committee, that would not commence
its work unless further decisions on the procedures and operational
arrangements are taken. This should take place, in accordance with the
same decision, at the second session of the Governing Body, after
discussion on outstanding issues. Pending such decision, the Governing
Body has also decided an, indeed rudimental, procedure for addressing
compliance; see Resolution 3/2006, Doc. IT/gb-1/06/report, p. 8.

• 2003 Kiev Protocol on Pollutant Release and Transfer Registers to the
Aarhus Convention (not yet in force) ('PRTR Protocol'); the Working
Group on PRTR at its third meeting considered a Draft decision on
Review of Compliance, doc. ECE/MP.PP/AC.1/2006/4, and referred the
issue to a Contact Group meeting intersessionally and further reporting
to the Working Group at its fourth Meeting.

Conclusion: return on the legal status of NGOs and on the methodological problems which arise for legal scholarship

Pierre-Marie Dupuy

In international law, NGOs remain legal objects which are difficult to apprehend. Neither subjects, nor objects, actors nonetheless! Neither even always formally recognized, which is to say possessing the status of observer at an international organization. NGOs irritate classical legal scholarship and worry states whose actions they watch and exactions they denounce.

NGOs are multiform, ambitious but also ambiguous. Some of them, the largest and better known, such as Amnesty International, the International Federation for Human Rights (FIDH) or Greenpeace, have been part of the landscape for some time. Their leaders, although they still retain a certain taste for contestation, aim at making it smoother. They more willingly comply with the rules of an international diplomacy of which they have become an essential part.

Others have more narrowly defined goals and limited means, but are nonetheless active in providing expertise, disseminating information or carrying out missions, humanitarian or other, at a more or less local level, depending on the situations. Others still show a capacity for stonewalling that reveals them for what they really are: groups created by states but disguised as NGOs, as a kind of mask for the counter-propaganda organized with more or less subtlety by those that the real human rights organizations regularly denounce for their repeated violation of their obligations.[1] It is thus important, here as anywhere else, to distinguish the genuine from the fake, the criteria being not primarily and not so much the sincerity of held beliefs, but an autonomous creation, devoid of any state control, and the sincere pursuit of a truly general interest, at the national level, but even more so at the international one. Real

---

[1]   See in this volume O. de Frouville, 'Domesticating civil society at the United Nations', p. 71.

NGOs are not only powers, they are also 'counter-powers'. They are civil society, not servile society. Some are expert, others merely gabby. Selecting them does, however, suppose taking a stand on their legitimacy, which involves resorting to criteria which are ideological and political before being legal. In any case, sorting out real NGOs from fake ones following the aforementioned criteria, as is regularly attempted by the internal organs set up by almost all big intergovernmental organizations (IGOs) to select and admit NGOs, often turns out to be unreliable.

Indeed, the selection of NGOs has itself too often become a question of political rivalry and haggling between governments within international organizations.[2] Civil society models the international society, but the reverse proposition has also become a reality. Governments, primarily those who feel less concerned with a certain 'democratization' of international relations, try to infiltrate the international civil society and use its subversive potential in their own interest. This is in particular the reason why the recent Cardoso Report (2004) rationally pleads in favour of depoliticizing the accreditation process within the UN as well as denouncing 'the growing phenomenon of accrediting non-governmental organizations that are sponsored and controlled by Governments'.[3] The problem here is to know how far rationality may, in the near future, meet with realism.

Whatever the case may be, having become indispensable to the efficiency of the more or less rigid structures of intergovernmental organizations, NGOs are organized in networks. They are themselves sometimes more structured than we might imagine and they weave an informal and computerized web between each other and between their agents that gives them the gift of ubiquity. Borders are hardly an obstacle to them and their nature allows them to go beyond the formal compartmentalization of competing nations.

The phenomenon of international associations is not new. It was already rather successfully taken into account by the International Labour Office in the inter-war years,[4] going through a revival after 1945 with the birth of the United Nations family. However, its decisive success is more recent, dating back to the 1980s. Since then, it has acquired an increasing importance. Already at the Earth Summit of 1992 in Rio, the national delegations of diplomats were joined by a sort of fringe conference settled just outside the walls

---

2   See in this volume E. Rebasti, 'Beyond consultative status: which legal framework for an enhanced interaction between NGOs and intergovernmental organizations?', pp. 29–30.

3   See *Panel Report*, UN Doc.A/58/817 at para.127 and Rebasti, *supra* note 2, at p. 55.

4   See Anna-Karin Lindblom (2005), *Non-Governmental Organizations in International Law,* Cambridge: Cambridge University Press, at 411.

of the city and took on a quasi-assailant aspect. The global village may still have a centre composed of state buildings, but it is now surrounded by grumbling and dissenting 'slums' calling for their recognition.

Here again, the phenomenon is not primarily legal. It is social. It is one of the aspects of the current phenomenon affecting the whole planet and which is for that reason called 'globalization'. It is by nature transnational. For the old society of states which goes back, beyond its successive transformations, at least to the 'good old' treaties of Westphalia, the phenomenon of the international civil society is living proof of the veracity at the international level of the analysis and predictions made by Alexis de Tocqueville at the beginning of the nineteenth century concerning democracy in America.[5] Political democracy leads to a democratization of the social practice of politics.

Faced with this evolution, confounded jurists search desperately in their toolbox for tools to apprehend the actions of entities which refuse to be tamed or seem immune to categorization. Are they *subjects* (of international law)? Certainly not! The classical reason for that is that they do not possess a legal personality, at least in the international legal order. 'But if they are subjects in national law, our colleagues in municipal private law should be the ones to handle the problem', will retort a good number of exasperated international lawyers, especially in continental Europe, and its Latin parts more particularly, who continue to determine the scope of their field by reference to state sovereignty as it was already conceived by the Permanent Court of International Justice in the *Wimbledon* case. They refuse to see that Gulliver is held down in an increasingly intricate web of national bureaucracies, intergovernmental organizations, various and varied pressure of interest groups, each one claiming from its specific viewpoint to contribute to the triumph of the general interest.

This formalism and narrowness of mind makes international lawyers from the Anglo-Saxon world smile. They do not shy away from extending the scope of their investigations beyond state actions and think they have found the solution. You claim they are not subjects? So what? They are simply 'actors', 'non-governmental actors' whose initiatives need to be included in the scope of our work, because they act both 'in favour of' and 'on' the law, based on the idea that they have of it. As a backdrop to this, what is reappearing is the old debate on a definition of the 'legal' based, not only on legality, but also on legitimacy, even if this term is not necessarily perceived in the same way on both sides of the Atlantic.

This contextualized approach, in particular of American international lawyers, seems in many ways better equipped to deal with the perception of NGOs in a legal world thankfully resituated in the ideological, political and

---

5   Alexis de Tocqueville (1835), *De la démocratie en Amérique*, Paris.

social context it is part of.[6] However, this type of analysis can lead to the use of a discourse which is not only versatile but also deeply ambiguous. In this discourse, the technical identity of law is all too often replaced by a self-referring meta-language in the production of which many authors are no longer aware that they are taking their desires for realities and want to think, like George Bush, that the word 'democracy' has necessarily the same meaning throughout the world.

Although we readily recognize that, owing to a lack of space, we have wandered on the side of simplification, the sketch we have just drawn at least illustrates the difficulties that the rapid development of NGOs has created for legal scholarship. One of the interesting aspects of the study of NGOs in international law is that the problems that arise for jurists are not only theoretical but also methodological, because, as the great physicist T. Heisenberg once said, 'there is nothing more practical than a good theory'. One could add that there is nothing less neutral, both ideologically and politically, than a method, even if it is called 'scientific', based on the idea that each person has, for example, of positivism.[7]

To illustrate what was said above, it is relevant to recall how, about a century ago, legal scholars had considered the question of how to analyse the birth and the nature of intergovernmental organizations which had appeared with the creation of the League of Nations and the International Labour Organisation (ILO). The phenomenon was not entirely new at the time, the nineteenth century having seen the creation of the first administrative unions, such as the Universal Postal Union, and even before that, the first fluvial commissions. These last examples illustrate how scholars were locked in the positivist logic according to which the law that, a little while earlier, Jeremy Bentham had suggested should be called 'international', was, 'by its nature', limited to states. Thus the European Commission of the Danube, because it

---

6   See the highly interesting presentation of NGOs in Michael Reisman et al. (eds) (2004), *International Law in Contemporary Perspective,* New York: Foundation Press, at 289–311; for a comprehensive approach, see Wybo P. Heere (ed.) (2004), 'From government to governance: the growing impact of non-state actors on the international and European legal system', *Proceedings of the Sixth Hague Joint Conference held in The Hague, 3–5 July 2003,* The Hague: T.M.C. Asser Press; P. Willets (2000), 'From consultative arrangements to partnership: the changing status of NGOs at the UN', *Global Governance,* **6**, 191–212.

7   See, for instance, S. Ratner and A.M. Slaughter (eds) (1999), 'Symposium on method in international law', *American Journal of International Law,* **93**(2), and, by the same authors (2004), 'The methods of international law', *ASIL Studies in Transnational Policy,* 36; to be compared with P.M. Dupuy (2002), 'L'unité de l'ordre juridique international – Cours général de droit international public', *Recueil des cours de l'Academie de droit international de La Haie,* **297**, 27–33, 396–9.

had normative powers which were fairly *avant-garde* for the time, was dubbed a 'fluvial state', which goes to show how much fiction is a privileged tool of legal technique.

In the early part of the twentieth century, authors would refuse to recognize the international personality of the League of Nations or the ILO. They were an association of states, but not themselves states. When he was asked in the 1930s about the legal statute of the International Office of Agriculture (ancestor of the FAO) the headquarters of which were already in Rome, the great Dionisio Anzilotti, President of the Permanent Court of International Justice and leader of the voluntarist positivist school refused to consider it as a subject of international law. For him, this body was merely a kind of ectoplasm or of a pipe-dream, if not an inconvenient mistake of international practice. It could only act through the 'directing state', that is, the state of the headquarters, which would use its own legal capacities to act in the name of this international administrative body which was itself 'legally incapable', that is to say devoid of any power of legal action in the international legal order. Only Sir John Fischer Williams, an ungratefully forgotten great British jurist, had had the audacity and lucidity to say that the League of Nations also was an international legal person, but one of a new kind.[8] What a stir this caused in the well-to-do circle of international scholars! At the time, it was considered that these were the slightly offensive words of an eccentric mind. The classical positivist analysis thought it was in principle based on scientific foundations, was in fact the prisoner of a quasi-mystical dogma: there is no light beyond the state. This precedent, which hovers on the border of drama and comedy, should in any case warn us of a simple fact: legal techniques and their use are very clearly informed, guided and inspired by an underlying ideology, even and sometimes primarily when they claim to be rooted in positivism. However, what is true of positivism is also true of various forms of sociologism or trans-Atlantic realism.[9]

In any case, to close the book on this telling precedent of academic short-sightedness when faced with the legal analysis of intergovernmental organizations, one should recall that, after the Second World War, it is to the International Court of Justice and not legal scholars that we owe the revelation that intergovernmental organizations possess an international legal personality.

In its famous and groundbreaking advisory opinion on *Reparation for*

---

[8]   John Fischer Williams (1934), *Some Aspects of the Covenant of the League of Nations*, Oxford: University Press, London: Humphrey Milford. See also, from the same author (1932), *International Change and International Peace*, London: Humphrey Milford.

[9]   See J.P. Cot (2006), 'Tableau de la pensée juridique américaine', *Revue Générale de Droit International Public*, **110**(3), 536–96.

Injuries Suffered in the Service of the United Nations,[10] the Court, acting inside the organization of which it is the main judicial organ, listed the clues which allowed it, based on a teleological reading of the United Nations charter inspired by the *effet utile* doctrine, to ascertain that the UN did indeed possess an international legal personality. The possession of this personality by international organizations was the result, not of an academic awakening, but of the judicial perception of its necessity. As for authors, they continued, unruffled, to forbid themselves to think outside the borders they had been taught to respect, just like children having fun in the playground.

What is even more interesting in this story is to observe that, when faced with the obvious necessities of the judicial practice, judges as classically positivist voluntarist as Jules Basdevant, when he was only a professor at the Paris law faculty, had no second thoughts in recognizing that an international legal personality could be attributed, even implicitly, to an international organization which, although composed of state members, is not a state, and even less a super-state. Necessity makes the law. However, we do know that for some time still, a last group of untouchables, led by the talented and fearsome Rolando Quadri, leading scholar at the University of Naples, refused, until late in the 1960s, to recognize that intergovernmental organizations, including the European Union, could possess a legal personality.[11]

Thus legal analysis is not neutral. It is never neutral. This remains true whether it claims roots in formalistic positivism, as in France or other Latin countries, or whether it calls for a more or less broader contextual approach, as in the United States in the form of several schools of thought; whether it comes from a belief that the law should not change, or, on the contrary, from a tendency, not to look at the law as it is, but as we would want it to be, forgetting along the way that law is first and foremost a formal technique.

Beyond these questions of methods or approaches to international law, the example of intergovernmental organizations could lead us to think that NGOs will receive the same treatment. They will be granted some form of legal personality, because, as was rightly underlined by the ICJ in the aforementioned 1949 advisory opinion, a legal order can be composed of legal persons possessing different powers and capacities.[12]

Such an evolution is indeed not at all impossible. It is even in some ways announced by the longstanding recognition that an entity such as the

---

[10]   ICJ Reports, 1949, pp. 174ff and http://www.icj-cij.org. For a commentary and analysis in relation to the general theory of subjects in public international law, see Dupuy, 'L'unité de l'ordre juridique international', *supra* note 7, at 107–16.

[11]   See R. Quadri (1964), 'Cours général de droit international public', *Recueil des cours, de l'Academie de droit international de La Haie*, **113**, 237–483.

[12]   ICJ Reports, 1949, at 178.

International Committee of the Red Cross possesses an international legal capacity, and therefore also an international legal personality.[13]

On the adjudicative front, such an analysis could be possible in the long run, especially if one considers, as did Luisa Vierucci, the already existing possibility for NGOs not only to participate but also to initiate international legal proceedings before jurisdictions such as the European Court of Human Rights. There is currently an increasing awareness on the part of the international judge of the fruitful contribution that NGOs may bring to international proceedings. This is particularly evident in the practice relating to *amicus curiae* ('friends of the court') submissions: not only those tribunals that are traditionally open to private parties (human rights jurisdictions) allow and make frequent reference in the judgments to such submissions, but also tribunals that traditionally adjudicate inter-state disputes (ICJ, arbitral tribunals) seem to become more open towards such type of third-party participation.[14] This awareness is giving rise to informal regulation of the type of participation that NGOs may have before the international judge.

In the silence of the constitutive instrument, the judge frequently decides himself whether or not to give access to NGOs. This practice is recently starting to give rise to formal ways of regulating in particular *amicus* participation.[15] Although NGOs are not specifically mentioned in those examples of formal regulation, in practice NGOs are allowed to participate as *amici*. In addition, although there is a generalized consensus on the need to allow NGO participation as *amici*, the modalities of such participation of NGOs necessarily vary from one jurisdiction to the other. The novelties in the *amicus* field, and in particular the increasing emphasis that is laid on the soundness of the arguments that NGOs put forward rather than on their formal legal standing, may constitute a model for a new type of interaction between NGOs and international tribunals also as far as NGOs right to file claims is concerned.

With respect to NGOs' *locus standi*, the reluctance of states to give leeway to non-state actors is certainly clear, even if some breaches may be singled out.[16] In general terms, the international status of NGOs in this area is more

---

[13]   See Mario Bettati and Pierre-Marie Dupuy (1986), *Les ONG et le droit international*, Paris: Economica.

[14]   See P.M. Dupuy (2006), 'Article 34', in A. Zimmermann, Ch. Tomuschat and K. Oellers-Frahm, *The Statute of the International Court of Justice, A Commentary*, Oxford: Oxford University Press, at 561–2.

[15]   See ECHR modification of the rule 44 in 2003, and art. 103 of the ICC rules of procedure and evidence in L. Vierucci, 'NGOs before international courts and tribunal', in this volume, p. 163ff.

[16]   For example, the newly created African Court for Human Rights allows NGOs to represent the public interest before the judge – an exercise in *actio popularis* that has to be evaluated in light of the judicial practice that the Court will develop. Ibid.

highly regulated than in the past – though by necessity subject to some conditions (conditional participation). Interestingly, this is happening despite the will of important NGOs (such as Amnesty International) and of states and leads to reflect on the increasingly legislative role of the judge in the international legal order.[17]

Whatever the case may be, one may also think that the more or less explicit granting of an international legal personality to NGOs, if it is a possibility, will not be of interest for a lot of them and will remain limited to just a few: the ones that, given their size and level of interaction with the traditional subjects of international law, states and intergovernmental organizations, are bound to be given, even in a restricted way, 'some form of international legal personality'.[18]

Other scenarios than a de jure or de facto granting of capacity to some qualified NGOs are however possible, including those for the larger NGOs. Indeed, there is an apparently major difference between IGOs before the recognition of the presumption of their international legal personality, and NGOs today. The former, especially the United Nations, actually wanted to act as states, that is, in particular, by being endowed with the legal capacity of passing treaties or claiming for reparation. They claim to possess such a personality.

As for NGOs, even the larger ones, they do not want to be like states. As underlined previously, they prefer, on the contrary, to go on acting according to a very different logic, flexibility and mode of functioning.

They want to retain a power to contest, propose and intervene, in short a liberty of style that protects their status as an effective 'counter-power' against the cumbersome red tape of bureaucracies and sovereignties. What matters for most of them is to preserve, expand and promote, depending on the situation, a power of pressure, influence and control over the acts of states, even if, in the case of compliance review mechanisms, it must accommodate itself to the respecting of certain procedures in exchange for its effectiveness. The study made in this book by Cesare Pitea definitely shows, in particular that, when NGOs are given the possibility of playing a meaningful role in the monitoring of treaty implementation, they have discharged with diligence and efficiently the responsibilities entrusted to them, furthering the effectiveness of the compliance review action.[19] However, the prevailing view among governments still remains that NGOs' participation, with special regard to their power to initiate adjudicative procedures, may undermine the non-confrontational

---

17 See Vierucci, *supra* note 15, at p. 173.
18 To use the words of the ICJ in the above-mentioned 1949 Advisory Opinion.
19 See in this volume C. Pitea, 'The legal status of NGOs in environmental non-compliance procedures: an assessment of law and practice', p. 181.

functioning of those procedures and bear negatively on their efficiency. There is an evident tension between the ever growing participation of NGOs in international legal relations and the reluctance of states to recognize that they are efficient and necessary.

Still, the different observatory statuses that NGOs have already been granted by IGOs, initially conceived at a time when these private associations were passive onlookers of intergovernmental debates, no longer correspond to the necessities of their active participation in the deliberations of the organs of these institutions. This explains the increasing bypassing, competition or simply discarding of established procedures in favour of more flexible empirical practices, elaborated on a case-by-case basis to allow the involvement of the more knowledgeable NGOs in the elaboration and application of norms. This practice leads to an increasing and progressive widening of the gap between the declared status of NGOs and their actual power of participation. The very existence of this gap explains why, in recent times, as diverse IGOs as the Council of Europe, in 2003, the UN, in 2004, the new African Union ECOSOCC, in 2004, the Organization of American States, in 2004 and 2005 followed in the same year by the World Bank, have reviewed the existing patterns of NGOs' participation in their work with a view to providing a framework for the current internal debates on how to improve co-operation with civil society organizations.[20]

As revealed in particular by the study of NGOs within the European Union as compared to other IGOs, there is almost in every case an inherent tension between the formalization and non-formalization of the involvement of NGOs in development policy. In the case of the Council of Europe, it has already been resolved in favour of the former.[21]

As a matter of fact, although the reluctance of governments, including those of the West, persists with regard to the potential extension of the scope of actions left to NGOs, there is at the same time a clear trend towards recognizing the high interest of co-operating with efficient emanations of the civil society, whether at the grass-root level or at the regional or universal ones. This tendency is illustrated, among others, by provisions such as Article 4 of the Cotonou Agreement between the European Union and its member states with the ACP Countries which recognizes 'the potential for contributions by non-state actors to the development process' and the possibility of involving them in the definition and implementation of cooperation policies.[22]

---

[20]   See Rebasti, *supra* note 2, at pp. 46–7.
[21]   See in this volume V. Bettin, 'NGOs and the development policy of the European Union', at p. 124ff.
[22]   Ibid., at p. 130.

The same inspiration can be found, among others, in Article 15 of the Aahrus Convention of 1998, the very purpose of which is to facilitate access of the public (mostly through NGOs) to information and justice as well as to ease its participation in environmental policy making, including when it comes to compliance review.[23] Article 15 of the Aahrus Convention must be, in this respect, put into perspective, in particular, with Article 9 of the elder Espoo Convention.

Nevertheless, it should not be assumed that such a trend is only manifest among European Countries. The newly established Economic, Social and Cultural Council (ECOSOCC) of the African Union provides us with an example of the complete integration of civil society in the institutional machinery of an intergovernmental organization. According to Article 3.1 of the ECOSOCC Statutes, the interaction with civil society is put in place through membership of an official organ which is statutorily vested with a role in the decision-making process of the organisation.[24]

In these different geographical and substantial contexts, the formal legal question of the international legal personality of NGOs might not actually be necessarily the right one, especially if one continues to understand this expression as a formalized pre-established set of competences. Indeed, for NGOs, their mobility is a guarantee of efficiency. By wanting to increase the legal certainty, they risk losing flexibility. All they need and mostly want, even if it is in a very empirical fashion, is to be recognized by states and IGOs as 'worthy interlocutors', that is to say, as useful and legitimate partners. This already is the case for a great number of them, without needing to take on the burden of an extremely formalized status. The problem here is more how IGOs can reach, among themselves, a sufficient and necessary harmonization of their accreditation and participation procedures.

This is probably where the whole issue of self-regulation becomes important.[25] This concept is understood as the initiative taken by NGOs themselves to subordinate their actions to the respecting of a code of conduct embodying a certain 'ethical responsibility', as defined by the philosopher Hans Jonas. In addition to limiting and adapting their initiatives to the specific scope of their speciality, NGOs must accept at least two things. On the one hand, they must satisfy a requirement of transparency concerning their origins, real objectives and financing. On the other hand, they must accept the necessary minimum control over the gathering and verification of the information provided.

These remarks apply both to the participation of NGOs in the deliberative

---

23 See Pitea, *supra* note 19, at p. 184.
24 See Rebasti, *supra* note 2, at p. 48.
25 Ibid. at p. 43ff.

organs of IGOs and to the contribution to legal proceedings. For the latter, it will however be necessary to modify at least the rules of procedure so as to allow the doors of the courtroom to be open to the 'friends of the court', certainly when the jurisdiction in question does not contain the relevant dispositions, as is already the case for the International Criminal Court and the African Court for Human Rights.[26]

In any case, and in other words, a reciprocal adjustment of the relevant partners involved can take place in an empirical and progressive way to improve and make clearer the conditions of NGOs' participation in the workings of international organizations, including compliance review mechanisms, without the question of the international legal personality of NGOs ever arising.

We are led back to the role of legal scholars faced with the paradox of NGOs: de jure these entities have no existence or a very narrowly defined one, if any; but de facto they do a lot, especially in the functioning of international institutions and the implementation of the law created in their midst. Given this situation, the only way for legal scholars to apprehend the reality of NGOs' involvement is to go beyond the rigid inter-state and voluntarist conceptions usually put forward by the positivist school of thought. The authors nonetheless must not succumb to a sort of logorrhoea in which the term 'law' is present on every line, but where is never made clear either its content, or the technical conditions by which it is elaborated and implemented, or what the sanctions of its non-application might be.

In this respect, it might be interesting to take into account the very recent trend, particularly in the United States, aimed at identifying global administrative law as a new field or branch of international law.[27] Linked to the concept of global governance, this trend considers a vast array of phenomena as related to each other through the emergence of a huge transnational bureaucratic web linking very different types of actors. This evolution is taking place by way of the development of diverse and multiple modes and procedures in particular for the elaboration of norms, whatever their legal status, as they transcend very largely classical distinctions of the public and the private, as well as the international and the national.

In such a broad context, there is considerable room for the analysis of the ways in which NGOs participate in the life of international organizations, the impact of this participation on the law-making procedures or on the work of the control bodies dealing with the implementation of the law. The focus is

---

[26]   See Vierucci, *supra* note 15, at p. 164.
[27]   See N. Krisch and B. Kingsbury (eds) (2006), 'Symposium: global governance and global administrative law in the international legal order', *European Journal of International Law*, **17**(1), 1–309, and Rebasti, *supra* note 2, at p. 70.

then less on the legal status of the organizations than on their action. What is important is the study of their participative action rather than the study of their pre-defined capacity, as would be the case if the eternal debate on their potential legal personality were brought back to the foreground.

This stimulating approach does nevertheless contain some dangers. One of them could be the birth of a new dogmatism. Moreover, this approach will bring to light various methodological difficulties, the complexities of which might currently not always be fully assessed by its followers. In any case, all jurists cannot claim to be sociologists, because, by going beyond the too narrow scope of formalism, they sometimes end up losing their command of legal techniques.

Vigilance thus appears to be necessary to guarantee lucidity. NGOs are the focus of an array of sociological analyses which are best left to those who are truly competent. As for jurists, they remain specialists, in theory at least, of the elaboration of norms, of their interpretation and of the control of their application. Even if they rightly broaden the scope of their analysis to encompass the socio-political context in which NGOs work, they must at the same time agree to focus their comments on the procedural and technical modalities of the partnership between, on the one hand, NGOs, and on the other, states and intergovernmental institutions.

They will then no doubt discover that the question of whether private associations possess (or not) international legal capacities is being progressively resolved, on the condition that the definition of this personality be reviewed and adapted to its true nature. It must be less a pre-established capacity to act legally than an effective and legitimate power to have a say on the content of international norms being elaborated or to play a part in the reality of their application.

APPENDIX 1 QUESTIONNAIRE ON THE LEGAL STATUS OF NGOS IN INTERNATIONAL LAW[1]

Please answer the following questions using the space provided. Feel free to use additional space if necessary. Kindly submit the questionnaire by 30 October to the following address: luisa.vierucci@iue.it and be ready to discuss it at the workshop.

Section 1 – NGOs and intergovernmental organisations (IGOs)
Section 2 – NGOs before international courts and quasi-judicial bodies
Section 3 – The legal status of NGOs in international law: general considerations

Section 1   NGOs and intergovernmental organisations (IGOs)

1. **Does your NGO have consultative status or equivalent with any of the following IGOs: United Nations (its organs and/or specialized agencies), European Union, Council of Europe? If yes, which? If not, why?**

2. **If your NGO does have consultative status, what rights does this status provide in practice?**

3. **Are there any rights your NGO is entitled to by virtue of its legal status which it cannot exercise in practice?**

---

[1]   European University Institute, Law Department, 'A Legal Status for NGOs in Contemporary International Law? A Contribution to the Debate on 'Non-State Actors' and Public International Law at the Beginning of the Twenty-First Century', 15–16 November 2002, Florence, workshop held under the responsibility of Pierre-Marie Dupuy, Professor of International Law, European University Institute and Université de Paris (Panthéon-Assas).

4. Are there systems for consultative status or equivalent which you find more useful than others? In which respects?

5. What has been your NGO's experience with the control exercised by the ECOSOC Standing Committee on NGOs and similar bodies? Is there a need to change the procedures in this regard?

6. Are you satisfied with the legal status your NGO has at present *vis-à-vis* the selected IGOs? If not, how do you think it should be changed?

7. Which IGOs or organs should be more open to NGOs than is currently the case?

8. Could the system for accreditation to and participation of NGOs in intergovernmental conferences and meetings be improved? If so, how?

Section 2   International courts and quasi-judicial bodies

9. Does your NGO believe that submitting complaints to international/regional courts and quasi-judicial bodies is a fruitful contribution? If so, why? If not, why?

10. Do you think that your NGO should be able to acquire legal standing before international jurisdictions or quasi-judicial bodies which are currently not open to NGOs? If so, before which bodies, and in what respects? If not, why?

11. Does your NGO consider submitting *amicus curiae* briefs to international/regional courts and quasi-judicial bodies to be a fruitful contribution? If so, why? If not, why?

12. In your view, should international courts and quasi-judicial bodies be more open to NGOs acting as *amicus curiae*? If so, which bodies? If not, why?

Section 3   The legal status of NGOs in international law: general considerations

13. Do you think that the legal status of NGOs within the international legal order should be clarified? If so, how could such a development be achieved? If not, why?

14. In your view, what new legal functions should be bestowed upon NGOs, if any?

15. According to which criteria should NGOs be selected for a different legal status in international law (in terms of internal structure, aims, functions, etc.)?

Thank you for your co-operation!

APPENDIX 2 SELECTED DOCUMENTS RELATING TO RECENT DEVELOPMENTS RELEVANT TO NGOS' STATUS UNDER INTERNATIONAL LAW

Participatory status for international non-governmental organisations with the Council of Europe Resolution Res(2003)8*

(Adopted by the Committee of Ministers on 19 November 2003 at the 861st meeting of the Ministers' Deputies)

The Committee of Ministers,

Recalling the Council of Europe statutory aim to achieve a closer unity between its members for the purpose of safeguarding and realising the ideals and principles which are their common heritage, and facilitating their economic and social progress;

Bearing in mind the missions entrusted to the Council of Europe by the Vienna and Strasbourg Summits and by the Budapest Declaration for a Greater Europe without Dividing Lines;

Considering that the achievement of this goal and the fulfilment of these missions cannot be realised without constant sensitivity to public opinion and to the driving forces in European society, which are constantly evolving;

Considering that the existence of an active civil society and its non-governmental organisations (hereafter NGOs), which are a vital component of European society, is an important and indispensable element of democracy;

Considering the essential role of counterbalance played by NGOs in a pluralist democracy, to intensify the active participation of all citizens in conducting public affairs, and promoting responsible democratic citizenship based on human rights and equality between women and men;

Convinced that initiatives, ideas and suggestions emanating from civil society can be considered as a true expression of European citizens;

Recalling that, in this spirit, the Council of Europe has, over the years, developed fruitful working relations with NGOs since it first created a consultative status for international non-governmental organisations in 1952;

Considering that the system of co-operation introduced by consultative status largely permitted the development and strengthening of co-operation between the Council of Europe and the voluntary sector, giving positive and particularly encouraging results for both parties;

---

* *Res(2003)8 on Participatory status for international non-governmental organisations with the Council of Europe*, reproduced with permission from the Council of Europe.

Considering that it is indispensable that the rules governing the relations between the Council of Europe and NGOs evolve to reflect the active participation of international non-governmental organisations (INGOs) in the Organisation's policy and work programme, and to facilitate INGO participation and access to such bodies as the steering committees and governmental expert committees, and other subsidiary bodies of the Committee of Ministers. This participation will allow the INGOs to continue to draw the Council of Europe's attention to the effects of changes in European societies and the problems facing them;

Noting that the development and reinforcement of this co-operation between INGOs and the Committee of Ministers and its subsidiary bodies, as well as with the Parliamentary Assembly and the Congress of Local and Regional Authorities of Europe has led to the 'Quadrilogue' which is, within the Council of Europe, an expression of democratic pluralism and an essential element for the further development of a citizens' Europe;

Wishing, through the present rules, to reflect the active and constructive role of NGOs, and to clarify, facilitate and intensify the co-operation between the Council of Europe and the INGOs, in particular underlining its participatory character;

Recognising the important role to be played by the Liaison Committee as the democratically elected representative body of all of the INGOs enjoying participatory status with the Council of Europe, and by the INGO thematic groupings as their collective voice and, thus, of millions of European citizens, working in each of the fields represented by them;

Recognising the importance of the co-operation between the Council of Europe and national NGOs, provided for in Resolution Res(2003)9 on the status of partnership between the Council of Europe and national NGOs;

Hereby decides to adopt the rules for participatory status appended to this resolution which replace the rules for consultative status established by Resolution (93) 38.

Appendix to Resolution Res(2003)8

Rules for participatory status for INGOs at the Council of Europe
1. The Council of Europe may establish working relations with INGOs by granting them participatory status.

Conditions to be met by INGOs
2. Participatory status may be granted by the Council of Europe to INGOs:
   a. which are particularly representative in the field(s) of their competence, fields of action shared by the Council of Europe;

b. which are represented at European level, that is to say which have members in a significant number of countries throughout greater Europe;

c. which are able, through their work, to support the achievement of that closer unity mentioned in Article 1 of the Council of Europe's Statute;

d. are capable of contributing to and participating actively in Council of Europe deliberations and activities;

e. which are able to make known the work of the Council of Europe among European citizens.

Modalities of co-operation

3. The INGOs with participatory status may be invited to be represented by the Liaison Committee or the thematic groupings at events organised by the Secretariat General.

4. The steering committees, committees of governmental experts and other bodies of the Committee of Ministers, may involve the INGOs enjoying participatory status in the definition of Council of Europe policies, programmes and actions in particular by granting observer status to the Liaison Committee and to the INGO thematic groupings, in accordance with the terms of Committee of Ministers' Resolution (76) 3.

5. The committees of the Parliamentary Assembly and of the Congress of Local and Regional Authorities of Europe are invited to study ways of intensifying co-operation with and facilitating INGO participation in their work, for example by granting observer status or by inviting the Liaison Committee or INGO thematic groupings to provide their expertise.

6. The Commissioner for Human Rights is also encouraged to maintain close co-operation with the INGOs enjoying participatory status.

7. Additionally, considering their role as advisers in questions concerning civil society, the Secretary General may consult the INGOs, the Liaison Committee or the INGO thematic groupings, in writing or by means of a hearing, on questions of mutual interest.

8. The INGOs enjoying participatory status:

a. may address memoranda to the Secretary General for submission to the committees mentioned above, as well as to the Commissioner for Human Rights;

b. may be invited to provide, through their specific activity or experience, expert advice on Council of Europe policies, programmes and actions;

c. shall receive the agenda and public documents of the Parliamentary Assembly in order to facilitate their attendance at public sittings of the Parliamentary Assembly;

d. shall be invited to public sittings of the Congress of Local and Regional Authorities of Europe;

e. shall be invited to activities organised for them by the Secretariat;

f. shall be invited to attend seminars, conferences, colloquies of interest to their work according to the applicable Council of Europe rules.

9. The INGOs enjoying participatory status shall undertake to:

a. keep themselves regularly informed of Council of Europe activities and developments in standards by means of the numerous sources of information available, including the Internet;

b. furnish, either spontaneously or at the request of the Council of Europe's different bodies, information, documents or opinions relating to their own field(s) of competence on matters which are under consideration or which could be addressed by the Council of Europe;

c. work to promote the respect of the Council of Europe's standards, conventions and legal instruments in the member states, and assist in the implementation of these standards, and this in close contact with local, regional and national NGOs;

d. give maximum publicity to the initiatives and achievements of the Council of Europe in their own field(s) of competence;

e. disseminate information on Council of Europe standards, instruments and activities, as well as information from the INGO thematic groupings, to their members, on a regular basis, and ensure that they too work actively to fulfil the requirements of the participatory status;

f. submit every four years a report to the Secretary General which should specify:

- their participation in the work of the various Council of Europe bodies (see paragraphs 4 and 6 of this appendix), the capacity in which they attended and their contribution;
- their attendance at events organised by the Secretariat General, the capacity in which they attended, the contribution they made and any follow-up action;
- their attendance at and contributions to the meetings of the INGO thematic groupings;
- any meetings which they themselves have organised, in particular those which have dealt with the promotion of the Council of Europe's aims, standards and legal instruments;
- any action they have undertaken with a view to ensuring respect of Council of Europe standards and to publicising its work.

Procedure for the granting of participatory status
10. The Secretary General shall keep the list of INGOs enjoying participatory status with the Council of Europe.

11. Any INGO wishing to be entered on this list shall submit to the Secretary General of the Council of Europe three copies of an application, in

French or English, and, preferably, in both of these official languages of the Council of Europe, which must contain the following documents:

    a. the INGO's statute;

    b. a list of its member organisations with a French or English translation of the title of these organisations as well as an approximate number of members of each of these organisations;

    c. a report on its activities covering the previous two years;

    d. a declaration to the effect that it accepts the principles set out in the statute and other basic texts of the Council of Europe;

    e. the official application form on which it states clearly:

– why it is applying for participatory status with the Council of Europe;
– how it considers it will be able to contribute to and participate in the activities of the Council of Europe (as set out in its current programme of activities);
– in what way it feels able to make such a contribution (studies, reports, previous work in the field concerned, expertise of its members in the area concerned, etc.);
– what practical co-operation has already been established with the Council of Europe departments concerned;
– by what means and to which audience it would publicise the work of the Council of Europe.

12. The decision to grant participatory status to an INGO shall be taken by the Secretary General of the Council of Europe based on the criteria mentioned above. The Secretary General may also take into consideration the main priorities of the Council of Europe's programme of activities and the possible proliferation of INGOs in a given sector of activity.

13. The Secretary General will communicate the list of INGOs to which he or she intends to grant participatory status to the INGO Liaison Committee for its opinion. The INGO Liaison Committee's opinion must be expressed within two months of the Secretary General's Communication.

14. At the end of this time-limit, the decision of the Secretary General will be submitted for tacit approval to the Committee of Ministers, to the Parliamentary Assembly and to the Congress of Local and Regional Authorities. This decision will be accompanied by the names of the INGOs concerned, those items from the relevant files which are necessary for the assessment of each case, the Secretary General's reasons for suggesting they be added to the list, as well as any comments received from the Liaison Committee. In the absence of any objection founded on the conditions set out in paragraph 15 below, the said INGOs will be added three months later to the list of those enjoying participatory status.

15. During the three-month period, a member of the Committee of Ministers or ten members of the Parliamentary Assembly from five different national delegations or ten members of the Congress of Local and Regional Authorities of Europe from five different national delegations may request that an examination be made of the file of any applicant INGO. In the former case, the examination shall be made and the decision to add the name to the list shall be taken by the Committee of Ministers. In the latter case, the Committee of Ministers shall defer its decision until it has received a recommendation from the Parliamentary Assembly or the Congress of Local and Regional Authorities of Europe acting on a report from their competent committees.

Withdrawal of participatory status

16. Any INGO already on the list may be removed from it by the Secretary General if, in his or her opinion:

a. it has failed to comply with its obligations under the rules set out in paragraphs 2 and 9 above;

b. it is represented twice as a result of affiliation to a larger organisation working in the same field of activity which is itself on the list;

c. no longer has any activity included in the Council of Europe's work programme;

d. it has taken any action which is not in keeping with its status as an INGO.

To this end, the Secretary General shall review periodically the list of INGOs with participatory status. The review shall be based on the report submitted by the INGOs every four years.

However, the Secretary General shall first inform the INGO in question of his or her intention to withdraw its participatory status in order to give it an opportunity to present its observations within two months.

17. The reasoned decision to remove an organisation from the list shall be taken by the Secretary General of the Council of Europe in accordance with the above rules.

18. The Secretary General will communicate the list of INGOs from which he or she intends to withdraw participatory status to the INGO Liaison Committee for its opinion. The Liaison Committee's opinion must be expressed within two months of the Secretary General's communication.

19. At the end of this time limit, the decision of the Secretary General will be submitted for tacit approval to the Committee of Ministers, to the Parliamentary Assembly and to the Congress of Local and Regional Authorities. This decision will be accompanied by the names of the INGOs concerned and his or her reasons for suggesting they be removed from the list of those enjoying participatory status, as well as any comments received from the Liaison Committee. In the absence of any objection founded on the

conditions described in paragraph 15 above, the names of the INGOs that have thus been communicated shall be removed from the list three months later.

20. During the three-month period, a member of the Committee of Ministers or ten members of the Parliamentary Assembly from five different national delegations or ten members of the Congress of Local and Regional Authorities of Europe from five different national delegations may request that an examination be made of the file of each INGO whose name has been communicated to them. In the former case, the examination shall be made and the decision to remove the name from the list shall be taken by the Committee of Ministers. In the latter, the Committee of Ministers shall defer its decision until it has received a recommendation from the Parliamentary Assembly or the Congress of Local and Regional Authorities of Europe acting on a report from their competent committees.

Sundry provisions

21. The procedures described above shall not restrict the right of the Council of Europe bodies to initiate any action concerning other NGOs in pursuance of their respective rules of procedure.

It should also not prevent the Secretariat of the Council of Europe from considering practical co-operation on an ad hoc basis with other NGOs in any field of mutual interest.

22. An INGO whose application has been refused or which has been removed from the list of those enjoying participatory status may submit a fresh application only after a period of two years following the date of the decision.

23. The present rules will enter into force following their adoption by the Committee of Ministers. From that date, the INGOs enjoying consultative status will have participatory status.

24. The INGOs enjoying participatory status will be required to submit their first report four years after the entry into force of these rules.

COMMUNICATION FROM THE COMMISSION, towards a reinforced culture of consultation and dialogue – general principles and minimum standards for consultation of interested parties by the Commission, COM (2002) 704*

I. Introduction

Interaction between the European Institutions and society takes various forms:

- primarily through the European Parliament as the elected representative of the citizens of Europe;
- through the institutionalised advisory bodies of the EU (Economic and Social Committee and the Committee of the Regions), based on their role according to the Treaties;
- and through less formalised direct contacts with interested parties.

In its White Paper on European Governance, the Commission undertook to help reinforce the culture of consultation and dialogue in the EU.

The Commission has prepared this paper on consultation of interested parties in order to meet those commitments. At the same time, the paper is a direct contribution to the 'Action Plan for Better Regulation' and the new approach to impact assessment.

Wide consultation is not a new phenomenon. In fact, the Commission has a long tradition of consulting interested parties from outside when formulating its policies. It incorporates external consultation into the development of almost all its policy areas.

Thus, the benefits of being open to outside input are already recognised. However, until now, there has not been a Commission-wide approach on how to undertake such consultation. Each of the departments has had its own mechanisms and methods for consulting its respective sectoral interest groups. While this has undoubtedly created many examples of good relationships between the Commission and interest groups, there is a general view, shared by many within the Commission and those whom it consults, that the process should be more consistent. The reactions of interested parties to the White Paper on Governance have confirmed this assessment.[1]

---

* *Communication from the Commission: Towards a reinforced culture of consultation and dialogue – general principles and minimum standards for consultation of interested parties by the Commission*, © European Communities, 1995–2007. Commission of the European Communities, Brussels, 11.12.2002 COM(2002) 704 final.

[1] These comments are displayed on the Commission's 'Governance' website at http://europa.eu.int/comm/governance/index_en.htm.

Through the present document the Commission therefore lays down a number of general principles that should govern its relations with interested parties, and a set of minimum standards for the Commission's consultation processes.[2]

The overall rationale of this document is to ensure that all relevant parties are properly consulted.

The principal aims of the approach can be summarised as follows:

- To encourage more involvement of interested parties through a more transparent consultation process, which will enhance the Commission's accountability.
- To provide general principles and standards for consultation that help the Commission to rationalise its consultation procedures, and to carry them out in a meaningful and systematic way.
- To build a framework for consultation that is coherent, yet flexible enough to take account of the specific requirements of all the diverse interests, and of the need to design appropriate consultation strategies for each policy proposal.
- To promote mutual learning and exchange of good practices within the Commission.

The general principles and minimum standards contained in this document were published in the form of a draft in June 2002 for comments by interested parties. The outcome of this consultation process is described in Part IV.

II. Overall rationale of the Commission's consultation processes

Consultation – a win–win situation all round

Consultation mechanisms form part of the activities of all European Institutions throughout the whole legislative process, from policy-shaping prior to a Commission proposal to final adoption of a measure by the legislature and implementation. Depending on the issues at stake, consultation is intended to provide opportunities for input from representatives of regional and local authorities, civil society organisations, undertakings and associations of undertakings, the individual citizens concerned, academics and technical experts, and interested parties in third countries.

There are already institutionalised advisory bodies established especially to assist the Commission, the Parliament and the Council, namely the Economic

---

[2] For the scope of the general principles of minimum standards, see Part V under the heading 'Nature and scope'.

and Social Committee (ESC) and the Committee of the Regions (CoR). The Commission attaches great importance to encouraging these bodies to take a more proactive role and has taken the necessary steps to achieve this (see Chapter III).

However, the essential role of these advisory bodies does not exclude direct contact between the Commission and interest groups. In fact, wide consultation is one of the Commission's duties according to the Treaties and helps to ensure that proposals put to the legislature are sound. This is fully in line with the European Union's legal framework, which states that '*the Commission should [. . .] consult widely before proposing legislation and, wherever appropriate, publish consultation documents*'.[3]

So there is no contradiction between wide consultation and the concept of representative democracy. However, it goes without saying that, first and foremost, the decision-making process in the EU is legitimised by the elected representatives of the European peoples. As the European Parliament stated in its Resolution on the White Paper on Governance:[4] '*Consultation of interested parties [. . .] can only ever supplement and never replace the procedures and decisions of legislative bodies which possess democratic legitimacy; only the Council and Parliament, as colegislators, can take responsible decisions on the context of legislative procedures [. . .]*'. The guiding principle for the Commission is therefore to give interested parties a voice, but not a vote.

On the other hand, the challenge of ensuring an adequate and equitable treatment of participants in consultation processes should not be underestimated. The Commission has underlined, in particular, its intention to '*reduce the risk of the policy-makers just listening to one side of the argument or of particular groups getting privileged access [. . .]*'.[5] This means that the target groups of relevance for a particular consultation need to be identified on the basis of clear criteria.

By fulfilling its duty to consult, the Commission ensures that its proposals are technically viable, practically workable and based on a bottom-up approach. In other words, good consultation serves a dual purpose by helping to improve the quality of the policy outcome and at the same time enhancing the involvement of interested parties and the public at large. A further advantage is that transparent and coherent consultation processes run by the Commission not only allow the general public to be more involved, they also give the legislature greater scope for scrutinising the Commission's activities

---

3   Protocol (N° 7) on the application of the principles of subsidiarity and proportionality, annexed to the Amsterdam Treaty.
4   A5-0399/2001.
5   White Paper on European Governance.

(e.g. by making available documents summarising the outcome of the consultation process).

The specific role of civil society organisations
Although the target groups of consultations vary according to the circumstances, all relevant interests in society should have an opportunity to express their views.

In this context, civil society organisations play an important role as facilitators of a broad policy dialogue. For this reason, the White Paper on European Governance stressed the importance of involving these organisations in its consultation processes. The Commission particularly encourages a coherent approach to representation of civil society organisations at European level.

This specific role of civil society organisations in modern democracies is closely linked to the fundamental right of citizens to form associations in order to pursue a common purpose, as highlighted in Article 12 of the European Charter of Fundamental Rights.[6] Belonging to an association is another way for citizens to participate actively, in addition to involvement in political parties or through elections.

White Paper on European Governance
'Civil society plays an important role in giving voice to the concerns of the citizens and delivering services that meet people's needs. [. . .] Civil society increasingly sees Europe as offering a good platform to change policy orientations and society. [. . .] It is a real chance to get citizens more actively involved in achieving the Union's objectives and to offer them a structured channel for feedback, criticism and protest.'

Problems can arise because there is no commonly accepted – let alone legal – definition of the term 'civil society organisation'. It can nevertheless be used as shorthand to refer to a range of organisations which include: the labour-market players (i.e. trade unions and employers federations – the 'social partners'[7]); organisations representing social and economic players, which are not

---

[6]   'Everyone has the right to freedom of peaceful assembly and to freedom of association at all levels, in particular in political, trade union and civic matters (. . .)'.

[7]   Because of their representativeness, trade unions and employers' organisations have a particular role. For instance, the EC Treaty requires the Commission to consult management and labour in preparing proposals, in particular in the social policy field. Under certain conditions, they can reach binding agreements that are subsequently turned into Community law (within the social dialogue).

social partners in the strict sense of the term (for instance, consumer organisations); NGOs (non-governmental organisations), which bring people together in a common cause, such as environmental organisations, human rights organisations, charitable organisations, educational and training organisations, etc.; CBOs (community-based organisations), i.e. organisations set up within society at grassroots level which pursue member-oriented objectives, e.g. youth organisations, family associations and all organisations through which citizens participate in local and municipal life; and religious communities.[8]

So 'civil society organisations' are the principal structures of society outside of government and public administration, including economic operators not generally considered to be 'third sector' or NGOs. The term has the benefit of being inclusive and demonstrates that the concept of these organisations is deeply rooted in the democratic traditions of the Member Sates of the Union.

III. Improving Commission consultation procedures – an ongoing process

The Commission is not starting from scratch when it comes to the involvement of interested parties. In recent years, it has undertaken a series of measures to improve the consultation process still further. Here are some examples.

Interactive Policy-Making Initiative (IPM)

On 3 April 2001 the European Commission adopted a Communication on Interactive Policy Making (C(2001) 1014), which aims to improve governance by using the Internet for collecting and analysing reactions in the marketplace for use in the European Union's policy-making process. IPM is one of the tools that will help the Commission, as a modern administration, respond more quickly and accurately to the demands of citizens, consumers and business.

The Interactive Policy-Making Initiative involves the development of two Internet-based mechanisms that will help the Commission assess the impact of EU policies (or absence of them) on the ground. These mechanisms are:

- a feedback mechanism, which helps collect spontaneous reactions in the marketplace. It uses existing networks and contact points as

---

[8] This description ties in with the analysis developed by the Economic and Social Committee in its opinion 'The role and contribution of civil society organisations in the building of Europe' (OJ C 329, 17 November 1999, p. 30)

intermediaries in order to obtain continuous access to the opinions and experiences of economic operators and EU citizens;
- a consultation mechanism, which is designed to receive and store rapidly and in a structured way reactions to new initiatives. This includes the setting up of standing panels to gauge views, such as the Business Test Panel.

CONECCS

Data on formal and structured consultative bodies have been collected in a database named CONECCS (*Consultation, the European Commission and Civil Society*).[9] The objective is to provide information on the committees and other Commission frameworks through which the civil society organisations are consulted in a formal or structured way.

Information on non-profit-making civil society organisations at European level is also available to the public on the CONECCS website on the Europa server. This directory of organisations is established on a voluntary basis and is intended only as a source of information, not a means of accreditation.

CONECCS is a dynamic tool, and is continually developing.

The Commission will continue this process of improving its consultation practices in the future. For instance, in a field that is of major importance to European citizens, the Commission is committed to implementing the UN/ECE 'Aarhus' Convention on Access to Information, Public Participation in Decision-making and Access to Justice in Environmental Matters.[10]

A more proactive role for the institutionalised advisory bodies
As indicated in the introduction, the Economic and Social Committee (ESC) and the Committee of the Regions (CoR) play a key part in the consultation process, in accordance with the Treaties. As institutionalised advisory bodies of the EU, they represent a deep-rooted tradition of consultation. The Commission is keen to draw upon their experience and encourage them to take a more proactive role.

---

[9] http://europa.eu.int/comm/civil_society/coneccs/index.htm.
[10] This might require additional implementing measures at Community level, and these are being considered.

Accordingly, in 2001, the Commission concluded Protocols on co-operation with the ESC and the CoR respectively. The rationale behind these Protocols is to reinforce their function as intermediaries between, on the one hand, the EU institutions, and, on the other, organised civil society (ESC) or the regional and local authorities (CoR) respectively. As far as the ESC is concerned, this new approach closely reflects the spirit of the Nice Treaty. The Treaty reinforced the ESC participation in the Community framework by stipulating that it '*shall consist of representatives of the various economic and social components of organised civil society*'. As regards the CoR, the Protocol on co-operation is essential because of the Committee's dual role: It is the representative body of regional and local authorities in the EU and acts as an indispensable intermediary between these authorities and the EU institutions.

Within the Commission, the Protocols are implemented[11] on the basis of an internal vade-mecum for the Commission departments.

According to the Protocols, these bodies will be asked, in the near future, to organise consultations on behalf of the Commission. It will then be necessary to discuss with them how they can fit into the framework laid down in this document.

IV.   Outcome of the consultation process

Following publication of the White Paper on European Governance, the Commission received many comments[12] welcoming its commitment to establish a coherent framework for the consultation of interested parties. However, many organisations expressed a desire to supply the Commission with more detailed comments on the basis of an actual draft consultation framework proposal.

The Commission, therefore, decided to publish such a draft in the form of a consultation document[13] and encouraged all interested parties to submit their comments on the proposed general principles and minimum standards. This approach was greatly appreciated by all those consulted. One of the

---

[11]   The implementation of these Protocols will entail, in particular: requests for exploratory opinions on cross-cutting issues in the framework of the strategic priorities of the Commission and systematic consultation on Green and White Papers; an increase in ad hoc co-operation (hearings, joint conferences, other events).

As far as the ESC is concerned, building upon its cross-cutting function to synthesise, other potential input aimed at enhancing its role as a facilitator of dialogue with civil society could also be considered.

[12]   These comments are displayed at: http://europa.eu.int/comm/governance/contributions/index_en.htm

[13]   'Towards a reinforced culture of consultation and dialogue – proposal for general principles and minimum standards for consultation of interested parties by the Commission' (COM (2002) 277 final).

contributors said: '*The fact that the Commission is consulting on the proposed general principles and minimum standards is in itself a demonstration of good consultation practice.*'

The Commission received a total of 88 contributions, consisting of comments submitted by governments of the Member States (Germany, Sweden, United Kingdom) and of a non-member country (USA), and by international, European and national organisations (covering both the private sector and NGOs), regional and local authorities, religious interests and churches, individual citizens and individual companies. There is a list of all contributors in the Annex. The full texts of the contributions are accessible on the Internet, together with information about the general objectives and structure of those groups that submitted comments on behalf of their organisations.[14]

Both the quantity and the very high quality of the various contributions show the clear interest of outside parties in the Commission's consultation practice.

All the reactions and comments the Commission received have been carefully analysed to see whether, and to what extent, they could be incorporated into the final design of the general principles and minimum standards the Commission is adopting through this document.

1.   Main features of the revised general principles and minimum standards
The revision of the initial draft has resulted in the following main changes:

- The scope of the general principles and minimum standards has been clarified.
- A clearer link between the Commission's impact assessment procedures and the use of consultation has been established.
- The operational implications of the general principles have been spelt out more clearly.
- The constraints on European and national organisations when preparing comments on Commission consultation documents on behalf of their members have been taken into account.
- The use of selection criteria for targeted consultations is explained in more detail.

In addition, the Commission will put in place a series of implementing measures in order to ensure proper application and monitoring across all departments (see Chapter IV.3).

---

[14]   http://europa.eu.int/comm/secretariat_general/sgc/consultation/index_en.htm.

2. *Feedback on the comments received*

In line with the guidelines laid down in the consultation document, the Commission intends to provide feedback on the main issues raised by the participants in the consultation process on these draft general principles and minimum standards.

NATURE OF THE DOCUMENT

Some of those consulted questioned the Commission's decision to set consultation standards in the form of a Commission communication (i.e. in the form of a policy document) instead of adopting a legally-binding instrument. They argued that this would make the standards toothless and the Commission would be unable to ensure the consistency and coherence of its consultation processes.

However, the Commission remains convinced that a legally-binding approach to consultation is to be avoided, for two reasons: First, a clear dividing line must be drawn between consultations launched on the Commission's own initiative prior to the adoption of a proposal, and the subsequent formalised and compulsory decisionmaking process according to the Treaties. Second, a situation must be avoided in which a Commission proposal could be challenged in the Court on the grounds of alleged lack of consultation of interested parties. Such an over-legalistic approach would be incompatible with the need for timely delivery of policy, and with the expectations of the citizens that the European Institutions should deliver on substance rather than concentrating on procedures.

Moreover, the fear expressed by some participants in the consultation process that the principles and guidelines could remain a dead letter because of their non-legally binding nature is due to a misunderstanding. It goes without saying that, when the Commission decides to apply the principles and guidelines, its departments have to act accordingly.

Finally, the Commission is of the opinion that improvement of its consultation practice should not be based on a 'command and control' approach but rather on providing the appropriate guidance and assistance to Commission officials in charge of running the consultation processes. The general principles and minimum standards should serve as a reference point for a permanent in-house learning process.

There is also an action plan providing for an annual report on 'better lawmaking' which will cover the application of the general principles and minimum standards.

SCOPE

Many of those consulted wanted a clearer explanation of the kinds of initiatives to which the new consultation framework will apply. In response, the Commission clarified the scope of the consultation standards.

However, the Commission has not taken up the idea proposed by some participants that the scope of the standards should be generally widened (to cover all consultation), or that they should be separated from the Commission's approach to extended impact assessments. This decision meets the overriding principle of proportionality, which must govern the Commission's administrative practice (see the general principles under the heading of 'effectiveness'). It is also linked to the fact that the Commission has to assess its consultation needs on a case-by-case basis in line with its right of initiative.

By the same token, the Commission must emphasise that consultation can never be an open-ended or permanent process. In other words, there is a time to consult and there is a time to proceed with the internal decision-making and the final decision adopted by the Commission.

ACCESS TO CONSULTATION PROCESSES

The Commission's consultation document made a distinction between open and focused consultation processes, which led many to ask whether access to consultations should be limited and how the quality of submissions by interested parties would be assessed.

There was a full range of positions: some argued that only representative European organisations should be consulted, while others felt that no interested or affected party should be excluded.

Accordingly, the Commission wishes to stress that it will maintain an inclusive approach in line with the principle of open governance: Every individual citizen, enterprise or association will continue to be able to provide the Commission with input. In other words, the Commission does not intend to create new bureaucratic hurdles in order to restrict the number of those that can participate in consultation processes.

However, two additional considerations must be taken into account in this context. First, best practice requires that the target group should be clearly defined prior to the launch of a consultation process. In other words, the Commission should actively seek input from relevant interested parties, so these will have to be targeted on the basis of sound criteria. Second, clear selection criteria are also necessary where access to consultation is limited for practical reasons. This is especially the case for the participation of interested parties in advisory bodies or at hearings. The elements listed under Standard B should be seen against this background.

The Commission would like to underline the importance it attaches to input from representative European organisations. In this context, it should be noted that the Economic and Social Committee has produced a set of eligibility criteria for the so-called 'civil dialogue'.[15] However, the issue of representative-

---

[15]   'In order to be eligible, a European organisation must: exist permanently at Community level; provide direct access to its members' expertise and hence rapid and

ness at European level should not be used as the only criterion when assessing the relevance or quality of comments. The Commission will avoid consultation processes which could give the impression that 'Brussels is only talking to Brussels', as one person put it. In many cases, national and regional viewpoints can be equally important in taking into account the diversity of situations in the Member States. Moreover, minority views can also form an essential dimension of open discourse on policies. On the other hand, it is important for the Commission to consider how representative views are when taking a political decision following a consultation process.

Therefore, the crucial issue for the Commission, when deciding on target groups for consultation, is to ensure that relevant parties are given the opportunity to express their views. The minimum standards have been redrafted and regrouped accordingly.

TRANSPARENCY AND INDEPENDENCE OF INTERESTED PARTIES
Several organisations expressed their concern that under the pretext of transparency the Commission could try to interfere in the internal structure of their organisations. The Commission wishes to emphasise that it fully respects the independence of outside organisations. On the other hand, for the consultation process to be meaningful and credible it is essential to spell out who participated in these processes. The general principles have been slightly adapted to make this clear.

TIME LIMITS FOR CONSULTATION
Many contributors to the consultation process urged the Commission to reconsider the minimum consultation period put forward in Standard D, arguing that six weeks was not long enough to prepare comments. In particular, European and national associations said they needed more time to consult their membership in order to produce consolidated contributions.

The Commission wishes to underline once more that consultation periods must strike a reasonable balance between the need for adequate input and the need for swift decision-making. Standard D has nevertheless been amended to cater, as far as possible, for the needs of interest group organisations.

---

constructive consultation; represent general concerns that tally with the interest of European society; comprise bodies that are recognised at Member State level as representatives of particular interests; have member organisations in most of the EU Member States; provide for accountability to its members; have authority to represent and act at European level; be independent and mandatory, not bound by instructions from outside bodies; be transparent, especially financially and in its decision-making structures.' (Opinion on 'European Governance – a White Paper' of 20 March 2002; CES 357/2002).

PROVISIONS ON FEEDBACK

The Commission reiterates that the main mechanism for providing feedback to participants in consultations will be through an official Commission document to be approved by the College of Commissioners, i.e., in particular, the explanatory memoranda accompanying legislative proposals.

The idea of providing feedback on an individual basis (feedback statements), as requested by some contributions, is not compatible with the requirement of effectiveness of the decision-making process. Moreover, interested parties should keep in mind that the Commission's decision-making is based on the principle of collegiality, that is to say only the College of Commissioners is entitled to weigh up the pros and cons put forward in a consultation process and to adopt a final position in the Community interest. However, this does not prevent individual Commissioners or Commission officials at the appropriate level from engaging in an open debate with interested parties on the policy fields within their remit.

SPECIAL FRAMEWORKS FOR SPECIFIC TARGET GROUPS

Several organisations emphasised the need to create specific consultation arrangements for their respective sectors.

Whilst stressing their role as democratically legitimised bodies, the regional and local authorities enquired about the state of play regarding the preparation of a framework for a more systematic dialogue with regional and local government associations in the EU, which the Commission announced in its White Paper on Governance. The Commission is preparing a working document aimed at identifying the framework, scope and modalities of such a dialogue. This document will be published and disseminated for consultation.

Churches also urged the Commission to put the dialogue with the communities of faith and conviction on a more stable footing and tabled a series of operational proposals to the Commission.

One NGO voiced the idea of concluding a 'Compact' between the European Institutions and voluntary sector organisations, following the example of existing arrangements in some of the Member Sates.

Both churches and NGOs advocated including in the Treaties an article designed to encourage more dialogue with religious interests and civil society.

It is apparent that these proposals go beyond the general principles and minimum standards for the consultation of interested parties. Currently, the Commission wishes to concentrate on proper implementation of the measures on better law-making, including the consultation standards.

3. *Implementing measures*

The abovementioned modifications are designed to make for smooth implementation of the general principles and minimum standards. However, to enable Commission staff to apply them correctly as well as to ensure the necessary ownership by staff, further measures are needed. Therefore, the general principles and minimum standards will be accompanied by the following measures:

- A Commission Intranet website will provide Commission staff with practical guidance, including examples of best practice.
- This will be accompanied by a help-desk facility using a mail-box, to which staff can send questions on the application of the general principles and minimum standards.
- Appropriate awareness-raising measures will be taken and, where appropriate, specific training seminars will be organised.
- The annual report on 'better law-making' will cover implementation of the Commission's consultation framework.
- Co-ordination of the above measures will take place in the context of the overall Commission network on 'better law-making'.

4. Conclusions

The Commission considers that the amended general principles and minimum standards, together with the set of implementing measures, constitute a further important step in the process of improving its consultation mechanisms.

Clearly these measures do not incorporate all the requests which interested parties put forward during consultations on the initial approach proposed by the Commission in June 2002. However, the Commission believes that the decisions taken in the present document strike the right balance between the expectations of interested parties and the need for a framework that, under the existing circumstances, is realistic and feasible in administrative terms.

The final set of general principles and minimum standards, contained in Part V, will apply from 1 January 2003.

V. General principles and minimum standards for consultations by the Commission

Nature and scope

The consultation relationship between the Commission and interested parties should be underpinned by certain fundamental principles. These principles define the environment within which they will both operate. They also constitute the basis for any future developments in the area of consultation policy. The principles draw primarily on the general principles guiding the conduct of the Commission's business. These key principles were highlighted in the

Commission's White Paper on European Governance: Participation, openness, accountability, effectiveness and coherence.

For the consultation relationship to succeed, the commitment to these principles cannot be unilateral: both sides involved in the consultation process have a role in applying them effectively.

When consulting on major policy initiatives the Commission will be guided by the general principles and minimum standards set out in this document, without prejudice to more advanced practices applied by Commission departments or any more specific rules to be developed for certain policy areas. Neither the general principles nor the minimum standards are legally binding.

As a first step, the Commission will focus on applying the general principles and minimum standards to those initiatives that will be subject to an extended impact assessment. Nevertheless, the Directorates-General of the Commission are encouraged to apply the general principles and minimum standards to any other consultation exercises they intend to launch.

The need for an extended impact assessment is decided by the Commission in the Annual Policy Strategy or at the latest in its Work Programme on the basis of the preliminary assessment statements. In deciding whether an extended impact assessment is required the Commission will, *inter alia*, take the following criteria into account:

- Whether the proposal will result in substantial economic, environmental and/or social impact on a specific sector, and whether the proposal will have a significant impact on major interested parties.
- Whether the proposal represents a major policy reform in one or several sectors.

The Commission Communication on impact assessment excluded various measures from the need for impact assessments, e.g. Green Papers because policy formulation is still in progress without producing any direct impact. In terms of consultation, Green Papers are by their very nature initiatives to which the general principles and minimum standards apply.

For the purpose of this document '**consultations**' means those processes through which the Commission wishes to trigger input from outside interested parties for the shaping of policy prior to a decision by the Commission. Consequently, the following fields are excluded from the scope of the general principles and minimum standards:

- Specific consultation frameworks provided for in the Treaties (e.g. the roles of the institutionalised advisory bodies; the social dialogue according to Articles 137 to 139 TEC) or in other Community legislation
- Consultation requirements under international agreements

- Decisions taken in a formal process of consulting Member States ('comitology' procedure).[16]

As flagged in the White Paper on European Governance, the general principles and minimum standards for consultation will be complemented, but not replaced, in the future by two other instruments that the Commission is developing at the moment:

- A set of guidelines on the use of expertise which will aim to encapsulate and spread good practice. In particular, they should provide for the accountability, plurality and integrity of the expertise used. They will apply notably whenever the Commission is faced with a policy issue that hinges to some extent on scientific assessment.[17]
- A framework for more systematic dialogue with European and national associations of regional and local government in the EU.

These instruments will correspond to the specific needs of the policy areas concerned.

General principles

PARTICIPATION
'[The] quality of [. . .] EU policy depends on ensuring wide participation throughout the policy chain – from conception to implementation.'[18]

The Commission is committed to an inclusive approach when developing and implementing EU policies, which means consulting as widely as possible on major policy initiatives. This applies, in particular, in the context of legislative proposals.

OPENNESS AND ACCOUNTABILITY
'The[European] institutions should work in a more open manner [. . .] in order to improve the confidence in complex institutions.'[19]

---

[16]   According to Council decision 1999/468/EC.
[17]   The guidelines will be implemented in co-ordination with the minimum standards, particularly since there is often a need in the policy process for an interaction between experts and interested parties.
[18]   White Paper on European Governance.
[19]   Idem.

'*Each of the EU institutions must explain and take responsibility for what it does in Europe.*'[20]

The Commission believes that the processes of administration and policy-making must be visible to the outside world if they are to be understood and have credibility. This is particularly true of the consultation process, which acts as the primary interface with interests in society.

Thus consultation processes run by the Commission must also be transparent, both to those who are directly involved and to the general public. It must be clear:

- what issues are being developed
- what mechanisms are being used to consult
- who is being consulted and why
- what has influenced decisions in the formulation of policy.

It follows that interested parties must themselves operate in an environment that is transparent, so that the public is aware of the parties involved in the consultation processes and how they conduct themselves.

Openness and accountability are thus important principles for the conduct of organisations when they are seeking to contribute to EU policy development. It must be apparent:

- which interests they represent
- how inclusive that representation is.

Interested parties that wish to submit comments on a policy proposal by the Commission must therefore be ready to provide the Commission and the public at large with the information described above. This information should be made available either through the CONECCS database (where organisations are eligible[21] for this database and wish to be included on a voluntary basis) or through other measures, e.g. special information sheets. If this information is not provided, submissions will be considered as individual contributions.

---

[20]   Idem.

[21]   In order to be eligible, an organisation must be a non-profit representative body organised at European level, i.e. with members in two or more European Union of Candidate countries; be active and have expertise in one or more of the policy areas of the Commission, have some degree of formal or institutional existence; and be prepared to provide any reasonable information about itself required by the Commission, either for insertion on the database or in support of its request for inclusion.

EFFECTIVENESS
'Policies must be effective and timely, delivering what is needed'.[22]

To be effective, consultation must start as early as possible. Interested parties should therefore be involved in the development of a policy at a stage where they can still have an impact on the formulation of the main aims, methods of delivery, performance indicators and, where appropriate, the initial outlines of that policy. Consultation at more than one stage may be required.

In addition, both the Commission and outside interested parties will benefit from understanding the perspective of the other. The Commission operates within a policy and political framework that is influenced by many factors. For example, it must take account of its obligations to the other European institutions under the Treaties, and of its international obligations to third countries and international organisations.

A prerequisite for effectiveness is respect of the principle of proportionality. The method and extent of the consultation performed must therefore always be proportionate to the impact of the proposal subject to consultation and must take into account the specific constraints linked to the proposal.

A better understanding of such factors and of how the Commission works will help outside interested parties to have realistic expectations about what can be achieved.

COHERENCE
'Policies and action must be coherent [. . .].'[23]

The Commission will ensure that there is consistency and transparency in the way its departments operate their consultation processes.

The Commission will include in its consultation processes mechanisms for feedback, evaluation and review.

This will be ensured through appropriate co-ordination and reporting in the context of the Commission's 'better law-making' activities.

The Commission encourages interest groups to establish their own mechanisms for monitoring the process, so that they can see what they can learn from it and check that they are making an effective contribution to a transparent, open and accountable system.

---

[22] Idem.
[23] Idem.

Minimum standards

A. CLEAR CONTENT OF THE CONSULTATION PROCESS

> **All communications relating to consultation should be clear and concise, and should include all necessary information to facilitate responses.**

The information in publicity and consultation documents should include:

- A summary of the context, scope and objectives of consultation, including a description of the specific issues open for discussion or questions with particular importance for the Commission
- Details of any hearings, meetings or conferences, where relevant
- Contact details and deadlines
- Explanation of the Commission's processes for dealing with contributions, what feed-back to expect, and details of the next stages involved in the development of the policy
- If not enclosed, reference to related documentation (including, where applicable, Commission supporting documents).

B. CONSULTATION TARGET GROUPS

> **When defining the target group(s) in a consultation process, the Commission should ensure that relevant parties have an opportunity to express their opinions.**

For consultation to be equitable, the Commission should ensure adequate coverage of the following parties in a consultation process:

- those affected by the policy
- those who will be involved in implementation of the policy, or
- bodies that have stated objectives giving them a direct interest in the policy.

In determining the relevant parties for consultation, the Commission should take into account the following elements as well:

- the wider impact of the policy on other policy areas, e.g. environmental interests[24] or consumer policy
- the need for specific experience, expertise or technical knowledge, where applicable
- the need to involve non-organised interests, where appropriate
- the track record of participants in previous consultations
- the need for a proper balance, where relevant, between the representatives of:
  - social and economic bodies
  - large and small organisations or companies
  - wider constituencies (e.g. churches and religious communities) and specific target groups (e.g. women, the elderly, the unemployed, or ethnic minorities)
  - organisations in the European Union and those in non-member countries (e.g. in the candidate or developing countries or in countries that are major trading partners of the European Union).

Where appropriate, the Commission encourages contributions from interested parties organised at European level.

Where a formal or structured consultation body exists, the Commission should take steps to ensure that its composition properly reflects the sector it represents. If this is not the case, the Commission should consider how to ensure that all interests are being taken into account (e.g. through other forms of consultation).

C. Publication

> **The Commission should ensure adequate awareness-raising publicity and adapt its communication channels to meet the needs of all target audiences. Without excluding other communication tools, open public consultations should be published on the Internet and announced at the 'single access point'.**

For addressing the broader public, a single access point for consultation will be established where interested parties should find information and relevant documentation. For this purpose, the Commission will use the 'Your-Voice-in-Europe' webportal.[25]

---

24 Article 6 of the Treaty establishing the European Community.
25 http://europa.eu.int/yourvoice.

However, at the same time it might be useful to maintain more traditional alternatives to the Internet (e.g. press releases, mailings). Where appropriate and feasible, the Commission should provide consultation documents in alternative formats so as to make them more accessible to the disabled.

D.   TIME LIMITS FOR PARTICIPATION

> **The Commission should provide sufficient time for planning and responses to invitations and written contributions. The Commission should strive to allow at least 8 weeks for reception of responses to written public consultations and 20 working days notice for meetings.**

The main rule is to give those participating in Commission consultations sufficient time for preparation and planning.

Consultation periods should strike a reasonable balance between the need for adequate input and the need for swift decision-making. In urgent cases, or where interested parties have already had sufficient opportunities to express themselves, the period may be shortened.

On the other hand, a consultation period longer than eight weeks might be required in order to take account of:

- the need for European or national organisations to consult their members in order to produce a consolidated viewpoint
- certain existing binding instruments (this applies, in particular, to notification requirements under the WTO agreement)
- the specificity of a given proposal (e.g. because of the diversity of the interested parties or the complexity of the issue at stake)
- main holiday periods.

When the deadline for transmission of comments has expired, the Commission will close the consultation and take the next steps in the administrative process (e.g. prepare for the decision by the Commission).

E.   ACKNOWLEDGEMENT AND FEEDBACK

> **Receipt of contributions should be acknowledged. Results of open public consultation should be displayed on websites linked to the single access point on the Internet.**

Depending on the number of comments received and the resources available, acknowledgement can take the form of:

- an individual response (by e-mail or acknowledgement slip), or
- a collective response (by e-mail or on the Commission's single access point for consultation on the Internet; if comments are posted on the single access point within 15 working days, this will be considered as acknowledgement of receipt).

Contributions will be analysed carefully to see whether, and to what extent, the views expressed can be accommodated in the policy proposals. Contributions to open public consultations will be made public on the single access point. Results of other forms of consultation should, as far as possible, also be subject to public scrutiny on the single access point on the Internet.

The Commission will provide adequate feedback to responding parties and to the public at large. To this end, explanatory memoranda accompanying legislative proposals by the Commission or Commission communications following a consultation process will include the results of these consultations and an explanation as to how these were conducted and how the results were taken into account in the proposal. In addition, the results of consultations carried out in the Impact Assessment process will be summarised in the related reports.

Guidelines for the participation of civil society organizations in OAS activities, CP/RES. 759 (1217/99)[*]

OEA/SER.G
CP/RES.759(1217/99)
15 December 1999
Original: Spanish

THE PERMANENT COUNCIL OF THE ORGANIZATION OF AMERICAN STATES,

HAVING SEEN the report by the Chair of the Committee on Civil Society Participation in OAS Activities and having studied the document prepared by that Committee, 'Guidelines for the Participation of Civil Society Organizations in OAS Activities' (CP/CSC-4/99 rev. 7); and

BEARING IN MIND:

General Assembly resolution 'The Organization of American States and Civil Society' [AG/RES. 1661 (XXIX-O/99)] containing the mandate for the Permanent Council to prepare guidelines for civil society participation in OAS activities and to adopt them before December 31, 1999;

The standards on cooperative relations between the Organization of American States and the United Nations, UN specialized agencies, and other national and international agencies contained in resolution AG/RES. 57 (I-O/71) and resolution CP/RES. 704 (1129/97) on the legal status of nongovernmental organizations (NGOs) in the Organization;

The General Assembly's recognition of the significant contribution of civil society organizations to activities of the OAS and its organs and agencies; and

The work carried out since 1995 by the Permanent Council and its subsidiary bodies to increase the degree to which appropriate nongovernmental organizations and civil society organizations might become more closely involved in, and contribute to, the activities of the Organization, as well as its examination of ways to implement the tasks entrusted to the OAS in the Santiago Plan of Action with respect to civil society,

---

[*]   *Guidelines for the participation of civil society organizations in OAS activities*, OAS permanent council resolution (CP/RES 759 (12/15/99), Organization of American States (www.oas.org), available at http://www.oas.org/consejo/resolutions/res759.asp.

RESOLVES:

1. To adopt the attached Guidelines on Participation by Civil Society Organizations in OAS Activities, which will supplement existing provisions in the Organization, will contribute to its modernization, and ensure the enhancement of relations between it and civil society.
2. To instruct the Secretary General to take the necessary measures to enable the implementation of these Guidelines and to report thereon to the Permanent Council prior to the thirtieth regular session of the General Assembly.
3. To encourage member states to disseminate information on these Guidelines among civil society organizations in their respective countries.
4. To congratulate the Committee on Civil Society Participation in OAS Activities for the efficient way in which it has complied with the General Assembly mandate in the preparation of the above-mentioned Guidelines.
5. To report to the General Assembly at its thirtieth regular session on the implementation of resolution AG/RES. 1661 (XXIX-O/99).

Appendix: guidelines for participation by civil society organizations in OAS activities

Introduction

The Organization of American States (OAS) has taken a special interest in potential contributions by civil society organizations to the activities of its organs, agencies, and entities. For that reason, the OAS Charter assigned the handling of possible special agreements or arrangements between the Organization 'and other American agencies of recognized international standing' to the Permanent Council in 1948. Over the past 50 years, the various organs, agencies, and entities of the OAS have developed, in the context of their institutional aims, various kinds of relationships with national and international institutions. This wealth of experience, which has given rise to some outstanding innovations in the arena of intergovernmental agencies, has also revealed the need to channel the contributions of those institutions and organizations by developing appropriate regulations.

That is why the General Assembly – which in 1971 had already adopted provisions to govern cooperative relations between the OAS and 'other international and national organizations' – came to adopt resolutions to complement the pertinent articles of the OAS Charter. The importance of such cooperation was firmly established at the 1994 Summit of the Americas in its declaration emphasizing the importance of civil society organizations in enhancing and preserving democratic institutions. At the Summit of the Americas on Sustainable Development, held in Bolivia in December 1996, various civil society institutions contributed experience that enriched the Plan of Action of Santa Cruz de la Sierra. The Plan of Action of the Second Summit of the Americas, held in 1998, indicates that the OAS could serve as a forum for the exchange of experience and information in connection with civil society organizations, and entrusts the OAS with promoting suitable programs to foster increased civil society participation in public affairs.

Thus began the second phase in the development of regulations and mechanisms for channelling the contributions of civil society organizations – an effort spearheaded by the OAS Permanent Council. The Committee on Juridical and Political Affairs conducted an exhaustive study of the subject and, in 1998, prepared a report on the legal status of nongovernmental organizations at the OAS. For its part, the Special Joint Working Group of the Permanent Council and the Inter-American Council for Integral Development on the Strengthening and Modernization of the OAS contributed to the development of guidelines for civil society participation in OAS activities.

For its part, in 1998 the General Assembly instructed the Permanent Council to study means of increasing the level of participation by civil society organizations in OAS activities and ways to implement the Santiago Plan of Action's mandates to the OAS relating to civil society. In 1999, the General Assembly decided to establish, within the Permanent Council, a Committee on Civil Society Participation in OAS Activities, whose tasks include developing rules to ensure such participation.

The OAS has thus acquired considerable experience with civil society participation in its activities. Initially, the different forms that participation took were developed by individual organs in accordance with their particular aims. Especially apt examples are the ties established by the Inter-American Commission on Human Rights, the Department of Sustainable Development (formerly Regional Development and Environment), and the Inter-American Telecommunication Commission. These different forms of relationship are reflected in the statutes and rules of procedure of those OAS bodies. In addition, civil society organizations traditionally attend the sessions of the OAS General Assembly.

This tradition of OAS cooperation with civil society organizations is based on the significant contributions these organizations can make to OAS work, since they can contribute knowledge and additional information to decision-making processes, raise new issues and concerns that will subsequently be addressed by the OAS, lend expert advice in their areas of expertise, and contribute to consensus-building in many spheres.

Bearing in mind recent changes in the responsibilities of non-state actors in public life and their increasingly important role at the national, regional, and international levels – trends acknowledged by the OAS and the Summit of the Americas – new mechanisms and methods must be identified to improve current standards and practices in order to adapt them to these new phenomena.

Within this framework, a new phase, i.e., efforts to facilitate participation by civil society organizations in OAS activities overall, began in 1994. In order to bear fruit, civil society participation must be oriented by a clear and yet flexible regulatory framework. Such flexibility is achieved by way of periodic review of participation in OAS activities. These Guidelines thus represent a further step toward enhancing civil society participation in OAS activities.

Guidelines

1. Purpose. The purpose of these guidelines is to govern participation by civil society organizations in activities of the organs, agencies, and entities of the Organization of American States (OAS), in accordance with the inter-governmental nature of the OAS and the provisions of the Charter of the Organization, in particular Articles 91.d, 95.d, 103, and 112.h, the statutes and rules of procedure of the corresponding organs, and the rules governing the conduct of OAS activities in pursuit of its essential purposes.

2. Definition. 'Civil society organization' is understood to mean any national or international institution, organization, or entity made up of natural or juridical persons of a nongovernmental nature.

3. Scope of participation by civil society organizations.

a. Civil society organizations may attend the activities of the OAS, make presentations, provide information, and, at the request of the organs, agencies, and entities of the OAS, provide expert advice, in accordance with these guidelines. They may also participate in operational activities relating to the design, financing, and execution of cooperation programs, in accordance with applicable regulations and specific agreements negotiated for this purpose.

b. The provisions of these Guidelines complement but do not modify the Rules of Procedure of the General Assembly, the Rules of Procedure of the Inter-American Council for Integral Development (CIDI), the rules governing the inter-American specialized conferences and organizations, and the rules governing the inter-American committees of CIDI.

4. Principles to govern participation by civil society organizations in OAS activities. Civil society organizations may participate in OAS activities in accordance with the following principles:

a. The matters with which they are concerned must fall within the competence of the OAS, and the aims and purposes they pursue must be consistent with the spirit, aims, and principles established in the Charter of the OAS.

b. Participation by civil society organizations in OAS activities shall have the purpose of enabling the organs, agencies, or entities of the OAS to benefit, in a manner consistent with their operational regulations, from expert advice or specialized information provided to them by those organizations on subjects in which those organizations have special competence or interest and from the cooperation such organizations may provide.

c. Participation by civil society organizations in OAS activities should further the activities of its organs, agencies, and entities without prejudice to the regulatory, policy-making, and policy implementation functions established by the instruments that govern those organs, agencies, and entities.

d. Participation by civil society organizations in OAS activities, while welcome, shall not be interpreted as a concession of negotiating functions – which are the exclusive preserve of the States – and shall not alter the intergovernmental nature of the organs, agencies, and entities of the OAS.

e. Arrangements for participation by civil society organizations in OAS activities are distinct from the rights accorded to member states, permanent observers, and entities and organs of the inter-American system.

5. Responsibilities of the organs, agencies, and entities of the OAS with respect to participation by civil society organizations in their activities.

a. The Permanent Council, through its Committee on Civil Society Participation in OAS Activities ('the Committee'), shall monitor the arrangements established between civil society organizations and the OAS within the scope of the functions conferred upon it by the Charter of the OAS.

b. The other organs, agencies, and entities of the OAS shall govern their relations with civil society organizations in ways that are consistent with their own governing provisions and that will best serve their purposes and specific mandates, with due regard to these guidelines.

c. The General Secretariat shall carry out the duties entrusted to it by the Permanent Council through the Committee, shall implement the mechanisms and procedures detailed below, and shall present recommendations as it sees fit to the Committee, with a view to improving the system once established.

6. Application to participate. In order for a civil society organization to participate in the activities of the OAS, it must direct an application to the Secretary General. The Secretary General shall refer the application to the Committee, which shall examine it, make such recommendations as it sees fit, and submit it to the Permanent Council for a decision. The application should contain the following elements:

a. Official name, address, and date of establishment of the organization and the name(s) of its directors and legal representative(s).

b. Its primary areas of activity and their relationship to the activities of the OAS organs, agencies, and entities in which it wishes to participate.

c. Reasons why it believes its proposed contributions to OAS activities would be of interest to the Organization.

d. Identification of the OAS work areas in which it proposes to support ongoing activities or to make recommendations on the best way to achieve OAS objectives.

e. The application shall be accompanied by the following documents:

- Charter or constitution
- Statutes
- Most recent annual report
- Institutional mission statement
- Financial statements for the previous fiscal year, including reference to public and private sources of financing.

7. <u>Registration of civil society organizations</u>. The General Secretariat shall establish a register of all civil society organizations approved by the Permanent Council for participation in OAS activities. The General Secretariat shall keep this register updated, and shall publish it on the OAS web site in the area pertaining to civil society organizations.

8. <u>Conditions of eligibility</u>. In examining the application to participate submitted by a civil society organization, the Committee shall take into account the following factors in preparing its recommendation thereon:

a. The civil society organization shall be of recognized standing within its particular field of competence and shall be of a representative nature.

b. The civil society organization shall have an institutional structure that includes appropriate mechanisms for holding its officers accountable and subject to its members. It shall also have a legal representative and an executive officer, as well as established headquarters.

c. The civil society organization shall obtain its resources primarily from its affiliates or individual members, and shall have provided a listing of its sources of financing and any donations received, including, in particular, those originating from government sources. Those organizations that are not membership-based shall also provide a listing of sources of financing and any donations received, including, in particular, those originating from government sources.

d. The Committee must satisfy itself in particular that the institutional and financial structure of the civil society organization is transparent and affords it a degree of independence.

e. The Committee shall not process applications to participate from civil society organizations that have their headquarters or conduct their principal activities in any territory over which there exists a sovereignty dispute between an OAS member state and a state outside the Hemisphere.

9. <u>Geographic origin of the civil society organizations</u>. The Committee should seek to ensure the registration of civil society organizations from all member states, in order to facilitate just, balanced, effective, and genuine participation by all regions of the Hemisphere.

10. <u>Comments and requests for reports by member states</u>. During the Committee's examination of applications to participate, member states may

submit comments and request information from the organization in question. These comments and requests shall be sent to that organization for a response.

11. <u>Responsibilities of registered civil society organizations</u>. By registering, the civil society organization assumes the following responsibilities:

a. Answer inquiries from the organs, agencies, and entities of the OAS and provide advisory services to them upon request.

b. Disseminate information on OAS activities to its members.

c. Present to the General Secretariat, before December 31 of each year, a report, containing an executive summary, on its participation in OAS activities during that year, its financial situation and sources of funding, and the activities planned for the coming year. This report shall be transmitted by the General Secretariat to the Committee.

d. Keep the information on its executive officers up to date.

12. <u>Participation in OAS conferences</u>. Participation by civil society organizations in OAS conferences shall be governed by the following rules:

a. A registered civil society organization may participate after notifying the General Secretariat of the name(s) of the representative(s) who will attend the conference.

b. A civil society organization that is not registered and wishes to participate in an OAS conference shall submit an application to that effect to the General Secretariat, which shall transmit it to the Committee. The application shall contain the information specified in item 6.

c. After the Committee has made a preliminary review of the application and has made such recommendations as it sees fit, the application shall be transmitted to the committee or working group charged with preparing for the conference, which shall take a final decision and, if appropriate, shall issue accreditation to the applying organization.

d. If a member state comments on or requests information with respect to an application to participate, the civil society organization referred to should be informed in time for it to be able to respond.

e. In all other respects, the participation of civil society organizations in OAS conferences shall be governed by the rules governing those activities.

13. <u>Attendance and participation by civil society organizations in the OAS at meetings of the Permanent Council, CIDI, and their subsidiary bodies</u>

a. Registered civil society organizations may designate representatives to attend, as observers, public meetings of the Permanent Council, CIDI, and their subsidiary bodies. Whether representatives of civil society organizations may attend closed meetings shall be determined by the chair of the meeting in question, in consultation with the participating member state delegations.

b. The Secretariat shall provide registered civil society organizations, in a timely manner, with information on the calendar of public meetings and, when available, the order of business of such meetings.

c. A registered civil society organization may present written documents, not exceeding 2,000 words, preferably in two of the official languages of the OAS, on questions that fall within its particular sphere of competence and appear on the agenda or order of business for the meeting. These documents shall be distributed by the General Secretariat to member states, insofar as possible, in two of the official languages of the OAS. Texts exceeding 2,000 words shall be accompanied by executive summaries in two of the official languages of the OAS, which the Secretariat shall distribute sufficiently ahead of time. The complete text of the document may be distributed in its original language or languages, the cost to be borne by the civil society organization in question.

d. In the case of meetings of committees of the Permanent Council or of CIDI, registered civil society organizations may distribute written documents in advance, in keeping with item 13.c, and, with prior approval from the committee in question, may give a presentation at the beginning of the deliberations. Civil society organizations may not participate in deliberations, negotiations, or decisions adopted by member states.

e. In the case of meetings of expert groups and working groups of the Permanent Council or of CIDI, registered civil society organizations that have special competence in the issue to be discussed shall receive the relevant documents in advance and, with the prior approval of the meeting, may present a statement at the beginning of the deliberations, the text of which may be distributed in advance to the member states. With such approval, they may also give a presentation once the consideration of the issue has concluded. Civil society organizations may not participate in deliberations, negotiations, or decisions adopted by member states.

14. Review of participation by civil society organizations in OAS activities. The Committee may conduct a periodic review of participation by civil society organizations in OAS activities, with a view to recommending to the Permanent Council any measures for improvement it considers appropriate. For this purpose, the Committee shall take account of the annual reports civil society organizations must submit under item 11.c.

15. Suspension or cancellation of registration. The Committee may recommend to the Permanent Council that it suspend or cancel the registration of any organization if it has concluded that such organization:

a. Has acted in a manner that is inconsistent with the essential aims and principles of the OAS;

b. Has failed to make a positive or effective contribution to the work of the OAS, as reflected in the reports submitted under item 11.c;

c. Has failed to submit reports for two consecutive years; or

d. Has furnished manifestly false or inaccurate information.

16. Term of suspension of registration. The Permanent Council may suspend registration, upon a recommendation from the Committee, as a result

of the review referred to in items 14 and 15. The Permanent Council shall determine the length of the suspension period, which in no case may be longer than one year. Any civil society organization whose registration has been suspended may apply to the Permanent Council to reinstate its registration, in accordance with the procedure established in item 7, after the period of suspension has expired.

17. Cancellation of registration. The Permanent Council may cancel the registration of a civil society organization as a result of the periodic review referred to in items 14 and 15. A civil society organization whose registration has been cancelled may apply again to the Permanent Council for recognition three years after the effective date of cancellation.

18. Notification of the procedure to the civil society organization. The Secretary General shall provide written notification to any registered civil society organization before the Committee recommends the suspension or cancellation of its registration. The Committee shall provide the organization in question with a reasonable opportunity to submit any comments, observations, or information it deems relevant.

Statement of the Free Trade Commission on non-disputing party participation, NAFTA, 7 October 2003[*]

A. Non-disputing party participation

1. No provision of the North American Free Trade Agreement ('NAFTA') limits a Tribunal's discretion to accept written submissions from a person or entity that is not a disputing party (a 'non-disputing party').

2. Nothing in this statement by the Free Trade Commission ('the FTC') prejudices the rights of NAFTA Parties under Article 1128 of the NAFTA.

3. Considering that written submissions by non-disputing parties in arbitrations under Section B of Chapter 11 of NAFTA may affect the operation of the Chapter, and in the interests of fairness and the orderly conduct of arbitrations under Chapter 11, the FTC recommends that Chapter 11 Tribunals adopt the following procedures with respect to such submissions.

B. Procedures

1. Any non-disputing party that is a person of a Party, or that has a significant presence in the territory of a Party, that wishes to file a written submission with the Tribunal (the 'applicant') will apply for leave from the Tribunal to file such a submission. The applicant will attach the submission to the application.

2. The application for leave to file a non-disputing party submission will:

    (a) be made in writing, dated and signed by the person filing the application, and include the address and other contact details of the applicant;

    (b) be no longer than 5 typed pages;

    (c) legal status (e.g., company, trade association or other non-governmental organization), its general objectives, the nature of its activities, and any parent organization (including any organization that directly or indirectly controls the applicant);

    (d) disclose whether or not the applicant has any affiliation, direct or indirect, with any disputing party;

    (e) identify any government, person or organization that has provided any financial or other assistance in preparing the submission;

---

[*] *Statement of the Free Trade Commission on non-disputing party participation*, NAFTA/Free Trade Commission statement of 7 October 2003, United States Department of Agriculture/Economic Research Service. Reproduced in *International Legal Materials*, **44**, May 2005 at 796–797.

(f)   specify the nature of the interest that the applicant has in the arbitration;

(g)   identify the specific issues of fact or law in the arbitration that the applicant has addressed in its written submission;

(h)   explain, by reference to the factors specified in paragraph 6, why the Tribunal should accept the submission; and

(i)   be made in a language of the arbitration.

3.   The submission filed by a non-disputing party will:

(a)   be dated and signed by the person filing the submission;

(b)   be concise, and in no case longer than 20 typed pages, including any appendices;

(c)   set out a precise statement supporting the applicant's position on the issues; and

(d)   only address matters within the scope of the dispute.

4.   The application for leave to file a non-disputing party submission and the submission will be served on all disputing parties and the Tribunal.

5.   The Tribunal will set an appropriate date by which the disputing parties may comment on the application for leave to file a non-disputing party submission.

6.   In determining whether to grant leave to file a non-disputing party submission, the Tribunal will consider, among other things, the extent to which:

(a)   the non-disputing party submission would assist the Tribunal in the determination of a factual or legal issue related to the arbitration by bringing a perspective, particular knowledge or insight that is different from that of the disputing parties;

(b)   the non-disputing party submission would address matters within the scope of the dispute;

(c)   the non-disputing party has a significant interest in the arbitration; and

(d)   there is a public interest in the subject-matter of the arbitration.

7.   The Tribunal will ensure that:

(a)   any non-disputing party submission avoids disrupting the proceedings; and

(b)   neither disputing party is unduly burdened or unfairly prejudiced by such submissions.

8. The Tribunal will render a decision on whether to grant leave to file a non-disputing party submission. If leave to file a non-disputing party submission is granted, the Tribunal will set an appropriate date by which the disputing parties may respond in writing to the non-disputing party submission. By that date, non-disputing NAFTA Parties may, pursuant to Article 1128, address any issues of interpretation of the Agreement presented in the non-disputing party submission.

9. The granting of leave to file a non-disputing party submission does not require the Tribunal to address that submission at any point in the arbitration. The granting of leave to file a non-disputing party submission does not entitle the non-disputing party that filed the submission to make further submissions in the arbitration.

10. Access to documents by non-disputing parties that file applications under these procedures will be governed by the FTC's Note of July 31, 2001.

Selected bibliography

NGOS IN GENERAL

Books

Alston, Philip (ed.) (2005), *Non-State Actors and Human Rights*, Oxford: Oxford University Press.

Archibugi, Daniele and David Held (eds) (1995), *Cosmopolitan Democracy; An Agenda for a New World Order,* Cambridge: Polity Press.

Bettati, Mario and Pierre-Marie Dupuy (eds) (1986), *Les ONG et le droit international*, Paris: Economica.

Clapham, Andrew (2006), *Human Rights Obligations of Non-State Actors*, Oxford: Oxford University Press.

Gherari, Habib and Sandra Szurek (eds) (2003), *L'émergence de la société civile internationale, vers la privatisation du droit international?*, Paris: Pedone.

Heere, Wybo P. (ed.) (2004), *From Government to Governance: the Growing Impact of Non-State Actors on the International and European Legal System. Proceedings of the sixth Hague Joint Conference held in The Hague, the Netherlands, 3–5 July 2003*, The Hague: T.M.C. Asser Press.

Hofmann, Rainer (ed.) (1999), *Non-State Actors as New Subjects of International Law*, Berlin: Duncker & Humblot.

Lindblom, Anna-Karin (2005), *Non-Governmental Organisations in International Law*, Cambridge: Cambridge University Press.

Martens, Kerstin (2005), *NGOs and the United Nations: Institutionalization, Professionalization and Adaptation*, New York: Palgrave Macmillan.

White, Lyman Cromwell (1951), *International Non-Governmental Organizations: Their Purposes, Methods and Accomplishments*, New Brunswick: Rutgers University Press.

Articles

Anderson, K. (2000), 'The Ottawa convention banning landmines: the role of international non-governmental organizations and the idea of international civil society', *European Journal of International Law*, **11**(1), 91–120.

Benvenuti, P. (1981), 'Organizzazioni internazionali non governative', *Enciclopedia del diritto*, Milano: Giuffrè, 407–13.

Burhenne, W. (1995), 'The role of NGOs', in Winfried Lang (ed.), *Sustainable Development and International Law*, London: Aspen, 207–11.

Charnovitz, S. (1997), 'Two centuries of participation: NGOs and international governance', *Michigan Journal of International Law*, **18**(2), 183–286.

Charnovitz, S. (2006), 'Nongovernmental organizations and international law (in Centennial Essays)', *American Journal of International Law*, **100**(2), 348–72.

Ranjeva, R. (1997), 'Les Organisations non gouvernementales et la mise en œuvre du droit international', *Recueil des cours de l'Académie de droit international de la Haie*, **270**, 9–106.

Ravi, N. (2000), 'Le problème des organisations pro-gouvernementales', *Moniteur des droits de l'homme*, **49–50**, 8–9.

Rechenberg, H. (1997) 'Non-governmental organizations', in Rudolph Bernhardt (ed.), *Encyclopaedia of Public International Law*, vol. 3, Amsterdam: North-Holland, 612–18.

Ruiz Fabri, H. (2000), 'Organisations non gouvernementales', *Repertoire de Droit international*, Paris: Dalloz.

Treves, T. (2007), 'Etats et organisations non-gouvernementales', in *Mélanges offerts à Jean Salmon – Droit du pouvoir, pouvoir du droit*, Bruxelles: Bruylant (forthcoming).

NGOS AND INTERGOVERNMENTAL ORGANIZATIONS

Books

Chiang, Pei-heng (1981), *Non-Governmental Organisations at the United Nations – Identity, Role and Function*, New York: Praeger.

Guillet, Sara (1995), *Nous peuples des Nations Unies. L'action des ONG au sein du système de protection internationale des droits de l'Homme*, Paris: Montchrestien.

Herrmann, Peter (ed.) (1998), *European Integration between Institution Building and Social Process: Contributions to a Theory of Modernisation and NGOs in the Context of the Development of the EU*, New York: Nova Science.

Lister, Marjorje and Carbone, Maurizio (2006), *New Pathways in International Development: Gender and Civil Society in EU Policy*, Aldershot, Hants, England, and Burlington, VT: Ashgate.

Orlando, Pietro Romano (1991), *La cooperazione dell'Europa comunitaria allo sviluppo dei Paesi ACP*, Napoli: Edizioni Scientifiche Italiane.

Ruzza, Carlo (2004), *Europe and Civil Society: Movement Coalitions and European Governance*, Manchester, UK and New York, US: Manchester University Press.

Smismans, Stijn (2006), *Civil Society and Legitimate European Governance*, Cheltenham, UK and Northampton, MA, USA: Edward Elgar.

Willetts, Peter (ed.) (1996), *The Conscience of the World – The Influence of Non-Governmental Organisations in the UN System*, Washington DC: Brookings Inst.

Articles

Armstrong, K. (2001), 'Civil society and the White Paper – bridging or jumping the gaps?', in Christian Joerges, Yves Mény and Joseph Weiler, *Symposium: Mountain or Molehill? – A Critical Appraisal of the Commission White Paper on Governance*, Jean Monnet Working Paper no 6/01, Florence and New York: Robert Schuman Centre for Advanced Studies – EUI and Jean Monnet Program – NYU, available at http://www.iue.it/RSCAS/research/OnlineSymposia/Walker.pdf.

Aston, J. (2001), 'The United Nations Committee on Non-governmental Organizations: guarding the entrance to a politically divided house', *European Journal of International Law*, **12**(5), 943–62.

Churchill, R. and G. Ulfstein (2000), 'Autonomous institutional arrangements in multilateral environmental agreements: a little noticed phenomenon in international law', *American Journal of International Law*, **94**(4), 623–59.

De Schutter, O. (2002), 'Europe in search of its civil society', *European Law Journal*, **8**(2), 198–217.

Elgström, O. (2000), 'Lomé and post-Lomé: asymmetric negotiations and the impact of norms', *European Foreign Affairs Review,* **5**(2), 175–96.

El Yazami, D. and A. Madelin (Spring 2002), 'Durban et les ONG', *Projet*, **269**, 25–32.

Fodella, A. (2003), 'Il vertice di Johannesburg sullo sviluppo sostenibile', *Rivista giuridica dell'ambiente*, **17**(3), 385–402.

Gray, K. (2003), 'World summit on sustainable development: accomplishments and new directions?', *International and Comparative Law Quarterly*, **52**(1), 256–28.

Guillet, S. (winter 1999), 'Les relations entre les ONG et l'ONU dans le domaine des droits de l'Homme: un partenariat en mutation', *L'Observateur des Nations Unies*, 7.

Gupta, J. (2003), 'The role of non-state actors in international environmental affairs', *Zeitschrift für ausländisches öffentliches Recht und Völkerrecht*, **63**(2), 459–486.

Iovane, M. (2005), 'Soggetti privati, società civile e tutela internazionale dell'ambiente', in Angela Del Vecchio and A.J. Dal Ri (eds), *Il diritto internazionale dell'ambiente dopo il vertice di Johannesbourg*, Napoli: Editoriale Scientifica, 133–83.

Ivanova M. (2003), 'Partnerships, international organizations, and global environmental governance', in Thorsten Benner, Charlotte Streck and Jan Martin Witte (eds), *Progress or Peril? Networks and Partnerships in Global Environmental Governance. The Post-Johannesburg Agenda*, Berlin/Washington D.C.: Global Public Policy Institute, 9–36.

Laroche, B. (Fall 1999), 'Maligned & excluded in a politicized process. HRIC denied consultative status', *China Rights Forum (publication de HRIC)*, 24–9.

Maljean-Dubois, S. (2003), 'Environnement, développement durable et droit international: de Rio à Johannesburg: et au-delà?', *Annuaire Français de Droit International*, **48**, 592–623.

Martines, F. (1998), 'Alcuni problemi relativi alla politica di cooperazione allo sviluppo della Comunità europea', *Diritto dell'Unione europea*, **8**, 891–4.

Morgera, E. (2005), 'An update on the Aarhus Convention and its continued global relevance', *Review of European Community and International Environmental Law*, **14**(2), 138–47.

Mutasa, C. (2004), 'The African Union – civil society contract. An act of democracy?', *Civil Society Observer*, **1**(5), available at http://www.un-ngls.org/cso/cso5.htm

Noortman, M. (2004), 'Who really needs Article 71? A critical approach to the relationship between NGOs and the UN', in Wybo P. Heere (ed.), *From Government to Governance: the Growing Impact of Non-State Actors on the International and European Legal Systems. Proceedings of the Sixth Hague Joint Conference held in The Hague, The Netherlands, 3–5 July 2003*, The Hague: T.M.C. Asser Press, 118.

Pallamaerts, M. (2003), 'International law and sustainable development: any progress in Johannesburg?', *Review of European Community and International Environmental Law*, **12**(1), 1–11.

Pisillo Mazzeschi, R. (1991), 'Forms of international responsibility for environmental harm', in Francesco Francioni and Tullio Scovazzi (eds), *International Responsibility for Environmental Harm*, London: Graham & Trotman, Dordrecht [etc.]: Nijhoff, 15–35.

Röben, V. (2000), 'Institutional developments under modern international environmental agreements', *Max Planck Yearbook of United Nations Law*, **4**, 363–443.

Sands, P. (1989), 'The environment, community and international law', *Harvard International Law Journal*, **30**(2), 393–420.

Varella, M.D. (2005), 'Le rôle des organisations non-gouvernementales dans le développement du droit international de l'environnement', *Journal du Droit International*, **132**(1), 41–76.

Wates, J. (2005), 'The Aarhus Convention: a driving force for environmental democracy', *Journal for European Environmental & Planning Law,* **2**(1), 2–11.

Wilkinson, M.A. (2003), 'Civil society and the re-imagination of European constitutionalism', *European Law Journal,* **9**(4), 451–72.

Willets, P. (2000), 'From consultative arrangements to partnership: the changing status of NGOs in diplomacy at the UN', *Global Governance,* **6**, 191–212.

Witte, J.M., C. Streck and T. Benner (2003), 'The road from Johannesburg: what future for partnerships in global environmental governance?', in Thorsten Benner, Charlotte Streck, and Jan Martin Witte (eds), *Progress or Peril? Networks and Partnerships in Global Environmental Governance. The Post-Johannesburg Agenda,* Berlin/Washington D.C.: Global Public Policy Institute, 59–84.

Yamin, F. (2001) 'NGOs and international environmental law: a critical evaluation of their role and responsibilities', *Review of European Community and International Environmental Law,* **10**(2), 149–62.

NGOS BEFORE INTERNATIONAL COURTS AND TRIBUNALS AND NON-COMPLIANCE PROCEDURES

Books

Beyerlin, Ulrich, Peter-Tobias Stoll and Rüdiger Wolfrum (2006) (eds), *Ensuring Compliance with Multilateral Environmental Agreements,* Leiden, Boston: Martinus Nijhoff.

Boisson de Chazournes, Laurence, Cesare Romano and Ruth Mackenzie (eds) (2002), *International Organizations and International Dispute Settlement: Trends and Prospects,* Ardsley, NY: Transnational Publishers.

Chinkin, Christine (1993), *Third Parties in International Law,* Oxford: Clarendon Press.

Ruiz Fabri, Hélène and Jean-Marc Sorel (eds) (2005), *Le tiers à l'instance devant les juridictions internationales,* Paris: Pendone.

Treves, Tullio et al. (eds) (2004), *Civil Society, International Courts and Compliance Bodies,* The Hague: T.M.C. Asser Press.

Articles

Ascensio, H. (2001), 'L'*amicus curiae* devant les juridictions internationales', *Revue Générale de Droit International Public,* **105**(4), 897–929.

Baratta, R. (2002), 'La legittimazione dell'amicus curiae dinanzi agli organi giudiziali della Organizzazione mondiale del commercio', *Rivista di diritto internazionale,* **85**(3), 549–72.

Beyerlin, U. (2001), 'The role of NGOs in international environmental litigation', *Zeitschrift für ausländisches öffentliches Recht und Völkerrecht*, **61**(2–3), 357–78.

Boisson de Chazournes, L., (1995), 'La mise an œuvre du droit international dans le domaine de la protection de l'environnement: enjeux et défis', *Revue Générale de Droit International Public*, 99(1), 37–76 .

Bothe, M. (1997) 'Compliance control beyond diplomacy: the role of non-governmental actors', *Environmental Policy & Law*, **27**(4), 293–7.

Brunnée, J. (2006), 'Enforcement mechanisms in international law and international environmental law', in Ulrich Beyerlin, Peter-Tobias Stoll and Rüdiger Wolfrum (eds), *Ensuring Compliance with Multilateral Environmental Agreements*, Leiden, NL, Boston, MA: Martinus Nijhoff, 1–23.

Cameron, J. (1996), 'Compliance, citizens and NGOs', in James, Cameron, Jacob Werksman and Peter Roderick (eds), *Improving Compliance with International Environmental Law*, London: Earthscan, 29–47.

Cygan, A. (2003), 'Protecting the interests of civil society in community decision-making – the limits of Article 230 EC, *International and Comparative Law Quarterly*, **52**(4), 995–1012.

De Schutter, O. (1996), 'Sur l'émergence de la société civile en droit international: le rôle des associations devant la Cour européenne des droits de l'homme', *European Journal of International Law*, **7**(3), 372–409.

Downs, G., D. Rocke and P. Barsoom (1996), 'Is the good news about compliance good news about cooperation?', *International Organization*, **50**(3), 379–406.

Dunoff, J. (1998), 'The misguided debate over NGO participation in the WTO', *Journal of International Economic Law*, **1**, 433–56.

Dupuy, P.-M. (2006), 'Article 34', in A. Zimmermann, C. Tomuschat and K. Oellers-Frahms (eds), *The Statute of the International Court of Justice: A Commentary*, Oxford: OUP, 548.

Ehrmann, M. (2002), 'Procedures of compliance control in international environmental treaties', *Colorado Journal of Environmental Law & Policy*, **13**(2), 377–443.

Fitzmaurice, M. and C. Redgwell (2000), 'Environmental non-compliance procedures and international law', *Netherland Yearbook of International Law*, **31**, 35–65.

Goote, M. (1999) 'Non-compliance procedures in international environmental law: the middle way between diplomacy and law', *International Law Forum*, **1**(2), 82–9.

Koester, V. (2005), 'Review of compliance under the Aarhus Convention: a rather unique compliance mechanism', *Journal for European Environmental & Planning Law*, **2**(1), 31–44.

Koester, V. (2007), 'The Convention on Access to Information, Public

Participation in Decision-Making and Access to Justice in Environmental Matters (Aarhus Convention)', in Geir Ulfstein, Thilo Marauhn and Andreas Zimmermann (eds), *Making Treaties Work. Human Rights, Environment and Arms Control*, Cambridge: Cambridge University Press, 179–217.

Koskenniemi, M. (1992), 'Breach of treaty or non-compliance? Reflections on the enforcement of the Montreal Protocol', *Yearbook of International Environmental Law*, **3**, 123–62.

Marauhn, T. (1996), 'Towards a procedural law of compliance control in international environmental relations', *Zeitschrift für ausländisches öffentliches Recht und Völkerrecht*, **56**(3), 696–731.

Marceau, G. and P. Pedersen (1999), 'Is the WTO open and transparent? A discussion of the relationship of the WTO with non-governmental organisations and civil society's claims for more transparency and public participation', *Journal of World Trade*, **33**(1), 5–49.

Marshall, F. (2006), 'Two years in the life: the pioneering Aarhus convention compliance committee 2004–2006', *International Community Law Review*, **8**(1), 123–54.

Ohlhoff, S. and H. Schloemann, (2001), 'Transcending the nation-state? Private parties and the enforcement of international trade law', *Max Planck Yearbook of United Nations Law*, **5**, 675–734.

Pineschi L. (2004), 'Non-compliance mechanisms and the proposed Center for the Prevention and Management of Environmental Disputes', *Anuario de Derecho Internacional*, **20**, 241–78.

Pitea, C. (2004), 'UN/ECE protocol on water and health – towards the entry into force', *Environmental Policy & Law*, **34**(6), 267–72.

Pitea, C. (2005), 'NGOs in non-compliance mechanisms under multilateral environmental agreements: from tolerance to recognition?', in Tullio Treves et al. (eds), *Civil Society, International Courts and Compliance Bodies*, The Hague: T.M.C. Asser Press, 205–24.

Pitea, C. (2006), 'The non-compliance procedure of the Aarhus Convention: between environmental and human rights control mechanisms', *Italian Yearbook of International Law*, **16**, 85–116.

Sands, P. (1991), 'The role of non-governmental organizations in enforcing international environmental law', in William E. Butler (ed.), *Control over Compliance with International Law*, Dordrecht: Martinus Nijhoff, 61–8.

Shelton, D. (1994), 'The participation of nongovernmental organizations in international judicial proceedings', *American Journal of International Law*, **88**(4), 611–42.

Stern, B. (2003), 'L'Intervention des tiers dans le contentieux de l'OMC', *Revue Générale de Droit International Public*, **107**(2), 257–303.

Sur, S. (1999), 'Vers une Cour penale internationale: la Convention de Rome entre les ONG et le Conseil de sécurité', *Revue Générale de Droit International Public,* **103**(29), 35–8.

Tanzi A. and C. Pitea (2003), 'Emerging trends in the role of non-state actors in international water disputes', in International Bureau of the Permanent Court of Arbitration (ed.), *Resolution of International Water Disputes,* The Hague: Kluwer Law International, 259–97.

Trachtman J. and M. Moremen (2003), 'Costs and benefits of private participation in WTO dispute settlement: whose right is it anyway?, *Harvard International Law Journal,* **44**(1), 221–50.

Udombana N. (2000), 'Toward the African Court on Human and Peoples' Rights: better late than never, *Yale Human Rights and Development Law Journal,* **88**.

Urbinati, S. (2003), 'Non-compliance procedure under the Kyoto Protocol', *Baltic Yearbook of International Law,* **3**, 229–51.

Wolfrum, R. (1999), 'Means of ensuring compliance with and enforcement of international environmental law', *Recueil des cours de l'Académie de droit international de La Haie,* **272**, 9–154.

Index

A Woman's Voice International 101
Aarhus Convention
   on Access to Public Participation in
      Decision-Making and Access
      to Justice in Environmental
      Matters, European
      Commission 232
   Almaty Guidelines 144–8, 197–200
   appointment of rapporteur 196–7
   environmental non-compliance issues
      184–5, 186, 188, 189–90, 194,
      195–200, 201, 203, 213
   and EU 197–8
   international environmental law 139,
      144–8
   and USA 197
Adair, A. 170, 171
Africa
   African Court on Human and
      Peoples' Rights 158, 159–60,
      170, 177, 210, 214
   Commission for Human and Peoples'
      Rights (AfrComHR) 158, 159,
      163
   EU, African, Caribbean and Pacific
      countries (ACP) aid 126, 130,
      131, 132–3
   Great Lakes Region 28
   Muslims Agency 88
   NGO Informal Regional Network
      (UN-IRENE) 91
   Organization of African Unity *see*
      African Union
Agence des cités unies pour la
   coopération Nord-Sud 96, 97
Agir ensemble pour les droits de
   l'homme 99
Algeria, complaints from, about NGOs
   95, 96
Alpine Convention, environmental non-
   compliance issues 185, 186, 187,
   201–2

Alston, P. 6, 156
amicus briefs
   European Court of Human Rights
      163–4, 166, 175, 177, 180
   ICSID 156, 164, 174, 175, 180
   and International Court of Justice
      (ICJ) 167–8, 174, 178–9, 210
   international courts and tribunals 8,
      16, 157, 162, 163–9, 171, 172,
      174–8
   international courts and tribunals,
      reasons for rejecting 179
   International Criminal Court (ICC)
      171, 210, 214
   Iran–United States Claims Tribunal
      175
   NAFTA 164–5, 175
   WTO 172, 175
Amnesty International 29, 32, 45, 57, 63,
   161, 204, 211
Anderson, K. 163
Angell, E. 164
Argentina, *Aguas Argentinas*, *S.A.* case
   (ICSID) 174–5
Armstrong, K.A. 62
Arria meetings 28, 54
Ascensio, H. 163
Asian Legal Resource Centre 99
Asociación Cubana de las Naciones
   Unidas 87
Association for the Prevention of Torture
   32
Aston, J. 25, 29, 30, 85, 143
Australia, Council for Overseas Aid
   Code of Conduct 170
Azerbaijan, NGO Informal Regional
   Network (UN-IRENE) 91–2

Bahrain, complaints from, about NGOs
   97–8
Bakker, Christine 1–17
Baratta, R. 178

Basel Convention on the Transboundary
    Movement of Hazardous Wastes
    and Their Disposal (1989)
    Mechanism for Promoting
    Implementation and Compliance
    184, 187, 188, 190, 201
Belgium
    Conka v Belgium (ECHR) 158
    NGOs, co-financing schemes 121
Bettati, M. 42, 210
Bettin, Valentina 10, 116–34, 212
Bosnia-Herzegovina, servile NGOs 87
Bothe, M. 193
Brazil, NGO Informal Regional Network
    (UN-IRENE) 91
Bretton Wood institutions 27
Brownlie, I. 2
Brunnée, J. 182
Bulgaria, *M.C. v Bulgaria* (ECHR) 166

Cameron, M.A. 38
Cameroon, servile NGOs 84
Canada
    NGO Informal Regional Network
        (UN-IRENE) 91
    Trail Smelter, United States v Canada
        141
    *United Parcel Service of America Inc
        v Government of Canada*
        (NAFTA) 165
Cannizzaro, E. 68
Cardoso Report 43, 52–3, 54–7, 63, 65,
    111–12, 205
Cartagena Protocol 188, 191, 199, 201
Catholic Group of European Caritas
        Agencies 119
Centrist Democrat International 93
Centro de Estudios Europeos 85–6
Centro de Estudios sobre Asia y Oceania
        85
Centro de Estudios sobre la Juventud
        86–7
Chayes, A. and A. 182
China
    All-China Women's Federation 78–9,
        80
    Care and Compassion Society 88
    complaints from, about NGOs 94, 95,
        97, 98–9, 101
    Disabled Persons Federation 79

Falun Gong 79
    Human Rights in China (HRC) 30,
        83–4, 94
    NGO Informal Regional Network
        (UN-IRENE) 92
    servile NGOs 73, 78–80, 83, 87, 88,
        92
    Society for Human Rights Studies 79
    United Nations Association of China
        79
Chinkin, C. 167
Chinkin, C. and R. Mackenzie 163–4
Christian Solidarity International (CSI)
        104, 105–6, 107, 115
civil society
    advisory roles, formal 34
    and EU policy formulation 60–62,
        123–33, 230–31
    institutional arrangements 23–6,
        37–43, 48–52
    multi-stakeholder dialogues 35–6
    organizations database, EU 62
    partnership policy with IGOs 37–9,
        65–6
    political and financial weight of
        organizations 33–4
    representivity of 43–4
    revolution 25
    see also NGOs
civil society participation
    African union ECOSOCC 48–52
    Council of Europe 57–60
    European Commission 60–62
    formalization, reasons for higher
        degree of 39–43
    formalized but not institutionalized
        52–60
    informal and administrative
        facilitation 60–62
    institutionalization 48–52
    participatory rights definition 16
    UNAIDS 36, 37
    UN Commission on Sustainable
        Development 35, 36
    UN ECOSOC 23–6
    UN General Assembly 27, 28
    UN Security Council 28
    World Bank 36, 47, 64, 112–13, 212
    WTO 64, 113, 168
Clapham, A. 4, 156

Coalition Gaie et Lesbienne du Québec
    109
Colombia, complaints from, about NGOs
    99
Conka v Belgium (ECHR)158
*Corfù Channel, United Kingdom v
    Albany* (ICJ) 141
Cot, J.P. 208
Cotonou agreement, EU 125, 130, 131,
    132–3
Council of Europe
    civil society participation 57–60
    Convention on the Recognition of the
        Legal Personality of Non-
        Governmental Organisations
        14
    human rights supervisory system 160
    international NGO (INGOs)
        participatory status 39–40, 46,
        57–60, 221–6
    Liaison Committee 58, 59, 60, 65,
        222, 224, 225
    NGO consultative relationships
        13–14, 40, 58, 59, 65,
        220–26
    NGO observer status 59
    NGO participatory status 39–40,
        57–60, 212, 220–26
    NGO Resolution (51)30F 13–14
    NGO Resolution (2003)8 40, 58, 59,
        65, 220–26
    NGO self-regulation 58, 59, 64–5,
        160–70, 177, 213
    Thematic Groupings 58, 59–60
Cuba
    complaints from, about NGOs 93–4,
        95, 96–7, 100–101, 102, 104,
        107–8
    Federation of Cuban Women 86
    NGO consultative status 73–4
    NGOs and conflict intervention 73–5
    servile NGOs 73–6, 85–7
Currie, D. 160
Cygan, A. 179

Danish National Association for Gays
    and Lesbians 109, 110
De Cesari, P. 179
de Frouville, Olivier 9, 15, 71–115, 204
de Schutter, O. 42, 44, 160

De Wet, E. 68
Disaster Relief, NGO Code of Conduct
    170
Dominicé, C. 3
Downs, G., D. Rocke and P. Barsoom
    182
Dunoff, J. 178
Dupuy, Pierre-Marie 173, 204–15

EC Treaty 117, 118, 179
    consultation procedures 230
ECHO Framework Partnership
    Agreement (FPA) 119–20
Ecopravo-Lviv case 192–4
Ehrmann, M. 181, 192
Elgström, O. 133
Enderlin, T. 186
environmental law, international *see*
    international environmental law
environmental non-compliance issues
    Aarhus Convention *see* Aarhus
        Convention
    Alpine Convention 185, 186, 187,
        201–2
    Basel Convention on the
        Transboundary Movement of
        Hazardous Wastes and Their
        Disposal (1989) Mechanism for
        Promoting Implementation and
        Compliance 184, 187, 188, 190,
        201
    Cartagena Protocol on Biosafety to
        the Convention on Biological
        Diversity (2000) 188, 191, 199
        201
    co-operation within treaty regimes
        182
    compliance procedures under
        negotiation 202–3
    and confidentiality 186
    and conflict of interest 195
    Ecopravo-Lviv case 192–4
    Espoo Protocol 184, 188, 189, 191,
        192–4, 213
    Implementation Committees 182
    institutional arrangements 185–6, 190
    International Treaty on Plant Genetic
        Resources for Food and
        Agriculture (under negotiation)
        202

Kyoto Protocol 187, 188, 190, 192, 198, 201
Montreal Protocol 181, 182, 184, 190, 201
Multilateral Environmental Agreements (MEA) 139, 143, 144, 145, 151, 182–3, 184–5, 189–90, 198
NGO accountability 199
NGO consultation 196
NGO legal status 181–203
NGO observer status 184, 185–6, 189–91, 195–6
NGO participation and lessons from past negotiations 197–200
NGO referrals 191–2
NGO role, formalizing 184–8
NGO role and policy considerations 183–4
NGO role, treaty provisions 184–5
NGOs, formal recognition, lack of 188–97
provisions on sources of information 187–8
public involvement 196, 197, 198, 199–200
Rotterdam Convention on Hazardous Chemical and Pesticides in International Trade (under negotiation) 202
trigger mechanisms 186–7, 192
Water and Health Protocol 184, 185, 186, 187, 190, 199, 200, 202
Espoo Protocol 184, 188, 189, 191, 192–4, 213
European Union (EU)
and Aarhus Convention 136, 139, 144, 146, 148, 151, 183–6, 188–90, 194, 195, 197–8
Action Plan for Better Regulation 227
African, Caribbean and Pacific countries (ACP) aid 126, 130, 131, 132–3
and Almaty Guidelines 144, 145
civil society organizations database 62
civil society and policy formulation 123–33, 230–31
Committee of the Regions (CoR) 229, 232–3

consultation processes 228–31
cooperation and knowledge transfer between non-state actors (NSA) 127–8, 130–31
Cotonou agreement 125, 130, 131, 132–3
Country Strategy Papers 127
Court of First Instance 158
decentralized co-operation 122–3, 126
development policy and NGOs 116–34
ECHO Framework Partnership Agreement (FPA) 119–20
Economic and Social Committee (EESC) 60, 124–5, 129, 228–9, 231, 232–3
European Charter of Fundamental Rights 230
European Communities – Measures Affecting Asbestos (WTO) 172, 173
European Development Fund 123
financial aid programmes 126
food aid 118–19, 121–2, 125
Humanitarian Aid Office of the European Community (ECHO) 119–20
humanitarian aid 119–20, 125
institutionalised advisory bodies 232–3
and Multilateral Environmental Agreements (MEA) 198
National Development Strategies 127
National Indicative Programmes (NIP) 126
NGO accreditation scheme 61, 70, 119, 122, 128
NGO consultation 29, 45, 60, 61–2, 131
NGO independence 120–21
NGO role evolution 117–24
NGO screening process 119
NGO-IGO relationship 61, 212
NGOs as aid implementers 117, 118–23, 125, 126–7
NGOs, co-financing schemes 121–3, 125
NGOs as development partners 121–4

NGOs and policy formulation 123–33
NGOs and policy formulation, formal
consultation 128–33
NGOs and policy formulation,
informal consultation 125–9
Nice Treaty 233
non-European NGOs, dialogue with
126–7, 130–31
North-South cooperation 96, 97, 119,
127–8
organised civil society 129–33
Pollutant Release and Transfer
Registers Protocol (PRTR
Protocol) 197–8
servile NGOs 88
*Stichting Greenpeace Council v
Commission* 158
UN Economic Commission for
Europe (UNECE) 139, 148,
185, 197
White Paper on European
Governance 116, 128, 227,
229, 230, 233–41
European Commission
civil society participation 60–62
Communication towards a reinforced
culture of consultation and
dialogue, COM (2002) 704 61,
131, 132, 227–47
CONNECS database 62, 232, 242
consultation procedures, improving
60–62, 231–3
consultation standards and principles
60–62, 239–47
governance consultation process
access 60–62, 236–7
governance consultation process
outcome 60–62, 233–9
Interactive Policy-Making Initiative
(IPM) 231–2
and UN/ECE Aarhus Convention on
Access to Information 232
Your-Voice-in-Europe webportal 245
European Convention for Human Rights
and Fundamental Freedoms 163
European Court of Human Rights
Conka v Belgium 158
Guerra and Others v Italy 142
Lopez Ostra v Spain 142
M.C. v Bulgaria 166

NGO involvement 156, 157–8, 161,
162–3, 164
NGOs and Rules of Procedure of the
Court 172, 175, 177, 180, 210
European Court of Justice (ECJ) 158
*European Parliament v Council
(Chernobyl)* 179

Falk, R. 5, 6
Federation of Cuban Women 86
Félix Varela Center 86
France
Aguas Argentinas, S.A. case 174–5
Lac Lanoux 141
NGOs, co-financing schemes 121
France-Libertés – Fondation Danielle
Mitterrand 98–9
Freedom House 75–6, 96, 97

Germany
complaints from, about NGOs 93
LaGrand (Germany v United States)
case (ICJ) 174
NGOs, co-financing schemes 121
Ghana, servile NGOs 84
globalization 25–6, 38, 39, 206, 214
Goote, M. 187, 188, 193
Greenpeace International 160, 204
Guerra and Others v Italy 142
Guillet, S. 81
Gupta, J. 149, 150

Heere, W.P. 207
Higgins, R. 5
Himalayan Research and Cultural
Foundation 88
human rights
African Commission for Human and
Peoples' Rights (AfrComHR)
158, 159, 163
African Court of Human Rights 158,
159–60, 170, 177, 210, 214
Agir ensemble pour les droits de
l'homme 99
Amnesty International 29, 32, 45, 57,
63, 161, 204, 211
Association for the Prevention of
Torture 32
Council of Europe supervisory
system 160

EU humanitarian aid 119–20, 125
European Court *see* European Court
  of Human Rights
Human Rights in China (HRC) 30,
  83–4, 94
Human Rights Watch 95
Inter-American Commission of
  Human Rights (AmComHR)
  158–9
International Committee of Peace and
  Human Rights 87
International League of Human
  Rights 94
International League for the Rights
  and Liberation of Peoples
  (LIDLIP) 94, 99
monitoring bodies 4, 156
Society for Human Rights Studies,
  China 79

IGOs
  access to 23–37, 62–70
  accountability 26, 68–70
  decision-making 26
  and GONGOs 15, 71, 72, 92
  international legal personality,
    reluctance to accept 2–3
  NGO cooperation with 8, 16–17,
    21–70, 214–15
  NGO Informal Regional Network
    (UN-IRENE) 91
  participatory status 39–40, 57–60
  transparency and informal
    participation 42, 43, 46
  and 'uncivil society' 42
  see also individual organizations;
    NGOs
India
  complaints from, about NGOs 94
  NGO Informal Regional Network
    (UN-IRENE) 92
  servile NGOs 73, 76, 77–8, 88
information technologies 25–6
Inter-American Commission of Human
  Rights (AmComHR) 158–9
International Association for the Defence
  of Religious Liberty 76
International Association for Democratic
  Lawyers (IADL) 96
International Association of Educators
  for World Peace 75–6, 95–6

International Centre for Settlement of
  Investment Disputes (ICSID) 156,
  164–5, 175
  Aguas Argentinas, S.A. case 174
International Commission of Jurists 32
International Committee of Peace and
  Human Rights 87
International Council of the Association
  for Peace in the Continents
  (ASOPAZCO) 76, 96, 97, 101,
  102, 104, 107–8
International Court of Justice (ICJ)
  and *amicus* briefs 167–8, 174, 178–9,
    210
  LaGrand (Germany v United States)
    case 174
  Practice Direction XII 167, 178
  *Reparations for Injuries Suffered in
    the Service of the United
    Nations* 2, 208–9
  Wimbledon case 206
international courts and tribunals
  advocacy NGOs 161, 162
  Aguas Argentinas, S.A. case (ICSID)
    174–5
  amicus curiae briefs 8, 16, 157, 162,
    163–9, 171, 172, 174–8, 214
  amicus curiae briefs, reasons for
    rejecting 179
  arbitral tribunals 180, 210
  dispute settlement 160
  *European Communities – Measures
    Affecting Asbestos* (WTO)
    172, 173
  *European Parliament v Council
    (Chernobyl)* (ECJ) 179
  LaGrand (Germany v United States)
    case (ICJ) 174
  M.C. v Bulgaria (ECHR) 166
  *Methanex Corporation v United
    States of America* (NAFTA)
    165, 177, 178
  NGO participation, codes of conduct
    169–71, 177, 213
  NGO participation and degree of
    regulation 169–75
  NGO participation, formal regulation
    171–5, 210–12, 213
  NGO participation, informal
    regulation 169–71, 210, 211,
    212

NGO participation, judicial
  regulation 172–5
NGO participation, safeguards of the
  rights of the parties 180
NGO representation 163
NGOs before 155–80
NGOs, conditional participation
  175–80
NGOs, direct participation, legal
  standing 157–63
NGOs, indirect participation 163–8
NGOs, legal standing 161
NGOs, overview of involvement
  156–68
NGOs, representation issues 177–9
and public interest 163, 166, 177–8
service-delivery NGOs 161, 162
Tadic case (ICTY) 168
*United Parcel Service of America Inc
  v Government of Canada*
  (NAFTA) 165
*United States – Duties on Certain
  Hot-Rolled lead and Bismuth
  Carbon Steel Products
  Originating in the UK* (WTO)
  173
*United States – Import Prohibition of
  Certain Shrimp and Shrimp
  Products* (WTO) 173–4
International Criminal Court (ICC) 26,
  155, 164
  amicus submissions 171, 210, 214
International Criminal Tribunals 155,
  164, 172
Tadic case 168
international environmental law
  Aarhus Convention (1998) 139,
    144–8
  Access Initiative 138–9
  Business Charter on Sustainable
    Development 140
  *Corfù Channel, United Kingdom v
    Albany* (ICJ) 141
  and corporate sector 140–42
  Global Ministerial Environment
    Forum 138
  Guerra and Others v Italy (ECHR)
    142
  Inter-American Strategy for the
    Promotion of Public

Participation in Decision-
    Making for Sustainable
    Development 138–9
  Lac Lanoux 141
  Lopez Ostra v Spain 142
  Multilateral Environmental
    Agreements (MEAs) 139, 143,
    144, 145, 151, 160
  NGO power and implementation of
    148–51
  NGOs decision-making development
    and 142–8
  OECD Guidelines for multinational
    enterprises 141
  partnerships and regulatory
    framework 150–51
  public participation developments
    135–52
  public participation principle 137–42,
    145
  Rio Declaration 137–8, 141, 144, 205
  and sustainable development 137,
    138–9, 140, 146
  Trail Smelter, United States v Canada
    141
  World Summit on Sustainable
    Development (WSSD) 36, 136,
    138, 140, 143, 148–50
International Federation of Free Trade
  Unions (IFTU) 94
International Federation of Human
  Rights (FIDH) 32, 45, 95, 96,
  97–8, 113, 158, 204
International Federation of Women in
  Legal Careers 96
International Human Rights Watch 32,
  45
International Islamic Federation of
  Students Organisations (IIFSO)
  76–7
International Law Commission 68–9,
  120
  Responsibility of States for
    Internationally Wrongful Acts
    (Article 33(2)) 6
International League of Human Rights
  94
International League for the Rights and
  Liberation of Peoples (LIDLIP)
  94, 99

International Lesbian and Gay
    Association (ILGA) 100, 102–4,
    108, 109, 110, 115
International Treaty on Plant Genetic
    Resources for Food and
    Agriculture (under negotiation)
    202–3
International Tribunal for the Law of the
    Sea 155
Iran
    complaints from, about NGOs 94, 95,
        96, 97
    Organization for defending victims of
        violence 88
Iran–United States Claims Tribunal,
    amicus submissions 175
Iraq
    complaints from, about NGOs 95
    General Federation of Iraqi Women
        88
Islamic African Relief Agency 104–5
Islamic World Studies Center 88
Italy
    Guerra and Others v Italy (ECHR)
        142
    NGOs, co-financing schemes 121
Ivanova, M. 151

Japan, NGO Informal Regional Network
    (UN-IRENE) 92
Jilani, H. 110

Kamminga, M. 14, 15
Kazakhstan, Aarhus Committee
    compliance 196
Koester, V. 186, 195
Koskenniemi, M. 182
Krisch, N. and B. Kingsbury 70, 214
Krislov, S. 164
Kyoto Protocol, environmental non-
    compliance issues 187, 188, 190,
    192, 198, 201

Lac Lanoux case 141
LaGrand (Germany v United States)
    case (ICJ) 174
Lapucci, A. 118, 121, 125
Latin American and Caribbean
    Continental Organization of
    Students (OCLAE) 86

League of Nations 23–4, 44, 207, 208
Lebanon, complaints from, about NGOs
    103
Lesbian and Gay Federation in Germany
    109, 110
Liberal International 75
Libération 96
Libya, complaints from, about NGOs 99
Lindblom, A.-K. 1, 8, 15, 22, 30, 48,
    159, 177, 205
Long-Range Transboundary Air
    Pollution Treaty (LRTAPT) 201
Lopez Ostra v Spain 142
Lowman, M. 164

Macedonia, NGO Informal Regional
    Network (UN-IRENE) 91
Marauhn, T. 181
Martines, F. 118
Mauritania
    NGO Informal Regional Network
        (UN-IRENE) 91
    servile NGOs 92
Mauritius, complaints from, about NGOs
    97
M.C. v Bulgaria (ECHR) 166
*Methanex Corporation v United States of
    America* (NAFTA) 165, 177, 178
Montagnard Foundation 101–2
Montreal Protocol 181, 182, 184, 190,
    201
Movement Against Racism and for
    Friendship Among Peoples
    (MRAP) 96
Movimiento Cubano por la Paz y la
    Soberania de los Pueblos 86, 87
Multilateral Environmental Agreements
    (MEA) 182–3, 184–5, 189–90,
    198

NAFTA
    amicus submissions 164–5, 175
    *Methanex Corporation v United
        States of America* 165, 177,
        178
    non-disputing party participation
        257–9
    *United Parcel Service of America Inc
        v Government of Canada* 165
Nair, R. 71

National Association of Cuban
    Economists 86
National Union of Jurists of Cuba 86
NATO, Parliamentarians for Global
    Action (PGA) 31
Netherlands
    NGOs, co-financing schemes 121
    *Stichting Greenpeace Council v
        Commission* (Court of First
        Instance and ECJ) 158
New Human Rights 96
NGOs
    accountability 4, 13, 15, 42–6, 56,
        58–9, 61, 64–6, 136, 174
    accreditation procedure 24, 25,
        29–31, 41, 53–7, 59, 61, 64–5,
        79, 205
    advocacy 22, 37–8, 161, 162
    amicus curiae briefs 8, 16, 157, 162,
        172, 210
    BINGOs (business interest NGOs)
        71, 136
    co-financing schemes 121–3, 125
    conflict intervention between states
        73–8
    consultative relationship 13–14,
        23–37, 40, 58, 59, 65, 73–4,
        220–26
    consultative status and participation
        control 27–31
    consultative status and participation
        facilitation 31–7
    and Council of Europe *see* Council of
        Europe
    decision making development and
        international environmental
        law 142–8
    defining, in international law
        12–17
    definition, absence of agreed 13–15,
        21
    development policy in EU 116–34
    and environmental non-compliance
        see environmental non-
        compliance
    EU *see under* EU
    flexibility 16, 17, 62, 65, 172, 175,
        211, 213
    GONGOs (governmental NGOs)
        15–16, 42, 71, 72

    governmental delegations, denied
        access 32–3
    IGO cooperation with 8, 16–17,
        21 70, 214 15
    independence, EU 120–21
    independent 16, 43–6, 82–3
    institutionalization 22, 23, 46–7,
        48–52, 89–92, 143, 185–6, 190
    and international courts and tribunals
        see under international courts
        and tribunals
    and international law, open attitude
        towards 3–5
    international legal personality,
        cautious recognition 5–7, 14,
        66
    international legal personality,
        reluctance to accept 2–3
    involvement, European Court of
        Human Rights 156, 157–8,
        161, 162–3, 164
    laudatory and imitative 78–81
    legal functionality requirements 6–7
    legal status 1–2, 22, 23–5, 37–9,
        39–43, 46–60, 62–6, 204–15
    legal status questionnaire 216–19
    legal status, selected documents
        relating to recent developments
        220–59
    lobbying 32, 33–4, 42
    and mainstream international law 1–7
    negative consequences of normative
        loophole 15–17
    network partners 56, 205
    NGO-IGO relationship, EU 61, 212
    NGO Informal Regional (UN-
        IRENE) 91
    non-legal category (servile society)
        71–2, 205
    non-profit aim 14
    observer status 25, 59, 143, 184,
        185–6, 189–91, 195–6
    participation formalization 37–46,
        48–52, 52–60
    participation formalization, dangers
        of 43–6
    participation formalization, reasons
        for higher degree of 39–43
    participation, multiplying patterns of
        46–62

participatory rights 16–17, 24–5, 32,
    33–4, 34–7, 54, 59–60
political weight, increased 25–6,
    37–9, 42–3, 62, 67
public interest (PINGOs) 135–6, 140
and Rules of Procedure of the Court,
    European Court of Human
    Rights 172, 175, 177, 180, 210
self-regulation 22, 43–6, 47, 53,
    55–60, 61–2, 64–5, 67, 147,
    169–71, 177, 213–14
service-delivery, international courts
    and tribunals 161, 162
servile society, creation of 73–92
servile in UN *see* under UN
UN *see under* UN
see also civil society
Nigeria, servile NGOs 84
Noortmann, M. 45
North Korea, human rights 84
North-South cooperation, EU 96, 97,
    119, 127–8

OECD Guidelines for multinational
    enterprises 141
Ohlhoff, S. and H. Schloemann 176
One World 120
Organization of African Unity (African
    (Union)
    civil society organizations'
        accreditation 29, 46, 48–52
    Cluster Committees, ECOSOCC
        51–2, 60
    Economic, Social and Cultural
        Council (ECOSOCC) 46,
        48–52, 65, 212, 213
    NGO consultative status 29
Organization of American States (OAS)
    civil society participation 24, 40,
        46–7
    Guidelines for Participation by Civil
        Society Organizations 14, 41,
        248–56
    NGO consultative status 25, 29
    NGO participation 159, 212
    Summit of the Americas on
        Sustainable Development
        249–50
Organization of the Islamic Conference
    106

Organization for the Solidarity of the
    Peoples of Asia, Africa and Latin
    America (OSPAAL) 86
OSCE (Organization for Security and
    Co-operation in Europe), NGO
    consultation 29, 113
Oxfam 119

Pakistan
    All Pakistan Women's Association
        76, 92
    complaints from, about NGOs 103
    NGO Informal Regional Network
        (UN-IRENE) 92
    servile NGOs and Kashmir conflict
        73, 76–7
    terrorist support 78
Parliamentarians for Global Action
    (PGA) 31, 32, 33, 46
Parmentier, R. 150
Pax Christi International (PCI) 95, 96
Pinochet case 162
Pitea, C. 11-12, 181–203, 211
Pollutant Release and Transfer Registers
    Protocol (PRTR Protocol), EU
    197–8
public interest
    environmental non-compliance issues
        196, 197, 198, 199–200
    and international courts and tribunals
        163, 166, 177–8
    international environmental law
        135–52
    NGOs 135–6, 140

Qatar Charitable Society 88
Quadri, R. 209

Ratner, S. and A.M. Slaughter 207
Rebasti, E. 9, 21–70
Red Crescent Movement, NGO Code of
    Conduct 170
Red Cross 3, 210
    NGO Code of Conduct 170
Reinisch, A. 3, 4, 15, 68
Reisman, M. 4, 207
Reporters Without Borders 100–101, 104
Rio Declaration, international
    environmental law 137–8, 141,
    144, 205

Röben, V. 143
Romania, NGO Informal Regional
	Network (UN–IRENE) 91
Russia, complaints from, about NGOs
	95, 101

Sachaiew, K. 181
Seary, B. 22, 23, 44
Senegal, complaints from, about NGOs
	103
Shelton, D. 139, 167
Simon Wiesenthal Centre 99
Society for Threatened Peoples 95, 96,
	98
South Africa, NGO Codes of Conduct
	171
Spain, *Lopez Ostra v Spain* 142
Sri Lanka
	complaints from, about NGOs 99
	Tamil Center for Human Rights
		(TCHR) 30–31
Stern, B. 168
*Stichting Greenpeace Council v
	Commission* (Court of First
	Instance and ECJ) 158
Sudan
	complaints from, about 97, 103,
		104–6, 107
	International Women's Muslim Union
		88
	RFK Human Rights Award 94
Sur, S. 2
Swinarski, C. 3

Tadic case (ICJ) 168
Tanzi, A. 10, 135–52
Thomas, L. 140
Thuerer, D. 5, 7, 14
Trachtman, J. and P. Moremen 176
Trail Smelter, United States v Canada
	141
Transnational Radical Party 98, 99, 101
Treves, T. 57, 67, 160, 161, 162, 179,
	189, 196
Tunisia
	human rights 80–81
	NGO Informal Regional Network
		(UN-IRENE) 91
	servile NGOs 73, 80–81, 87, 92
Tupaj Amaru 100, 102

Turkey, complaints from, about NGOs
	99
Turkmenistan, Aarhus Committee
	compliance 196

Udombana, N. 159
UK
	*Corfù Channel, United Kingdom v
		Albany* (ICJ) 141
	NGO Codes of Conduct 171
	NGOs, co-financing schemes 121
	*United States – Duties on Certain
		Hot-Rolled lead and Bismuth
		Carbon Steel Products
		Originating in the UK* (WTO)
		173
Ukraine
	Aarhus Committee compliance 196
	Ecopravo-Lviv case 192–4
UN
	Agenda 21 28, 34–5, 144
	Arria meetings 28, 54
	Assembly of States Parties of the
		Rome Statute 31
	Cairo Conference (1994) 27–8
	Cardoso Report 43, 52–7, 64, 65,
		111–12, 205
	civil society domestication 71–115
	Commission on Human Rights
		(UNCHR) 32, 36, 42, 71–2,
		73, 75–6, 77–8, 80, 81, 94, 96,
		97–8, 99, 100–101, 111, 114
	Commission on International Trade
		Law 165
	Committee on NGOs 25, 29–31,
		44–5, 55, 65, 73–4, 81, 83–8,
		90, 93, 95–6, 102, 104–8,
		110–11
	Conference on Environment and
		Development (UNCED) 34,
		143
	Conference of NGOs (CONGO) 63,
		66, 89, 106
	Development Programme (UNDP) 36
	Economic Commission for Europe
		(UNECE) 139, 148, 185, 197
	Economic and Social Council 23–6,
		27, 32, 34, 36, 39, 72, 81, 84,
		88, 89, 97–8, 101, 115
	Global Compact 39, 140

Global Environment Facility 39
Global Policy Reform (GPR) 63, 66
and GONGOs 15–16, 92
Group of 77 27
HIV/AIDS Programme (UNAIDS)
36–7, 48, 50, 65
Human Rights Council (HRC) 57,
67–8, 71–2, 73, 81
International Labour Organization
(ILO) 39, 44, 48, 49, 51, 64,
205, 207, 208
NGO access and cooperation 27–8,
29–30, 52–60, 212
NGO accreditation procedure 24, 25,
29–31, 53–7, 112
NGO consultative status 23–37, 40,
54, 81–4, 85
NGO Informal Regional Network
(UN-IRENE) 73, 89–92
NGO Planning Committee 28
NGO sanctions 100–108
NGO self-regulation 55–7
NGO space allocation 32–3
NGO status withdrawal 104–8, 115
NGO trust fund for developing
countries 56, 90–91
Non-Aligned Movement 27
Non-Governmental Liaison Service
(NGLS) 41
Office on Drugs and Crimes
(UNODC) 36
Oil for Food Program 69
Panel of Eminent Persons on United
Nations-Civil Society
Relations 46, 52–7, 112
*Reparations for Injuries Suffered in
the Service of the United
Nations* (ICJ) case 2, 208–9
Security Council 27, 28, 54, 68, 69
security measures 33
servile NGOs, application and
passive voting 87–92
servile NGOs, application support for
85–7
servile NGOs, introduction into
system 81–4
servile NGOs, oral attacks on
92–100
servile NGOs, special reports 95–100
and servile society 73–92, 114–15

servile society, institutionalization of
89–92, 166
Specialised Agencies 24, 25, 27, 36,
40
UN reform proposals 57, 67, 69, 71,
111, 112
UNAIDS Program Coordinating
Board 36–7
Universal Declaration of Human
Rights 4
World Summit on Sustainable
Development (WSSD) 36, 136,
138, 140, 143, 148–50
UN Charter
Article 71 13, 22, 23, 45, 67–8, 143
UN, ECOSOC (Economic and Social
Council) 13, 14, 23–6, 27,
29–31, 32, 55–7, 66
accreditation procedure 25, 29–31,
40–41, 54–5
accreditation requirements 40–41
Commission on Sustainable
Development (CSD) 34–6
Committee on NGOs 25, 29–31,
44–5, 55, 65
NGO consultative status 23–37, 40,
53–7, 79, 81–2, 84–6, 87–8,
91, 96, 106–8, 110
NGO consultative status,
recommendations to deny 109–10
NGO observer status 25, 143
Permanent Forum on Indigenous
Issues 34, 43–4, 48, 50, 51, 65
Resolution 1296 – 1968 27
Resolution 1994/50 103, 115
Resolution 1995/2 36
Resolution 1996/31 27, 30, 31, 40,
41, 79, 81–2, 84–5, 88, 93,
96–100, 103–9, 113, 114, 115
Resolution 1996/297 27
Resolution 2000/22 34, 43–4, 49
Resolution 2002/225 90
UN General Assembly 27–8, 41, 54,
55, 56–7, 67–8
decision A/52/453 27
decision A/60/1 69
decision A/60/251 67–8, 72
Special Session, 19th 28, 35
United Arab Emirates, NGO Informal
Regional Network (UN-IRENE)
91

USA
  and Aarhus Convention 197
  AFL-CIO 93–4
  complaints from, about NGOs 100, 102–4, 105–6, 107
  foreign policy and selective indignation of servile NGOs 88
  Iran–United States Claims Tribunal, *amicus* submissions 175
  LaGrand (Germany v United States) case (ICJ) 174
  Methanex Corporation v United States of America (NAFTA) 165, 177, 178
  NGOs and conflict intervention 73–5
  servile NGOs 73, 75–6, 85, 93
  Trail Smelter, United States v Canada 141
  United Parcel Service of America Inc v Government of Canada (NAFTA) 165
  United States – Duties on Certain Hot-Rolled lead and Bismuth Carbon Steel Products Originating in the UK (WTO) 173
  United States – Import Prohibition of Certain Shrimp and Shrimp Products (WTO) 173–4, 180

Valencia-Ospina, E. 168
Victor, D. 190
Vierucci, L. 1–17, 155–80, 210
Vietnam
  complaints from, about NGOs 99, 101–2
  servile NGOs 84

Water and Health Protocol, environmental non-compliance issues 184, 185, 186, 187, 190, 199, 200, 202
Wates, J. 189
Wedgewood, R. 6, 7
Weiler, J. 176
White, L.C. 24
Willetts, P. 27, 28, 44, 66, 207
Williams, J.F. 208

Wimbledon case (ICJ) 206
Witte, J.M., C. Streck and T. Benner 149, 150–51
Wolfium, R. 102
Women's Human Rights International Association 96
World Association of NGOs, Code of Conduct 170–71
World Bank
  civil society participation 36, 47, 64, 112–13, 212
  Inspection Panel 69
World Confederation of Labour 96, 97
World Conference on Human Rights 79
World Council of Churches 119
World Federation of United Nations Associations 90
World Muslim Congress 76, 92
World Organisation Against Torture 32
World Serbian Union 87
World Summit on Information Society 92
World Summit on Sustainable Development (WSSD) 36, 136, 138, 140, 143, 148–50
World for World Organization 92
WTO
  Additional Procedure (2001) 172
  amicus submissions 172, 175
  civil society participation 64, 113, 168
  Dispute Settlement Understanding 168, 173–4, 175, 176, 180
  European Communities – Measures Affecting Asbestos 172, 173
  notification requirements 246
  statutory powers 171
  United States – Duties on Certain Hot-Rolled lead and Bismuth Carbon Steel Products Originating in the UK 173
  United States – Import Prohibition of Certain Shrimp and Shrimp Products 173–4, 180

Zagorac, D. 161
Zimbabwe, complaints from, about NGOs 95